TO MY MOTHER.

# CONTENTS.

# EIRENE.

## I.

### LEAVING HOME.

"GOOD-BY, Rene."

"Good-by, Win." Here the soft voice broke, and a pair of brown eyes looked through gathering tears, while the young girl who owned them leaned across a rough gate and kissed a boy who stood inside.

"Good-by, Pansy," she said, turning to a little girl. "Be a good girl to mother till I come back, and I will bring you a new dress as blue as the sky. Think of it, Pansy, and don't cry!"

This promise of a new dress stopped Pansy's tears. She opened her purple-blue eyes wide and laughed with delight. She threw her arms around her sister, and exclaimed: "Rene, how long before you will come back and bring me the new frock?"

"Very soon," said Rene, and she kissed the child on her yellow hair.

"Mother! You will pray for me?"

"Yes. Always."

"Come! We shall be too late for the cars! They never stop for *good-bys*," said a kind voice a little impatiently. This call came from an elderly man who sat waiting in a rickety buggy. As he spoke he mildly jerked the reins, as if to impart a little of his own impatience to his horse; but the jerk only made the meek old mare stretch out her straight neck a little straighter, stiffen her legs as if they were riveted in the sod, and she herself willing to stand till the end of the world without stirring.

At the sound of her father's voice Eirene turned to her mother with a sudden, deep embrace, then hurried from the gate, climbed up into the ancient vehicle, tucked herself into a corner of the rusty seat, and without looking back said, "Now, father."

"Get up, Muggins!"

But Muggins was decidedly averse to "getting up." She seemed to know that it involved carrying Eirene away.

"Muggins, I say, *get up!*"

The injunction this time was accompanied by so decided a jerk, that Muggins did "get up;" that is, she began to move away at the slowest of all paces. The aged, straight-necked horse, the old wagon, the gray-haired man, the young girl, went shaking together along the stony hill-road.

### A COUNTRY RAILWAY-STATION.

The October sun had filtered its gold through a hazy heaven till the wide spaces of air palpitated with topaz mist. An uplifted veil, it trembled above the faces of the hills, and floated in luminous nebulæ far down the valley.

On the mountain-sides, in the deep gorges, in the wide woods, the carnival of color had begun.

The maples fluttered their vivid ambers and scarlets; the oaks wore their garnet; vines, ruby and yellow, festooned the rugged boulders with flame-like hues.

Armies of ferns stood by the way with nodding plumes and crimsoned falchions. Through the mellow air rained the ripe leaves of October.

With a low stir of melody, they rustled down into the stony road, and the ruthless wagon-wheels passed over them and crushed them. They were full-juiced, and their exuding wine filled the atmosphere with a faint, delicious fragrance. The air was sweet also with the perfume of the pines, distilling their balsams amid the stillness of the hills. The world was all athrill with murmurous music—the quick rustle of the squirrel running through the loosely-meshed leaves, the shrill trill of the cricket, and the low hum of insect-wings astir on the borders of silence. Over all bent the azure-amber firmament,

It was one of the rare days which God makes perfect.

"How sweet the pines smell, father. I can't make it seem that I am not going to see these dear old woods any more;" and as she uttered these words, Eirene, who had been silently taking in color and odor and sound, gazed around her with an expression of unutterable love and sadness, strangely at variance with a face so young.

"Yes, you will, child. You will see the old woods at Thanksgiving. You know that I am coming down after you then," said her father.

"Yes, but at Thanksgiving the leaves will all have fallen. The woods will be gray—not my woods, all in a glory as now. But then I am going to something better. I am glad of that, father," and the girl looked anxiously into his face, as if sorry that she had uttered a repining word.

"I wish that you were going to something better, Rene. I haven't said any thing about it before, because I felt that I couldn't. It is very hard for me to send my Rene out into the world to earn her bread, instead of sending her to school, and giving her the start in life which I always intended that she should have. But I have done the best that I could, child. It is not my lot to be lucky."

There was a pathos in the man's voice and utterance which brought the swift tears back into Eirene's eyes.

"Oh, father, I didn't know that you felt so bad about my going away," she said, "or I am sure I would not have spoken a word about leaving the woods. You know that I want to go. I am young and strong; why shouldn't I do something? After my work is done, I shall find some time to study. And if Win and Pansy can be educated, it does not make so much difference about me.

"Now, father, don't feel bad any more, because there isn't any reason why you should," she continued, as looking up she saw that her words had failed to bring any smile into the sorrowful eyes. "Father, mind me;" and with an effort to be playful, she took the corner of her shawl and wiped away the solitary tear that was making its way down a groove of the furrowed cheek.

It was only two miles to the railroad-station, down-hill all the way. Eirene and her father had ridden in silence but a little way, when the most uninteresting of all material objects, a country railway-depot, confronted them at the angle of two roads. It looked like a diminutive barn painted a blackish brown. Inside it boasted of a dirty floor, a spittoon half filled with sawdust, a rusty stove, a bleared looking-glass, two unsteady benches, and a hole in the wall, in which was set the red face of a man waiting to sell tickets. Yet this depot was the centre of attraction for miles around. It was the grand hall of reunion for all the people of the scattered town, not second in importance even to the meeting-house. Here, twice a-day, stopped the great Western and Eastern trains, the two fiery arteries through which flowed all the tumultuous life of the vast outer world that had ever come to this secluded hamlet. Its primitive inhabitants in their isolated farm-houses, under the hills and on the stony mountain moors, could never have realized the existence of another world than the green, grand world of nature around them and above them, and would have been as oblivious of the great god "News" as the denizens of Greenland, if it had not been for the daily visits of this Cyclops with the burning eye. Now twice a-day the shriek of his diabolical whistle pierced the umbrageous woods and hilly gorges for miles away, and its cry to many a solitary household was the epoch of the day. Hearing it, John mounted his nag and scampered away to the station for the Boston journals of yesterday. Seth harnessed Peggy, and drove off in the buggy in all possible haste to see if the mail had brought a letter from Amzi who was in New York, or from Nimrod who had gone to work in "Bosting," or if the train had brought Sally and her children from the city, who were expected home on a visit. Here, under pretext of waiting for the cars, congregated the drones and supernumeraries of the different neighborhoods, lounging on the steps, hacking the benches with their jack-knives for hours together, while they discussed politics, and talked over their own and their neighbors' affairs.

A walk to the station on a summer evening was more to the boys and girls of this rural region than a Broadway promenade to a metropolitan belle. Their day's tasks done, here they met in pairs, comparing finery, and indulging in flirtations with an impunity which would not have been tolerated by their elders at the Sunday recess in the meeting-house. Then, besides, it was such an exciting sight to see the cars come in, to see the long rows of strange faces, and to catch glimpses of the new fashions at their open windows. Besides, at rare intervals, a real city-lady would actually alight at the rustic station of Hilltop, followed by an avalanche of trunks, "larger than hen-houses," the girls would afterward affirm to their astonished mothers, when it was discovered that the city-lady, in her languishing necessity for country-air, had really condescended to come in search of a remote country-cousin. Besides the fine lady, sometimes small companies of dashing young gentlemen, with fishing-rods and retinues of long-eared dogs, or a long-haired artist with a portfolio under his arm, all lured by the mountains and woods and streams to seek pleasure in far different ways, would alight at the station and inquire of some staring rustic where they could find the hotel.

The question invariably called forth the response,

"Thar' ain't nun'; but Farmer Smoot accommodates."

The dog-star, whose fiery rays sent these pilgrims of the world to the cool bosom of the hills, had long set. It was October now. No one was expected. But the girls and boys of Hilltop had heard on Sunday, "at meeting," that on Monday Eirene Vale was going down to Busyville to work in a factory, and they had come to the station to see her off.

She stood in the midst of a group, her plain brown dress and shawl, her dark straw bonnet, with its blue ribbon, affording a striking contrast to the glaring finery of her companions.

"Now, I say, Rene, if you don't bring the Fashion Book when you come hum at Thanksgivin', you'll see what you'll git. You know we've sech lots of company tu our house, I've got to be dressed," said a coarse, red-haired girl, who rejoiced in the mellifluous appellation of Serepty Hepzibah Smoot.

"See here, Rene!" and a tall girl with glowing red cheeks and flaming black eyes took her by the arm and drew her aside with an air of impenetrable mystery. "See here, Rene, and don't you tell, for if it gits out, mother'll set her back agin it, and I can't bring it round. But I'll tell you what, if you like it down to Busyville, I'm coming tu. I'll work and board with you. I know thar' ain't no need on't. Father's forehanded. He sez I can go tu school, but I ain't goin'. I never could larn; now I'm eighteen, I ain't goin' to try. I'm goin' to have clothes. Father don't half dress me, so I'm goin' to work tu earn 'em. I ain't goin' to live and die on this old mountain. I'm goin' whar' I can see and be seen!" and the rustic beauty tossed her head with a self-conscious and defiant air.

"Let *me* speak!" said a squeaky voice, in an imploring tone. "The cars'll come and I shan't have no chance;" and black-eyed Nancy Drake made way for Moses Loplolly, a tall, lank youth, with a crotchet in his shoulders, yellow locks, and small, pale eyes of a gooseberry green.

"Rene, here's a keepsake fur yer to remember me by," he said, thrusting into her hand a small metallic cage, inside of whose swinging ring sat a little green parrot, muffling its bill in its feathers, and peering and blinking with great solemnity from a pair of yellow eyes.

"Yer can't guess the lots of time I've spent a-larnin' on't, and it's learnt. Say your lesson, Polly: 'Pretty Rene. Poor Mo—, Poor Moses Lop——"

As it heard these words, the bird plucked its bill from out its breast, nodded its head, winked on one side, then on the other, and with a shrill scream called out, "Say your lesson, Polly. Pretty Rene, poor Mo—, poor Moses Lop——;" at which utterance the boys and girls of Hilltop broke forth into simultaneous laughter. All but Moses Loplolly; he, with a very sorrowful visage, leaned over Eirene, and whispered: "When it screeches, you'll think of me, won't yer, Rene? Yer won't forget me 'mong the scrumptious fellers you'll see down in Busyville, will yer? You know I never sot so high by nobody as I set by you, Rene?"

"I shan't forget you, Moses," said Eirene. "You have been too kind to Win and Pansy, as well as to me."

"Why should I forget any one because I am going to Busyville?" she asked. "I shall think of you all, and of the pleasant times that we have had together." This was an exceedingly popular remark. The young Hilltopers naturally wished to be held in remembrance by their young companion amid the splendors of Busyville, and they gathered closer around her with parting injunctions and ejaculations.

"Wal, neighbor Vale, so yer goin' to send yer little gal out to seek her fortin'," said red-faced Farmer Stave to the sad-eyed man who stood leaning against the door, gazing at his child.

"I reckon she hain't goin' far to find it. Shouldn't wonder if she'd be merrid afore this time next year. Sech eyes as hern warn't sot in no gal's head for nothin'. I tell yer what, neighbor Vale, they're mighty takin', them are eyes, leastwise they'd be to me, if I was a youngster. 'Tween me and you, neighbor Vale, if your little gal wasn't jest sech a gal as she is, I should say it's tarnal risky bus'nis a-sendin' on her down into the pomps and vanities and tem'tations of Busyville, and not a blessed soul to look arter her but herself."

"Here they are, the cars! you must be on the platform, or you'll get left," exclaimed a voice, and all rushed out as the shrieking whistle, piercing the gorge, announced the arrival of Cyclops. He condescended to tarry but a moment at the unimportant station of Hilltop. There was just time for Eirene's father to lift her upon the platform. In another moment, with her satchel in one hand, and Moses' bird-cage in the other, with a tremulous "Good-by, father," and a strangely palpitating heart, Eirene had vanished through the car-door. In another, the engine with a scream and a snort was off; and in another the long train had darted behind the sharp curve of an aggressive mountain, leaving the little group upon the station-steps still gazing in its wake.

As they turned, each instinctively felt that there was nothing to be said to the silent man who was slowly untying his horse from a tree near by, and who, with a kind "Good-day, all," mounted into his ancient vehicle, and drove away without another word.

"Neighbor Vale seems clean cut up about his little gal's goin' away," said Farmer Stave, looking after him; "and I think myself, she might as well a-staid to hum. It's mighty risky bus'ness a-sendin' on such a purty cretur into sech a sink-hole as Busyville, and neighbor Vale is jest clean cut up about it. It doesn't seem more nor a year ago, sence me and him sot eatin' doughnuts, and noonin' it, on the meetin' 'us steps, and the purty little cretur was a sittin' in the middle; and neighbor Vale was a-starin' at her. And sez he: 'Neighbor Stave,' sez he, 'this child shall be eddicated. She's a destiny to fill in the world, and it haint triflin'. I can afford to be of small account if my child is eddicated and look'd up to in the world.'

"I looked at him so kind a-droopin'-like, and sez I, in'ardly, her destiny's mighty doubtful if it depends on the eddication that you'll give her. For you all know, though neighbor Vale has the best heart in the world, he haint a mite of kalkerlation; and none of the Vales never had, as ever I heerd on. When he thinks of what he said to me about her eddication and sees her when she ain't no more than eighteen, goin' behind that screechin' enjin' to arn her bread and butter in Busyville, it ain't no wonder he's clean cut up."

"No, 'tain't no wonder," chimed in a crony. Then these two old gossips, with the assistance of occasional data from half-a-dozen others, began to enumerate how many times Neighbor Vale's crops had failed; how many mishaps had befallen him since the beginning of his career; how large a mortgage there was on his farm; "for nuthin' under the sun," they said, "only for the want of kalkerlation." "Yes!" cried Farmer Stave, bringing his heavy stick upon the dirty floor with great emphasis, and growing very red in the face. "There ain't no better man, no more feelin' man in the world than neighbor Vale, and it's a thousand pities for him and hisen, that he hain't a mite of kalkerlation."

###### THE VALES.

"Ef he'd only tuk to larnin' that had a-brought in su'then," Farmer Stave continued, "ef he'd only tuk to larnin' that he could ha' turned to account, there's the pint! He needn't be diggin' in the rocks now, and nuthin' to show. I tell ye, Deacon Smoot!"

"It's a myst'ry to me, with sech a little schoolin', how he's picked up sech a lot of larnin.' I tell ye thar' ain't nuthin' from doctorin' a child all tuckered out with teethin' to namin' on the stars, but he knows suthin' about it. Wall! larnin' doos wall enough, when it brings in a fortin'; but what the deuce's is its vally if a chap's got to be a poor cuss all his life, with a mortgage on his farm? I'm glad I allas *was* back'ard. I hain't had nuthin' to hender me gettin' forehanded. Like enuf, if I'd tuk to larnin' as Vale did, me and my folks might a-ben a-livin' from hand to mouth as well as him and hisen. The matter with him is, he hain't no kalkeration. But all the Vales never had, none as ever I heerd on; they was all cracked for larnin', that's my idee."

It is true, the Vales were a cultivated and gifted race, long before one of its sons brought his moderate temporal fortune, his elegant tastes, and rich mental possessions across the Atlantic. They were opulent in those days. Then the wealth which maternal ancestors had garnered for them (a Vale never could have accumulated a fortune) was not nearly exhausted.

Nothing in their necessities prompted them to coin their large gifts into gold for their own uses. Each generation slipped away devoted to religion, to science, and to the æsthetic arts, and every son found himself a little poorer than his father. At last it came to pass, upon a later day, one Aubrey Vale found himself, upon his twenty-fourth birthday, an orphan; his only inheritance a University education, a learned scroll (proclaiming him to be a Doctor of Medicine), his father's library, and his father's spotless memory. With a Vale's abilities, any one but a Vale would have planted himself in a flourishing place; there investing this capital as a sure guarantee for future success.

But a Vale had never been known who knew how to struggle for his own fortune or his own fame. The town of his nativity was amply provided with physicians, but Aubrey Vale knew that the not-distant hamlet of Hilltop did not possess one resident medical man.

He said: "What a quiet spot for a home! what magnificent scenery! Its practice will afford me support, its retirement opportunities for study. If I ever want the world, I know where to find it."

But the air of Hilltop was bleak, too bleak for Aubrey Vale, too bleak for Alice Vale, the young wife, the tropical flower transplanted from a richer and a sunnier soil. They never saw their summer. It was yet their spring when all that was left of them mortal was laid away in one grave in the neglected graveyard of Hilltop, a desolate place half overgrown with blackberry bushes, and left open as a pasture for cows. It was many years afterward that the briers were torn away from the else forgotten grave by a strong man's hands, and the new turf planted with violets and lilies of the valley by the hands of a child—a child wondrous-eyed, with a low, vibrating voice. She was Eirene Vale, and the dark-eyed man was her father.

Lowell Vale was left an orphan when but six years old. After the small homestead was sold, to provide in part means for his support, nothing was left the child but the Vale library. There were no near kin to claim the little boy.

Thus it came to pass that Lowell Vale was thrown from the track of life over which his ancestors had glided so smoothly and gracefully for centuries.

Doubtless he had his own niche in the world; but as there was no one to tell him what it was, he never found it.

It was a sad, sad childhood for a child of such a nature—no father, no mother!

No one was cruel to him, but who was tenderly kind? They would have liked him better—those sturdy farmer-women—if he had borne a closer resemblance to their own tow-headed urchins. "Such a queer cretur, to be sure!" they said to each other. "So still and mopin'. Why didn't he thrash about like Hezekiah?" Thus he was tossed from farmhouse to farmhouse till he came to man's estate. Then why did he not fly from this desert-bondage? you inquire. Oh, he could not; he was a Vale.

The infirmity of his race was in his blood, its weakness in his brain. With a little more self-reliance, a little more hope, a little surer faith in himself, only a little more of positive qualities, he would have gone forth into the world where he could have wrestled with men for the world's prizes, and he would have won them. His comprehensive mind would have compassed success; his lack of executive power made his life a failure.

Here was a Vale at last, who, with the lack of business qualifications which marked his family, had been denied the liberal culture which had helped many of them to eminence in the professions. He bought a little rock-bound, rock-sown farm, and his life shrank into one hopeless effort to wring from the stony soil gold enough to make this sterile piece of earth his own and his children's. To fail even in this, what a fate for a Vale!

When Lowell Vale said to Eirene, "I have done the best that I could. It is not my lot to be lucky," he told the whole story of his life. We see many men who never learn to fit their natures to the groove of life in which they find themselves. At Hilltop life had gathered itself into one narrow channel for generations. Here human nature had repeated itself in one phase for centuries. The railway cut its first path out to the great world. Cyclops was the first screaming herald of progress, the first innovator upon the unutterable dulness of Hilltop.

Yet even now the topics of conversation were very scanty; its people had little to talk about but each other. One variety in the *genus homo* made an inexhaustible theme; thus it happened that Lowell Vale and his affairs were more talked of than of all others put together. It was of no account to these sturdy yeomen that his organization was more delicate, his instincts finer, his aspirations higher, while his house remained smaller, his stock poorer, and his crops scantier than their own.

Of these spiritual facts they were very dimly conscious; but the material ones stood with painful palpability before their scrutinizing eyes. They beheld them, to gaze with ever-renewed complacency upon their own possessions, and to exclaim for the ten thousandth time, with pharisaical commiseration: "Poor neighbor Vale! a better critter never lived, nor none more feelin', and it's a thousand pities for him and hisen that he hain't a mite of kalkerlation."

### LEFT.

The unfortunate object of all this mingled criticism, commiseration, and good-will, slowly urged Muggins up the mountain-road, through the forest, under the scarlet rain of leaves, just as he did an hour before when Eirene sat by his side. No, not just as he did then. He was alone now. He had never felt so alone in all his life before. In spite of himself, he felt as if he had lost his child.

"And yet," he reasoned, "she has only gone to Busyville. I can drive down there after her any day. It is only twenty miles away." The fact that she was there did not seem in itself sufficient to fill him with such a sense of loss. For eighteen years his meagre life had absorbed grace and beauty, poetry and love, from this child. But never until now had he realized that she was the very soul of his soul; that to him the very light of the world had gone away with her eyes.

As he emerged from the forest-road and saw his home before him, he thought that he had never seen it look forsaken and desolate before.

He remembered that all the fine houses in Busyville had failed to disgust him with this lowly abode; that it never turned such an inviting face toward him as when he returned from that handsome but commonplace village. With a thrill of joy he had always caught the first glimpse of its dormer windows, of its low roof, of its brown walls. He could see nothing which filled him with such positive delight as the sight of those trees and flowers and vines planted by his own hands. Then all his loved ones awaited his return within this home. Now for the first time one was wanting, and for the first time the little house looked dreary. This look must have been the reflection of his own feelings; for any traveller would have said at this moment, that in all the scattered town of Hilltop there was not another abode so lowly and yet so homelike in its aspect. A painter would have seen before him a picture of such brilliant autumn beauty that he would have longed to transfix it on canvas forever.

Everywhere the red maples had cast down their scarlet leaves, now lying in glowing drifts in the hollows of the roads. The yellow maples ripening slowly in the soft shelter of the hills, still fluttered their green skirts edged here and there with gold; while others, standing in the crisp air of some open space, spread out their tremulous panoplies of unbroken amber.

The old vines, which festooned the gables and dormer windows of the cottage, hung in vivid relief beside the dark green of the dappled English ivy—an ivy sprung from the immemorial vine which an elder Vale had brought across the seas and planted; a souvenir amid the rocks of New England of his old English home.

The Swiss larches which Eirene's father planted when she was a baby waved their green plumes above the russet grass in the yard before the house, while on each side of the path stood the sturdy autumn flowers which had defied the early frosts. A few marigolds still flaunted their brazen splendor, here and there a garnet dahlia looked down from its blackened stalk, and, each side of the porch, beds of crysanthemums brightened the air with their delicate bloom. On one side, the meadow sloped down to a narrow river running swiftly away from the far mountains in its rear; on the other, the little farm stretched away to the woods that crowned the hill. Before it, far below, spread a lovely valley, while beyond it, another chain of purple mountains bound the horizon.

For the first time in his life, Lowell Vale was blind to the beauty of the world around his home; he thought only of the little group about its hearth, and that one was wanting.

Win and Pansy heard the wagon-wheels, and ran out to meet their father, their eyes still swollen with weeping; and as if to console themselves, began to quarrel as to who should drive Muggins into the barn. Pansy ended the discussion as her father alighted, by scrambling up one of the wheels, and quickly seizing the reins, which feat being accomplished, she turned to her amazed brother with an indescribably triumphant air, and exclaimed:

"There, Mister Win, who'll drive now?"

He sprang forward as if to seize the bridle, but Pansy's sudden pull of the reins sent Muggins off at a frantic gallop toward the barn—a gallop which proved that Muggins was a susceptible animal in spite of appearances; that she thrilled to her very shoes with the nervous, wilful pull of Miss Pansy, although no amount of mild orthodox jerks could ever induce her to "get up."

"For shame on a girl driving a horse! I wouldn't stoop to quarrel with a girl anyhow!" cried the discomfited Win.

A moment after, he saw Muggins in her unprecedented momentum not only knock the buggy-shafts and her own nose against the door of the barn, but toss the triumphant Pansy from her seat against the front of the vehicle; seeing which sight, this young man of fourteen turned and walked slowly away with a lofty, injured, yet satisfied air.

Nevertheless, the moment he reached the house, he quickened his steps, and exclaimed: "Oh, father, I'm afraid Pansy is hurt! Won't you go and see?"—an act which he very much desired to perform himself, only his pride and sense of injury would not let him.

At supper, Pansy had a black eye, and her pretty nose was very much swelled. But little Win looked away from her with a severe, offended air. He was too magnanimous to say that he was glad, yet altogether too angry to say that he was sorry.

Pansy's nose ached, so did her heart. She had a confused feeling that she had already forfeited the blue frock, and that every thing was going wrong. The peacemaker who had always poured oil on their naughty tempers was gone; her seat between the scowling brother and sister was empty.

The most eventful day that ever comes to a New England household had come to the lowly home of the Vales.

The first child had gone out from its shelter into the world. Sooner or later this day comes to every country New England home: its sons and daughters must go forth to be educated, or to work. The secluded farm, the scattered town, afford scanty advantages and few employments. Thus the girls and boys must go elsewhere to work in shops, to study in college, to teach school; and to those who are left, home never seems quite the same that it did before they went away.

It was a sore trial to this father and mother to know that their young child had gone, not to the Busyville Academy, but to the Busyville factory; that from morning till night she was to be shut up to work in a close shop, with little choice of associates, and with none of the amusement and interest so indispensable to the young. But the poor, who have never learned the trick of making life easy for themselves, can hardly do more for their children.

Eirene had gone; what was left for them now but resignation?

Pansy's little purple nose was bathed in camphor, and she had mounted the confessional of her mother's knee, there to confess her sins and say her prayers before going to bed. She was very penitent at first.

She had been naughty, she said; she was sorry, and would be good to-morrow.

Suddenly another mood swept over her. She wouldn't have been naughty if it hadn't been for Win. Mister Win needn't think that *he* was always going to drive Muggins, and leave her standing on the ground. Her head ached, her nose was sore—"it was Muggins who was wicked to bump her against the barn there!" Thus, with a passionate sob, the penitent suddenly passed into a severely abused child bewailing its grievances without stint. She refused to be soothed, till at last her mother said:

"What would Rene say to see Pansy so angry with Win? How sorry it would make her!"

These words were magical. Pansy saw as in a vision the receding outline of a sky-blue frock, and the eyes of her sister full of tears.

Thus together love and selfishness triumphed; so early does the mingled essence of good and evil enter into human motive.

Pansy suddenly wiped her eyes, threw her arms around her mother's neck, and whispered,

"I *am* sorry that I was naughty."

Then the little sinner in the round night-cap and long night-gown marched off to bed.

At family prayers that night, Lowell Vale for the first time prayed for the absent. As he prayed the Good Shepherd still to hold in his keeping the beloved lamb that they had sent out from the fold, his voice trembled, and at last broke.

Mary Vale was very quiet in her grief. All her life she had been relinquishing desire; not so much desire for that which she had lost, as for that which she had missed. It was a gift conferred upon her, this power of self-renunciation. She had not been always thus; her soul had been eager and importunate once. Then it had seemed to her that she must beat her way out of the restricted sphere in which she was born.

The life which she read of in books she was very sure was only the faint reflection of a richer life to be found somewhere in the world. It was very different from the life of Hilltop; to her she was certain it would be more satisfying. There were books and pictures and music in this life. There were gay cities, cathedrals, and resonant organs; all the wonderful sights of strange lands, rivers, and oceans that she had never seen! There was wealth and leisure and beauty in the world; why might she not have something of it all in her portion?

Had she married an ambitious and successful man, he could have conferred upon her no honor that she would not have grown to adorn. As it was, before her youth had passed, Mary Vale knew that this life which she saw in dreams would never become real in her earthly lot. It was a natural transition when her hopeless longings turned from the delights of earth, which she knew could never be hers, to the joys of the heaven which she felt sure would one day be her portion. It was such happiness to know that she could imagine nothing of this unseen world that would transcend the reality. She could afford to live in a poor house here, and even have a mortgage upon that, while she felt certain that after a little while she would enter into a building of God, a house not made with hands, eternal, and in the heavens.

She loved to read over to her children its description in Revelations, all glowing with gems. And when she had ended the inspired story, she would turn to her husband with softly dilating eyes, and say: "My dear, the heirs of *such* an inheritance can afford to wait." "Father!" This one word comprehended her entire idea of God. To her He was a tender, an all-pervading, ever-guarding Presence. Every one of His promises she seized with child-like trust. He might deny her, might bereave her, yet she never doubted His love. Every morning she prayed for His strength to bear the cross of that day; every night she laid it down at the feet of her Lord with tearful thanks that the burden had been so light. There was no object on earth dearer to her than her first-born child. To-day she had relinquished her without one repining word. Yet what a different lot she would have chosen for her, had it been possible. A few tears dropped upon her pillow ere she slept. Then the lids drooped over the soft eyes, and with a tender smile she passed out into the limitless realm of dreams, this mother, to walk hand in hand with her child.

Lowell Vale waited till she slept, then taking the candle from the stand beside which he had apparently been reading, he walked quietly up-stairs to Eirene's room.

If a room can reflect the character of its occupant, how pure must have been the nature of this child. The windows of the little dormer chamber faced the east, looking out upon the valley with its ribbon-like river, and the great mountains which girded the sky. They were draped with white, and between them stood the white toilet which Eirene's own hands had fashioned. Over it hung a little mirror festooned with golden tissue-paper, falling like flakes of flame against the pale-blue walls.

At one end of the room, commanding the view from the windows, stood Eirene's table. This, too, was covered with white, and on it still stood her work-basket and a glass filled with pink and white crysanthemums. Over it hung a swinging bookcase filled with relics of the Vale library.

Here were Shakespeare and Milton and old George Herbert in antique bindings, stained and worn by time. Here were Rollin and Gibbon, and volumes of the Spectator and Rambler. Thomas à Kempis, Jeremy Taylor, and holy old Baxter stood on the same shelf with Byron and Burns. Ivanhoe and Old Mortality, with other of Scott's magic creations were the only novels; but there was a shelf filled with old Latin books which Eirene had always treasured as if they were gold, because they looked so wise; and another filled with French books, which the child had studied many a night when all in the house were sleeping. Under the bookcase where the sweet face always looked into hers as she sat there, Eirene had hung an engraving of St. Elizabeth of Hungary in a frame of dark wood which her father had made for her. How well he remembered her look, and the kiss that she gave him, when she took it from his hands, that frame so deftly fashioned, so fit a setting for her treasure.

Over the mantel opposite hung the portrait of a young and most lovely woman. The beauty of this face was not of mere tint and outline, although both seemed faultless. It was not ruddy and rustic, but a high-born face, with the exquisite profile which we see cut in antique gems. But what were this to the soft splendor of the half-veiled eyes, and the tender smile brooding in the curves of the gentle mouth! It was a mouth to which childish lips would turn and cling in the loving innocence of infancy. And the rippling hair of nutty brown just touched with gold,—how a child's hand would love to lose itself in its silken luxuriousness!

It was the face of a woman that no manly man could behold without love; of a woman for whose sake such a man would live and die, nor desire a happier destiny. It was the face of one in the first lustrum of womanhood, else it might well have been taken for the portrait of Eirene Vale.

It was the portrait of Eirene's grandmother. How unlike the other grandmothers of Hilltop, sitting in their mouldy frames in high caps, sausage curls, and bagpipe sleeves, was this tutelary saint who passed from the world in the undimmed lustre of her youth! The image of Alice Vale was repeated in her grandchild. Perhaps this was one reason why the heart of Lowell Vale seemed bound by so close a tie to his first-born child—that her face recalled in vivid reality the living face of the young mother so dimly remembered.

Lowell Vale, with the light in his hand, walked slowly around the room, pausing before every object, each one in his eyes sacred for the sake of his child.

Every thing was left as if she had gone out for an hour, and might return any moment. There was the unfinished work in her basket, the glass filled with flowers, the last book that she had read with the mark in it as she had laid it down on the table; the low chair where she had sat.

Lowell Vale looked long, looked with a sigh that swelled almost to a groan, as he turned to the low cot with its white counterpane and untouched pillow. Since he first laid her down there himself, a tiny child, fourteen years before, when Win was born, this was the first night that the cot had been empty, and the fair child-head sheltered by the roof of strangers.

He knelt down, buried his face in

her pillow, and did what the strongest and weakest of mortals are almost sure to do in their moments of extremity. This father, who felt that it was beyond his faltering power to take care of her himself, again committed his child to the care of God.

THE GIRL UP-STAIRS.

While her father knelt beside her pillow at home, Eirene sat alone in her new room at Busyville. She sat like one in a daze, as if stunned by the strangeness of her surroundings. Her eyes were fixed upon Moses Loplolly's little parrot, now fast asleep on its perch; yet she did not see the bird nor the hard, bare outline of the new room. No, she saw her own little chamber with its azure walls; saw her own little bed; saw her father kneeling by its side; then again the soft eyes swam in tears, and she started as if she had just wakened from a vision.

"Father," she murmured, stretching out her arms as if to enfold him. "Dear father, for your sake, and for yours, dear mother, I will be brave and patient and hopeful."

She felt strangely alone. Surely that angular little room could never seem home-like to her; it was so cold and cheerless. Its very atmosphere was repelling. Its bare walls were covered with coarse whitewash; its one window covered with a stiff paper curtain; its floor was painted a bright yellow; its furniture consisted of a very diminutive looking-glass, a pine washstand on which stood a tin basin, a straight-backed wooden chair, and a bed covered with a glaring patchwork-quilt. As Eirene's eyes wandered over these meagre appliances, she started, for the first time remembering the words of a metallic voice, uttered while the door was closing upon her for the night:

"Remember, we breakfast at six. We never wait. You are to be in the shop by seven o'clock."

Eirene took from her head the silken net which covered her hair, and as she shook and brushed out its waving length, repeated to herself the Bible verse which her mother had marked for her in the morning.

The young head touched the strange pillow, and the young lips murmured as they had murmured from infancy:

"Now I lay me down to sleep,
I pray the Lord my soul to keep."

Thus, and with a prayer in her heart for each beloved one at home, the young eyes closed in innocent sleep.

But there was somebody very wide awake down-stairs. This somebody sat in a large family-room, a commodious room which reflected the competence and the thrifty housekeeping of its owner.

Yes, it was a very comfortable room, although not a single picture, not one artistic touch, suggested a love for the beautiful in the one who had furnished it. The walls were hung with yellow paper; the windows were covered with yellow shades. The great lounge and stiff-backed rocking-chair were covered with chintz of large device, and glaring hue.

The floor was covered with that home-made carpet indigenous to New England, which is never seen in perfection out of it—a carpet in which stripes of violent yellow, red, and green run side by side in acute lines till they cover the floor.

The slumbering fire of an autumn night dwindled upon the hearth. Before it stood a large table, on which was a shaded lamp and a work-basket piled high with work. On each side sat a man and woman, with a cradle between them, in which a baby slept. The woman slowly moved the cradle with her foot, while her busy hand plied the needle in and out through the heel of a stocking, which had been mended till not even imagination could conjecture which had been its original yarn. This woman had restless, eager eyes; greedy eyes you would have called them, had you looked into them closely. They had a taking-in look, as if they had grown hungry gloating over objects of desire and of possession.

Yet they were handsome eyes, and in certain moods could suffuse with tears of motherly feeling. The watery tendency of these handsome eyes had won a popular reputation for their owner among the matrons of Busyville. "There never was a more feeling woman than Tabitha Mallane," they would say. "Such a capable woman! What a family she has, and how she has brought them up. What a mother she is, to be sure!" Her face was deeply care-lined. Every motion indicated disquietude, as if in all her anxious, workful life she had never earned the right to Heaven's own boon—repose.

It was not thus with her husband. Time and care had furrowed his face also; but in its intellectual lines, so much more intellectual than his wife's, you could trace the capacity for rest as well as for work; and now with a remote look in his eyes he was buried in the oblivion of his newspaper.

Perhaps his wife was more restless than usual. She gave a spasmodic rock to the cradle, she moved her chair, she pushed the lamp, she pulled her needle with such violence through the stocking that the yarn broke. From time to time she looked round the side of the newspaper into the face of her quiet husband with an expression of positive annoyance. At last the silence became unendurable. Again she jerked the cradle, pushed the lamp, and in a peremptory tone said:

"Father!"

No reply issued from the voluminous depths of the Boston Journal. Mr. Mallane was absorbed with the affairs of his country.

"Father!"

This time the endearing appellation was uttered in such a keen tone of acerbity, that it penetrated the thick rime of national affairs.

Mr. Mallane slowly laid down his paper, slowly took his spectacles from his eyes, slowly took his silk handkerchief from his pocket, slowly wiped his glasses, and as slowly said:

"Well, mother?"

"I should think that you would say 'Well, mother!' Where are your eyes, Mr. Mallane?"

"In my head, I believe, Tabitha."

"You know what I mean! Are you crazy, John Mallane?"

"No. I am perfectly sane, Tabitha."

"No, you are not. You are either blind or crazy; or you never would have brought that girl up-stairs into this house."

"Why not? She is a very pretty girl, mother. I should think that you would like to have her in the house for the sake of the children."

"For the sake of the children! Why do you aggravate me, John Mallane? Isn't Paul coming home in a week? Hasn't Paul eyes in his head?"

"Yes, Paul has eyes in his head, very handsome eyes, too; just such eyes as yours used to be, Tabitha, before you began to worry; and he knows how to use them, too," said Mr. Mallane; and a smile of parental pride passed over his face as he spoke of his first-born son.

"I'll tell you how he'll use them, John Mallane;" and in her eagerness the mother leaned forward with distended eyes and ominous voice:

"He'll use them the very first thing to fall in love with that girl up-stairs. If there's no running away and getting married, and all that, it will be a pretty story to go about town, that Paul Mallane has fallen in love with one of his father's shop-girls. I warn you, John Mallane."

"Tabitha, why will you always borrow trouble? As you say, Paul has eyes in his head. He will see that the girl is pretty. He can't help that. But Paul has common sense. Paul is long-headed; he has any amount of foresight. He is just as ambitious for wealth and for position as you are. He is the last fellow on earth to make a fool of himself by running off with a poor shop-girl. And I don't see that he is very much inclined to fall in love with any body. Here he has been flirting a whole year with Tilly Blane, the prettiest and the richest girl in town. She would like to have him fall in love with her; but he hasn't. And she is pretty, and I don't know but prettier than the girl up-stairs."

"Yes, she is prettier, perhaps," answered the mother, dubiously. "But it is only flesh and blood pretty, pink cheeks, blue eyes, curly hair. At thirty she will be as ugly as her mother, who, you know, twenty-five years ago was the belle of Busyville. But this girl upstairs has an uncommon face. Didn't you notice it, father? Why, with that expression on it, she will be beautiful at fifty. When those great brown eyes look up through those long lashes, there is a look in them that would take the heart out of any young man, and they'll take the heart out of our Paul. And she'll turn them up, and cast them down. She'll make good use of those eyes, the artful——"

"Be reasonable, be reasonable, Tabitha. Don't call the poor child names; for she's only a child, and whatever arts she may learn, she hasn't learned them yet. You could see that at supper. She felt so strange and frightened, she could scarcely eat. She has never been away from home before. Let us show her the same kindness that we would like shown to our Grace if we had to send her away to earn her bread."

"Show her kindness? The greatest kindness that we can show her, is to send her out of this house. It is no place for *her*. I cannot have her here. I will not have her here. She shall go to-morrow. I have set my foot down, John Mallane."

"She shall not go to-morrow," said Mr. Mallane, quietly, but in a tone which could not be contradicted. It usually happened that when Tabitha Mallane "set her foot down," John Mallane set his down also.

Coolly and quietly he asserted his will; but having once asserted it, it was as fixed as a rock. His wife's temper, like a stormy wave, chafed and fretted in helpless anger against the immovable mountain of will. Poor wave! it soon beat itself weary. Baffled, worn-out, it always subsided in sullen passivity at last.

Yet John Mallane was not a tyrannical husband. As he allowed no one to interfere with "his business," so he was careful not to encroach upon his wife's prerogatives in the management of the household where she reigned supreme. Thus, this sudden invasion of her territory, with his last declaration of authority, seemed as unpardonable as it was unexpected. Yet he had said it—"She shall not leave to-morrow"—and Tabitha Mallane knew that now there was nothing for her to do but to smother her rage and submit.

John Mallane read on awhile in silence, giving time to the chafed and fretted temper of his wife to subside into calmness. She, too, was silent, knowing well that at the present crisis no added word of hers could avail in gaining her end. John Mallane was wise; he never talked with his wife when she was angry; and thus, without any serious matrimonial combats, he managed to have his own way whenever he chose.

When he thought that the proper moment had arrived, he laid down his newspaper, took off his spectacles, took his red silk handkerchief again from his pocket, deliberately polished his glasses, deliberately reset them upon the high bridge of his imperturbable nose, and as deliberately said:

"Tabitha, I have no desire to be unreasonable. I know that you have care enough, and I don't want to increase it. But I promised this little girl's father she should have a home in my family. I feel sorry for Vale. He is one of the kindest men in the world, but he isn't a manager. I am. I've been successful; he hasn't. I'm rich, he's poor. I send my boy to college; he sends his little girl to work in my shop. And he'll have to take her small wages to help pay the mortgage on his farm. I am not willing to advance money on the mortgage, but am willing to give a comfortable home to his little girl, who will help earn it. I am perfectly able to do the first, I am only willing to do the latter. It is no stretch of generosity, you see, Tabitha?"

Mrs. Mallane made no reply. But the needle in the stocking seemed to listen, and the cradle moved with a slow, thoughtful motion.

Her husband continued: "Poor Vale! The tears came into his eyes when he spoke of his little girl. I thought of our Gracy; what it would be to us to send her out into a strange place to work in a shop, and I said: 'Vale, I'll do the best that I can for your child. She needn't go into the boarding-house with the other hands. She shall stay in my family, and eat at my table, and I'll ask nothing extra.' To have said less would have been inhuman. You don't want me to be inhuman, especially when it don't cost any more to be human, do you, Tabitha?"

Under ordinary circumstances, Tabitha Mallane's better nature would have responded to this appeal, and she would have said: "Yes, father, you are right. I have been unreasonable. I don't complain that you take your own way."

But against this act of her husband's, against this child whom he had brought into her home, was arraigned the strongest instinct of her nature, the instinct of maternity, fierce, selfish, prevailing.

In and out through the heel of a fresh stocking flew the glittering needle with spasmodic haste, while the jerking cradle, the working of the strong features, the movement of the large frame, all told of an inward struggle. There was a silence of moments before she spoke; then the anger had gone out of her voice, but its tones were deeply troubled.

"I have feeling for the girl," she said, "when I think of our Grace in her place. I should be willing enough to have her stay, if it was not for our Paul."

"Nonsense!" said John Mallane, in an incredulous voice. "Tabitha, let me tell you once for all that our Paul will take care of himself;" and with these words, John Mallane again took up the Boston Journal, and soon forgot the existence of the girl up-stairs in the excitement of reading about "South Carolina Fire-Eaters."

## II.

### PAUL.

OUR Paul had come. Without being told, you would have known the fact, by the changed atmosphere of the house.

He strode about like a king, and all the children were afraid of him.

To tell the truth, there were altogether too many children in the house to please this royal young gentleman. Not but what he had some fraternal affection for each individual brother and sister, but in the aggregate they were troublesome, "so many young ones."

They brought more or less of noise and confusion into the house, and his princeship craved order and quiet.

Their numerous wants absorbed much of the time and attention of his mother, which he wished to appropriate to himself.

Every other summer when he came home, he found a new baby in the cradle —it was very aggravating.

If a portion of the aggravation was born of the fact that each newcomer lessened the amount of his prospective fortune, Paul had never acknowledged it, even to himself. It was enough that they annoyed him in the present; they made a noise, they were in the way, they filled up the house, which the young gentleman had already pronounced "a mean, pinched-up box."

Paul made no effort to hide the fact that he was dissatisfied with the appearance of his home, and his dissatisfaction was an affliction to his mother. She remembered the time when he looked upon the family sitting-room, with its striped carpet and yellow walls, with great complacency, and thought it a very fine affair. That was before he went to Harvard, or had seen the splendid drawing-rooms of Beacon street and of Marlboro Hill. Out in the great world he had stepped upon the plateau of a higher life, a life of leisure and ease, a life of culture and of graceful repose. It was very hard for him to step down again to the level on which he was born. He did it very unwillingly and very ungracefully. Ever since he could remember, his mother had been drudging and saving, his father delving and making money. He was determined to do neither. He wanted money only for the gratification that it would purchase; for the life of luxury and splendor which were unattainable without it. Each year the streets of Busyville looked narrower, its houses lower, his own parental domain smaller than the year before. Settle in

Busyville! Never. The whole kingdom of Busyville could not tempt the ambition of this young prince.

On the afternoon of his arrival, after having condescended to kiss his mother and patronize the children, Paul sauntered into his father's shops. Paul liked to saunter through the shops, looking at the work-people, and talking with them in a half supercilious, half hail-fellow way; it added to the consciousness of his own importance. Especially he enjoyed lounging in the "Girls' Room." More than any place in the world, there he was king. To a company of young girls shut up in a close room, to ply one monotonous task from the beginning of the year to its close, the advent of a handsome, polished young man was a very pleasant event. It must have been humiliating, if they remembered the fact that outside of that shop he never recognized them; they did not belong to "his set." Tilly Blane and the other fair maidens of the mansion houses did not speak with shop-girls in the street; then why should he, the petted beau for whom these maidens were ready to give their fortunes or break their hearts? But in the shop! Ah, that was a different matter. Here no king amid his court could be more graciously condescending. Gay, graceful, debonair, he loitered through the long room at his leisure, chatting with all, giving a smile to one, a subtle compliment to another, a witty sally or repartee to another, making each one feel that he was especially pleased with her individual self, indeed, that she was the object of his particular admiration. Thus each one was delighted with him.

Was it wonderful? He was young and handsome and rich, with a charm of manner unwonted among the men of their acquaintance. They were young and pretty and poor, and women. Thus they yielded to him involuntarily the homage of smiles and blushes and eloquent eyes. It was very pleasant to Paul. Nowhere else did he feel so positively sure of his importance and power in the world as in the girls' shop.

He felt perfectly secure of himself in this intoxicating atmosphere; felt sure that his armor of pride was proof against all their pretty weapons. "They are none of them *my* style," he would soliloquize. "The mountain girls are too rustic, and the town girls too pert. Nearly all of them use two negatives in a sentence, and their verbs rarely agree with their nominatives. What else could be expected of shop-girls? But, after all, some of them are deuced pretty, and how they admire *me!* How delighted they are with my notice, poor things. There's Lucy Day, she really thinks that I am serious, and will call upon her on Sunday evening. The devil! I am going to see Tilly Blane, of course."

On this afternoon, he had nearly completed the length of the long apartment; had paused in his leisurely way to exchange coquetries with every fair worker, before he discovered Eirene Vale standing busy at work beside a window, in a remote corner of the apartment. He could not see her face, yet knew her at once to be a stranger. A "new hand" always possessed a degree of interest to Paul, yet on this occasion he forbore to manifest it, lest he might arouse feelings of jealousy in the hearts of others of his fair subjects. Thus he asked no questions, seemed as if he did not see the stranger. "Is she pretty?" This question he determined to answer for himself. From the moment of his discovery, he thought only of reaching the spot where she stood—it was gained at last.

"Miss ———?" he said, with a mixture of suavity and effrontery which he would have used only to a shop-girl in his own father's shop: "Miss ———?" hesitating as if he knew her name, yet could not that instant recall it.

Eirene turned her face. The clear eyes met his with a simple look of surprise. She was neither frightened nor flattered. The innocent face expressed only wonder that an utter stranger should accost her with the familiarity of a friend, while she waited for the young gentleman to conclude his sentence.

"I beg your pardon. I thought ——."

"I thought ——;" but the utter nonfusion of the youth prevented him from telling what he thought.

The conceited boy of the world stood abashed before the guileless look of a young girl's eyes. He was totally unprepared for such a look, it was so different from the one he had anticipated. He had expected smiling confusion, blushing vanity, with spontaneous and undisguised admiration of his own imperial self. This apparent unconsciousness of his magnificence, this utter lack of self-consciousness, with the look of wonder and inquiry in a pair of eyes—the loveliest, he thought, that he had ever seen—was too much for Paul's equanimity, notwithstanding the large amount of his self-possession.

To his astonishment he saw before him a lady, and was disgusted that he had proved himself to be less than a gentleman.

"I ——. I am mistaken. Pardon me," for the third time stammered our discomfited Adonis, as, with a profound bow, he withdrew. He felt an impulse to rush directly out of the shop. He was not used to appearing at disadvantage. He was more than mortified at losing his self-possession, and that to a shop girl—he who had never blushed before the beauties of Marlboro Hill, and had borne without flinching the full blaze of the drawing-rooms of Beacon street. Yet amid his confusion he did not forget that the eyes of his fair subjects were upon him. What would they think? What would they say, if they saw that one of their own class had the power to embarrass the young prince and send him in disconcerted haste from their presence? That would be indeed a fall from his lofty position.

Thus he sauntered down the other side of the room and endeavored to chat in his wonted manner. But somehow he felt the gaze of those innocent eyes still fixed upon him, though if he had dared to look, he would have seen that they were bent steadfastly upon their work. The amusement of flirting had suddenly lost all its zest. He found himself judging these buxom beauties by a new standard—the face that he had just left behind him. How coarse their voices sounded, how inane their words seemed now. He was thankful when he came to the end and had made his last pretty speech.

He went out, and but one face went with him. He did not know the name of its possessor, he had not enquired. He could have asked the question carelessly enough to have gratified an idle curiosity. But it was not idle curiosity, it was interest which he felt. Should he, Paul Mallane, betray interest in one of his father's shop-girls? Oh, no. He could not forget so far his high position.

"Mother could tell me," he said to himself as he stepped into the street. "She knows every girl that comes and goes from these shops. But she is the last person on earth that I would ask."

Paul was too well aware what his mother thought of his visiting the shops.

"It is undignified and beneath you, Paul," she would say, "to lounge away so much of your time with the shop hands. Besides, it is dangerous. It is very pleasant, I know, to bewitch those pretty mountain girls. I am sure you do," and the mother would look with gratified pride upon the young, handsome face. "But by-and-by one may bewitch you. I know you think not; but you don't know how foolish a pretty face might make even you, Paul, with all your ambition."

"Mother, you need not worry about me," the young man would say, with a conscious air. "I have never seen a shop-girl yet, no, nor any girl, who could make me forget what is due to my position."

After his promenade through the shops, Paul had intended to show his handsome face and air his immaculate broadcloth on Main street. He knew that Tilly Blane would see him as she looked through the blinds of the squire's house, at first with eager hope, and then with tearful disappointment, as he, the imperial Paul, strode past in sublime unconsciousness of being opposite her paternal mansion. He knew also that Abby Arnot would peep through the blinds of the house across the street, and as she watched him pass by, exclaim with a toss

2

of triumph: "There! There goes Paul Mallane! He doesn't even look toward Squire Blane's. Talk to *me* of he and Tilly being engaged."

He thought, too, how old Deacon Nuggett, sitting in his shop door, would call out as he passed by: "Ah, Paul! Paul Mallane, is that you! Well! well! how fine ye're lookin'. A son any father might be proud on. Y'u'll be in Congress in ten years, eh? Paul!"

But when he rushed forth from the factory door, Paul had forgotten all these anticipated triumphs. He walked straight across the street to the white house under the trees. He entered it, but did not go into the family sitting room, where he knew that his mother sat rocking the baby. Instead he walked into the prim parlor and threw himself down upon the stiff high-backed sofa. Paul was disgusted with himself (a most unusual state of mind), therefore it was not strange that he soon grew equally disgusted with every thing that he beheld. "What a shabby, shut-up box this parlor is, any way," he said to himself. "There is nothing spacious, nor elegant, nor easy about it. And yet before I went away from Busyville I thought it splendid, just as mother thinks it is now. The pattern of this carpet is entirely too large for the room, it looks as if it was crowding the walls back. And the walls are too low for these great pictures, and the pictures are in dismal taste. Washington's Deathbed; and Calvin, preaching his gloomy theology; and Grandmother Bard in a frizzled wig looking as black as thunder. They say that I look like her too, and —— how that centre-table looks, with that square of daguerreotypes piled around the astral lamp. That is Gracy's work. If there is no one else, I will teach her how to take a little of the stiffness out of this room. She should see the drawing-rooms at Marlboro' Hill; then she would know how to arrange a parlor. But to make an elegant room of this is impossible," and Paul gazed about with an expression of increased contempt. "Dick Prescott expects to come here, too. He shan't. He shan't see this parlor. He shan't see ——." What? Paul did not see fit to say. He threw his head further back, fixed his eyes upon the ceiling, and as the rich color stained his cheek, impatiently exclaimed: "I am an ass."

It was a most unwonted state of mind which could make the young prince of the house of Mallane declare himself to be "an ass."

The bell rang for tea. Paul did not stir. "Let those children get seated with their confounded clatter;" said this amiable young man, with eyes still fixed upon the ceiling. When the shuffling of little feet and the shouts of eager voices had subsided a little, and the click of tea-cups and the tinkling of tea-spoons and the fragrance of tea reached his nose and ears instead, Paul arose, and, half lazily, half ill-naturedly, sauntered forth.

"Here, Paul, here's your seat by me," said Mrs. Mallane, as turning with her most benignant mother-look, she saw Paul, with an expression of annoyance and embarrassment upon his face, standing in the open door. When he opened it, a pair of clear eyes looked up from a tea-cup. The young face whose guilelessness had so abashed his impertinence in the work-shop, wearing the same expression, looked up to his from the home supper-table. His astonishment at seeing it there, with the recollection of his behavior, again overcame Paul's self-possession. He stood perfectly still, as if he thought there was no seat for him at the table. Not till after he had taken the place proffered by his mother, did Paul become conscious that he was sitting on the same side with the young stranger, his sister Grace between them, while his accustomed seat opposite was filled by little Jack. Again he was vexed. Much as it had disconcerted him—strange to say, he felt the most insane desire to look on the face again.

"Mother intended that I should not, and so seated me here," he thought, looking full upon that matron's countenance. The gray eyes were fixed upon him with a penetrating gaze.

"Will you take tea, Paul?" was all that she said.

Paul began to sip his tea in silence,

and all the children began to stare at him, wondering if this could be our Paul who was so silent; when suddenly, rallying his forces, he commenced rattling on in his old, gay, careless manner.

It was his usual vacation talk, all about the Prescotts and Appletons and Marlboro Hill; the distinguished men and beautiful women whom he had met. This talk was usually very interesting to both John and Tabitha Mallane; to the father, because he felt a genuine interest in the persons described; to the mother, because it gratified her ambition to know that her son was admitted into such illustrious company.

There had been a grand reunion at Cambridge of philosophers and poets of the transcendental order. Paul, with a few other young bloods of the law school, had managed, through the prestige of Dick Prescott, to gain admittance, and had thus caught a glimpse of the savants and seers. Paul had seen Thoreau, and Hawthorne; E—— and H—— and L——, and gave brilliant descriptions of them all. "L——," he said, "with his hair parted in the middle, looks as much like the picture of Christ as ever." Eirene was thinking what a grand young gentleman this must be, who was on such familiar terms with the great men of whom she had read all her life, but whom she never hoped to see; when this last remark struck her sensitive soul like blasphemy. She looked up, caught the eyes of the speaker as they turned and gazed over the head of his sister Grace. Once more they grew disconcerted and fell before the child-like glance. Again Paul inwardly pronounced himself an ass; but turning toward his mother, he ran on more pompously than before; while the children, their eyes distended with wonder, and their cheeks distended with pie and cheese, listened, inwardly exclaiming: "What a great man our Paul must be."

###### PAUL AND HIS MOTHER.

TEA was soon dispatched. Eating in this New England household was merely a business affair, and as such dispatched as soon as possible.

The æsthetic phase of tea-drinking, the toying with tea-spoons, the lingering over tea-cups to tell pleasant stories of the day, Tabitha Mallane had never learned. To give her family enough to eat, to have them eat it as quickly as possible, and to have her table cleared in the briefest space of time that could be, was to her the Alpha and Omega of eating.

Although Paul had just returned and seemed to have much to tell, this meal was no exception to others. Indeed, the atmosphere of hurry seemed more positive than usual.

Eirene found herself swallowing her tea with great trepidation, and wondering why she felt that there was not time to drink it, and why each individual there was doing the same, as rapidly as possible.

With a feeling of relief, she saw Mr. Mallane push back his chair. No one had introduced her to Paul. Nobody but Mr. Mallane had spoken to her through the meal. No one seemed to notice her as she walked quietly out of the room; yet two persons at the table were keenly conscious of her departure.

"Rene! Rene! Poor Mo——" cried out the parrot as she opened the door of her little cell. At the sound of his name, the image of lank, awkward, yellow-haired Moses rose before her, in contrast to the handsome young stranger down-stairs.

"Strange that there can be such a difference in two," she ejaculated involuntarily, as taking up her book, she sat down on a low stool beside the window and commenced the translation of a French exercise. It was an extract from Bossuet: "*Quoique Dieu et la nature aient fait tous les hommes égaux en les formant d'une même bone, la vanité humaine ne peut souffrir cette egalité.*" "Although God and Nature have made all men equal in forming them of the same earth, human vanity cannot bear that equality." She paused, the pencil poised in her suspended hand. A young manly face set in dark hair, lit with dark eyes, seemed to look up into hers from the page before her. "How it would have grieved mother to hear the Saviour's name spoken with such indifference," she said simply, murmuring the sentence aloud after the manner of people much alone. "But why should I think of it?" she continued, bending her eyes once more upon the page, and resuming her task. But the vagrant thought refused to be called back to the study of French. "Then *he* is Paul of whom I have heard so much," it whispered. She looked up from her book, out upon the garden; there under the old cherry-tree, on the grass was stretched the same Paul, gazing up as if he saw a vision.

There he was! and she was thinking of him! This consciousness sent the quick blood into the young girl's cheeks for the first time.

Paul saw it, this maiden-blush, saw it as the first recognition of his own princely self, and it sent a new thrill into his heart, a thrill that went into his dreams. For a number of moments he had been gazing without interruption on this fair picture above him; on the pure profile of the young face in the open window within its frame of dark vines. The long gaze could hardly have come to a more delightful termination than this, caused by the uplifted face, the vivid blush. And yet he felt once more abashed that he had been discovered. He arose with a bow, then threw himself down again and fixed his eyes with a look of profound meditation upon the sky. "He came out to think," reflected Eirene, and that she might not seem to intrude upon his meditation, she moved her seat from the window, and in the interior of her cell once more invoked the eloquence of Bossuet to assist her in studying French.

To do Paul justice, he did not throw himself upon the grass for the purpose of gazing at Eirene's window; he came into the garden solely to escape his mother and himself. The pretty picture of the window had been an unanticipated delight, enjoyed the more keenly because unexpected and stolen. He knew that if his mother could have foreseen this pleasure, he would never have enjoyed it.

Tabitha Mallane had hastened supper and the children out of the way, in order that she might have a talk with Paul.

The young gentleman would have gladly escaped, but he knew that it was useless to try to evade his mother; he might delay it, perhaps, but the talk would come.

"Sit down, Paul," she said as she seated herself in her low chair and began to rock the cradle, her invariable employment when she had "something to say." "What, going out?" "How uneasy you are. You will have plenty of time left to see Tilly Blane if you do sit a little while and talk with your mother."

Then she began to question him concerning his studies and his prospects for being graduated with honor. "No mother's boy should stand before him," she declared, as her questions were promptly and favorably answered. Yet she did not seem satisfied, and began to rock the cradle violently in the silence.

"What do you think of the new hand, Paul?" she asked abruptly.

"What hand?"

"Why, the one that your father will have eat at our table. Isn't she pretty?"

"Pretty? ra——ther," answered the young gentleman, with the imperturbable air which he always summoned to his assistance in such conversations with his mother. "You took care that I should see only half of her face, that looked well enough," he continued.

"But what *do* you think of her, Paul?"

"Think! I think she is dressed like a dud. Can't say how she would look in the costume of the present century."

"Don't try to evade, Paul. You know that I am not talking of her dress. What do you think of the girl?"

"What time have I had to think of her?" "Ten minutes at supper."

"Half the afternoon, Paul."

"What an idea! Why should I think of her more than of any other shop hand?"

"*Why*, Paul? The girl's face answers that question. You can't deceive me. I saw you go into the shops. I saw you come back. Something unusual happened there, or you would not have come and shut yourself in that dark parlor, instead of going into the street. Then, when you came in to supper and saw her sitting at the table, your face told me of whom you had been thinking."

"Mother, you need not begin to hold guard over *me*," exclaimed the young man, angrily. "You need not watch me through the blinds, when I go out, and when I come in. I am not one of your babies. I know what belongs to my position."

Poor Paul! No matter what his annoyance, it was such a support for him to fall back upon his "position."

"I know you, Paul," said his mother, leaning forward, eagerly, rocking the cradle more violently, as she always did when excited. "Because I know you, I warn you, in the beginning, against this girl up-stairs. She is sly and deceitful, such still people always are. She intends to captivate you with her quiet ways and her great soft eyes, and she *will* captivate you in spite of all your pride and all your ambition, unless you are on your guard. Of course, my son, you know what is due to your position, you know what your mother expects of you; but it will be hard for you to be true to your knowledge until you are older."

"Mother, who under heaven *is* this girl that you are making such a fuss about?"

"Her name is Vale. Eirene Vale. Her name is as outlandish as her family. She comes from a shiftless, poverty-stricken set, up on the mountains. Her father whimpered about her having to go to work, and so your father took a notion to be kind to the girl. You know what your father's notions are? They can't be changed. He will have her here. She is a nuisance. I hate the sight of her."

Paul leaned back in the rocking-chair, yawned, and then began to whistle. He was not as fluent upon the subject of the "new hand" as upon his favorite topics of the Prescotts, and Marlboro Hill. He had nothing to say; he looked bored and sleepy.

"Well," he said at last, in a careless tone, "you are making a great ado, and I am sure I don't know what for. You say that this girl is 'sly, poverty-stricken, and a nuisance.' Do you think that there is the slightest danger of my committing myself to such a person?" and with this disclaimer Paul thrust his hands into his pockets, sauntered forth into the garden, and threw himself down under the old cherry-tree.

"Mother will overdo everything," he said to himself, angrily. She ought to know more of human nature than to think such talk will make me dislike the girl. Why did not she let her alone? and let me alone? It is enough to make a fellow say that he *will* make love, even if he had not thought of it before. Of course, there is every reason why I should never commit myself to one in her position. But I don't like to be balked. I won't be balked, not by my mother. Why didn't she leave me to my reason? Then I could have taught myself to have looked on this face without—well, without such a flutter. Such a face!"

"Such a face!" Surely. As Paul threw his head back to look up into the sky, he caught a glimpse of it in the frame of vines in the open window above him.

What was it in this face which so held his gaze? It was not its youthful loveliness alone, Paul was used to beautiful faces. It did not please his senses only, it seemed to touch his soul, it rested, it soothed, it satisfied. What a contrast to the eager, restless, life-worn face which he had just left. The worldly, selfish, blasé boy gazed on, till through the evening air something of the serenity of the pure young brow stole down to him. As he gazed, he felt within him the promptings of his better angel telling him that with such a face to light his life, purity and peace would be possible even to him.

Tabitha Mallane looked out of the window, saw her son, then walked back to the cradle and rocked it as if she were frantic. The baby must have thought so, for it awoke with a terrific scream, which instantly brought Paul back from Elysium, and made him say, "Curse that child!"

Tabitha Mallane *did* know Paul better than his father knew him; better than he knew himself. When she said: This girl's face will take the heart out of our Paul, she spoke from the depth of her consciousness of his nature. He had taken this nature from his mother, he was like her.

She remembered her own impulsive youth, when even interest and ambition went down before the one, importunate want of a young, passionate heart. Well she remembered when she turned from the goodly lands and the pimply face of Benoni Blane to marry John Mallane, though all Busyville held up its hands, rolled up its eyes, turned up its nose and exclaimed in wonder, because "Tabitha Bard looked no higher than a journeyman worker, and he a Yorker."

She remembered the struggling years of her early married life, when Paul was a baby. She had not forgotten, when she drew him through the village streets in his little wagon, how she used to meet young Squire Blane's pretty wife with the infant Tilly in a fine carriage.

She could see distinctly now, the nod, half condescending, half disdainful, which the young beauty would throw her as the carriage rolled on. She remembered how she used to stand in the dusty street, with the handle of the little wagon in her hand, gazing after the fine phaeton, thinking it might have been hers, if she had only been willing to have accepted with it the pimply face of Benoni Blane.

She was not sorry. Although her share in the old homestead was long withheld from her by an angry mother; although she had borne the disgrace, terrible in New England, of being poor: she would not have exchanged John Mallane for Benoni Blane with all his possessions. She wanted John Mallane, but she wanted the equipage, the mansion, and the honored position also. "I *will* have them," she exclaimed, gazing after the receding carriage. "The day will come when your baby will be glad enough of the notice of my boy; when you won't toss your head at *me* like that, Belinda Blane."

Tabitha Mallane had divining eyes. They foreread the future; her prophecy was fulfilled.

The poor journeyman worker was now one of the wealthiest manufacturers in Busyville. His opinions carried great weight in the councils of the church, and in "Town meeting." He had reflected great credit upon Busyville in the State legislature, and for all these weighty reasons, Busyville had forgiven him for having been born poor, and in another State.

Tabitha Mallane's handsome son, the Harvard student, the incipient lawyer, the prospective member of Congress, the possible President of the United States, all in all considered, was the finest "catch" in Busyville. There were young men there with purer hearts, and brains quite as clever, but they lacked the money, or the beauty, or the grand, imperial air of Paul. He assumed so much indifference and hauteur, and was withal so very graceful and handsome, that there was not a girl in all the mansion houses but what felt flattered when he condescended to bestow his attentions. All this was a misfortune to Paul. He stood sorely in need of a little humiliation. The consciousness of supreme power over women is so very dangerous to any man. His mother's great anxiety came from the fear that he would not make the most of his advantages. She was so afraid that, in some moment of impulse and passion, he would do precisely as she did once: marry for love without asking his mother's permission. She had never repented her own course. When she looked back into the years, she always said: "I would do the same if I were to live my life over again. I could never love another man as I love John Mallane; besides, I always knew that he would die rich. It is very different with Paul. He could never work and wait as I have done, for a fortune. He was made to enjoy and to spend one. Besides, my boy shall never drudge and suffer what I have, in struggling up to prosperity. He must marry a rich wife. If we could give him all we have, it wouldn't be much with his taste and habits. He thinks that we live in a very poor way" (and here the poor mother would sigh).

"What will our property be, divided among eight?" "One eighth! What would that be to our Paul? Of course, he will settle in the city. Before that he must marry Tilly Blane. She is longing to give herself and all that she has to him. I knew that she would, long ago. Belinda Blane, it's a long time since you tossed your head at me.

"And now that girl up-stairs! I hate her, she is in the way."

BUSYVILLE—ITS BRAHMINS AND BUSTLERS.

BUSYVILLE was a fair type of a small manufacturing New England village. Its Yankee friends called it "a smart little town." It was, in truth, an enterprising, energetic, money-getting place.

Within a limited range of thought and action, its people were intelligent, but its arc of life was very narrow. Its besetting sin was littleness. Its factories, its schools, its churches, its houses, its people, all betrayed this tendency toward contraction.

Their life was shaped by the belief that Busyville, having arrived at a state of absolute perfection generations before, could not by any possibility be improved.

Family branches which had struck out and taken root in the great world, sometimes strayed back and informed their kindred on the parent tree that Busyville was behind the times; information which said kindred resented as an insult. In their opinion, any knowledge which was not known in Busyville, was not worth knowing. In their old Academy, the formula of study had not varied in fifty years. Within a certain range, it was excellent; but it never advanced, never grew larger. To its denizens Busyville was the Eden of this world. To have been born in another town, was a misfortune; to have been born in another country, was an ineffaceable disgrace. The poor stranger, the lonely foreigner who alighted here to look for work, had a sorry time. It did not occur to the pious women who sent boxes of clothing to the Congoes, and sometimes stinted themselves to help support the missionary whom they had sent to civilize the Hottentots, that there might be mission work to do even in Christian Busyville.

There were crowded lanes and by-ways in this town swarming with wild, ill-cared for children. It would have been a mercy to have clothed and cared for them, and to have led them by the hand into the commodious Sabbath-schools filled with the smiling, singing children of the church; but the women devoted to the Congoes had no time left for little white sinners at home. In close chambers and in little tenements, lonely stranger-women lived out their crushed existence;—overtaxed, sore-worn wives and mothers whose weary tasks were never done. To one of these a call from a prosperous sister-woman—one kindly expression of personal interest, would have been as the cup of cold water to one of Christ's thirsting little ones. Alas! it was rarely proffered. The lady absorbed in the Hottentots had nothing left for the "common woman" who washed her husband's shirts and mended her many children's scanty clothes in the shop tenements of Busyville. The bustling, well-to-do wives of Busyville were too busy with their societies, and schools, with their churches and houses, their own and their neighbors' affairs, to have either time or capacity left to devote to "outlandish people."

The sin of being a stranger in Busyville was never more keenly felt than by the newcomer on commencement day at the Academy. Then the daughters of the Busyville Brahmins, the maidens of the mansion-houses, the buxom beauties of the old homesteads proceeded to the seats which they had occupied from their earliest recollection and proceeded to pass judgment upon all aliens. With supercilious and mocking eyes they measured the rustic youths and maidens from the mountain-towns, and the young strangers from other States. After the first session, the fair Sanhedrim met in solemn conclave and decided whose outward aspect entitled them to be "one of ourselves."

Woe to the girl who "looked poor." Woe to the pale student whom they suspected of having emerged from one of the village shops, she never became "one of ourselves."

No one proffered to assist *her* in the solution of Algebraic problems. No sweet girl-voice which had parsed triumphantly through Paradise Lost, offered to lead her through pages of involved analyses. She watched the cliques of pretty girls laughing and playing under the trees at recess, or looked with wistful eyes as they recited their lessons in groups in the old Laboratory,—but no welcoming word or smile ever made her feel that she was one of them. She passed in and out of the long halls as alone and lonely on the last day of school as at its beginning.

The lines of caste were as rigidly drawn in orthodox Busyville, as in Pagan India.

One had to probe through the family soil for two or three generations to appreciate duly the prerogatives of the Brahmin order.

Methuselah Blane, a stout and unlettered yeoman came across the ocean, perhaps in the *Mayflower*—the Blanes say that he did. For a few pounds, he bought a large tract of land in the new valley, built a log-house and proceeded to subdue the stones, while his wife Mehitabel proceeded to subdue the tempers of her snub-nosed boys and to prepare them by a course of rigorous discipline for a life of vigorous labor. Methuselah and Mehitabel sleep together in one grave, in the old graveyard, beneath a brown tablet from which time has nearly effaced a very remarkable epitaph. They had gone back to dust, and their snub-nosed boys were gray-haired men, before Busyville grew into existence. Then the land of the "Blane boys" was cut into village lots; at last the iron path of the rail-horse was laid through their domain; money flowed into old stockings till they overflowed, and the Blanes and their children became Brahmins forever.

The present representative of the race, Benoni Blane, was a well-enough man, with a brain as neutral-tinted and as pimply as his complexion. It was not easy to point to any mischief he had done in the world, and equally difficult to discover any good.

Had any one asked a good-natured Brahmin: Why does Benoni Blane stand at the head of his order in Busyville? Is he of large public spirit? Has he endowed a school? Has he founded a library? Has he assisted poor young men to obtain an education? Does he support missionaries or build churches? Is he remarkable for talent, culture, or piety?

The good-natured Brahmin would have replied, "No, he has done none of these things. He is not distinguished for genius, learning, or goodness. Benoni Blane is a man who minds his own business, he is descended from one of the first settlers—and the Blanes have always been well to do."

To have had an infinitesimal portion of your being brought across the Atlantic by a remote ancestor in the *Mayflower*—was, of course, a superlative honor—it constituted you a person of exalted birth. But, if only your grandfather sailed over the ocean in a fast-sailing modern-built ship, oh, that was a different matter—a misfortune, if not a disgrace, which made you "foreign," if not outlandish.

To the Brahmins, by natural birthright, belonged the emoluments and dignities of Busyville. They supplied the town with professional men; the lawyers, doctors, and squires were all Brahmins. The clergymen were not equally blessed. Men had preached in Busyville whose ancestors did not sail to this country in the *Mayflower;* but they did not preach to the Brahmins. As you recognized the mansions of the Brahmins by their venerable gables, time-stained walls, and the deep shadow of their patriarchal trees, so you knew the ambitious "villas" of the wealthy Bustlers by their stark, staring newness, by their tumorous bay windows, astounding porticoes, and stunning cupolas, threatening the frail fabrics beneath with constant annihilation. But if these rich Bustlers did not know the vulgar from the beautiful, they had ample means to educate their children to higher tastes. Occasionally a decayed Brahmin family were thankful to sell their magnificent prerogatives, and uncomfortable poverty for new money and a new domain, even if they had to accept with it a new name.

With such recompense, more than one fair Brahmin concluded that she could afford to ignore the obscurity of her husband's ancestry, while she still retained the splendid memories of her own! The wealthy Bustlers who thus allied themselves with the "first people" invariably turned their backs upon their own class, and lifted their eyes and aspirations alike toward the Brahmins. But the small Bustlers, never rich, always comfortable, who were perfectly satisfied to remain Bustlers forever, were largely in majority, and it was they who gave to Busyville its peculiar character and tone. On every corner stood their little workshops, all astir with the hum and whirr of machinery, with the buzz of busy hands and voices. The streets were lined with their houses; little houses glaring in vivid white and green—pretty "pine boxes" in which they flourished in happy mediocrity.

The boys and girls worked together in the shops; made love, married, and then with laudable thrift, made haste to earn and build one of these habitations for themselves and their children. Thus as the years went on, little streets reached out over the meadows, and new white boxes were set in parallel rows, blistering and blinking at each other in the sun. Each house, as it stared, beheld its counterpart in its neighbor, and all of them alike, in their smallness, and sameness, and snug comfort, reflected fairly the average condition and character of their owners. The matrons of these boxes found them quite large enough for their small ambitions and emulations. Whose house should be paid for earliest; who should have the prettiest garden, the brightest "three-ply" carpet, the most wonderful "riz cake," the most transcendent baby, were all objects dear to their hearts, and to them worthy of all desire and struggle. To see all the family cotton flying on the clothes-lines by breakfast time each Monday morning was a triumph, whose winning called more than one housewife to her washtub a little past midnight. Every chore was done, and she working for the shops and rocking baby, before it was time for her to get her dinner. In the long afternoons, many little shiny-topped baby wagons, precisely alike, issued from the gates, drawn by mother-hands. These matrons then found the recreation of their day, in going to each other's houses, comparing babies, and serving to each other delectable dishes of small gossip. Women endowed with such a remarkable amount of New England "faculty" that they could dispatch every household affair of their own in one fourth of the day, necessarily had some time left for the affairs of their neighbors.

Socially, the Brahmins and Bustlers were as far apart as if they lived on separate planets. The shop-girl from her window watching the academy girl pass to school, mocked her dainty airs, and when she met her on the street with "I'm as good as you are," toss of head, took care that the pretty Brahmin did not have more than her share of the sidewalk. Meanwhile, the Brahmin averted her pretty nose, and gathered up her delicate robes, lest they should be contaminated by the touch of the working-frock of "that dreadful shop-girl." Yet both of these were American maidens, Christian maidens, born in New England Busyville.

The Bustlers and the Brahmins rarely worshipped God together. The Brahmins were all orthodox, and praised their Maker in a proper manner in an imposing structure. From serene heights they looked down with pious pity or disgust, according to their dispositions, on the happy Bustlers, whose devotions they deemed of an unnecessary, vociferous, and hysterical character. All the time, the Bustlers considered themselves not only sound in faith, but as a city set upon a very high hill in the spiritual kingdom, with light enough in it to illuminate the entire race. With holy triumph they referred to the place and the moment where they "got religion." With warm compassion they prayed for the groping Brahmins, who only "hoped that they had a hope." And for no one with so profound an unction as for old Dr. Drier, the Brahmin divine, the meekest and most blameless of men, yet one so utterly undemonstrative and unlike themselves, that they were sure "he know'd nuthin' what religion wuz."

Thus, the Brahmins ignored the Bustlers, and the Bustlers alternately envied and pitied the Brahmins. Each possessed qualities which the others lacked, which, had they been blended together, would have made a more harmonious type of manhood and of womanhood. The Brahmins needed the stamina and activity of the Bustlers. The Bustlers lacked the refinement and capacity for repose which crowned the Brahmins. But there could be no exchange of gifts and graces, for in social life they rarely met, and never mingled. Neither class ever knew half the good that was in the other.

Hero came bounding down the road to meet them. Mary Vale, with Win on one side and Pansy on the other, stood outside of the gate. Again the loose wheels of the old buggy rattled, and for once in her life Muggins hurried.

Eirene had come home, had come home to spend Thanksgiving—what joy there was in the dormer cottage.

A month had wrought a great change in the aspect of nature. The maples had dropped all their scarlet and amber, and stood discrowned in the wood. A few garnet leaves still clung to the sheltered boughs of the oaks. The larches in the yard still waved their feathery plumes, and the pines on the hill still swayed their evergreen branches with the old soughing sound. The English ivy, dappled and warm, still festooned the brown walls and dormer windows; all else was bleak and bare. Piles of wind-whipped, rain-beaten leaves filled the hollows of the road. The marigolds and dahlias had ceased to parade their splendor, lying prone and ragged upon the ground. Even the crysanthemums had vanished, and now smiled in snug boxes in the sitting-room windows.

How was it with Eirene? Had she changed, as well as the garden? Do we ever come back from the world to any beloved spot just the being that we left it?

One moment in her mother's arms—then the happy little company followed Eirene into the house.

---

# III.

## GOING HOME.

EVERY thing was bright for Thanksgiving. The white curtains were newly hung, branches of laurel and holly, bright with scarlet berries, garnished mantel and pictures; little Sir Don, the canary, was trilling a throat-breaking welcome amid a bower of greenery, while his wife, as she could not sing, went plunging into her glass bath-tub for joy. Out from the pantry issued a compound of savory odors, in which an epicure could have detected the aroma of roast fowls, of mince and pumpkin pies, and spice-cakes.

"What have you brought for me? Have you brought me the new frock? I've waited and waited!" cried the excited Pansy, her nervous little fingers already trying to open Eirene's satchel.

"Is that all you've wanted? How selfish you are," said Win, in a stern tone of reproof; "I should think that you'd want to see Rene."

"I do want to see her as much as you do, Mister Win. But she promised me a frock. You want to see what she has brought *you;* I know you do."

"No, I don't want Rene to spend a cent for me. It's bad enough that she has had to go away and work, without spending her earnings for us, Pansy."

"But I must spend something for you,—see what I have brought you!" said Eirene, her face all flushed with happiness, as she took a little key from her pocket and unlocked the satchel, taking out first a red, rotund volume. "See, Win, this is the book you wanted so much, 'Washington and his Generals.'"

Win's dark eyes kindled. He *did* want this book so very much! Could he find fault if his sister had spent her money to gratify this desire of his heart? "O Eirene! some time!" He did not finish the sentence, but he thought—"Some time I will repay her, she always remembers me."

Pansy had commenced to pout. Why should any body be remembered before this little princess?

Win had a book! Where was her blue dress? "She didn't believe she had any, there!"

"You promised, you did!" cried the child with a passionate sob.

"Yes, and here it is," said Eirene. "See, haven't I brought you a pretty frock?"

Like a rainbow through a shower looked forth the glittering eyes of the child. Pansy had never had such a dress, had never seen one even half so lovely; it was merino, blue as the sky.

"Azure and amber. See, mother," said the happy Eirene, as she laid a soft fold of the fabric against the gold of the child's hair. "What a lovely contrast! Oh, I must stay at home long enough to make it for you, Pansy;" and with an impulse of love, she threw her arms around her sister and kissed her.

The mother's impulse had been to set the teakettle in the polished stove, to draw out the table and cover it with her whitest cloth; and when Eirene looked around, she was already setting some of the viands which her loving hands had compounded for her absent child, while she thought of the coming of the most joyful of all Thanksgiving days.

Just then, Lowell Vale having paid his last necessary attention to Muggins, came in to behold his happy household group.

"See, father! see my new dress! Rene brought it to me," cried the exultant Pansy, as, wrapped in the blue merino, she stood perched on tip-toe upon a chair, surveying herself in the looking-glass.

The father's eyes grew misty as he took

the gifts into his hands one by one—the blue dress, the red book—and then looked from one child to the other. "Rene earned these for you," he said; "will Pansy ever earn any thing for Rene?"

Pansy had not thought of that. "I can't work; Rene *can*," was the little beauty's conclusive reply.

It seemed a rich compensation for separation and absence—the dear home-supper that came after. To hear her mother say, as she set some delicate dish before her, "I made this for you;" to be the object of so much tender solicitude, of so many loving looks and words, brought tears into Eirene's eyes. It made her remember the last four weeks of her life, in which she had sat a scarcely tolerated presence at the dismal table of strangers.

She knew that she had felt strangely lonely at that table. But the neglect and unkindness which she had received, came to her now as a positive thought for the first time, forced into her mind by contrast to all this home-love. The beloved child, the unloved stranger—she knew, now, what it was to be both.

"Oh, it is so pleasant to be at home once more!" she said with overflowing eyes. "Not but what I have had every thing necessary at Mr. Mallane's, but it is not like being with you all at home, you know."

She forbore to complain; she did not say once that she had been lonesome, or homesick. In answer to all her mother's anxious inquiries, she said that she had had every thing that she had needed. She had a comfortable room. The Mallanes were good people. It was better for her to be with the family, because out of the shop, she had no one to disturb her in her studies. It would be quite different at the boarding-house, the girls were very gay and noisy. She did not find her work hard; indeed, she was perfectly satisfied.

Thus she silenced every misgiving of her mother's heart, and no shadow fell on the happy supper of Thanksgiving eve.

"Tell me about the children," said Pansy, with her pretty lisp. "Is Grace Mallane so pretty? Has she very fine frocks? Any finer than mine?" And the dimpled hand smoothed fondly the blue merino, which she had laid within arm's reach, before sitting down to her supper.

Then Eirene told her sister every pleasant thing that she could remember about Grace Mallane, and all the "children,"—save one. She scarcely mentioned Paul. She did not know why, but it did not seem easy to talk of him, perhaps because he was not at all a child.

How long they lingered around the little table! At last Eirene, with wondrously smiling eyes, took from her pocket her little purse, and poured its contents upon the table.

"It is not much, but there will be more another month. I could not come home for the first time, without bringing Win and Pansy something. But I intend to be very saving; and if you are prospered, father, the old place will be saved."

"But what have you bought for yourself, child?" asked the mother, with the suggestion of tears in her voice.

"Nothing," said Eirene. "I have not needed any thing."

"We thank God for our child," said Lowell Vale, as soon as he could command his voice; "but we cannot take all your earnings, Eirene. What you do not need, put in the bank at Busyville. Another year's crops such as this year has brought us, and Hillside will be saved. If not,—for your mother's sake, and your's and the children's—that we may not lose our home, we must take what you have saved; but not unless we *must.* If not, it will pay for you at the academy at Busyville. You can go to school a long time, Eirene."

Eirene seeing that it was hard for either father or mother to talk about money, slipped out of the room to look for Win. She proceeded to the old barn, within which she had seen him vanish a few moments before.

It was chilly without, but as she opened the door, the air within seemed warm and sweet with the smothered fragrance floating out from piles of clovery hay. As she entered, old Blossom and young Daisy, who stood quietly waiting to be milked, rubbed their noses against her hand, and Muggins, in her stall, looked up and whinnied a welcome over her half-eaten oats. Eirene climbed up above the great mounds of hay into the loft! She knew Win's haunts; knew that after the November rain and damp had fallen on the beloved woods, his chosen sanctuary was this little chamber in the loft. It had one window looking out upon the west; upon the great hills of amethyst, behind which the sun went down. Against the rough boards hung Win's rifle and all the accoutrements of hunting. On the other side, some hanging shelves, neatly covered with paper, were filled with Win's books—more relics of the Vale library. And here, with the pale late rays of the November sun falling on his dark hair, with Hero by his side, stretched upon some fresh hay, lay Win, devouring with his eyes "Washington and his Generals." He started half abashed, half delighted, as he saw his sister Eirene's face, her loving wistful eyes. But Win was not demonstrative; he was strangely shy and reticent, even with those whom he knew and loved the best. The love which he felt for his sister, Eirene, was nearly blended with worship. She was finer and lovelier to him than any other being in the world. He would sit and gaze on her with a strange mixed feeling of awe, admiration, and love, which could not be expressed in language. It was the involuntary reverence for womanhood, born of the unconscious manhood stirring in the boy's heart.

"Hero, will you take up all the room when you see who has come?" he said to his dog, as he jumped up and made room for Eirene on the hay by his side. When she was seated he opened his new book, then looking up, said abruptly,

"Rene, do you think that there will ever be another war in this country?"

"Why, Win, how can there be? Why do you think of such a thing?"

"Because I would rather be a soldier than any thing else in the world."

"Oh, Win, how could I live and think of you suffering all that a soldier must! I was reading the other day what the soldiers suffered in the Crimea, and I thanked God when I thought that there never could be war in this country. England will never trouble us again. France likes us. Who else could fight this country?"

"We may fight each other, some time, Eirene. I never should have thought of such a thing, but the other day I found among the old books, a pamphlet with the great speeches which Webster and Hayne made in the Senate, in 1830—before we were born. I read them through, and learned an extract from each for a declamation in school. There are sentences in them which keep ringing through my mind. Do you want to hear them, Rene?"

"Yes," said his sister, with a deep interest kindling through her eyes.

The boy arose, and with all a boy's unction of feeling—and less than most boys' stiffness of declamation—with a rich voice that made the old barn ring, he exclaimed:

"Good God! Mr. President, has it come to this? Do gentlemen estimate the value of the Union at so low a price, that they will not even make one effort to bind the States together with the cords of affection? And has it come to this? Is this the spirit in which this government is to be administered? If so, let me tell you, gentlemen, the seeds of dissolution are already sown, and our children will reap the bitter fruits."

"Now shall I recite Webster's answer?" asked the excited boy. And Eirene answered "yes," gazing on him as if she saw him in a dream, when he once more exclaimed:

"I have not allowed myself, Sir, to look beyond the Union to see what might be hidden in the dark recesses behind. I have not coolly weighed the chances of preserving liberty, when the bonds that unite us together shall be broken asunder. I have not accustomed myself to hang over the precipice of disunion, to see whether with my short sight I can fathom the depth of the abyss below.

"While the Union lasts, we have high, exciting, gratifying prospects spread out before us, for us and our children. Beyond that, I seek not to penetrate the veil. God grant my vision never may be opened on what lies behind.

"When my eyes shall be turned to behold, for the last time, the sun in heaven, may I not see him shining on the broken and dishonored fragments of a once glorious Union; on States dissevered, discordant, belligerent; on a land rent with civil feuds, or drenched it may be with fraternal blood!

"Let their last feeble and lingering glance, rather, behold the gorgeous ensign of the Republic, now known and honored throughout the earth—still full high advanced, its arms and trophies streaming in their original lustre, not a stripe erased or polluted, nor a single star obscured—bearing for its motto no such miserable interrogatory as, *What is all this worth?* Nor those other words of delusion and folly — Liberty first, and Union afterwards; but everywhere spread all over in characters of living light blazing on all its ample folds, as they float over the sea and over the land, and in every wind under the whole heavens, that other sentiment, true to every American heart — Liberty *and* Union, now and forever, one and inseparable!"

"How you feel all this," said Eirene, as Win sat down, with the perspiration on his face and a scarlet spot on his cheeks. "I have never thought of any of these things. All that I have thought of our country is, that it is beautiful, and great, and free, and must always remain as it is now — only growing greater.

"But I have thought a great deal about you, Win, and about your future life; I want you to go to college. I want you to study a profession, and be happy and successful. I am going to help you: I am older than you, you know."

"Eirene, I don't want you to help me. I am a boy, and ought to be able to help myself. But I have heard father say that no Vale has been successful for generations. I don't know whether I could get on in the world any better than father or not; but I know that I could be a soldier, and fight for my country."

"But, Win, if the great words which you have just spoken should come true, you would have to fight against your own countrymen. *That* would be dreadful."

"My own countrymen? They would not be my own countrymen if they had broken the Union. I think it would be splendid to fight for *that*."

"I hope it will never need your life, Win. You have been reading 'Washington and his Generals' till you want to be a hero. You can be heroic without a war."

"Rene, you think that the Union will never come to an end," said Win, still pervaded by Webster and Hayne. "Don't you remember, in the histories that we read last winter, each one of the old republics had something in it which destroyed it?"

"Yes; but they were heathen republics. This is a Christian nation, Win."

"Yes, I suppose it is," said Win, dubiously. "But it don't seem to me very Christian. Its great men are fighting all the time, I should think by the newspapers. The South has grown rich and saucy living on negroes; and the North has grown rich and greedy on manufactures and trade. We are down on the South for its Slavery; and the South is down on us for our Tariff. We pity the ignorant Southerners, and they despise us peddling Yankees; and we'll come to a fight some day, or I don't understand what I read."

"Don't you think that we are too young to understand these great questions, or to tell what is going to happen? If this country is ever to be torn by war, I don't want to think of it till I must. Let us talk of something cheerful, Win."

"I don't want to make you feel bad, Rene, and I'm sure I don't know what will happen to the country. But the only thing I feel sure of is, that some day I shall be a soldier."

There was a strange commingling of incredulity and sorrow in Eirene's gaze as Win uttered these words.

The possibility of Win's being a soldier had never entered her mind. She did not believe that he would ever be one, yet the mere suggestion was enough to fill her eyes with a brooding sadness.

As they sat, gazing upon each other, they looked strangely alike — this boy and girl. Win's forehead was brown, his cheeks bronzed by exposure; while Eirene's low brow was white, and on her cheek trembled the delicate bloom of the blush-rose. But both had the same wavy hair of nutty-brown, touched with gold, and the same mouth, in whose exquisite curves trembled all the sensibility, the purity of an entire race. Their eyes, too, were as the eyes of one face — in their oneness of expression consisted the remarkable likeness which each bore to the other. They were the Vale eyes, of a limpid brown, winsome and winning. They were not melancholy eyes, for they overflowed with light — not with the light which exults and triumphs, but rather that which hopes and believes— the light which kindles the eyes of martyrs and of saints. They were not restless, anxious eyes, they were serene in their very wistfulness, yet they had a deep, far gaze, as if looking on toward something distant, for some joy that they had missed, or for some treasure which they had never found; not that these young lives were conscious of any such longing, but their eyes reflected the souls of their ancestors. It was as if Aubrey and Alice, and Lowell and Mary Vale, were all looking out from the eyes of these children. They were sealed with the family soul, they were signs of the family fate. Superlative eyes, suffused with soft sunshine, they still suggested sadness rather than smiles. In their deep lovingness they drew hearts toward them like magnets, yet in their too deep tenderness you read the prophecy of tears, not of triumph.

As they sat, the setting sun sent his last rays above the hills. They poured through the little window of the barn, and covered the children sitting upon the hay with glory. Through the chinks of the loose boards they floated in, and for a moment seemed suspended in the form of a cross over their heads. Was it the augury of destiny?

TWO CHUMS.

That same sunset which made the old barn-loft glitter like the chamber of a palace, lit up the venerable walls and windows of old Harvard just as two young men met in one of the innumerable walks which intersect each other in the grounds of the University.

"Well, old boy, you have come at last," said one, as he switched the sleeve of the other with a rattan cane; he was a small, fashionably-dressed, *blasé* young man. "Just in?"

"Yes, in the last train," answered Paul Mallane, who, from his altitude of six feet, looked down upon his insignificant companion, as handsome and as nonchalant as ever.

"Why didn't you stay up-country all winter, and be done with it? You have stayed so deuced long I have made up my mind that something has been to pay. Come, now! Why haven't you been in more of a d—l of a hurry?"

"I thought I'd stay and help my Governor take inventories and cast accounts."

"A likely story! You've been touched, I know. Nothing but a girl could have kept you so long in a town that you curse. And the term commenced, and all your chums eating nice little suppers, and enjoying all sorts of nice little pleasures. I'll swear that nothing but a girl could have kept you from us a whole month."

"Pshaw, Dick, I am not always chasing a girl's shadow, because you are. You don't believe, then, that I have turned dutiful son, and have been posting my father's books?"

"Not I. Come, my boy, you may just as well own up first as last. You want my advice; you know you do. *Who* is it? Not pretty Tilly? She'd never wake you up. Come, now!" And the wise old-young man slipped his arm into Paul's, and they sauntered on toward the colleges.

"You are a bore, Dick Prescott, yet I suppose that I do need your advice," said Paul, in a half annoyed, half impatient tone. "I want you to suppose a case. Suppose you should meet a young lady, to you exquisitely lovely, not handsome in just the flesh-and-blood sense, but in figure, in coloring, in expression, and in manners to you perfectly lovely"—here Paul paused as if he were interrupted.

"I have it; 'to you perfectly lovely!' Go on, I am supposing the case," said Dick.

"Well, suppose you should meet her in a place, and in company utterly at variance with her nature, in the midst of a crowd of ignorant, noisy girls. Suppose that you should meet her in —— well, in your father's shop: what would you do?"

Dick Prescott broke into a loud laugh. "Prince Mallane," he said, "I did not think that you could be such a spooney."

"I don't know why you should call me a spooney," Paul replied, angrily; "I have only asked you to suppose a case."

"Suppose a case? I can't suppose any such case. I can suppose a perfect lady, and a perfect beauty; but I can't suppose her at work in a shop in the midst of a pack of noisy, ignorant girls. It's all in your eye, Prince. She is just like all the rest, only you are touched."

"Touched! by heaven, I *am* touched," exclaimed Paul, in a passion. "I've never been in love in my life—although I've tried to be, hard enough. I am *not* in love now; but I am haunted by a face. Her eyes follow me wherever I go. If I have a mean thought it seems as if she saw it, and the pure face makes me ashamed and uncomfortable;—but only uncomfortable when I feel that I am mean and unworthy. No woman's face ever made me feel so before. I can't get rid of the look in her eyes. But then I have not tried very hard. I am willing to own up, I have stayed in Busyville a whole month, just to look at it."

"Do you think me verdant enough to believe *that?*" asked Dick. "You have made love, and proposed an elopement, I will bet my head."

"Then you will lose it. I spoke to her the first day I went into the shops, but it was before I saw her face. I wanted to see what she was like. She turned and looked, and her surprise and her face made me so ashamed of my impertinence that I never more than bowed to her afterwards. You may laugh if you please; I am telling the truth. As we were situated I could not meet her as I did other ladies; and I would not, indeed I could not, talk to her as I did to the rest of the shop-girls."

"Well, Prince, I never expected to see *you* so far gone. That's all I have to say. What do you propose to do?"

"That's just *it*. What am I to do? To me she is a lady; to every body else she is a shop-girl. I don't go with shop-girls, I can't go with her; it would drive my mother mad. Besides, I can't afford it. I am not an only son, like you, Dick. I shall only have an eighth of my Governor's money; and he is not a millionaire, like your parental relative. I am not going to begin life in any shabby way; I must marry either position or a fortune when I do marry. Confound it! I can never propose to this little girl, if I want to. Not that I am at all sure that I shall ever want to, but it maddens me to think that I can't, if I do. One thing I never could bear—that is, to be balked."

"Mallane, you talk like an idiot. I never before suspected you of being such a fool," said Dick. "You can't propose to this belle of the shops, of course you can't. Of course you don't want to; you wouldn't if you could. You are only mad at the fact that you can't, that's all. You cannot perpetrate matrimony, but you can amuse yourself, that's enough better. You can make *her* believe that you are going to marry her; the excitement of such fun will be worth a dozen weddings. When you are tired of it, leave her (she will get over it), and take somebody else. If you married her—think of it! you'd have to stare at her at least three hundred and sixty-five times a-year for the rest of your life, no matter how much she bored you. Take my advice—amuse yourself, my boy. I'd like to know what the d—l is to pay that I have to exhort Prince Mallane to amuse himself. It is the first time."

"Dick Prescott, I feel as if I could knock you down. You show that you know nothing of my case, when you name *her* in such connections. Yet, I suppose I should have talked just the same a month ago. I have amused myself, and perhaps I may again. But it would be easier for me to cut off my hand than to trifle with this girl. She seems so lifted above all evil, that I feel ashamed of myself every time I come into her presence. I feel like an inferior being, I do! You may laugh if you want to, but I *am* inferior, and so are you. When we think of all the disgraceful things that we have done, we ought to stand abashed in the presence of such purity. Yet you dare ask me to amuse myself! Trifle with *her!* No; I never saw a lady at Marlboro Hill, nor anywhere else, that I would treat with more consideration. I used to think that I could talk agreeably to women. I can, can't I? But this innocent girl has taken a little of the vanity out of me. I have not the slightest reason to suppose that she even admires me. The flattery which I deal out to other girls of her condition, would serve me no purpose with her. I should stammer and forget all my fine speeches, the moment I looked in her eyes."

"Mallane, I told you you were touched. I knew that; but, by Jupiter! you are clear gone. You are dead in love. You rave like a madman," replied Dick Prescott, as he looked up into his chum's face with a surprised and quizzical expression. "I think you are past my advice, but I'll give it; you may do as you please about taking it."

"I am aware of that," answered Paul haughtily. "You can't give advice where you can't even suppose a case. Every word you say only convinces me the more, that you have no conception of the loveliness and purity of the one that I have tried to describe to you."

"Oh, your loveliness and purity be hanged! Your sentiment don't go down with me, Prince. I know too much of the world and of women. You are sappy. You betray the fact that you are from the rural districts. After all my instructions, you haven't learned the world, Mallane, nor women. Let me tell you again, they are all alike. There was never one since Eve that could not be reached by flattery. You have let this little plebeian see that you are smitten. She has been using her power, by making you feel that you must get down upon your knees. But don't tell *me* that she can't be flattered! A smaller quantity and finer quality she may demand, I admit. But all you want is tact and insight, to administer to her case and be master of the situation. You need not tell her so outright; there are a thousand ways by which you can make her believe that you think her the loveliest of her sex. Make her feel that you remember her. In short, make yourself necessary to her, and then show her that *you* are perfectly able to live without her. And Paul, my boy, the game is yours."

"I am very much obliged to you for your instructions, although I have heard them all several times before, and they don't apply in this case," said Paul coldly. "I have made all your moves and won my game more than once. They might win all other women, but they won't her. No sham will live in her presence. Any thing short of utter sincerity, would shrink before the truth in those eyes. I sha'n't do a thing that you've told me."

"Very well, then, don't come to me again for advice. You are as unreasonable as a donkey. The trouble is, it is a foregone thing. You are in love already, and won't listen to common sense till you are out of it."

"No, I am not in love, and I don't intend to make love. I have made up my mind not to take any advantage of this girl, never to arouse any hopes in her life, that my position will not allow me to fulfil, even allowing that I could teach her to like me; and I am not sure of that," added Paul, with a strange touch of humility. "I will do her justice, and all the more because she is so poor,—but I am not in love with her; I want you to understand that, Dick."

"Oh, no, you are not at all in love. I understand that. But do you know how many times you have contradicted yourself since you commenced to talk about this girl?"

"No, and I don't care. I only know that I have told the truth. She—"

"There! don't begin to enumerate her perfections again, Prince, or we shall never get out of this yard. I am going to Marlboro. Will you go, too?"

"No, thank you," said Paul. "I am going to my room;" and he set his face toward Cambridge.

## IV.

### NOT IN LOVE.

PAUL went back to his books but not to very patient study. He had never dreamed that Coke and Blackstone could be such bores.

Dick Prescott's ridicule forced him to two conclusions: the first, that he had made a goose of himself in so nearly falling in love with a girl so much his inferior in station. Paul would not acknowledge even to himself that he *had* fallen in love—of course he had not. But he had come to the conclusion to do justice to all, no matter how lowly their condition, and to do justice to this girl, he said he must acknowledge that she was lovely, and a lady, and very superior to her situation. The second conclusion was, that while he would not demean himself by attempting to follow Dick's advice, he would be equally careful to give Dick no opportunity to say that he was committing himself seriously to a shop-girl. He would study harder than he had ever done before, and think no more about her. The oftener he said that he would think no more about her, the more continually he thought of her. He had been attracted before by many pretty faces, that he had found it easy enough to forget when it became convenient.

"It will be the same with this one," he said to himself. "In a week or two I sha'n't think any more about it than about Tilly Blane's, and really this time last year Tilly looked wonderfully pretty. I hadn't seen her in so long a time, that she struck me as something quite new and charming. But I was soon tired enough of her pink and white, and today she seems perfectly insipid. I shall be tired of this face as soon as I see one that will please me better." In the midst of these very thoughts, a voice far down in his heart would say to him, "You will never see a face that will please you better." And even while he exclaimed, "I will think no more about her," he was eagerly recalling every lineament, till the whole face seemed to rise through a mist between his eyes and his book. It was not outline and color, nor the gleam of waving hair, on which his eyes were fixed. It was the pure brow, the appealing eyes, the gentle mouth, which drew nearer and nearer to his, till a thrill of delight ran through his heart, and he closed his eyes as if before an ecstatic vision.

Paul often asked himself, "I wonder if she sometimes thinks of me?" But for once his complacency failed him. He by no means felt certain that she thought of him with any of the exquisite pleasure with which he remembered her. Not even the memory of the blush in the window reassured him. No wonder she blushed when she thought of my rudeness, and saw me still staring at her, he said, for the first time in his life thinking of a woman without an atom of self-conceit.

Christmas came. Paul in his impatience thought it never would come, yet it did in that year of grace as early as in any other. When he thought of going home for the holidays, his heart gave a great throb. Never had any thought of home so moved it before. And strange to say when he thought of it, he only saw one window and one face in it. The stiff parlor, the staring sitting-room, the baby in the cradle, no longer rose up and annoyed him, for he did not think of them. And when his worldly self said: "Paul Mallane, you are a fool. You can never marry this little girl. You respect her too much even to flirt with her. You could not make love to her even if you were in love, and you know you are not. You can only go and look at her. What a fool to be so anxious for only that."

Yet for only "that," Paul refused

manifold invitations to Beacon-street, and a special one to Marlboro Hill. "Thank you, Dick," he said, "but I must go home this Christmas; it will be the first time, you know, since I entered college."

"Don't I know? I know, too, you are spooney yet over that shop-girl, or you would not go for all Busyville. Own up, Prince!"

"I've nothing to own. I am going home because I want to, that is enough."

"Well, go ahead. We'd like to have you at the Hill, though. We shall have a jolly time and no mistake. Bell is just home from Madame Joli's, 'finished,' and she has brought a school-mate to make my acquaintance; a Cuban beauty with a cool million. What do you think of that, Prince?"

Paul had several thoughts concerning "that" which drew him Marlboro Hill-ward, when Dick's concluding sentence sent the tide back in full force toward Busyville.

"Bell says she thinks that it is time that she knew Prince Mallane. And when I was coming away she said, 'Be sure and bring him back, Dick. I want to see how many fibs you have told about him!' But of course, Bell Prescott's desire to know you is nothing while a pious shop-girl is waiting to sing psalms to you in Busyville! I know by the look of your eyes that you don't intend to take my advice—and fool her. No! you will let her fool you into downright love-making. Then there'll be a scrape you won't get out of so easy. Mark what I say. Prince Mallane won't marry a shop-girl, if he does fall in love with her."

"I am not going to fall in love with a shop-girl nor marry her; but I am going to spend Christmas in Busyville, Dick. Carry my regrets to Miss Prescott; tell her I shall lose no time in calling upon her when I return, and that may be before the holidays are over."

The moment Dick's grating voice uttered the word "shop-girl," Paul saw again as distinctly as if before his actual eyes the young face of the window, in its frame of summer vines, and the very chords of his heart seemed to tremble and to draw him toward it. Besides, another feeling influenced him. He saw that Dick was really anxious that he should become acquainted with his sister.

When they first became chums, Dick used to patronize Paul. More than once he had made him feel most keenly the difference in their antecedents; the distinction between having one's grandfather a poor carpenter, or having one's grandfather a distinguished gentleman. He had taught Paul the advantage of possessing an illustrious name, and the disadvantage of owning one the world never heard of before. Yet, in spite of the obscure name, and in defiance of rank and of ancient lineage, some way the sceptre had slipped into Paul's hands. Dick had learned that the prestige of a fine physique, of graceful manners, and of a brilliant brain, are quite as potent as the memory of one's grandfather. Everywhere he saw Paul possessing himself of attention and of admiration, by the charm of his own personality. He saw, too, that it added to the reputation of even a Prescott, to be on intimate terms with this popular youth. He acknowledged his claim as a rising man; spoke of him always as his particular friend, the prince of fine fellows; and though he still lectured and gave him advice as a man of the world, it was no longer with the assumption of superiority or the arrogance of earlier days. Still Paul had not forgotten the snubbings and condescensions which used to bruise his self-love, and he always remembered them most keenly when Dick, by some word or act, made him aware of his present importance. He was flattered at Dick's eagerness that he should meet Miss Bell, yet this very eagerness prompted him to show his own indifference as proper pay for old patronage in the past. In characteristic fashion, if there had been no Eirene Vale in Busyville, Paul Mallane would probably have gone to that not brilliant winter-town, when he found that Dick Prescott was really anxious that he should become acquainted with his sister.

Without one yearning for Marlboro

Hill he went to Busyville. He saw the daguerreotypes which he despised, still piled around the astral lamp. He saw the bright stripes of the sitting-room carpet, the hateful yellow of its oak paper; indeed, he saw most clearly every thing which he disliked, for all that he had longed most to see was wanting.

The girl "up-stairs" had gone home to spend Christmas-week, and Paul had his old seat at the table with the ordinary countenance of his sister Grace for a perfectly safe *vis-à-vis.*

Great would have been the delight of Tabitha Mallane at the prospect of Paul spending his holidays at home, if she could have believed that the unwonted visit had no connection whatever with the girl "up-stairs." Her instincts all bore opposite testimony. Thus she said to her husband,

"Father, give the poor girl a week, and let her wages go on. She can't afford to lose any thing, but I think that she is homesick."

"She can go home, and welcome. I am glad that you are getting more kindly disposed toward the little girl. I'm sure she makes no trouble," said good-natured unsuspecting John Mallane.

But Paul and his mother knew each other intuitively. The other girls were at work; if Eirene had a holiday there was a special reason, and his mother was connected with it, Paul knew. Yet he said nothing; he did not mention the name of the "new hand;" he was only more ill-natured than usual, found fault with every thing.

He had intended to be very munificent—to present to each of the children and to his mother an elegant Christmas gift. Besides, he had resolved for once to be as smiling and gracious at home as he had ever been in Beacon-street or Marlboro Hill, and not to swear at the baby once, no matter how loudly it screamed. Poor Paul! the result was that he forgot all about the presents, and he made himself so disagreeable, and the atmosphere of the whole house so perfectly uncomfortable, that at the close of the third day his mother felt relieved when he informed her that he should go and spend the remainder of the week at Marlboro Hill.

"Very well, Paul," she said in a perfectly undisturbed tone. "I should think you would like to meet Miss Prescott, and the next time you come home I hope that you will be happier."

"That will depend on circumstances, mother," answered her son, looking her fully in the eyes.

The gray eyes looked back with as wide and deep a gaze.

They understood each other.

When Eirene heard Grace and the children talk of Paul's coming home at Christmas, it was with a feeling of relief that she thought she should not meet him, and she felt more than ever grateful for Mr. Mallane's unexpected permission to spend the holidays at Hilltop.

If she had been asked why she felt relieved at the thought of not meeting Paul, I doubt if she could have told—for she spent very little time analyzing her own emotions; but in a dim, unconscious way, she felt that while he was most pleasant to behold, he was an object so entirely above her own lowly life, that it were wiser for her not to contemplate him, lest what seemed brilliant and desirable in his lot, should make her less patient of what was distasteful in her own. In the weeks that had passed since his handsome face vanished from the house, its memory had at times come back, and brought with it something like light and warmth into the cold little chamber.

If Eirene had been a wealthy schoolgirl, with nothing to do but to learn her lessons, and no object of interest dearer than her own pretty self, doubtless she would have spent as much time meditating on this princely youth as he did in thinking of her.

Amid such circumstances this manly face, the most brilliant that she had ever seen, would probably have shone upon her often enough to have satisfied the utmost vanity of its owner.

But life's hard conditions saved Eirene from even the temptation of idle dreaming. They had filled her young heart with desires and anxieties too deeply rooted to be displaced by any passing fancy.

To her already life was a fact whose penalties she did not seek to escape, but to fulfil, faithfully and patiently.

Already her labor had found a purpose and an end; thinking of these, the young feet might faint, and the young hands grow weary, but the true heart never faltered nor murmured.

There was the mortgage! that dreadful mortgage that she had heard of ever since she could remember. It was certain to be foreclosed before very long; for the man who held it was very aged, and his heir, who lived in a distant city, had already announced that if the little farm was not redeemed by the time of the old man's death, it would be sold in the settlement of his estate. Eirene knew that this day could not be very far off; that unless her father was prepared to meet it, Hilltop would be lost; and she thought with a shudder, of the family going out from the only home that it had ever known; of her father, more incapable and discouraged than ever, seeking vainly to begin his fortune anew with all the world's odds against him. Then there was Win's profession! His life must not be a failure, as his father's had been. No Vale had ever been known to succeed in business; his tastes and habits were intellectual; he might succeed in something connected with books, she felt quite sure that he would. And there was a little education for herself! It could never be finished or thorough, she knew, but by improving all her moments out of the shop she could learn considerable.

The Vale instincts were strong in the girl's nature. Culture was a necessity. She longed to hold the key of knowledge, and unlock for herself something of the mystery of the universe. Into this preoccupied heart, so full of care for others, so busy with loving thoughts for father, mother, sister, and brother, in strangely brilliant contrast sometimes stepped the image of the handsome Paul; but it was by no means the absorbing and undivided presence which that individual desired.

The Harvard law-student, after he had dismissed his books and his chums, often sat far into the night alone in his handsome bachelor's room in Cambridge. His indulgent father had denied him nothing, and the apartment reflected without stint Paul's love of luxury and beauty. Rich books and pictures were scattered around him in profusion. A velvet carpet covered the floor; a sumptuous lounge was drawn near the open fire, on which our young gentleman reclined, smoking his meerschaum. The blue velvet cap upon his head, whose silver embroidery and glittering tassel afforded such fine relief to his dark hair, and which in itself was so strikingly becoming, was wrought by Helena Maynard, a Beacon-street belle. The delicate buds and roses blooming on his slippers had been worked with tenderest thought for him by the pretty fingers of Tilly Blane. Even the watch-case on the wall with its delicate filigree, and the cigar-stand upon the table with its golden frettings, were gifts from her and the beautiful Maynard, meet examples of the prodigal presents which fond and foolish girls are forever making to young men; presents which are sure at last to find their way into the hands of mistress or wife, while the ungrateful masculine says, "*You* shall have this, sweetheart. Isn't it pretty? —— gave it to me. *She* was in love with me, poor thing!"

Paul sat in true bachelor reverie, gazing into the clear flame and down into the red core of the wood-fire, which was one of his special delights.

With the perversity inherent in man, with the silver-embroidered cap upon his head, and the rose-wrought slippers blossoming on his feet, his thoughts were not of the Beacon-street belle, nor of pretty Tilly Blane, but of a girl who had never given him any thing at all. The young eyes into whose depths he seemed to gaze, had a look in them which he could neither fathom nor understand, yet it haunted and fascinated him. It was the look of eyes which saw further down into the deeps of life than he could divine, reflecting the emotions of a nature which had felt already the mystery, the tenderness, the pathos of existence; as he, in his strong self-centered life, had never felt them. Her years were fewer, yet in all that really makes life, in doing, in feeling, in being, she had out-lived him. To Paul, these eyes were full of mystery, guileless as a child's; they still suggested to him gentleness, tenderness, and love, deeper than he had ever dreamed of in woman. This was why, in spite of himself, they followed him always. It never occurred to him to inquire, "Is there ought in *me* to suffice these large, tender, asking eyes?" His thought was, though he was not conscious of it, "What is there not in this heart for *me!* Somebody will woo and win it! Why not I—I want it. I will have it," he said, at last, but not then.

At the same hour, when the luxurious student leaned back amid his cushions, dreaming over pipe and blaze, the young shop-girl sat in her bare chamber without a fire. Feet and fingers were numb with cold, and she shivered in the shawl which she had wrapped around her, but it was the only time that she had for quiet study; and, though the eyelids would droop sometimes, and the book almost fall from the stiffened fingers, she studied on till the lesson was learned.

The frozen air was hardly as favorable to love-dreaming as the summer atmosphere of the Cambridge parlor.

During the three days spent at home, Paul had stalked into this room, impelled by angry curiosity. He was strongly suspicious that it was the most comfortless room in the house; and in the absence of its inmate, he deliberately opened the door and walked in to see if his suspicions were correct. When he looked at the bare painted floor, the cold whitewashed walls, the scanty and shabby furniture, strange to relate, the aristocratic youth thrust his hands into his pockets, and in his wrath swore aloud, because the apartment of this shop-girl was not as comfortable as that of his sister Grace. He had no very generous ideas of what was necessary to the comfort of shop-girls in general, but some way these ideas did not seem to apply in any way to this particular one. He had supposed the room was meagre enough, and yet he was not prepared to see it look quite so barren, so utterly devoid of all comfort.

"There are rolls and rolls of carpeting in the garret that have never been used, and yet mother won't lay a strip down here," he said deprecatingly, as he looked on the painted floor. "Even old Beck can have a warm fire in her chamber over the kitchen, and *she* hasn't had one this winter. She sits here and studies, too, in the cold. Curse it!" he exclaimed, still more bitterly, as he looked at the stand by the window on which Eirene had left a few books and a work-basket. Paul took up the books one by one, and found them to be Fasquelle's French Grammar and Dictionary, Fénélon's Telemachus, a small volume of extracts of Bossuet's sermons, and a French Testament. The two latter were very small, very richly bound, and very old. On the fly-leaf of the Testament he read in round delicate characters,

"ALICE VALE, 1820.
Spes mea Christus,"

and below, in a clear, graceful hand,

"EIRENE VALE, 1856.
En Dieu est ma fiance."

Paul looked long and thoughtfully on these two names and sentences, the first brown and faded, the last clear and bright, as if lately written.

"Well," he at last soliloquized: "I am glad you have somebody to trust in. It would be very little comfort to me though, to trust in God, if I had to work in a shop and burrow in a hole like this, and be snubbed by my inferiors. For we *are* her inferiors. I am her inferior, I know it, and d—n my position!" he exclaimed, as proud in his sudden humility as he had ever been in his self-conceit. He laid the books down on the white cover with which Eirene had sought to hide the deformity of the old pine stand, looked at them a moment, and then with a low whistle walked out of the room and out of the house. He knew that his mother had heard him walking on the bare floor over her head; indeed, he was in such a defiant mood, he had made all the noise that he could. It was partly to punish his mother for sending Eirene away, that he had gone up there in the first place; he knew that nothing could vex her more; but having done as he chose, he now had no desire to return to the sitting-room and listen to a lecture from over the cradle. If he did, he knew that he would say in reply something perfectly savage, and Paul did not like to be impertinent to his mother, however much he enjoyed punishing her by his actions for thwarting his wishes.

Tabitha Mallane rocked the cradle and listened to Paul walking in Eirene's room overhead; heard him come down stairs and go out, shutting the front door with an angry slam. She then left the baby in the cradle and walked quietly up to the room that he had left.

"It does look comfortless, sure enough," she said, as she gazed around. "I should have made the girl more comfortable if I had not taken such a dislike to her on *his* account. I foresaw all this. I knew how it would be. I was sure of it; because I knew that, with all his fancies, Paul had never loved any girl, and that what is peculiar in this one, is just what would seize and hold him. It is no trifling matter for a Bard to love, and Paul is all a Bard in his passions. I wanted to save him trouble and her too. It is too late. Love her he will, in spite of me; but marry her he won't. It is not too late to prevent *that*. You needn't study French for him, young lady!" she exclaimed, as she gave the grammar a contemptuous push; "he will never marry you, never!"

When Eirene returned, great was her surprise to find upon her little stand a package which had come by express, directed to

"Miss Eirene Vale,
Care of Hon. John Mallane."

She opened it, and found within two cabinet pictures in half-oval rustic frames, the one a photograph of one of the most exquisite marbles ever conceived by human soul, or wrought by human hand—Palmer's statue of Faith before the Cross. The other was an engraving of Longfellow's Evangeline. As she took these treasures from their paper wrappings, Eirene's hands trembled so with delight that she could scarcely hold them. Who had sent them? Who could have thought of her? How perfectly satisfying they were. How happy she was. She had never seen her name before written by a strange hand. Indeed, in all her life she had never received a communication from any one outside of her own family. Thus she read the superscription over and over, trying in every letter to catch a clue to the writer. But no, she never saw that bold, full hand before; that ostentatious quirl at the end of the "e" did not afford the slightest idea of its maker. She only knew that somebody was *so* kind, and it was so strange because she thought that no one knew her outside of Hilltop.

Could it be? Could it be Mr. Paul Mallane, who, in making presents to all the family, had so unexpectedly included her? Oh no, that was not possible. He had never spoken to her but once,—and his mother! His mother she feared did not like her. Thus, she knew that Mr. Paul would not send a present to her directed to the care of his father, when he must know that to do so would displease his mother! Besides, Mr. Paul Mallane himself was rather haughty, and she,—she worked in a shop! No, it could not be he. She did not know who had sent it, but she would save the direction.

What companionship and comfort she would find in these faces! already they changed to her the entire aspect of the room. Her surprises were increased when turning around she saw, what she had not discovered before, a small stove, and behind it a box filled with wood ready for burning.

"Oh dear, how pleasant every thing is," she exclaimed; and in her overflowing gratitude, quite forgetting all her fear of Mrs. Mallane, she ran down-stairs, and appearing before the lady, exclaimed:

"How kind of you, Mrs. Mallane, to put that dear little stove into my room! It will make it so pleasant to study evenings. I thank you so much."

"You needn't thank me," said that truthful woman. "Thank Mr. Mallane; it's his work. I shouldn't give you any stove to injure your health by. It is a very bad thing for you to sit up as you do nights, using candles and your eyes besides. When you have eaten your supper you ought to go to bed."

"It is the only time I have," said Eirene beseechingly.

"It is the only time you have to sleep, and you ought to use it for that purpose. What do you want more education for, any way? You have enough now for all practical purposes; unless you want to teach school, and that's a dog's life. You had better stay in the shop. In your situation in life the more education you have the more discontented you'll be. If I've heard the truth, that is the curse of your whole family. You are none of you willing to come down to your circumstances. You are all trying to be more than God intended you should be, and to get out of the place in which He put you. My advice is, earn an honest living, and be contented. You've got all the learning you need for that now." With these cruel thrusts Mrs. Mullane looked up, and the white quivering face before her moved her perhaps to a stony compassion, for she said:

"There! you needn't cry. You'll hear harder truths than I have told you before you get through the world. There's no use in being so tender, it don't pay. Study all night, if you want to, but I thought I'd do my duty."

Just then came a knock at the door, which opened an instant afterwards with Mrs. Mallane's "come in;" and there appeared the well-fed form and florid face of young Brother Viner, the Methodist clergyman. Tabitha Mallane was born a Brahmin, and one of the sacrifices which she had made to her love for John Mallane was to forsake her high estate in the Brahmin church, to take up her cross and become a Methodist. But sister Mallane had "a gift." She could speak and pray in meeting with profound effect.

The encouragement given her talent, the powerful influence it gave her among her brethren and sisters in the church, more than compensated her for a place and a pew lost among the Brah mins.

Brother Viner was a special favorite. He was young, well-looking, talented enough to command the first churches. Besides, his father was rich. Sister Mallane had more than one reason for wishing to ensure his good graces. For a moment his attention seemed fixed upon the white face in the open door opposite, and as it vanished he was still looking after it, when Mrs. Mallane said:

"Do sit down, Brother Viner; you are just the one that I want to see. The Lord must have sent you. I am sorely tried."

"What is your trial, Sister Mallane?"

"My sense of duty, and the difficulty of doing it. You saw that girl in the door?"

"Yes, a sweet face."

"Well, I suppose you gentlemen would call it sweet. I am sorry, Brother Viner, to tell you that it is a deceitful face. I know it has a look in it such as you see in pictures, and you gentlemen are attracted by it, that is why it is dangerous; but it belongs to a weak-minded, inefficient person. She belongs to a family miserably poor, and she is going the way to make them poorer. I feel it to be my duty to tell her so, to instruct her in the right way; but it is hard to the flesh to do so. I am a mother, Brother Viner. I have a daughter. I have a mother's feelings. When I look on this girl, and think what would be the state of my mind if my Grace were like her—"

"What does the poor girl do, sister? I thought she seemed to have a very innocent face; but then I only caught a glimpse of it as she shut the door."

"Well, I must say that gentlemen are all alike in one thing—they will think that a face is innocent and every thing perfect if it is only young and pretty. Even Mr. Mallane, sharp-sighted as he is, cannot see a fault in this girl. And God knows the trial she is to me!"

The concluding sentence was perfectly sincere, and uttered in the pathetic mother-quaver which was entirely absent from the first portion of the reply. Brother Viner was a young man, and not profoundly experienced in the ways of women. His own mother, a sweet-tempered, unworldly woman, never torn by conflicting ambitions and passions, could not have been moved to such a show of distress by any thing less than death, or an equally overwhelming calamity. Men measure all women by the particular woman whom they know best. Thus, Brother Viner, thinking the while of his own mother, felt sure that Sister Mallane had profound cause for being "sorely tried;" but some way, it was difficult for him to connect the cause of such trial with the face which he had just seen in the door. He was exceedingly puzzled. In seeking explanation, he very naturally fell back upon his ministerial functions.

"Have you asked wisdom from on high?" he asked. "That is our only help, Sister Mallane. Don't you think that it would bring comfort to your soul if we should have a season of prayer?"

"Yes, Brother Viner, that is my only refuge. But wouldn't you like to have me call Grace? Dear child! I think her heart is very tender just at this time. I feel certain that she is serious, for last Sabbath, after your sermon to the young, she said, 'Mother, I shall read a chapter in the Bible every day;' and after prayer-meeting in the evening, she said, 'it goes right through my heart to hear Brother Viner pray.' I wouldn't have her miss hearing you now. You may be the means of bringing the dear lamb into the fold of Christ. Oh, Brother Viner, you little know the feelings of a mother's heart!"

Brother Viner was very sure that he did not. Therefore he made no reply, but began to compose his countenance for his coming prayer, which he intended should contain an eloquent appeal for the conversion of the young girl's soul, while Sister Mallane went to the door and called Grace.

Grace appeared with downcast eyes and maiden blushes, and with tremulous devotion prostrated herself upon her knees, while the young minister in sonorous tones said, "Let us address the Throne of the Heavenly Grace."

In the meantime, the cause of this family prayer-meeting,—who, strangely enough, was left entirely out of it,—the girl up-stairs—wrapped in her shawl,—was gazing steadfastly upon her new picture, Faith before the Cross.

The utter repose of the figure, the beautiful serenity of the uplifted countenance, seemed to steal over the trembling frame of the young girl; the tears faded from her eyes, the quivering lips grew still, and without being conscious of it, she began to grow calm and strong again, to take up the cross of her own little life.

At the same hour Paul sat in one of the lecture-rooms of Harvard. He gave slight heed to the Professor's learned disquisition; his thoughts were far away. He was wondering if Eirene had come back; if she had received the pictures; if she liked them; if his father had attended to the stove. Then he thought how he would like to take a peep into the little room, just to see her enjoy the comfort of being warm; indeed, how he would like to sit down there, beside the little pine stand, and help her to read Télémaque. Paul had studied French in the old academy, and later had acquired the faultless accent of Monsieur de Paris, and felt sure that he was perfectly qualified to be her teacher in the *beau* language. The more he thought of it, the more he longed for the privilege; the stronger grew the attraction in the bare little room at home, the more tedious grew the Professor, and the more intolerable his learned disquisition on the law. Paul at last felt as if he could not stay where he was another minute.

Great had been the astonishment of good John Mallane a few days before, when he received, with the package directed to Miss Eirene Vale, a letter to himself from Paul, which ran in this wise:

"Dear Father:—You will oblige me

by delivering to Miss Eirene Vale the accompanying package. And you will oblige me still more, if you will see that a stove is put up in her room, that the poor girl may be made more comfortable. When I was at home I accidentally stepped into her room, and was shocked, yes, I must say shocked, to find that one, thought worthy to have a home under my father's roof, should occupy a room no better furnished than a prison-cell; and have absolutely nothing done for her comfort. I saw books which she must sit up at night to study, yet she has not had a fire in her room this winter.

"The girl is nothing to me. But as I sit before my cosy fire in my cushioned chair, in a room full of luxuries, I must confess that I feel mean, to think that all these things have been given to me, a *man*, to make my student-life more attractive, while a young girl, trying to study under every disadvantage, sits shivering and freezing over her book, and that in my own father's house. I tell you, father, it takes away more than half of the comfort of my fire; and I should despise myself if it did not.

"As I said before, the girl is nothing to me, personally, for I have not even spoken to her since she entered your house. Yet please say nothing to mother about this letter, for you know her weakness. She thinks that I am in love with every girl that I look at, except Tilly Blane. You, dear father, know better. You know that I make the request simply from a feeling of humanity; because I like my ease too well to have it disturbed by my conscience, at least in this case. And I know, father, that you want every body in your house to be comfortable. I think mother does, too,—every one except this little girl, whom she dislikes because she thinks that I shall fall in love with her, of which there is not the slightest danger.

"Your affectionate son,

"PAUL."

John Mallane took his spectacles off, wiped and re-wiped, set them on his high nose, took them off and set them back again numerous times, before Paul's letter had received its last reading and was shut away in his inside pocket. Then he said to himself: "The girl must have the stove, of course. She could have had it before if I had known that she hadn't one. But it seems to me this is new business for Paul, prowling around in his mother's chambers, looking after the comfort of their inmates. But I consider his letter an encouraging sign. He has been indulged so much himself, and has so many wants of his own, I have thought sometimes that he would never think of other people's. I am glad to be mistaken. It is really kind in him to think of the little girl's comfort, when, as he says, she is nothing to him. He is right, too, in saying that he knows I want every body in my house comfortable. I do. He is right about his mother, also. Tabitha *is* very unreasonable about this little girl; but then all women are unreasonable sometimes. I shall not tell her about this letter. It would only make her fret, and do no good, for the little girl must have the stove." And without further meditation, honest John Mallane went and ordered that a stove should be put up immediately in the small bedroom.

Paul's letter *did* make Tabitha Mallane "fret" that very evening.

When husband and baby were asleep, she laid down the stocking which she was mending beside the cradle, rose, took down John Mallane's coat from its accustomed hook, and placing her hand in the inside pocket, drew forth all the letters which the mail had brought him that day. This act usually closed her day's work. John Mallane confided to her very little of his business affairs. Early in their married life he had said, in reply to one of her questions, "Mother, you attend to the house, and I will attend to the shop. You would not half understand business matters if I should try to explain them, and then you would be all the time worrying over what you knew nothing about, and that would worry me. Leave me to attend to the business; the house and the children are enough for you." Tabitha Mallane thought otherwise. Although she had a passion for that employment, her eager faculties reached out beyond her nightly stocking-darning. What was the yearly income? Was money being made? Was money being saved for all these children, or would they some time come to want? All these were vital questions to her; the last a spectre that often rose up and horrified her in the midst of plenty. The fear of coming to want, the selfish insanity which has made miserable so many lives, poor Tabitha Mallane had inherited from her mother, who lived and died in the midst of abundance, yet never enjoyed the good things of this world for a single moment, for fear that some day she might wake up and find them gone. Tabitha Mallane knew her husband too well to trouble him further with financial questions. Yet she determined to be answered, nevertheless. Thus she commenced the nightly practice of extracting from his pockets and private desk, his memoranda and business letters. By reading orders, receipts, and bills of sale; by additions and deductions, she managed to give herself a partial yet tolerable knowledge of the financial status of her husband's affairs. If her conscience ever reproved her for the deceptive means which she took to obtain this knowledge, she re-assured herself with the thought that she made no bad use of it. Besides, in reality, was it not *her* business quite as much as it was his? Was not her share of the Bard homestead invested in this business? Had she not a perfect right to look after her own money, if John Mallane, like all other men, did think that no woman could understand the complicities of trade? John Mallane slept too soundly and snored too loudly for his wife to incur any risk in the time of looking over his business accounts. But to-night she could scarcely wait till the nasal trumpet began to sound in the adjoining bedroom. That afternoon the stove had been put up in Eirene's room, and she had taken in her own hand, from the pine stand, a package directed to that troublesome girl, "care of Hon. John Mallane," in Paul's boldest writing. Nothing had been said to her about either package or stove, yet she was sure that both came from her son. She felt abused and indignant. Would that perverse boy be the death of his mother? Were husband and son combined to destroy the dearest ambition of her lifetime?

She would see. Her hand trembled, and the lines about her wide mouth grew more rigid, as she drew the package of letters from the coat-pocket.

She had only heart for one to-night; she singled it out immediately and dropped the others back into their receptacle.

She sat down again by the cradle, and her pale face grew still paler as she opened the letter and read: "Dear Father: You will oblige me by delivering to Miss Eirene Vale the accompanying package;" and further on, as she came to—"Please say nothing of this letter to mother, you know her weakness, etc." the rigid lines grew almost ghastly, and she said: "It is what I expected." And when she read to the concluding sentence she reiterated: "'Afraid that I will fall in love!' Afraid that you will! Foolish boy! You *are* in love, and your father is as blind as a bat. You will have your way for a while. Your fever will run itself out. But you shall never marry her, never."

The next day, when Eirene returned, as Mrs. Mallane heard her step in the hall and thought of Paul's letter, her first impulse was to open the door and drive her from the house.

But twenty-five years of life with John Mallane had taught her at least something of self-control. To send the girl from the house now, she knew would be to madden Paul, and drive him to some extreme act, and to call down upon herself the only wrath which she feared upon earth—the wrath of her husband. She had resolved to control both husband and son, and to do this, she knew that she must first, in part at least, control herself. If Eirene could have conceived of the contending passions in this woman's heart, and of her pitiless anger toward herself, she would no more have dared to approach her with thanks and gratitude than she would have dared to rush into the face of any infuriated animal.

In comparison with what she felt, Tabitha Mallane's words to Eirene were merciful; and her exclamation to the minister, "God only knows the trial she is to me!" was no exaggeration.

Paul counted the cost of angering his mother when he wrote the letter and sent the package. But she had angered him so much in sending Eirene to Hilltop, that the satisfaction of inflicting punishment upon her entered into the purer pleasure of purchasing the pictures.

He saw them in Williams & Stevens' window on his way back from Marlboro Hill. And the face of Evangeline, that love of all college youth, her seeking eyes so full of tender quest, the homely dress she wore, made him think of Eirene. Thus, as so many young men more or less romantic have done, he bought one copy for his Cambridge room and another for her. "It will brighten up that den a little," he said to himself. "And this figure of Faith, how like her's! the same pure girlish outline, though with her the cross is not before her, but on her shoulders. She shall have this picture too. How angry it will make mother. I am glad of it. She needn't have sent her off. She will find she can't balk me."

Paul had a pleasant visit at Marlboro Hill. If he had been in his wonted mood, it would have been to him a season of marked triumph. The Cuban beauty was altogether too dark for his fancy. Even her million in sugar and slaves was not altogether to his fastidious taste. But Isabella Prescott, who someway he had fancied would be as bony and freckled as Dick, to his surprise he found his opposite; a round-limbed blonde, with a head covered with tiny feathery curls; a creature full of kittenish pranks and coquettish ways, with a twinkle in her small eyes which might have been called a wink in any body but a Prescott, and which in her was the sign and seal of the coquetry which she had already cultivated and consummated as an art.

Six weeks earlier, this gay creature would have set Paul's nerves tingling with her witching ways, and he would have opened a campaign of flirtation which would have ended in his subjugation or in hers for the time being. But to his own astonishment, and to her extreme mortification, for once he found himself indifferent. He was by no means in a normal mood; he was preoccupied, and found himself constantly comparing these brilliant beauties of the world to one whose preëminent charm was her unworldliness, and her utter unconsciousness of all the little arts which world-taught women practice to fascinate men.

Dashing young ladies of the world who carried with them the prestige of family, of wealth, of beauty, were the only ones that Paul had ever aspired to conquer. Thus it was an utterly new sensation for him to find himself measuring all women by a new standard, and that one which he had never found in the merely fashionable world. He was vexed with himself, and tried to banish from his thoughts the haunting face which continually came between him and all Bell Prescott's dangerous ways.

"*Here* is a match for me," he said to himself. "The heiress of Marlboro Hill! Dick says that she inherits this magnificent place from her mother, to say nothing of a fortune in railroad stock, and her charming self. She is a proper match for me. Confound it! Why am I not making the most of my chance? Dick is willing, and she—well, one can't be certain of such a witch of a girl in three days. What she's up to now, is to captivate me. But in the end, I'll make her love me, that is if she *can* love, which I rather doubt. Why am I not about it? Why——?"

At the close of the visit, Miss Isabella Prescott found herself piqued and disappointed. Youth, and wealth, and beauty, are not accustomed to indifference, and cannot bear it patiently. Yet Bell Prescott had borne it from one whom she had expected to conquer, and whom she had intended, although in a lady-like manner, to treat with condescension.

"Dick!" she said to her brother, after Paul's departure, "I thought you said that your chum was a *parvenu?*"

"Well, I meant that his father came up from nothing. Of course, if I hadn't considered *him* a gentleman, I shouldn't have invited him here. His mother, I believe, is of old stock, but ran away and married a journeyman mechanic. The old fellow is tolerably well off now, and very influential in a small way. I've seen him."

"Never mind his father or mother. *He* has the air of a grandee, of a prince of the blood, and he don't take it on; its natural. Why didn't you tell me he was so high and mighty? Why, he was as cool and indifferent to me as could be. I don't think he likes me a bit. I wouldn't mind if he wasn't so handsome and clever. You did not overrate him, Dick."

"Of course I didn't," said Dick.

"Really his manners are quite European, yet you say he has never been abroad? But I blame you, Dick, I do, for talking to me as if he would be ready to kneel at my feet the moment he reached here. You knew better. You shouldn't have told me such a story. I can tell you, it will be no every-day conquest to subdue him."

"Don't take on, Bell. Wait your time. He's in love with a shop-girl now, but he'll get over it."

"A shop-girl! What do you mean?"

"Why, I mean that he has done what I thought he never would do; he has fallen in love with a girl who works in one of his father's shops. You ought to hear him rave about her. But he'll never marry her. He is too sensitive on the subject of position. I am perfectly certain that he has always intended to contract a marriage that would strengthen and elevate his own, not one that would drag him back to old antecedents. But for the time being he has lost his wits over this girl."

"Indeed!" was the young lady's only reply.

"If you want to make a conquest, Bell, you can do it just the same; only wait till he gets over the shop-girl, then take your turn."

"Indeed! Take my turn *after* a shop-girl! Where's your family pride, Dick Prescott? I am not so poorly off for admirers, I can tell you." And the young lady perked up her piquant nose, and puckered up her pretty little eyes in a fashion which made her anger very comical.

"Oh, you will always have all the beaux you want, Bell. But you seemed piqued over Mallane's coolness, and I was explaining it. Of course, you must wait for one flame to subside before you can expect that he will feel another. Wait your time, then conquer him. I'd like to punish him for this shop-girl nonsense myself. He's fallen in love contrary to all my advice. Of course, Bell, under any circumstances, you wouldn't be in a hurry to commit yourself. You know that you can make a higher match. In one sense, it would be a coming down for a Prescott to marry a Mallane, especially to bear the name. But there's no denying one thing, Prince Mallane would make a deucedly presentable husband. You might marry a name and a fortune and all that sort of thing, and the man belonging to them be a cursed bore, you know. So take time to decide which you want most,—the man, or the accompaniments. The chances are against your having both. It will be worth while for you to bring Mallane to your feet, whatever you do with him afterwards."

"Indeed!" again said Bell, as she made a mouth at him and a courtesy, and vanished.

A few moments afterwards, she stood prinking and making pretty faces, and throwing herself into graceful attitudes before her mirror.

"A shop-girl, ah! I never had to wait for a shop girl before. I wonder what she's like? Of course, he thinks that she is prettier than I am! She's a common little rustic, I know. Then this is why you were so cool to me, Sir Knight? This is why you watched me dance, and sing, and do all manner of pretty things, as unmoved as a stone? Very well, you won't always. My day will come. Then I'll teach you whether you will sit by my side like your grandfather carved in alabaster! I'll go and tell Delora about you," and with these words she capered off to the boudoir of the Cuban heiress.

# V.

EIRENE'S SUMMER.

IN the Spring, Eirene left the house of Mr. Mallane and went to live with her friend, Tilda Stade, in the family of Brother Goodlove, John Mallane's foreman. From the advent of the store and the pictures, Eirene felt that she must go away from the presence of Mrs. Mallane, for she had every reason to feel that she was only a tolerated member of that lady's household.

"She dislikes me," said the child, "because she thinks that I am trying to make myself more than God intended I should be. And she thinks that is the trouble with all my poor family, that we are not contented with our condition, and yet are not efficient enough to better it. 'Poor and shiftless,' she called us; *that* sounds hard. Poor father don't know how to get on, but he has always worked hard; sowed, and others have reaped his harvests. Oh, if he could only get on well once! But I must go away from here. It hurts me to stay where I am not wanted. Father thought it would be so nice for me to live here, because Mr. Mallane seemed so pleasant. Mr. Mallane *is* pleasant; he doesn't seem to think so poorly of us. I noticed he was very kind to father the other day; urged him to stay to dinner. I said nothing, because I feared that Mrs. Mallane would not like it. I will go to the boarding-house. I have dreaded to go there because it is so noisy. But I will give up my French. I *can* give it up, although I like it so well. I never studied it because I thought it fine, but because I love the language. I will tell Tilda, to-morrow, and see if I can room with her."

Tilda Stade worked next to Eirene in the shop. She was a good girl—a zealous Methodist, whose piety held her apart from her more rude and boisterous companions. Although she regarded Eirene as an unconverted sinner, still "in the gall of bitterness and bonds of iniquity," she had become personally warmly attached to her. Her gentleness and refinement, showing in such striking contrast to many of those around her, were very attractive to Tilda, and from the first she established herself as the uncompromising friend of the new hand upon every possible occasion.

When Eirene told her that she was going to leave the house of Mr. Mallane, she replied that she was glad of it, and there was something better in store for her than that wicked boarding-house, where she herself could scarcely find a moment's quiet for secret meditation and prayer. Brother Goodlove had offered her the front chamber in his house, and she had only been waiting to find a quiet girl to share it with her, so that she could afford to take it.

Eirene, who had a terror of the boarding-house, was made quite happy by this proposition.

Thus, one May evening not long after, Brother Goodlove himself carried her small trunk across the street to his story-and-a-half house, which stood in a gay little garden beside the shops. Eirene followed, carrying Moses Loplolly's parrot, which, for the sake of the giver, she had named Momo. Momo was as pretty and prating as ever, and, greatly to Eirene's discomfiture, went out of the house crying: "Paul! Paul! Pretty Rene! Mother! mother! no you don't! Pretty Paul!"

Mrs. Mallane had never objected to the presence of Momo, because he afforded much amusement to the children. He had a remarkably facile tongue even for a parrot, and caught new words and phrases from the little ones every day. Tabitha Mallane had heard him sing out "Paul," hundreds of times, but it never sounded as it did to-night, coming back through the street, and even from Brother Goodlove's door. She stood in the open window, with the baby in her arms, watching Eirene's departure. And as she heard the parrot's cry, her whole face darkened.

"Oh, the hateful huzzy, to teach the bird such talk as that! And she'll hang the little wretch in her window, to call my boy in, will she!"

"Mother! mother! no you don't!" screamed the parrot.

"She taught it that in my own house!"

Tabitha Mallane, in her anger, was entirely forgetful of the fact that Momo had learned this precious bit of satire from her youngest son, her own little impish Jack.

"Well, she's gone," the mother went on, "out of my house, at least, but only across the street. She is cunning. She knows that she will have a better chance to see him there than here. But you have a long head, young lady, if you think you will outwit me."

If Tabitha Mallane's hate had allowed her reason any action, her own good sense would have told her that all her accusations were false. She knew better even when she made them. She knew enough of the simplicity of this girl's nature, to know that she had laid no traps to entice her son; that all such devices were unknown to her thoughts. She knew, in her inmost heart, that she only hated Eirene because there was that in her face and in her nature which would be attractive to Paul; that she hated her because she was lovely, and because her loveliness was in the way; and the more conscious she felt of her own injustice, the more bitterly she accused its object.

Eirene reached her little chamber, with Mr. Momo screaming at his utmost voice. She gave the cage a very humane and positive little shake as she set it down, and said:

"Momo, how can you—how *can* you be so naughty?"

Momo, conscious that he was in disgrace, thrust his bill into his breast, shook his head, and blinked solemnly, first with one eye, then with the other, and at last said, in a very subdued voice, "Pretty Paul!"

"Who taught him *that?*" asked Tilda, abruptly.

"He learned it of the children. You can't think how soon he picks up words. The first thing we know, he will be repeating our talk."

"Well, if I were you, I would rather have him repeat any thing than 'Paul.' In my estimation, Mr. Paul Mallane is a very wicked young man, and I shouldn't want any bird of mine calling out his name."

"Oh, I hope he is not wicked," said

Eirene, with feeling, as she looked at the two pictures which he had sent her, already hanging in their assigned places. "His father and mother seem to live in him; they would never get over it, if he were to disappoint them."

"Oh, he won't disappoint *them!* Haven't they brought him up to be what he is?—though, how they can, they both praying and speaking in meeting, is more than I can understand. If Sister Mallane had spent her time praying for his soul and fitting him for the itinerant ministry, instead of bringing him up as she has done, then she would have done her duty. Jack's to be the minister, I believe. They'll give the first son to the world and the devil, and the last one to the Lord."

"How do you mean that they have brought him up?" asked Eirene, doubtfully. Notwithstanding his thoughtful kindness to her, she felt an unwilling consciousness that Mr. Paul Mallane might not be quite as good as he ought to be, and she was naturally anxious to lay the fault to his parental training.

"I mean," said Tilda, "that they have always indulged him in every thing. They have made him feel that nobody else is quite as handsome or quite as smart as he is. He has grown to think that nothing in the world is quite good enough for him, and has come to look down even on his own flesh and blood. If the other girls felt as I do, they wouldn't seem so pleased and flattered every time he comes into the shop and notices them. His very notice there is an insult, for he never speaks to one of them outside of it. He knows better than to make any of his fine speeches to *me.* I want nobody to speak to me in the shop, that can't speak to me out of it. I don't believe he'd turn his white hand over to help a shop-girl if she were dying."

"Oh, you judge him too hardly," said Eirene. "He can be very kind. He sent me those two pictures which you admire so much, and I am nothing to him at all. He never spoke to me but once, and then it was through a mistake. You know I have not the slightest claim upon him, and it seemed very good of him to remember me in such a way."

Tilda looked amazed and exceedingly displeased.

"Eirene Vale!" she said, with deep solemnity, "if Mr. Paul Mallane sends you presents, he does it for no good purpose. If you had known what is due to yourself, you would have sent them back as soon as they came."

"I did not know who sent them when they came, nor for a long time after," said Eirene, her voice trembling slightly, as it always did when she was frightened. "I only knew that Mr. Paul sent them to me, when the first number of this magazine came. On it was written, 'From Paul Mallane,' and then I saw that it was the same hand which directed the pictures. If it was wrong to keep them, I am sorry that I did; but nobody but father ever made me a present before. It does not seem as if a person who thought any harm would send me such a picture as 'Faith.'"

"You know nothing of the wickedness of men," said Tilda, compassionately, in a tone which indicated that *she* knew all about it. "Mr. Paul Mallane is very old for his years. Of course, he can see what you are; any one with half an eye could see that. If he sent you anything, it would be something which he knew would please you. What are the magazines? Trifles,—full of foolish travels and fashions and comic pictures, to make you laugh and forget your soul's salvation. When the next one comes, I advise you to send it back. Show him there's one shop-girl that don't want any of his attentions."

Eirene made no answer. Her gaze was fixed upon "Faith," and, as she looked, she seemed to be far away.

Tilda turned toward her her small, keen eyes, and narrow, perceptive forehead, which had no power of reflection in it, and came to two conclusions. The first was, that the beauty of the face before her, without doubt, was very attractive to Mr. Paul Mallane. The second was, that she, Tilda Stade, in virtue of six years' seniority and vastly superior knowledge of men, would defend and save this innocent lamb from the impending wolf, even when he came in the unexceptional clothing of a young gentleman of the world.

Brother Goodlove's front chamber did not prove to be a paradise. The afternoon sun shone full upon its low roof and unsheltered windows, fading its cotton carpet, blistering its cheap furniture, and making its air stifling with heat. In the evening, when their day's work was done, Eirene found it scarcely easier to breathe there than in the close atmosphere of the overcrowded shop. Weary with her ten hours' toil, she would sit on a low chair by the open window, vainly waiting for a breeze to come in to cool her throbbing temples, and rest her a little for the lesson which she so much desired to learn. Across the street, through the boughs of the apricot tree, she saw the window where she used to sit, half hidden within its cool curtains of summer vines; and she might have wished herself back again in the bare little room, if it had not been for the memory of Tabitha Mallane's unfriendly face.

Tilda Stade said that *she* " desired only the wisdom which cometh from on high," and, therefore, had very little sympathy with Eirene's pursuit of earthly knowledge. Indeed, it was only on class-meeting and prayer-meeting nights, when Tilda was absent telling " what the Lord had done for her soul," that Eirene could study at all. Tilda's favorite anxiety was for Eirene's conversion; and as her zeal was not at all according to knowledge, she felt it to be her duty to labor perpetually for this much-desired object. No matter how high the thermometer stood, nor how tired Eirene might be, nor how hard she herself might have worked, this devout young woman always had vitality enough left to exhort her friend by the hour to repent of her sins and " give her heart to Jesus." She acknowledged to herself that she did not understand Eirene's case; and the more it puzzled her, the more extreme grew her unction, and the more fearfully long her lectures. While Eirene sat beside one window, she usually sat by the other, on a high, straight-backed chair, ostensibly to sew. But in a very few moments the work was sure to drop into her lap, and, with her feet firmly fixed on a high stool before her, she would plant her elbows upon her knees, thrust her chin in her hands, and set her sharp, inquiring eyes upon the face drooping below the level of the stand which divided them. It never remained for any length of time a silent gaze. The large, patient look fixed upon the difficult page always provoked Tilda to exhortation, and all the more because it in no way coincided with the expression which she thought an unconverted sinner's countenance ought to wear.

" How you can look like *that* over a Catholic French book, is more than I can understand," she would exclaim. " If it was your Testament, Rene, and you were reading about your Saviour, then I should know."

At the first exclamation, Eirene always laid her book down, knowing well that any further attempt to study would be useless.

" If you would only fall down before your Saviour, confess your sins, and get the evidence that you were accepted, I shouldn't be troubled about you any longer," Tilda would say.

" I have prayed ever since I can remember, and every day ask my Saviour to forgive my sins, and give me strength to do right," Eirene answered.

" That makes you all the worse. You pray in your own strength. As long as you are not converted and haven't received the witness, your prayers don't get through the ceiling."

Eirene did not understand these fine points in Tilda's theology. The faith of the gospel, as it had been taught to her by her mother, was very simple. " Ask, and ye shall receive; seek, and ye shall find; knock, and it shall be opened unto you," were words which she believed with unquestioning faith, and obeyed with the simplicity of a child. Almost from babyhood she had been accustomed to carry all her little sins and sorrows to this Saviour, whom she had been taught to regard as an Elder Brother, who loved little children, and who was interested in all that concerned their happiness. Now, to be told that He cared nothing for her, and would pay no attention whatever to her prayers because she was so wicked, was to her a view of Christ unprecedented and appalling. The lack of self-poise was a weakness in her character. Her delicate, work-worn nerves, her tender and humble heart, were no match for Tilda's pugnacious persistency. Thus this devoted missionary often enjoyed the partial satisfaction of seeing the eyes before her suffused with tears, and the head bowed in bewildered sorrow. For, after all, Eirene knew no other way than to go on praying and believing, just as she had always done.

Then Tilda would exclaim, in joyful enthusiasm :

" You are almost in the kingdom, Rene. If you were only under conviction, and would give up all for Jesus—if you could only feel that you were willing to be lost, if it were His will, then you would *have* the evidence. But your own goodness is only filthy rags. It'll *never* save you. Are you willing to give up every vanity for the Saviour ? "

" I hope so," was the humble reply.

" Are you willing to take that ribbon out of your hair ? "

" Oh, yes."

" Are you willing to have the small-pox, and look like a fright ? "

" I—don't know."

" Then you are NOT a Christian, and you won't be till you are willing," was Tilda's conclusive rejoinder.

" Yet she is outwardly more consistent than many professors," Tilda would ejaculate to herself. " But, then, that's natural goodness ; it won't save her ; she has never been under conviction—never received the witness. She is in a state of nature. She can't be saved any more than I could before Christ pardoned me."

In order to feel certain of Eirene's safety, she wished to see her pass through precisely the same spiritual travail and triumph which had been vouchsafed to herself. Her mind could comprehend no reason why Eirene's finer mental and spiritual organism would receive religion through the process of silent growth, rather than by any sudden and violent demonstration such as she herself had experienced. The great object of her daily labors was to make Eirene feel as she did. To gain this end, she would tell over and over her own religious experience : how the sudden death of her cousin, a gay young man, had transfixed her with terror in the midst of her winter dissipations of quilting-bees and apple-parings ; how she suddenly discovered that she had loved nothing in the world so well as this young man ; how she had lived for him and for herself ; how she had done all in her power to injure Betsey Boyd, because she feared that this young man loved Betsey better than he loved herself ; how, over his coffin, she was suddenly overcome with a consciousness of her sinfulness, and the fear of hell, whose terrors she did not feel willing to share even with the gay young man ; how, for weeks, she was under conviction ; how she wept and prayed at protracted meeting ; how she wrestled day and night, yet saw only the blackness of darkness, and God seemed to have forsaken her ; how, at last, at the " anxious seat," she cried out, " O Lord ! I deserve to be lost ! " And, with these words, a great light shone about her. All the brethren and sisters shouted " Glory ! " She herself cried, " Praise the Lord ! " fell down in a vision, and had the " power." In which she saw her Saviour come down from the skies, with a white book in His hand, on whose front leaf, in gold letters, she read : " Tilda Stade, thy sins are forgiven thee." How, when she came to herself, she felt peace unspeakable, and knew that she had received the white stone and the new name. She had received the witness. Thus she could point Eirene to the spot —to the very moment when the Saviour forgave her sins ; and this Eirene must be able to do before she would be fit for the kingdom of heaven.

Eirene, whose childish moods had been of a milder sort, who had never tried to injure any young woman, and had never been violently in love with any young man—who had never experienced any of Tilda's vehement passions—naturally felt a less violent though no less sincere sorrow for her sins. As she listened wonderingly to Tilda's spiritual story, she felt sure that she could never feel like *that;* she did not believe that anything so wonderful could ever happen to her. In conclusion, she would drive Tilda almost distracted, by saying that she never felt that she herself was good—she knew that she was not—but when she went to her Saviour, He always seemed near and ready to help her, and that she trusted in Him for strength to do right.

In August there was to be a camp-meeting in the woods of Southerly, and this became Tilda's final hope for Eirene's salvation.

"I'll take her there," she said, with an energetic jerk, as if the taking would involve corporeal lifting, and Eirene was to be carried in her arms to the camp ground. "I'll take her there, and when the Spirit of the Lord comes down, as it did at Pentecost, it will pierce her through and through. Then she'll see her sinfulness, but not before. Such blindness! such blindness! But when she is a Christian, she will be a bright and shining light. I haven't a doubt but she'll receive the blessing of sanctification."

PAUL'S SUMMER.

Paul had not been at home all summer. He had a strong will, and it had kept him away from Busyville. During the winter the desire to go there, the desire to see Eirene, had often rushed through his heart. Head and heart wrestled together, but in the end the head had always been victorious. More than once he sat over his meerschaum gazing into the fire till he saw the face that he sought rise and look forth on him through its heart of flame. Once as he beheld it thus, he turned aside to his table, took his pen and began a letter to Eirene; more, he wrote on to the end, a long letter into which he poured his heart at flood-tide. He told her how she seemed to him in her innocence; how different from the young ladies of the world; how her face and her presence rested and satisfied him; how it made him happier and better, indeed how it made all goodness seem possible even to him!

For he was not good, he told her; he was guilty of sins of which she had no comprehension; but that the look in her eyes made the pleasures of the world hateful to his very thought.

He needed the influence of such a nature in his life. She could do everything for him, if she only would; if she would only care for him, if she would only care for him a little; if she would think of him, and write to him sometimes. And he hoped that he could do something for her—it pained him to think that she, a young and delicate girl, was struggling against such hard odds for an education, while he, a young man, had opportunities given him which he did not improve. He could assist her a little at least in the way of books. Would she let him? Would she let him be her brother? Would she be to him a sister? Paul had never written anything in his life so purely noble and sincere as this letter, till he came to the last sentence. "Sister! brother! Pshaw! A pretty brother I'd make to *her!* I dare say she could be my sister, but I never could be her brother. To her I can only be a lover or nothing. I cannot be her lover. Then I will be nothing. But I won't send *her* any such lying humbug." And in his self disgust Paul tossed into the fire the letter in which he had put the very best of his heart.

Instead of the letter he sent her a magazine! Paul's shrewd, worldly head domineered over his passionate and importunate heart. Thus he carried in himself two conflicting and keenly-defined natures which were constantly warring with each other. Like all men of intellect eager for power and distinction in the world, his plan of life was distinctly marked out, and in the end he meant to fulfil it at any cost to mere affection. In his cool moments he was quite as ambitious for himself as his mother was for him.

But she knew him well when she said: "It will be hard for you to be true to your position till you are older."

Now life was eager within him. His youth was in the way. It was the youth in his heart which cried out and would not be defrauded of its right.

But as the winter wore on, Paul found it easier to submit to what he called his "reason," and he began once more with a will to bend all his desires to his old plan of life.

Time dropped its barrier between him and the fair presence which for a single month had so pervaded and possessed him. The sweet face began to seem picture-like, something to remember and half worship as he did the Evangeline before him.

As it grew more dreamlike, he found it easier to reason over his feelings, and began to console himself with the conclusion that he had not been such a foolish fellow after all.

"I never saw a face that moved me like that, and I don't believe that I ever shall another," he would say to himself. "I came very near falling in love. But I left Busyville just in season. I knew enough to know my danger, and I have had sense enough to keep out of it. I shan't go home again till I am sure I can look at that face without a single flutter, and criticise it as coolly as any other."

Paul found Marlboro Hill a valuable assistant to his sensible resolutions. He accepted all Dick's invitations, and spent his Saturdays and Sundays there. Like most men, he was powerfully controlled by his senses. What he saw and felt this moment moved him more than what he remembered.

We have no gauge which can measure the power of personal contact,—the influence of voice and eye, of look and touch, laying siege to the soul through the outworks of the senses.

We do not half realize how potent is the subtle atmosphere of presence sheathing every human body, repelling or attracting with inevitable magnetism.

Rare as wonderful is the personality of that being who can so pervade another,—that neither time nor absence nor rivals, the cruelest foes to love, can dethrone or banish it from the heart into which it has entered and in which it is enshrined. Not more than one man in a thousand is strong enough to be perfectly loyal in thought and in deed to the absent love, when beguiled by the looks and words and tones of a charmer whose living presence makes the absent one pale into a memory and a dream.

Paul would have been a very different Paul from what he was had he proved to be an exception to his sex. Besides, bound by no vow, feeling himself subject to no law but that of his own nature, he threw himself with all the force of his will into that side of the balance which held the whole of his interest, if only a part of his feeling.

Feeling is usually a rebel against mere expediency. And Miss Isabella Prescott's cause would have prospered more surely if Paul's practical head had not been constantly reiterating to his rebellious heart: "You must fall in love with Bell Prescott, because it is for your interest to do so." As he had made up his mind to obey his head, he did it as far as he was able, and he would not have been Paul if he had found that obedience wholly disagreeable.

To a young man of his tastes it was by no means an irksome task to be the escort of a belle, a beauty, and an heiress. It pleased his vanity to roll about the country with her in a showy carriage; or on a mettled thoroughbred to canter through the streets of Cambridge by her side; or to promenade with her down Beacon street, and thus send a pang through Helena Maynard's heart as she beheld them seemingly absorbed in each other, from the windows of her stately home. Paul attended Miss Prescott to church, he waited upon her to the opera. He danced with her, sung with her, in fine flirted with her, and the world looking on said that it was a high game that either one, or both were playing, and wondered which would win.

And yet every week Paul spent one evening at least with Helena Maynard, in which he neither waltzed nor sung—but sat in cosy tête-à-tête in a classical and luxuriant library, talking metaphysics and ethics, ethnology, psychology, theology, art, poetry, and love, with one of the most noted girls in Boston. Not a week but one or more of her exquisitely scented missives, witty, sentimental, dashing, to the verge of coarseness, free beyond the conventional limit of maidenly freedom, yet certainly clever, and unmistakably tender, found its way to the law student's parlor in Cambridge. Paul would read it over more than once, and say thoughtfully: "With all her conquests, and all her offers, she undoubtedly loves *me*. And she writes the cleverest letters that I ever read—they are really company." And in proportion to his estimate of their cleverness, he felt flattered by their homage. And what kind of letters did he write in reply? Not love letters in the openly declared sense, and yet love letters still, in all subtle and undefined expression.

No single sentence committed him to any positive declaration, yet every word was full of implied interest, sympathy, and tenderness toward her, and all that concerned her happiness. Helena made him her confidant. She uncovered to his vision her inner life;—told him of her many lovers, of the numerous offers of marriage made her;—of her refusals of every one;—revelations not at all unpleasant to a vain young man, when the inevitable conslusion was, that these refusals were all made by a heart pre-occupied with his own absorbing self. It pleased him to call himself and Helena "friends." He believed in men cherishing female friends *à la* Récamier, and thought it of immense value to his own development to be the intimate companion of a gifted woman of society. Besides it afforded him a flattering estimate of his own superior strength and wisdom, to be able to accept this unequivocal homage unveiled even of maidenly reserve, and yet to be strong to inform her, in return, that his heart was not his own—that he was her true and devoted friend, but could be no more. And yet while making this avowal in words in a thousand ways more expressive than all language, he made her feel constantly, after all, that if less than a lover, he was more than a friend.

He would say to himself: "I shall never love Helena Maynard. Her nature is too exaggerated, too over-wrought. She is too full of passionate unrest, it would worry me to death to live with it; but I admire her, and I am not going to give up such letters."

Poor Paul! he did not know that it was almost impossible for him to give up any thing which in the slightest degree ministered to his own pleasure. These letters were a gratification to himself. He did not think to inquire how far they might grow to compromise the peace of their writer.

Still, his intercourse with Helena Maynard was only the side play of life, its positive entertainment was derived from the society of Bell Prescott. To him, in this, there was just enough of the play of passion to make it pleasant. There was no deep yearning of heart, no sympathy of spirit, no holy love, but there was personal attraction hovering in look and gesture; fluttering in the touch of her dainty hands, and in the twinkling of her dancing feet.

She played about him perpetually, and fascinated his senses. If he sat by her side he wanted to touch the jewel quivering in her ear, or to toy with the golden chains fettering her delicate wrists: or he felt an insane desire to catch some tiny feather of a curl floating out from all the rest. The pretty hand so playfully yet coyly given, so quickly withdrawn, he liked to take it in his, and hold it an instant longer than necessary. He liked to dance with this airy sylph—for she swayed him with her movement, now dreamy and languid, now sprightly and gay. And for the time being she would fascinate him with her eyes,—one moment languishing with tenderness, the next sparkling and teazing with merriment. Then she was so full of pretty pranks and whims which are as charming in a youthful beauty as they are tedious and irritating in a plain, elderly woman.

One moment she would say she "could waltz forever," and the next would declare she was "*so* tired she could not take another step. Mr. Mallane *must* take her fan and bouquet, her vinaigrette and her *mouchoir*." But as soon as she saw him fairly laden she wanted them all back again.

When Dick remonstrated, and told her that she was "silly," as he always did when he was about, she would look at him with an audacious twinkle in her cunning eyes, and a vexed pout on her childish mouth, and tell him that she "liked to be silly, it was vastly pleasanter than being wise," which was very true in her case. She was too perfect an artiste in her art not to know precisely the effect of all these foolish, yet bewitching ways. She had practised those charming gestures and made those pretty mouths too long not to know exactly their influence upon susceptible young men.

Her prophecy was already fulfilled—Paul no longer sat by her side unmoved as his "grandfather carved in alabaster." Indeed, her moods were so full of contrast, such a perpetual surprise, that he was in a half-astonished, half-admiring, and wholly-bewildered state whenever he was in her presence. But her empire did not extend beyond her personal atmosphere. Fairly outside of that, Paul was alone with himself, and then it was not of her that he thought. Or if he did, strange to say, he felt no longing to return to her side—and it was with a feeling of vexation toward himself, that while he was conscious that she fascinated him, he was equally conscious that he did not love this girl.

He would sit and wonder if Eirene had translated Telemaque yet, or if she had read all of Bossuet's sermons; or if she liked the Magazine, or the copy of Beranger's songs which he had sent her.

He would think of her as he saw her once standing by the window, at the end of the long shop, the sunshine falling on her hair touching its brown with gold.

He wondered if she ever fancied where her pictures and books came from, and if she ever thought of him! Then came the thought which always came at last, and which was a longing also—that the pictured eyes could only look on him once more from the living face.

"Bell Prescott is the gayest of all company," he would say to himself; "and her ways are fascinating, very, and when I am with her I don't know whether I am in love with her or not; but as soon as I get away I know that I am not. It looks cunning in a girl of her features—but I don't think that I should fancy having my wife winking at me out of the corner of one eye, or making mouths at me—as she does. It's odd, but what one thinks very charming in a coquette, and a young lady of fashion, is not at all what one would fancy in one's wife! These are the eyes to spend one's life with!" he said, looking down into the face of his Evangeline—eyes that would never upbraid except with their tenderness, that would never mock save with their purity. "These are the only eyes to save *me* from the world and the devil. If I could look down into them and see them full of love for me, the eyes of my wife! and see them looking up at me again, some day, from the eyes of my children—that would be joy enough! How I could love that girl! What a cursed fate! What a cursed nature that will not be satisfied with less than all!"

When he reached this climax Paul usually snatched Blackstone and went to studying with all his might; or if he could, he did what was better still for self-forgetfulness, he went to sleep, and in a short time found himself in his dreams perfectly happy, living like a king at Marlboro Hill; but, strange to say, the queen who shared all fortune and beauty with him was not Bell Prescott, but a shop-girl named Eirene Vale.

Bell Prescott was perfectly certain that she had made great advances in his favor since Paul's first visit to Marlboro Hill—indeed that she had gained a positive power over him; still she was equally certain that it was only a partial power, and therefore she by no means felt satisfied. Notwithstanding she made her presence so engrossing, there were moments, perhaps when she was most brilliant and fantastical, when an absent look would creep over his face as if he saw something far distant, It is true at these times another face did rise before his vision by sheer force of contrast to the one before him.

This look never escaped Bell's quick eyes, and she would inwardly say: "There! he is thinking of that shop-girl! It seems very hard to get *her* out of his head. If I can't, nobody can." Sometimes while toying with her jewels he would drop them suddenly, with a sense of self-disgust, and a look of positive weariness. He was playing with the charms in her chatelaine one day, when he let them fall listlessly, and this look so unwelcome to his companion stole over his face.

"Who are you thinking of, Sir Knight?" she asked in her softest voice. This unexpected question, the first of the kind which she had ever put to him, brought the color into Paul's cheek.

"Ah!" she said archly, "you are thinking of some Busyville beauty. It's nobody very near I know, for your thoughts seem a long way off. Come, Sir Knight, tell me. *Have* you a little loveress?"

"No indeed, *ma belle*. I am solitary, with no lady to love me. But I *was* thinking of a lovely girl, one of the loveliest that I ever saw, and she does live in Busyville."

"Indeed!" was the involuntary exclamation, and this time the pouting of the little mouth was real not affected. Miss Bella was not quite prepared for this unanticipated confession. The vexation of lip and tone were not to be mistaken, and for an instant Paul experienced the keen masculine delight of making one woman miserable by praising another.

His triumph was only momentary. Miss Prescott was quite as well aware of his weakness as he was of hers, and before Paul could choose any new adjective of praise for the unknown rival with which to torment her, she had recovered all her wonted art and exclaimed:

"Oh, I know who it is! Dick told me all about her. He said you were in love with her; she works in your father's shop."

This was extremely mortifying, and would have seemed almost rude if it had not been uttered in the most innocent and charming tone in the world.

Paul never mentioned the "shop" at Marlboro Hill. The Prescotts had never been "in business;" and Paul himself felt a repugnance to trade which was rather at variance with his New England origin. When he heard his companions boasting of their pedigree, he often wished that he could refer to a long line of illustrious ancestors whose white hands had never been soiled by coming in contact with gross products; and whose lofty intellects had never come down to accounts in stock, but who had lived and died in the practice of high and wise pursuits, or in the serene atmosphere of affluence and leisure.

It was but a partial consolation for him to remember that the Bards had always been freeholders and rich, while he could not forget that the grandfather whose name he bore, had been only an honest, industrious carpenter, and that his father's wealth had all been acquired in the shops where in earlier days that same father had worked with his own hands. This false pride, ever alert, stung him once more at Bella Prescott's words; but he was too haughty to betray his weakness for more than an instant, and thus said very deliberately: "Yes, she does work in one of my father's shops. But she is very superior to her condition. Indeed, I have reason to think that she comes from an old and educated family who have become reduced," and his mind referred to the little antique testament with its Latin phrase. "But, Miss Prescott, personally she is nothing in the world to me, and never will be. Her face comes back to me like pictures that I have seen and admired, and as it has a peculiar kind of loveliness I like to look at it, that is all. She makes a pretty picture, and yet she has not the style of beauty that I most admire in a woman, you may know, for her eyes are brown." He said this with a look of unmistakable meaning fixed upon her eyes.

"Are you sure that is all?"

At the very beginning of this question the gay voice melted into a tender vibration which must have been irresistible, for Paul answered quickly: "Yes, I am sure. Don't you think that I am old enough to know my own mind? Brown eyes may be lovely in a picture, but in the living woman give me the blue."

A moment afterward Paul despised himself for a liar, and Miss Prescott, feeling the emanation of his discontent, mused silently over his words. "I don't believe it! No man would ever spend so much time in growing absent-minded over a picture. He has told me a fib, and dotes on brown eyes, and has told *her* so."

## VI.

### THE PLEASURE MONTH.

AFTER Commencement Dick made up a gay party for his new yacht the Nautilus, which sailed from Boston for an island off the coast of Maine.

The Cuban heiress went, accompanied by her brother Señor Oredo, and Helena Maynard went also as one of the bridesmaids of a bridal party. Miss Bella Prescott's nominal protector was her brother Dick, but her escort of course was Mr. Paul Mallane.

The real history of that pleasure month off the coast of Maine cannot be written in words; for with some of its actors it was all lived in heart-throbs, in thrills of joy, in deep stabs of pain, and while these must be lived they can never be told. After a sunny voyage the Nautilus rested in a quiet cove, and its festal party retreated to a summer cottage on the island open for guests. But this was only a partial retreat, where they slept and sometimes eat,—their holiday was spent in the open air.

They fished and boated, rode and drove; picnicked, loitered, and rested, after the fashion of all pleasure parties; and in the sultry July nights the gentlemen swung hammocks from the trees and went to sleep under the stars. The island was full of lovely and lonely haunts, where Nature wrought her delicious alchemies alone, and only her voices were heard.

Her crickets piped in the long waving grasses; her birds twittered to each other from their solitary boughs; her waves ran up and talked with the rustling sedge and pearly pebbles on the shore, and there were none to molest or to make them afraid. What wonder that beauty and youth, that love and romance, discovered these unaccustomed haunts, and made them their own!

What roads were those running through cool forests, bordered by broad beds of fragrant fern, walled and festooned with wild vines, roofed with panoplies of interlacing leaves through which the midsummer sunshine twinkled in stars! And what paths were those winding through groves of cedar and spruce and pine, ending at last on the sheltered beach, where you might sit and rest while the waves of the ocean played with the shells at your feet. I must believe that God meant such a spot as this for love and rest, and for that serene content which is the fulness of peace. But since sin has come into His world, wherever His creatures go, goes also discontent, unrest, and that mighty yearning of the heart for what is not, and for what cannot be, which so often destroys the satisfaction of all present possession.

Thus, excepting the newly-married pair, who were thoroughly in love and wholly absorbed in each other's society, it is doubtful if in all Dick Prescott's gay party there was one who at heart was perfectly satisfied and happy. Where half a dozen human beings meet and mingle, and the give-and-take of society is going on, it is curious and often sad to watch the subtle forces which move them; the secret passions which draw them together, and drive them asunder; which make them love and hate, misjudge and wrong, bless and destroy each other!

Dick and his Cuban heiress were probably the best contented of the company. For he had Delora entirely to himself, and although she did not care a fig for him, she was too indolent to trouble herself about any body else. In a sort of a sleepy way she admired the Señor Malane, but it did not annoy her at all to see him constantly by the side of another, while her own *cavalier servante* was so exclusively devoted, that he anticipated all her desires, and saved her the exertion of thinking at all. Thus she had nothing to do but to enjoy; to drink in all light and warmth, all odor and sound through her luxurious senses. Her most positive emotion was manifested when the wind swept cool from the sea; then she would shudder in her thick wrappings of India shawls, and wonder "how people *could* live so near the North pole." Her brother, the Señor, was not quite as content. This dark Don had conceived a positive admiration for the white beauty of the Massachusetts blonde; her vivacity was in pleasant contrast to his own heaviness, and charmed him exceedingly.

Paul, who was in no way oblivious to the Cuban's admiration, redoubled his own attentions through sheer rivalry; otherwise he would certainly have conferred at least half of them upon Helena Maynard.

But as he graphically expressed it, "with that confounded Spaniard always about," Miss Prescott received his almost exclusive devotion, and Helena Maynard and Señor Ovedo were left to make the most of each other. The latter was not devoid of a latent admiration for her Cleopatra-like beauty, which might have been greatly enhanced if she had taken the slightest pains to please him, which she did not do. Helena had devoted years to flirting and was tired of it, and now the real passion in her heart admitted of no room for pastime.

Besides, the Don was heavy and slow both in thought and movement, with a positive preponderance of the senses in his organism; just the style of man which she did not admire. Helena, though a belle, was also a Blue, and was much vainer of her intellect than of her beauty. Yet the mental cleverness on which she prided herself was that portion of her being to which Señor Ovedo was perfectly oblivious. He could appreciate mirth and vivacity like Miss Prescott's; but real intellectual acumen in a woman was a power of which the Señor had no comprehension. Thus the finest quality of a Boston belle was all lost upon the dull Don. Miss Maynard had the mortification of perceiving that the man who escorted her, could only regard her as a fine animal to admire or as a pretty toy to entertain him. Her most brilliant repartees quickened in him no like response; the little glancing arrows of her wit flew all about him—yet he did not seem to see, much less to feel them, although it was very evident that he saw with perfect distinctness the saucy curls dancing under Bella Prescott's little hat. It was very aggravating to be doomed to such a companion, even if he were a rich and high-born Don—while she saw constantly before her eyes, wasting his brightness on "that silly Bell Prescott," a young man whom she admired, yes, much more than admired, although he advanced many lawless ideas, and did not believe in the New Testament miracles.

The charming discussions which she had anticipated with him, which her imagination had presented to her so many times with all the poetic accessories of summer woods, and of the sighing sea blending with gentle tones and tender looks and soft silences, did not take place. In these discussions the young lady had intended to have taken very orthodox grounds against Paul's Spinoza. Paul was all the more interesting to her for his religious unbelief. It was very becoming to a clever young man to be sceptical; it indicated an original and investigating mind; but she as a woman must of course believe in the Bible. Besides being safer, it was much pleasanter to do so; it enabled her to be in one sense a missionary and a defender of the Faith to this erring youth, who was audacious enough to question Moses and the prophets. But contrary to all her expectations Helena found very slight opportunity for setting Paul right in the Christian faith. Purposely he seemed to keep himself remote from her. Yet not a day passed but she witnessed some act of his which seemed more than she could bear. He and Miss Bella had a fashion of separating from the remainder of the party, and of wandering away by themselves. Often, some unexpected turn in the road brought the Don and Helena into the presence of this devoted pair, and a pang like a stab would strike through her heart when she beheld the fair hair of her rival crowned with flowers by the hands which she loved. Or when she saw the eyes whose meaning looks were so dear to her, turned upon the trivial face before her in apparent unconsciousness of her presence, something very like hate swelled in her breast toward the aggravating creature who had come between her and her supreme joy. How keenly she felt this hate one day when Bell called out in a tone of tantalizing sweetness: "O Helena! see these lovely wild flowers which Mr. Mallane has gathered for me! Do take enough for a bouquet!"

Any casual observer seeing Don Ovedo and Helena Maynard cantering side by side through those wooded roads would have thought them a perfectly stylish and satisfied pair. The light laugh that came back on the breeze, which each heard so distinctly, seemed in no way to break the tenor of their talk or to arrest their attention. Yet each heard it with a startling distinctness; and as they listened, each became more assiduously polite to the other, from the very consciousness one felt that he longed to go in search of that gay laugh, indeed that he was defrauded by its being bestowed upon another; and the consciousness the other felt that she hated it, with an almost irresistible impulse to rush on and take the place which she felt was her own beside Paul Mallane. Yet to a superficial glance they seemed perfectly contented, and were probably as well satisfied with each other as most people are who get together in this world.

At last there came to Helena a moment of triumph to set against her long days of waiting and disappointment. One evening, tho last before they went away, Paul asked her to walk on the beach. They walked slowly down the path winding through the fir-balsams, and Miss Prescott, sitting on the veranda, watched them as they went with no slight vexation of heart. Señor Ovedo was by her side, and his heavy countenance wore an unwonted degree of illumination at the unusual prospect of a tête-à-tête free from the presence of the handsome Paul.

The band on the lawn were playing the sweetest airs in Il Trovatore, yet the pretty blonde neither looked on her devoted cavalier, nor listened to her favorite music. There was no mistaking the pout on her childish lips, nor the look in her twinkling eyes, fixed for once, as they followed the two figures, now lost, now visible amid the trees, as they went slowly on toward the sea.

She knew it was said in their party that she and Paul Mallane were "a match," and hitherto appearances had been very positively in favor of such a supposition. This young lady had taken great delight in making the most of these appearances, yet in her secret heart she by no means felt sure of her conquest.

With all Paul's attentions she still felt dissatisfied. She knew that he had one sort of admiration for her; knew there were moments when she almost enthralled him; yet what came of it all? She never felt sure of her power. In the very midst of her spells did he not seem to slip far away, as if thinking of some one afar off? She knew that he had some positive motive for paying her so much attention, as she had hers in receiving it. What was it? He was her admirer certainly, but not her lover. Bell knew this certainly also, although she would not have owned it to any one else in the world but herself.

All this uncertainty concerning her own relation to Paul made her watchful and even suspicious of the slightest attention which he paid to another.

"What *is* there between him and Helena?" she soliloquized, as her eyes still followed the receding figures.

"There *is* something. If he were to deny it forever, I should not believe him.

I know he told me this very morning that she is not his style. But what of that? Why do they look so conscious whenever they meet, especially she? What a look she gave me, to be sure, the other day when I asked her to take some of my flowers! I knew that she would not touch one, unless to tear it to pieces the moment she was out of sight. For an instant she looked as if she would like to tear *me*. It was delightful. I love to torment her. Helena has queened it long enough. It is time that she should see somebody else admired besides herself. Why, she is twenty-five! I hadn't long dresses on when she came so near killing Dukehart. I remember Dick telling about it, when I was home at vacation, and of thinking how splendid it must be to have a very handsome man frantically in love with one. And I remember, too, how long it seemed before I should be through school and have my chance. Well, it has come at last. And I intend to make the most of appearances. I will have so much compensation for the real fact that my knight is not half so much in love with me as he seems. I will teaze Helena every chance I get. I will have that consolation—no very satisfactory one, if I am to see them very often walking in this style. I'll pay you for this, *mon prince*, some day."

"Señor, will you walk with me on the beach? See, it is a perfectly lovely evening!" she asked in a pleading tone, as if a walk on the beach had been the one subject of her desire and of her meditation.

Nothing save a promise to become his wife could have made Señor Ovedo so happy as this unexpected request. It brightened his face wonderfully, and all the more that a moment since he had stood beside her perfectly disconsolate, because he could think of nothing whatever to say or do that would make the pouting blonde look less discontented.

### THE FLIRTATION.

By this time Paul and Helena were slowly walking up and down the beach. The scarlet fires of sunset had gone out upon the sea, and lovely twilight ripples ran along the waves, that plashed with a cool, soughing sound against the warm pebbles and shells on the shore.

This was the first time that Helena had been alone with Paul since their coming to the island, and they were to go away to-morrow! She realized it all, as she looked down at the Nautilus still resting in the cove below.

She fancied already that there was something of expectancy and of eagerness in its gay streamers as they rippled out to meet the home-sailing breeze. Then this was to be the end of the beautiful excursion which she had dreamed so vainly would give her heart not only rest, but certain joy!

The perfect days and nights had mocked her with their peace. They were burdened with their own content; while she, she was unrest itself, in her passionate longing for the love which she did not possess. She had trifled with plenty of hearts; she had even trampled on them, not maliciously, but heedlessly, even cruelly, because she did not care, and because her own time to love had not come. But she knew all about it; she felt it now, that exquisite torture of spirit, born of the neglect or the indifference of the one loved best.

For, mortifying as it was to her pride, cruel as it was to her love, there was no evading or forgetting the fact that he had neglected her; indeed, at times had seemed studiously oblivious of her existence. She could not forget this, although now he stood by her side, and talked with all his old-time familiarity and interest, just as if he had conversed with her every day since their coming in the same manner. Every word that he spoke only made her more keenly conscious of the companionship that she had missed; and they were to go to-morrow! She could not forget this. And as she looked again toward the Nautilus, she saw him already promenading the little deck, with Bella Prescott by his side, and she once more playing the farce which had grown to be so pitiful—that of appearing gay and happy with the Don. She had succeeded, she knew, and had hidden her torture from all eyes but his. She did not wish to hide it from him; she wanted him to know that she suffered for his sake. She would not humiliate herself before the world, for she was a proud woman; but the proudest woman is humble with the man whom she loves. In proportion as she prized her love as a very high gift, which many had fruitlessly sought to win, she took pleasure in making him realize that she had withheld it from all others, that she might lavish it wholly upon him! She was one of those exceptional women, by no means the most sensitive nor the most delicate-natured, yet romantic and passionate women, who do not wait to surrender their hearts in coy return to man's long wooing, but who choose rather the bliss to give them up unclaimed. She felt no maidenly shame that a man who had never positively sought her love, still should know that she loved him with all fervor and passion. She gloried in the thought that to him she gave her love: "As God gives light aside from merit or from prayer."

Yet, in proportion as she compared the gifts which she lavished upon him, with the scanty measure doled out to her in return, she suffered.

As she looked toward the Nautilus, Paul saw where her eyes rested, and divined their meaning, yet he asked:

"Why look so sad, Helena?"

"How can I look otherwise, Paul?" she answered, "when I remember that, to-morrow, the Nautilus will carry us from this lovely spot, and that this is the first time that you have walked with me, and must be the last? Why have you neglected me so utterly? As a friend, how could you treat me so unkindly?"

Something like compunction rose up in Paul as he felt the real pain which vibrated through her voice. But the haughtiest woman, when she makes a man conscious that she is dependent upon him for happiness, makes him feel also that he is her master, and in so much she loses something of her finest power—the power which makes the unaccepted lover seek a woman's love as the supreme object of his desire, if only because it seems remote and almost unattainable.

Paul was man enough to know and to accept his advantage, and answered her accordingly in a wise, superior voice:

"Helena, you are too dear a friend for me to treat unkindly. I have only taken that course which seemed to me to be the wiser. You know, it is dangerous to our happiness that we should be much together. Your feelings run too deep to admit of the surface intercourse of society, at least with me. You know, when together, you and I always fall upon the most serious themes. If we begin away out in the universal, we always end in the personal. And your emotions are so absorbing, so magnetic—I may say, so tragic—they affect me very much; indeed, they wear upon me, and upon yourself, and you know we came here for rest and recreation. Do you know, I thought Don Ovedo a godsend to you. He is too sluggish to rouse in you any emotion whatever, so your whole nature has had a chance to rest."

"Rest!" Helena did not finish the sentence. A fine ripple of scorn ran along her scarlet lips, which would have broken into brilliant sarcasm if any one else had spoken thus to her.

There was nothing but the most painful anxiety in face and tone when she spoke again, and asked:

"Tell me the simple truth, Paul: what *is* there between you and Bella Prescott?"

"Nothing."

"You are *not* engaged to her?"

"No."

"Shall you propose to her?"

"I have not decided to do so."

"Do you love her?"

"No, I do not love her."

"Then, if she is only a friend, no more to you than I am, why are you hovering about her continually? Why do you pay her every attention, while you neglect me altogether? She does not, she is not capable of loving you as I do, Paul."

"I know that, Helena, and I don't want her to love me *as* you do. It would oppress and torment me, if she did. You know you have grown to be exacting and melancholy. Bell is bright and amusing, and makes me forget unpleasant things. Your feelings have become so intense, that now you upbraid me whenever we are alone. When shared with others, I enjoy your society as much as I ever did; but I have spared myself all *tête-à-têtes*—acting on the rule I adopted long ago, whenever it is possible, to avoid every thing disagreeable."

Helena made no reply. But, as she looked on him, her memory reached back over their years of acquaintance, and took up a few of the numberless looks and words and deeds by which Paul Mallane at the first made himself attractive, then necessary, and, at last, infinitely dear to her. She could not forget that, when her heart was free, and she ruled a queen in her little realm, happy in the devotion of her willing subjects, that this young law-student, whose only prestige was his fine person and showy talents, looked up and made her preference the object of his special pursuit. And for what? Was it that, after he had made the attentions of other men seem to her insipid and spiritless—after he had won her heart, and he knew it—that he might neglect her for a girl as trifling as she was pretty?

True, he had never told her that he loved her. No, he had studiously impressed upon her mind the fact that he was only her friend. Then why had he taken the course and exerted just the influence which he, with his psychical knowledge, must have known would cause her to love him? And now that she did love him, her love was only irksome; it fretted and annoyed him! She had ceased to be the merely brilliant companion, and he had forsaken her because he wished only to be entertained! She would give her whole life to him, and he—he was not willing to share with her one unhappy moment.

All this thought and emotion rushed through her brain and heart in conflicting tumult, and would have found utterance in burning words, only love made this high-strung creature timid. If she spoke at all, she knew how passionate would be her reproaches, and she saw before her a man who would not hear them. No, at the very first utterance he might rush from her presence; and only to stand so near him, and to gaze on him, sent a trembling delight quivering through all her pain. She looked on him as Venus might have looked on Adonis.

The moon, just coming up from the ocean, threw a shifting bridge of flame across the waves to their feet.

The air was full of shimmering radiance, and as it fell on Paul, it enveloped him in a halo which at once brightened and spiritualized his beauty. There was nothing effeminate in it. It was the beauty of rare statue and of symmetrical form. All the alluring charms of color trembled in the warm tints, contrasting and blending on lip and cheek, in the bearded bloom and in the deep shadow of his waving hair. Intellect, passion, and youth looked together from his eyes. As he gazed on Helena, unmistakable admiration brightened his whole expression, but not a ray of love kindled in its light. The same subdued atmosphere which spiritualized his beauty, softened hers refining an outline which, in the coarser daylight, all lovers of a spirituelle loveliness would have called too strongly pronounced and positive.

Paul thought that he had never seen her look so beautiful before—and he never had. He had never beheld her through such a radiance, nor seen her when her whole being was moved with emotion and passion, and all for him!

The hood of the scarlet cloak which she had thrown over her white robe, had fallen from her head, loosening the jetty bands, which now rippled about cheek and throat. The passion in her heart had given a -ch bloom to her olive cheeks, and an intenser glow to eyes in which there seemed always to burn a half-smothered flame. There was every thing to move him—the breathing swell with which the scarlet mantle rose and fell; the dimpled hand which held it across her bosom; the Circean face turned up to his. As he looked, he felt a sense of oppression. Something in her seemed almost to stifle him, like the over-burdened atmosphere of a midsummer noon. She increased his own unrest, because he found in her the same qualities which already existed to excess in himself. She could influence, she could oppress him; she could never soothe him, nor give him peace.

Yet she made a glorious picture, standing there in the moonlight beside the sea! And all this love and passion was for him! He could not forget this. He did not love her; but he was a man, and no man is ever insensible to the delicious flattery of a beautiful woman's love, even if he does not love her in return. The very thought, "She loves me," makes him unconsciously tender. As Paul looked into those brooding eyes, with their burden of unshed tears, he experienced a sensation half regret, half delight, that this impassioned creature, who had triumphed over so many men, was now suffering all this torture of love for him! "For me!" he thought, as he felt once more the consciousness so delightful to him, that he was gifted with an inherent power over women of the higher type. He was man enough and weak enough to be ambitious for this power, and vain when he had won it. It was very flattering, this picture before him. Vanity and sense were satisfied. When he spoke again, all loftiness had vanished from his voice. It was low and tender, as he said:

"Helena, if you could know how dear you are to me, how sincerely I desire to see you happy, you would never allow any seeming neglect to trouble you. It is not because I do not care for you, but because you have such power over me, that I do not trust myself with you oftener. You know why it is; we are too much alike. We might love each other passionately, but it would always be a troubled, maddening love. Neither can give the repose which the other craves. Yet you *know* you are more to me than a hundred Bell Prescotts. You could think and feel more in one hour than she could conceive of in a lifetime. She entertains me—she keeps me from feeling too serious; but you are perfectly certain that she could never be to me the absorbing creature that you are. You know, before I tell you, that she is not at all the woman whose love could satisfy me. Indeed, I do not believe that she *can* love as you and I understand love, Helena."

The white hand rising and falling on the scarlet cloak—its tantalizing jewels, which seemed at once to mock and to allure him toward it—was here irresistible to Paul. He took it gently into his, that too willing, that too happy little hand.

And then that mysterious silence which falls on a man and woman only where one or both love; that subtle silence, so much deeper, so much more dangerous than all speech, covered them with its spell.

The sudden revulsion from anguish to triumph, from the most exquisite pain to the more exquisite happiness, for a moment seemed to Helena more than she could bear. In a calmer moment she would remember that no promise of coming happiness, no assurance of such a love as she yearned for, had been expressed in one word that he had uttered. But she was not conscious of this now; she only knew that he had said what she at this time had longed most and hoped the least to hear—that *she* was more to him than Isabella Prescott!—that, after all, Bell Prescott was only a pretty toy, that wiled him for the time to forget Helena Maynard's deeper power. He had acknowledged this power, and what was it but the power of love!

If he was compelled to shun her in order to find strength to resist it now, in time might she not win from him the utmost that she desired—his undivided heart? At the very thought, she felt her own beat as if it would escape from her breast; her eyes grew more luminous, her face radiated a joy which no language could declare. Her whole being, brain, and spirit were eloquent with emotion. That moment there was a dangerous splendor in her beauty, an almost fatal magnetism in the hand which fluttered in Paul's. He slowly said:

"Bella Prescott is a pretty plaything, but you!"

That delicious sentence was never ended.

A light, mocking laugh broke through the cedars. Paul dropped her hand as if he had been struck. Quickly as he did it, the act was seen by the acute eyes of Bell Prescott.

The artless young lady, who had made it her business to approach very quietly, that moment appeared upon the beach, leading Don Ovedo by a handkerchief which she had tied to one of his wrists. With the most innocent air possible, she led the delighted and apparently demented Don up to the conscious couple, exclaiming, with all her usual *naïvete:*

"Helena, here's your prisoner. I have done my best to comfort him, and he is inconsolable. So I have brought him back to you."

Don Ovedo was too gallant a gentleman to deny this accusation in the presence of the lady for whom he was said to mourn. Nevertheless, he hardly knew how to bear this finale to the last heavenly half hour. When Bell Prescott tied her laced and perfumed handkerchief around his wrist, with so many bewitching glances, the Señor thought that he would like to have her lead him up and down forever, provided she would continue to look at him from under her lashes as she did that moment.

It was a sore disappointment to be led directly back to the handsome Miss Maynard. Pretty Miss Prescott not only entertained, she delighted him; how cruel of her, then, to doom him again to the overpowering company of *la petite duchesse*, just because she herself was uneasy out of the society of the handsome Yankee. Even the stupid Señor was bright enough to know this.

Other parties coming up, the company became general, to the great relief of Paul, who felt any thing but comfortable standing between two young ladies, to each of whom, during the last twenty-four hours, he had committed the pleasant little confidence that the other was not at all the style of woman that he admired, and, consequently, nothing at all to him!

Helena's love, so intense and real, had moved him to a half pitiful, half passionate tenderness which had not been simulated, therefore he did not find it easy to rebound instantly to the surface of Bell Prescott's chatter. She was the only one of the three perfectly unconstrained. At the sight of her, a pang of positive hate shot through Helena's heart. She could not bear the sight of the trivial face that had come once more between her and her joy. For the first time in all their intercourse the intensity of her feeling made her powerless to feign a kindliness which she did not feel. She regarded Bell's intrusion as unpardonable, almost an insult. *She*, with all that she had suffered, had never broken in upon any of Paul and Bell's *tête-à-têtes*. She had been too proud and too respectful, at least toward him. The disgust and indignation which she felt were perfectly apparent upon her haughty features. Paul saw the expression, and it made him very uncomfortable. Isabella Prescott saw it, and the sight filled her with delight. Her gayety increased Paul's discomfiture. He by no means felt certain of so much unconscious artlessness. Somehow he could not rid himself of a mortifying consciousness, that, after all he had said to her of his non-admiration of Helena's "style," that Miss Bella did see him hold and then drop Helena's hand; for he remembered that his face had been turned from her, and that she and the Don were very near before he heard them at all. Was it to convince her that what she had seen meant nothing whatever, that, a few moments after, he allowed her to obtain precisely what she had all the time intended to secure—himself as an escort back to the cottage?

Helena returned with the Don, the perfect bliss of a few moments before supplanted by a bitterness which could not be fathomed.

Was it true, or was it only a dream, that she stood with him alone, so near in person, so near in spirit, in joy so complete? Why had he been so near, now only to be so far—so far, that all the universe seemed to be between them?

Her keenest pain came from her distrust of him—from a stinging consciousness that, in some way, he was playing a double part between Isabella Prescott and herself. She could not forget, at the sound of Bell's voice, with what a shock he dropped her hand, nor how constrained he looked at the sight of Bell's face; nor, after all that he had said, how ready he had been to leave her and walk back with her rival.

Meanwhile, Bell, coquetting by his side, delighted with her triumph, was thinking as well of the lover-like attitude in which she had seen him stand by Helena—of the way in which he held her hand. "He is a flirt," she said, mentally. "When he finds an opportunity, he says the same fine things to Helena which he says to me; and, no doubt, says sweeter things to the shop-girl than he says to either. Never mind, Sir Knight! I shall punish you in the proper time."

Each girl distrusted him thoroughly, and each was affected according to her nature. Helena's tortured love cried out, and only loved him the more for its cruel doubts. Bell's piqued and angry vanity leaped out to the future, and foresaw his punishment and her own triumph.

As for Paul, he walked on perfectly conscious that, while he had spoken truth to both of these girls, he had been sincere with neither. After the evil in his soul had triumphed, his good angel always came back to him and told him, with tearful pity, just how he had sinned. Some over-mastering bent of his nature was forever forcing him on to do that which he afterward regretted. For, no matter how far he was carried by impulse, his brain never let him commit any act unconsciously. He would do some ignoble deed, and then despise himself, hate himself, and resolve to do better. Yet he invariably went and did the same thing again, or something worse, if at the time it only pleased him so to do. Thus nearly the whole of his life had been spent in sinning against his better nature, and in hating himself for doing it.

An hour or two after the walk from the beach, Bell Prescott having seen the sleepy Dolores close her eyes for the night, turned to her mirror and commenced brushing out her curls and making pretty mouths to herself in the glass. But every few moments an expression would come over her face which contrasted oddly with her unthoughtful features. Yet it must have meant something positive; for at last she exclaimed: "Yes; he will do it yet! Then I will have *my* revenge. Bell Prescott, *you* can afford to wait."

At the same time Helena Maynard was sitting alone in an adjoining room. A candle was burning dimly on the table by which she sat, or rather leaned, her cheek resting on her hand. Her loosened hair fell over her white draperies and about her whiter face, its blackness making her beauty seem almost ghastly. She held one hand on her heart, and her breath seemed stifled, as if she were suffering physical pain.

"Retribution! retribution!" she said slowly. "I deserve it all. I trifled with Dukehart. I trampled on him, and he was a noble man; he was truth itself. I made him wretched; I shortened his days because he loved me. This is my recompense. *Then*, how was I to know that I could ever love like this? Had I known how a heart can suffer because it loves, at least I should have been pitiful, I should have been kind. I was cruel, and I take my reward. How true it is, that no wrong which we do another can escape its penalty even in this life. Paul, Paul!"

Paul, who had refused Dick Prescott's invitation to play a game of billiards, was also in his room sitting alone in the dark. The glowing crest of his cigar revealed where he sat, leaning back in his chair, his feet on the low window-ledge. To turn away, to flee from whatever chafed or annoyed him, was an instinct of his nature. After the evening's experience, he was beginning to feel that both Bell and Helena teased him more than they amused him; and that moment he felt heartily tired of both, and glad that the pleasure-trip was nearly at an end. Beside, as he sat there smoking and thinking, he despised himself more and more, as he realized the pitiful subterfuges to which a man is driven, who, in order to retain a certain power over both, without loving either, acts a double part between two women. He realized, too, the pettiness of word and deed to which two women sink, who regarding each other as rivals, struggle against each other to possess the exclusive devotion of one man. Oh, the littleness, the bitterness, the misery born of rivalry, insincerity, and misplaced passion!

Paul made no ejaculations over it, yet felt conscious of it all. He liked to flirt—it was his favorite pastime; but the moment it merged into any thing serious, it ceased to amuse him, it fatigued and worried him, and then his supreme desire was to be well rid of it. He felt no compunction over Bell. "She is quite my match," he said to himself. "I must keep my eyes open, or the little minx will play me a game.

"But Helena! Who could have believed that love would so subdue *her*. And for me! How superbly handsome she looked on the beach. I think that I showed great self-command in only taking her hand. Yet I cannot love her. I will not marry her; she would torment me to death. But I'll stop treating her meanly. I am a scamp to do it, when she is so generous to me. Yet I could never help it, if Bell Prescott were near us. I believe there is a devil in that girl. She certainly sets me to acting like one. There's something in her that calls out the worst in me. Confound it! How *did* she make me walk back with her to-night? I did not intend to do it. It was a shabby trick, leaving Helena after I had invited her to a walk. The trouble was, I had told Bell so many times, that Helena was not my style; and yet I *know* she saw me holding her hand and standing beside her like a lover; and more is the wonder if she did not hear me tell Helena the very same thing about herself, that she, Bell Prescott, is not at all my style; *that* was what I call 'a fix.' I was caught, sure enough; and served me right for being two-faced. Yet it is for my interest to keep Bell good-natured. She is a match. Once married, we could quarrel to our heart's content. It wouldn't hurt her, nor me either; she could go her way, and I mine. But that could never be with Helena; we should kill each other."

The longer he thought of each, the more weary he felt of both. He had been playing a part, and for the present, at least, was very tired of it. But it was a necessity of his pleasure-loving nature always to possess some object toward which he could turn with satisfaction, if not delight. In the same proportion that the complication between Bell and Helena grew annoying, came back the face which for weeks and months he had persistently banished. This moment he did not resist it; he welcomed it. He was no longer amused, nor even pleasantly occupied. No, he was fretted and discontented, and the supreme mission of this face was to soothe and to satisfy. His restless heart yearned for something to rest on; and what in all his life had he found so sufficing as this face, with its promise of utter love, and of perfect peace? With the soft sea-air flowing over the pines it came in to him, with the old vividness, the old thrill, half wonder, half ecstacy which strikes through a man's being, when for the first time in his life he feels that he supremely loves.

"Darling, my brown-eyed darling,

5

*I love you.* You I will never deceive. To you I will be only true," he murmured, leaning forward, as if an actual presence came in through the darkness from the outer air, to whom he gave this greeting.

His mind was too wearied to assert its wise plans, his heart too eager to be denied. It might all be different to-morrow. But this night, at least, the dear vision remained with him, and Paul passed out into the realm of sleep, gazing into its eyes.

One week later, the Nautilus had folded its sails, and rested on the low tide below the Charles.

Dick Prescott and Dolores, Bell and Don Ovedo had gone to Saratoga. Helena Maynard was with her parents in their cottage at Nahant. Both girls thought of Paul more than of any body else; one with a latent hope, the other with a clearly defined and secretly avowed purpose.

Paul had written a long letter to Helena, in which he called her "dear girl" and "dearest sister." In this letter he sincerely intended to make some reparation for the subtle wrong which his conscience very clearly informed him that he had done her. The result was, that he made the matter worse by unconsciously causing himself to seem to her more noble and precious than ever before. Her reply was full of characteristic generosity. She exonerated him from the faintest blame. It was not *his* fault that he possessed so many manly qualities; so many mental and personal attractions that she could not choose but love him. She had been unreasonable, she had done him injustice. He must forgive her. She saw so distinctly now that his course on the island was pursued only for the good of both; a fresh proof of his fine sense of honor, and his kindly care for her happiness. She had chosen her future life. She should never marry. Life spent alone for his sake, would be dearer and happier than any life could be shared with another. She felt that hitherto her whole existence had been artificial and false.

She had lived to allure men; to win their homage, to conquer them; yes, to trifle with them.

She should never do this again. She had ceased to care for admiration, and longed only for the love of one. She had been a great sinner, but had repented, and henceforth should live a life devoted to piety and good works. Like all women of her nature, weary of ambition, or disappointed in love, Helena turned for consolation to religion. She almost wished herself a nun, that she might retire to a convent for a season. But as it was, she should seclude herself from society; she should devote the winter to teaching in ragged schools, in visiting the poor, in attending meetings for prayer, and in writing articles for the magazines. Before Helena knew it, she found not only unconscious consolation, but real delight in these pictures of a new life.

For some way in the foreground of all she saw a very handsome young woman, whose strong beauty was subdued by a nun-like garb.

What was stranger still, not very far in the background there hovered a handsome young man. And there still lingered in Helena's heart, though she did not know it, a delicious hope that when the young man crossed the path of this beautiful sister of mercy, as he surely would, that he would succumb to the subdued eyes and the dovelike dress, as he never had done when she loved him and sought him in the apparel of the world.

### AT BUSYVILLE AGAIN.

One week from the evening when Paul walked with Helena on the beach, the dépôt-coach of Busyville rolled up to the white house under the maples, opposite John Mallane's factories, and Paul alighted.

He had entered the gate, and was passing with quick steps toward the house, when he heard his name called with a clear, shrill cry: "Paul! Paul! pretty Paul!" Turning around, he saw Momo sitting in his cage in Seth Goodlove's window, and beside it, on a low seat, apparently busy with something before her, he saw Eirene.

She looked up when the coach stopped; but this same coach, with its roll and rumble and bustle of disburdening luggage and passenger had started Momo from his blinking meditation into this loud outcry, and she did not look up now. If Paul had been near enough, he would have seen that her cheeks were scarlet with blushes.

She saw Paul when he alighted, and Momo's cries filled her with consternation. "Oh Tilda," she said involuntarily; "*will* Mr. Mallane think that I taught Momo to call his name in such a saucy way?"

Whereupon Tilda commenced a lecture upon the folly of possessing a parrot, and the sin of caring *what* Mr. Paul Mallane thought, ending with an ejaculation of pious gratitude that to-morrow morning was "camp-meeting morning," and then, she "blessed the Lord." This camp-meeting was her only hope of saving Eirene from destruction. The wolf had come, and she was ready to fly with her lamb to the arms of the Good Shepherd.

Meanwhile, Mr. Paul Mallane had disappeared inside of his father's house. He did so, saying to himself: "Can it be that she has taught that bird to call my name?" An instant afterwards he thought: "No. Confound it! It was the young ones. I remember, I heard them at it myself. But, I think that she might have looked up," he added, with a sense of injury. "She knew that it was I."

## VII.

### CAMP-MEETING.

EIRENE sat by the window, filling a basket with cakes and sandwiches, which Sister Goodlove had given to her and Tilda to carry to camp-meeting the next morning. How she had counted the days, and longed for the coming of this camp-meeting morning! If she had analyzed her emotions (which she never did), she would have discovered that she had scarcely thought of the camp-meeting at all as a religious service. Having never attended one, she might have fancied that it would be pleasant to hear people pray and sing in the open air—only she did not think of the people at all. She longed for her old friends, the woods, the air, the summer sky. From babyhood these had been her closest companions, and this was the first year of her life that had shut her away from them all. From this low seat, where she sat now, she had watched the sunset scarlets glinting through the trees of Mr. Mallane's garden. Above the window, in the shop where she stood at work, spread a narrow slip of sky; and, looking up, she had sometimes seen the peaceful clouds come sailing down the valley, and this was all that she had known of the summer. Often, in the languid evenings, she had dropped her book and turned a wistful face away from Tilda Stade's scrutinizing gaze and wearying voice, and, looking beyond the trees out to the serene West, a soft desire had stirred in her heart for something sweeter and better than she had ever known—she knew not what. We, who know her well, know that it was the first mysterious stir of the soul of the girl-woman, dimly yearning for companionship, for sympathy, for tenderness, such as had never entered her barren life in Busyville. The summer should have given some holiday to seventeen; it had given none to her. But going to the woods for a single day, she thought, would be a good deal better than nothing. Thus, light of heart, at five o'clock the next morning, she ascended, with Tilda, into the vehicle of Brother Goodlove, which was to carry his brethren and sisters to the camp-ground for twenty-five cents a person. It was a high, springless wagon, with boards laid across for seats, and, this morning, was crowded with passengers. A number of sisters bore witness to its being a very uncomfortable equipage, by sundry little groans concerning their aching backs. Eirene, sitting at one end, where the boughs of the bending trees brushed her as she passed, thought of nothing but the pleasures of the ride. The road ran by sequestered farms and through the woods, all the way. The young light shimmered through the leaves above and around them; the air was full of soft sounds and of pleasant smells; of the fragrance of resinous branches and juicy ferns crushed beneath the wagon-wheels. Eirene took it in at every pore, and grew as glad as the birds singing over her head. After a two hours' drive, they entered a new road cut through the woods, and a distinct murmur of human voices reached their ears; and then what seemed to Eirene to be an extraordinary sight for such a place, greeted her eyes. Under the trees, all along the roadside, booths had been erected of green boughs, and under them men and women seemed to be driving an astonishing trade in small-beer, gingerbread, candies and doughnuts, and other harmless commodities. New-comers were constantly arriving. Wagon-loads of the sisters and brethren of the church; young men and their "girls," in buggies, arrayed in their best, nearly all of whom stopped at the stalls to regale themselves with ginger-pop, peanuts, and other innocent refreshments. At last, through the shifting leaves, Eirene caught glimpses of white tents, forming a semicircle under the forest-trees, surrounding an amphitheatre of rude seats facing a rude pulpit canopied by the boughs of beeches and elms. Their wagon stopped outside of this inclosure. Tilda Stade, hurriedly alighting, assisted Eirene to do the same, informing her, at the same time, that this was the "blessed camp-ground, and yonder was the very spot where she received the blessing of sanctification—where Jesus spoke perfect peace to her soul." Taking Eirene's hand, she led her toward a large tent bearing the name of "Busyville" above the door. They were now fairly on the camp-ground, and Eirene beheld what was to her a most unwonted and picturesque sight. Tiny fires, made from dried boughs, were crackling in the rear of every tent; and on these, kettles were boiling and meats were frying. Extempore tables, set under the trees, were spread with white cloths, garnished with flowers, and loaded with viands. Pretty young sisters in white sun-bonnets, white aprons, and gay frocks, superintended these tables; while matrons in close "shakers" and demure dresses hovered about the fires, guarding the meats and watching the tea-pots and coffee-pots, lest their delicious liquids should run too low to supply the numerous hungry people waiting for breakfast. The air was full of the most varied sounds. Birds twittered in the trees. Girls chattered and laughed with each other, and flirted in a half-subdued, half-pious way, with the young brethren, whose plates they piled and whose cups they filled; while the women by the fires talked in low, mysterious tones to each other, as women will. From manifold tents issued the sounds of morning devotions. Old hymns and old tunes of every conceivable rhythm and metre met in mid-air in inextricable confusion. In one tent could be heard the sobs of a sore soul wailing over its sins, amid a Babel of prayers rising to heaven in its behalf; from another came a solitary voice, fervent and sonorous, going up to God in early thanksgiving; while from every direction came choruses of voices shouting, "Bless the Lord!" "Glory to God!" The whole scene bore witness to what it was—a great religious picnic, in which material pleasure and human happiness blended very largely with spiritual experience. The appearance of Tilda Stade on the camp-ground was a signal for rejoicing to the more zealous Christians, for it was a sure promise of increased zeal in the prayer-meetings. As they gathered around to welcome her, Eirene was left standing alone for a moment; and, looking about her, saw, for the first time, an individual who had seen her from the first moment of her appearance. It was good Brother Viner, standing at the head of the table, evidently just concluding his breakfast. He looked red in the face, and uncomfortable, as if the sisters were overfeeding him that warm morning. He was literally besieged by women, young and old, each one producing, from her particular basket or from her particular fire, some viand, hot or cold, setting it before her minister, with the exclamation, "Oh, Brother Viner, do taste this; I made it on purpose for you!" "Oh, Brother Viner, where's your appetite gone to? You *must* eat your breakfast!" Brother Viner did not like to appear ungrateful, and thus kept on tasting each dish set before him. It was a sight to behold them—the dishes of pork and beans, cold ham, succotash, omelets, doughnuts, crullers, pies, preserves, pickles, all heaped up before the unfortunate minister. Brother Viner had an excellent appetite, and, at first, attacked this conflicting mass of food with all the zest of a young and vigorous stomach; but even he was no proof against the ignorant kindness of women—a kindness that has caused more sour stomachs and sour theology than the most powerful imagination ever conceived. Brother Viner looked up from the mass on his plate, and beheld Eirene looking toward him with wondering eyes. He recognized her at once as the innocent-looking little sinner who had caused the prayer-meeting at Sister Mallane's. Here she was on the camp-ground—the place of all others for her conversion, the most appropriate in which to reclaim her from the error of her ways; and what an interesting subject! Brother Viner could not help seeing this. He was a young man, and, like any other young man, could not help feeling a more spontaneous interest in a lovely girl than in an ugly one. But Brother Viner was also an intelligent man, and perfectly conscious of the relative fitness of things. How could he labor with her concerning her soul? How could he appeal to her, with pathetic tones and tears, to forsake her sins and give her soul to her Saviour? How could she regard him solely as a spiritual teacher, now that she had seen him there, devouring, with such gusto, such quantities of food? Not but what he thought that he had a perfect right to his breakfast—as good a right to enjoy it as any other man—but not to such a breakfast. In his over-fed condition, there was something incongruous in passing directly from the feast to the prayer-meeting, to pray for a girl who, in her white frock and innocent face, "looked like a lily out with nature." At least thus poetically thought Brother Viner, notwithstanding Mrs. Mallane's account of her wickedness still remained in his memory. "Why didn't I sit down under a tree, and make my breakfast from a bowl of bread and milk, in true pastoral fashion?" he asked himself in tones of self-disgust, his eyes still fixed upon the white dress and sun-bonnet.

At this time Eirene's attention was called away from the young minister by a rustic young convert, who, in his new-born spiritual joy, was oblivious of breakfast and of all human want. Spying Eirene standing alone, he immediately came to the conclusion that she was "a sinner," and not "a sister;" therefore, a proper subject for missionary zeal. He walked up to her, and, without a single preliminary, asked, "Do you love the Lord?"

Eirene, startled by the abrupt question, saw before her a lank, long-haired youth, the exact counterpart of Moses Loplolly. Had that young man of peddling propensities concluded to study for the Christian ministry?

"Do you love the Lord?" was the solemn question again propounded to the wondering girl.

"I hope I do," was the timid answer.

"You hope you do!" [In a tone of deep disgust.] "You hope you do!

Do you hope yer love yer father and mother? No! Ef yer love um, yer know yer luv um. Yer don't hope nuthin' 'bout it. Yer *know* it [tones rising]. So, ef yer love the Lord, yer know it. Ef yer only hope yer love Him, 'tain't no luv 't'all. Yer goin' down the road to perdition, straight. [In a milder tone.] Don't yer want religion?"

"Yes; I have wanted to be a Christian ever since I can remember," answered Eirene.

"How bad do you want to be one? Bad enuf to give up all yer pride, and confess yer sins?"

"I hope so."

"Hope! agin [in tones of despair]. I can try yer hope in a minnit. Do you want religion bad enuf to enable yer pride to get it? Then yer willin' to kneel down on this very spot, and let me pray fur yer soul. Will yer do it?"

"Oh, not here, please!" said Eirene in a tone of entreaty, with the instinctive shrinking from publicity which was natural to her.

"Now where's yer hope? [In a tone of triumph.] It don't amount to nuthin'. But I'll pray fur yer jest the same; there's them that's brought into the kingdom of heaven by force. I'll pray fur yer jest the same" [with profound spiritual condescension]. Thus the youth knelt down and lifted up his voice in prayer. The sound immediately attracted the attention of the sisters who had gathered around Tilda; when they turned, and saw Eirene leaning against the tree, with her head bowed, as if overcome by some emotion, and the young evangelist kneeling before her, calling upon God to have mercy upon her soul, Tilda believed that her dearest wish was about to be realized —that her friend, struck with conviction the moment she reached the camp-ground, was now to be converted. She, with the other sisters, hastened to the spot, and, immediately kneeling down, formed a circle outside the evangelist, with Eirene, leaning against the tree, the central figure. Joining the youth, all commenced ejaculating and praying together; thus a special prayer-meeting was at once inaugurated. "Oh, do, Lord!" "Yes, Lord!" "Come, Lord!" "O, blessed Jesus, speak peace to her soul" "O Christ, forgive her sins!" "O God, show her her wickedness!" These were the expressions, in every possible tone, producing one wild discord of supplication, which now smote the ears of the bewildered Eirene. Each communicated excitement to the other: every moment the cries grew louder, the groans deeper, the entreaty more importunate, till, at last, overcome by pure nervous excitement, Eirene sank upon her knees, sobbing as if her heart would break. This prostration was the signal for a still more clamorous outbreak. Cries of "Lord, have mercy on this poor girl!" "O Lord, save Eirene Vale!" rent the air with a perfect tornado of sound.

This scene was witnessed by one person with extreme displeasure. It was Brother Viner, who had left the breakfast-table, notwithstanding the entreaties of the sisters, and seated himself within the Busyville tent. He was an ardent lover of Methodism; his mother, a saint of the Mrs. Fletcher type, had nurtured him in the love of its memories and in devotion to its principles. In his inmost heart he believed that the vitality and zeal of his sect was the salt of the Christian world. But he was too intelligent to believe that zeal born of ignorance was as worthy as that tempered by knowledge. While believing it to be a necessity to some, he was so gentle a gentleman himself, he could no more be boisterous in sacred worship than he could be loud and vulgar in the expression of any sentiment whatever. He was too sensitive to the nature of others not to see, by the aspect of this girl, that she was more overcome by fear and grief at being thus assailed, than by any conscious conviction of sin. "She would make a lovely Christian, I know," he said to himself; "we need more such women in our church. She must not be repelled and driven from us by a repulsive manner of approach." Yet, as he looked, he saw some of his young converts and some of his most zealous members in this praying circle, and knew well that, if he were to manifest any disapprobation of their meeting, he could not, by any possibility, explain to their satisfaction such a course. Such a procedure, he knew, would bring them to the sudden conclusion that their minister had "backslidden." Yet, *as* their minister, he must either join their circle, or break it; he concluded to do the latter. The first season of prayer was over; they refreshed their fearfully-taxed energies by singing a hymn, and were beginning their cries anew, when Brother Viner walked quietly up to their circle, and said, "Brothers and sisters, we must do all things decently and in order. I understand your feelings. You are so happy in prayer, and so moved for the salvation of souls, that you wish to pray continually. This you may do. You may lift your hearts silently to God without ceasing. But some of you have ridden many miles this morning. You all need your breakfast. After you have refreshed yourselves, come to the prayer-meeting in the tent, at eight o'clock." Their minister had said it. They must go to breakfast, notwithstanding this precious soul was not yet saved. They did so, all shaking hands with their minister as they passed, till no one was left with him but Tilda Stade, standing by Eirene. As Eirene rose from the foot of the tree where she had knelt, she seemed like one coming out of a dream. She opened her eyes, still glistening with tears, and drew a deep breath of relief. Tilda thought it the sigh of conviction—a hopeful sigh—and hastened to introduce Eirene to her minister. This good woman had not the acute perception which announces instantaneously to its possessor when he or she may not be wanted. As Eirene's special protector and spiritual guide, she waited to hear what the minister had to say to her. Great was her amazement when he said, "Sister Stade, will you be so kind as to allow me to say a few words to this young lady alone?" What Brother Viner could have to say to Eirene "alone," was more than she could divine; nevertheless, as it was her minister—not Paul Mallane—who made the request, she passed on. Then Brother Viner addressed Eirene for the first time, by asking her if she had been educated a Methodist. She told him no. "Then," he said, "our manner of worship may seem strange, even rude, to you. But do not let our ways disturb you, for they are only outward forms of expression. In every human heart, religion can be but one essence—that of love to Christ and love to one another. If you feel your soul pervaded with this love, you are a Christian. The personal manifestations of religious joy differ as much as our natures differ. No two persons give expression in precisely the same terms to any human experience; the law of temperament forbids it. Therefore do not be offended at the zeal which you see manifested here, even if it seems to you a little intemperate. And do not be discouraged if you yourself feel prompted to display none of this outward fervor. Without any reference to any other human being, receive the Spirit of God as it comes to you. Receive it as if you were alone with God in His universe. It can come to you only in accordance with your nature; you can respond to it only in the same way.

"Do you hear, in your inmost heart, the still small voice calling you to follow your Saviour?—to cast your burden on Him?—to love Him?—to be like Him?"

"Oh, yes, sir; I have always heard it."

"Do you try to resist it, or do you seek to obey it?"

"I seek to obey it, and it is my dearest comfort. It cheers me when I am sad, and it strengthens me when I am weak."

"And you give your heart to God?"

"Yes, sir. Every day I give myself anew to Him. Am I not safe in His love?"

"My sister, I feel that you are a Christian. What you need is encouragement, not conviction or loud expression. I see how it is. You have a gentle nature; your religion is as gentle as your heart. Come into the eight-o'clock prayer-meeting, and I will see that you are not again disturbed. Now, shall I go with you to the breakfast-table?"

His voice was so kind and assuring, his words so helpful, that, when he had finished, Eirene felt like another creature. With the elasticity which belongs to the quickest sensibilities, her heart leaped to her eyes in a joyous smile, as she exclaimed, "Oh, I feel so much better!"

As Brother Viner saw this inward illumination spread over every feature, he thought it not only the most innocent, but the brightest face that he had ever seen; but he only said, "Now we will find Sister Stade."

This young woman was standing devoutly before a bowl of blueberries and milk, as Brother Viner led Eirene up to her side. When she saw the serene light which covered both faces, she was forced to the conclusion that their conversation had been of a heavenly sort, although she had not been permitted to listen to it. She received her charge back with much demonstration, while Brother Viner returned to his seat in the tent, to meditate and prepare for the morning prayer-meeting. He did not find it as easy as usual to fix his mind on the chapter in the Bible and the hymn which he was selecting; involuntarily his eyes wandered back to the breakfast-table under the trees, and rested on the slight figure in the white frock standing by Tilda Stade. He had forgotten all about Sister Mallane's lamentations over this girl's wickedness, and thought only of her face, all radiant as it looked up to his last. "She has just the face that would please mother," he said to himself; "and, if I am not mistaken, she has just the nature that would please mother. What a companion she would make for her! for mother will come and live with me." Then, suddenly conscious that he had arrived at very rapid conclusions, considering his very slight knowledge of this young lady, he turned his back and commenced searching for hymns with redoubled assiduity, selecting, at last, "Jesus, lover of my soul," "Rock of Ages, cleft for me," and others, whose sweetness, purity, and divine fervor lift them so far above the rampant rhymes sometimes called camp-meeting hymns. After breakfast, the brethren and sisters gathered in the tent, some sitting on benches, some in the clean straw which covered the ground, some on piles of bedding on which many had slept the night before. Brother Viner offered Tilda and Eirene a seat in a corner, where it was impossible that a crowd should gather around them, as they had done outside. He opened the meeting with the hymn which all young people love:

"Jesus, lover of my soul,
Let me to thy bosom fly."

His pure tenor-voice gave all its sweetness to the singing. Eirene did not listen; she worshipped. Every pulse in her heart sung with rapture the matchless lyric of the Methodist poet. Brother Viner followed with prayer, and, as he prayed, utter silence pervaded the tent, broken only by low-murmured "Amens." In the fervor of his youth, in the fulness of his faith, he prayed, as if he knelt face to face with his Lord. He said, "We rejoice to come to Thee with all the freedom of favored children—with all the sweet familiarity of love, openly and joyously." He prayed that to all might be granted a clearer vision to discern the exceeding loveliness of Christ—a deeper consciousness of their need of Him, who was at once their Friend and Saviour. He prayed for "sinners and seekers," and at last for one whose feet trembled in the narrow way, but whose heart yearned toward all pure and lovely things. He prayed that to the young heart might be granted strength to cast aside every weight, every besetting sin, every allurement of the world; that this young soul might run with patience and cheerful alacrity the whole Christian course, and receive the clear witness of its acceptance and fellowship with Christ. Eirene felt that this prayer was for her; it was the very prayer that she would have offered for herself, yet prayed with an unction and a fervor which she felt her own prayers had not. There was an earnestness, an assurance of faith in the tones which strengthened and helped her. As her heart ascended with it, a deep peace came down into her soul—a peace so pervading that none of the discord which came after had the slightest power to disturb it. Brother Viner, a true Methodist, believed that where the Spirit of God is, there is liberty. Thus, aside from the general supervision of the prayer-meeting, he did not attempt to control the boisterous element around him. Thus the meeting did not advance very far before men and women were praying, groaning, and singing together. Some were groaning for their sins, some praying for their companions, others singing and shouting because they themselves felt happy. Among the latter was Tilda Stade. She shouted "Hallelujah" till she had "the power," or, in more intelligible language, swooned from pure physical exhaustion; falling back, her head dropped into Eirene's lap. Eirene was less alarmed than she would have been if she had not already seen several others drop in the same way. She tried to lift her friend's head, and support it, when Tilda, opening her eyes, uttered the piercing cry of "Glory," falling again; whereupon Eirene let the head rest, where it fell, till the meeting closed. The brothers and sisters, who had formed themselves into the special Praying Band, seeing the peaceful expression of Eirene's countenance, concluded that she had received the blessing, and at last began to importune her to tell what the Lord had done for her soul. She was beginning to tremble with something of her first fear and excitement, when Brother Viner again came to her help. He told the Praying Band that he had conversed with this sister, and believed that she had received in her heart the witness of the Holy Spirit, but that they must remember that, while the fruits of the Spirit were always the same, its personal manifestations were very different; that in some it bore witness by the very expression of the face, in perfect silence; that it was not this sister's duty to speak openly, unless she felt moved to do so from within. This form of conversion was by no means the most satisfactory to the Praying Band; but, as their minister sanctioned it, they felt bound to accept it. Those who knew her personally went forth from the prayer-meeting and announced to all the Busyville brethren outside that Eirene Vale had "experienced religion, and received the blessing;" but they thought it pretty queer that she wouldn't speak. With a feeling of inexpressible relief Eirene walked forth from the tent to attend the morning service in the grove. The mode of worship in the prayer-meeting had been sincere; she believed *that*, yet she could feel none the less that it was discordant with her feelings, and outraged many of her ideas of what was harmonious and fit in sacred worship. But the public service in the grove seemed a complete realization of all that such worship should be. Out from their tents came the great congregation, and took their seats in God's sanctuary. His own power had reared the columns of this mighty cathedral. Along its high leaf-woven dome soft winds rippled. In its verdurous arches birds sang; from its mossy floors flowers sent up their praise in perpetual perfume. When the preacher stood up in the rude pulpit beneath two patriarchal elms, and invoked the blessing of God on the vast assembly; when more than a thousand human voices joined the winds, the birds, and the blossoms, singing,

"There seems a voice in every gale,
 A tongue in every flower,
Which tells, O Lord, the wondrous tale
 Of thy Almighty power,"

Eirene beheld, at last, in its perfect form, the wonderful charm and devotional significance of the Methodist camp-meeting.

In the afternoon Brother Viner preached an earnest, dramatic, magnetic sermon, whose fervor and power astonished his own congregation, and electrified all. Brother Viner was a good man, besides being a young man of decided talents; and under any circumstance, with such a congregation before him, would have preached more than a common sermon. How much added inspiration and unction he received from the consciousness of a single presence, from the gleam of a white frock, and the glimpse of a golden-brown head, leaning against the rough bark of a tree—with a sweet, serious face looking forth toward his, which seemed to him singled and separated from all that vast congregation—Brother Viner did not know, nor did any body else. Eirene, like all persons of very sensitive organization, took in joy as well as suffering through every nerve. Every leaf that rippled, every bird that sang, every flower distilling incense, every breeze, sailing by laden with the honey of the pines, added something to this large delight. So, too, did the anthem, the prayer, now the sermon. True, holy, helpful words were these of Brother Viner, full of the vitality of human life, piercing to the depth of human experience, and reaching upward to the height of all Christian aspiration; few could listen and not receive from them somewhat of the help that they needed. Eirene no longer wondered that Tilda found the camp-meeting such a sanctuary of joy—this portion of camp-meeting, certainly, was very delightful. Eirene no longer thought of the young evangelist, of the extempore prayer-meeting, or of any annoyance, any more than Brother Viner thought of *his* morning vexation amid the spiritual and oratorical exaltation in which he now stood, with which indigestible breakfasts intermeddled not.

The morning and afternoon service, even the evening prayer-meetings, were ended, and yet the congregation once more gathered beneath the trees to listen to a third sermon, before going to rest. Eirene was tired. During the day she had experienced so many new sensations—had been so overcome and pervaded by them, it seemed to her that she could take in no more. Thus, when the brethren and sisters went out in a body to the evening service, she, with a few aged mothers in Israel, remained behind in sole possession of the tent. Placing a camp-stool just outside the curtain, she sat down to listen, where she was. The scene upon which she now looked forth was even more picturesque and impressive than that of the day. The many lamps, hung to the swaying boughs of the trees, threw long lines of flickering light and shadow upon the great congregation seated beneath. The wavering lights on the pulpit, the dipping branches of the elms above their heads, gave a weird look to the faces of the preachers, while the prayers that they uttered, and the hymns which they sung, softened by the slight distance, floated out through the evening air to the few listeners in the tent with a strange and sweet solemnity.

Perhaps it was a desire to hear more distinctly the words of the sermon, or perhaps it was the wonderful beauty of the night trembling down to her through the forest-trees, which after a time allured Eirene to leave the little camp-stool and step out into the air. She walked a few paces from the tent and leaned against the tree where, in the morning, she had been attacked and prayed for by the young evangelist. The words of the preacher came distinctly to her ear, and with them blended the scattered moans and amens of the congregation. She listened a few moments; then, looking back to the green inclosure beside the tent, she felt the old impulse to wander out, as she used to do in the woods at home. Since her coming this was the first moment that she had been alone with herself. True darling of nature, the old charm of freedom, the old spell of the woods, was on her. Still the preacher's voice, and the amens of the congregation, came to her ear, and yet she heard them not. The very leaves of the trees seemed to turn toward her, whispering to her to come, as she turned and walked slowly out over the trodden grass. Presently she came to high banks of ferns, which no camp-fires had reached and no feet had crushed, walling her in and pervading the air with fragrance. She paused under a tree with low-bending boughs, and listened. She heard the birds stirring in their nests,—the tiny chirp of the mother-birds soothing their broods; but otherwise the little choristers of love were still. She listened to the clear cry of the katy-dids in the branches high over her head, and to the slender horn of the crickets piping in the grass. She heard the hum of insect-folk—the murmuring natives of the summer air all a-thrill with life and love, stirring, with their low, pervading music, the wide realms of silence. Storms gone by had given the night-air that pure rare quality which makes the August of New England the most delicious month of the year. Eirene leaned her head against the old tree, and looked up through its umbrage to the sky, conscious of nothing but utter content. She only knew that she was happy, and did not question wherefore. Too young to analyze emotion, too innocent to dream of ill, she took in, through soul and sense, the exceeding beauty of God's world, and was glad. How could she know—this girl-woman—that she had come there to meet her fate. How could she, whose heart had never known another love than that of child and sister, know that even now her feet trembled on that perilous border-land of passion, from which, once touched, there is no retreat.

A quick rustle of leaves, a stir in the air, a consciousness of a second presence, came to her together. She started; and that instant a squirrel jumped through a mesh of leaves near her feet, and began to scamper up an adjoining tree.

"Bun, was it you?" she asked, with a low laugh.

"Bun, it is time to go to bed;" and, again leaning her head against the rough bark of the tree, she watched Bun as he went jumping to the very top of his green ladder. Yet she only did so for a moment, when a sound—a sound of positive steps—not still and stealthy, but light, quick, eager steps, she heard approaching very near to her. From what direction—the foliage was so dense—she did not see, nor did she wait to do so. For the first time conscious that she was alone, and at some distance from the tent, she was alarmed, and started from her leafy thicket to retrace her steps. She had not taken two when a long shadow fell across the grass before her, and she heard her name spoken in slightly tremulous yet assuring tones. She turned, and there, just dividing the walls of fern, almost at her side, stood Paul Mallane.

"Don't be alarmed. Don't go away, I beg of you, Miss Vale. Pardon me, if I intrude—and I know that I do—yet you will be doing me the greatest kindness if you will remain for a moment; then I will escort you back to the tent."

No human being could doubt the sincerity of his words, uttered in such tones of anxiety and entreaty. Eirene, frightened by his sudden and unaccountable appearance, could think of nothing but that he must be the bearer of some unexpected and imperative message to herself, exclaimed, "What has happened, Mr. Mallane? Have they sent for me from Hilltop? Oh, tell me what it is! How kind of you to come!" Already her affectionate heart and excited imagination had leaped to the conclusion that some misfortune had befallen the loved inmates of the dormer cottage.

"Nothing has happened at Hilltop which has sent me after you, Miss Vale," answered Paul, in tones which he tried to make calm and soothing. "Nothing has happened, and yet I have come here on purpose to see you. I have been here all day. I don't care a fig for the camp-meeting—though Viner's sermon, this afternoon, was really a model of oratory. I came here on purpose to speak with you. Don't look frightened. Don't think me rude if I am abrupt. I have waited so long, I have wanted so much to speak with you, I can't stop now for preliminaries or conventionalities. It is now nearly a year since I saw you first. All this time I have been trying to forget you. The result has been that I have thought of you twice as much as if I had not tried to put you out of my mind. I knew that I had no right to intrude upon you, and yet I could not refrain from sending you those pictures, as tokens of my remembrance, and the magazines, hoping that they might brighten your life a very little. Did you receive them?"

"Yes, and thank you for them so much," said Eirene. "I cannot tell you the pleasure they have given me."

"I am glad of that," replied Paul, with an expression of intense gratification. "That was all I sent them for,—not as advances toward acquaintance. Indeed, I came home yesterday with no definite expectation of finding myself any better acquainted with you at the close of this vacation than when I went back last autumn. But when I found that you were gone, I felt so angry at the thought of the unkindness which you had endured, I resolved that I would see you, and tell you that I, at least, have lifted my voice against the unjust persecution which followed you during all your stay in my father's house."

At these words a look of pain and of entreaty came into Eirene's eyes. Paul saw at a glance that whatever her life had been in his father's house, she could not talk of it.

"But that is not all I wished to say to you," he hastened to add. "For months I have wanted to tell you what you have done for me, and what you can do for me, if you only will. Very likely, if I had found you still in our house, I might have refrained from telling you. But when I saw that you were gone, I felt more than disappointed—I felt ill-tempered—for I knew that you had been really driven away by unkindness. Then I made up my mind to let you know what you had done for me, and that I was your true friend. I saw you when you started for camp-meeting this morning; till then I had not a thought of going. But it occurred to me that here would be a good place to tell you what has been so long in my mind; and I should have told you, before I left to-night, though it had been in the presence of all those pious old ladies in the tent, who would have gone back and published it to all Busyville to-morrow. It is due to you to know what you have done for me."

"What I have done for you," slowly said Eirene, in astonishment. "Why, Mr. Mallane, I have never been able to do any thing for any one in all my life, except for those at home, and very little for them. What could I do for you?"

"I will tell you what you have done," said Paul, reverently. "You have made all women more sacred in my eyes. It is not your fault if you have not made me a better man. I think of you all the time; more than of all other human beings put together. When I have remembered you, studying alone in your cold little room, I have been ashamed of my own indolence beside my warm fire. When I have thought of you, so young and tender, working hard with your hands for others, I have been ashamed of my own selfishness. When I have thought of your innocence, I have been ashamed of my own wicked thoughts and evil ways. For, if any one has told you that I am not a very good fellow, they have told you the truth. I am not. But if any one can improve me, you can."

"You make me feel very much ashamed," said Eirene. "I never feel certain that any thing I do is the very best thing to be done. I am always afraid that I might do better. I can't tell you, Mr. Mallane, how very uncertain I feel. But it will make me very happy to think that I may be of service to you, if you will only tell me how I can do it."

"Why—if you will only take a little interest in me," said Paul; "if you will care a little whether I am good or not, or happy or not. In short, if you won't be perfectly indifferent to me;

that will help me. I can tell you it will be a great incentive to try to do right, if I know that you care."

"But I do care, Mr. Mallane. I have cared ever since—"

"Ever since when?"

"Ever since Tilda said—"

"What did Tilda say?"

"She said, Mr. Mallane, that you were not quite good."

"I am not quite good," said Paul, penitently. "But, then, you cared!" he added, with a quiver of delight in his voice.

"Yes, I cared very much. Some way, it hurt me just to hear it. I thought, for the sake of your brothers and sisters, and for your father's and mother's, who are so proud of you, that you ought to be very noble, Mr. Mallane."

"You did! I ought to be noble for their sakes? Yes. I ought to be, I suppose. But *you* haven't the faintest idea what a fight it is—the world tugging at you outside, inside the devil. Why, it is the hardest thing on earth for a man to do, to be noble. If you were only in the world, you would know it. But *you* can't know it. You see it as you find it in good books, and in your own heart. But if you care, I'll try. I'll try to be just what you would like me to be."

Helena Maynard and Bella Prescott, could they have heard the tones in which these words were uttered, would have found nothing of their haughty Adonis in this humble youth. But Paul Mallane was by no means the first worldly man who has stood contrite before the innocence of a girl.

"You have promised to care, to take some interest in me," he went on. "Now, if you will promise to think of me—under all circumstances to think of me as—as your friend, it is all that I can ask."

It was not in eighteen girlish years, not in a girl with such a guileless and loving heart, to look up to the face which gazed down upon hers, quivering and luminous with feeling, full of entreaty, at once manly and tender, and, seeing it, to say that she did not want such a friend. No. Her heart thrilled with a new delight as it asked, how could one so strong and radiant for a moment need her sympathy, or pause in his bright life, to proffer his friendship? Thus, with her large soft gaze unconsciously lifted to his, she said, "I am sure it will make me happy to think of you always as my friend; and it will make my life seem wider and brighter if I can only believe that I help another."

"Help another! You can make me what you please," was Paul's passionate ejaculation.

As he spoke, the first lines of Charles Wesley's inspired hymn,

"Love divine, all love excelling,
Joy of heaven to earth come down,"

came rolling through the air on the joyful voices of the congregation. Never could it have sounded more expressive and sacred than in the soft air of that August night; never more triumphant, as in great waves of melody it rolled up through the forest-trees. Paul was irreverent, more through cultivation and habit than from nature. This moment the anthem was in perfect harmony with the place and with his feelings. Now the mother moon, who before had been peering through the branches of the trees, sailed forth into the open space of sky, and looked directly down into these children's faces, as if to see them and listen to what they were saying. They stood silent, listening. The hymn ceased. Words of worship—a strange commingling of religion, devotion, and love—began to surge into Paul's very throat for utterance, when the crackling of boughs, crushed by rapid footsteps, called him suddenly back to earth and to his senses. There, rushing through the branches broken off for the morning fires, Paul, to his dismay and anger, beheld Tilda Stade coming directly toward them. The hymn, which had just filled the air with such joyful peace, had closed the evening service. The moment it was ended Tilda hastened to the tent—but to find Eirene gone from the camp-seat, where she had left her. She questioned one of the mothers of Israel, and the old lady's reply was by no means satisfactory: "She went off more'n an hour ago, and I hain't seen nothin' of her sence." Tilda, who considered Eirene poetic, or, as she called it, "childish," to the verge of irresponsibility, thought now that she had gone out sky-gazing, but was prepared for nothing worse. Imagine, then, the shock which this worthy young woman received, when rushing into the green inclosure back of the tent. In the moonlight, bright as a second day, she beheld, with terrible distinctness, this child of her care standing under a wide-spreading tree, and by her side an "awful man." Imagine her increased horror when, drawing near enough to discern his features, she discovered that this man was no other than that young wolf of the world, against whom she had warned her lamb so long.

"Eirene Vale!" she exclaimed in her astonishment and anger. "Eirene Vale, was it for this you didn't feel able to go to meetin'? So you stayed back to meet a man—and this man! Haven't I warned you?" [Losing all self-control.] "Paul Mallane, you'd better be in better business!"

"Miss Stade," interrupted that youth, in lofty tone, "you don't know what you are talking about. But I request you to speak more respectfully to this lady. She stay to meet me! to meet any one! You know better. I intruded myself upon her, because there was something which I thought necessary to say to her. I have heard of you as being very zealous in your efforts to do good. Let me tell you that nothing could do me more good than the privilege of speaking with this young lady. If you are such a missionary, take care how you interfere with the only chance I have on earth of becoming a Christian. Miss Vale, may I accompany you to the tent?"

Tilda, who had started to seize Eirene by the arm, and lead her back as a culprit, was confounded by the overpowering manner of this young man, and all the more that the thought crowded into her mind that she remembered him when he wore frocks and aprons. The tone of deference with which he addressed Eirene was not to be mistaken. The most exacting lady in the land could not have demanded more, as he walked by her side, while the discomfited Tilda followed behind. When, at the door of the tent, he bade her good-night, with his hat in his hand, he had not the air of a man who was ashamed of himself, or ashamed of his company, although he made his adieu before the amazed eyes of the gossips of Busyville. One of them declared, in the shop, next day, "Where he dropped from, at that time of night, the Lord only knows; but there he was, in the tent-door, bowing good-night to that Vale girl, as if she had been a queen."

"So all I brought her to camp-meetin' for was to meet that man," groaned Tilda, as she tumbled about on a cotton comforter which she had spread over the straw on the ground.

---

## VIII.

PAUL'S WOOING.

Paul did not know whether he was in the body or out of it. He had but one consciousness—this: that he had seen her—been near to her—spoken with her; that her eyes had looked up to his, full of a gentle kindness—yea, more than a kindness—were they not full of an unspeakable sympathy? He had seen her, he had been near her. Now, his only desire was to see her, to be near her, again.

"Why are you so still? If you are happy in the Lord, I should think you would say something," said Tilda to Eirene the next morning, as the great Moloch of a wagon once more went on crunching roots and branches beneath it through the woods before sunrise. "It wasn't my way, when I received the evidence. I was so happy, I couldn't keep quiet. But you are different" (in a tone of disparagement).

"Yes," said Eirene, in a voice too far away to be reached by Tilda's reproof.

A few hours later, as she stood in her old place at work in the factory, John Mallane came to her side, and asked her if she had enjoyed the camp-meeting. When she answered that she had, he asked her if she didn't feel the need of a little vacation. "I noticed, several weeks ago, that you were looking very tired," he said. "If you would like to go home for three or four weeks, you can, and your wages may go on."

"Oh, Mr. Mallane," she exclaimed, in an effusion of gratitude, "that would be too much; the others—"

"Never mind the others," he interrupted; "they are no concern of yours. If you would like to go, I think it will be better all around. You certainly need the rest."

What he meant by the statement that her going would make it better all around, John Mallane did not explain. Had he so chosen he might have done it, by the fact that, an hour before, he had submitted to a very unmerciful attack from Mrs. Tabitha.

"You will go on deaf and blind, John Mallane, till that girl is tied to the family. You don't realize it; but I tell you, even now, there is no living with Paul because she is out of the house." And she went on waxing more and more enraged at every word she uttered, until her husband ended it with his usual, "Well, well, Tabitha, what do you want done?"

"I want you to send her home as straight as she can go; and, if you listen to me, you will never let her come back."

"To do that would be too cruel," he replied; "but I will give her a vacation while Paul is at home, if you say so, mother."

"I *do* say so." And she would have said a great deal more, but she knew that John Mallane "had put his foot down," and that it was perfectly useless to make further demands.

That evening, at twilight, Paul sat on the door-step, smoking his cigar in a very uneasy state of mind. He did not know what to do with himself. Every impulse in him impelled him to walk over to the little house across the street, and yet he compelled himself to remain where he was.

"Haven't I said every thing to her that I have a right to say?" he asked himself. "I told her what she had done for me—what she could do for me; asked her to be my friend. Of course, there is nothing more to be said."

But this conclusion did not soothe him any. He felt an insane desire just to see her again.

"If I could only sit down where she is, if I didn't say a word, I should be contented," he ejaculated mentally, as he sent some sudden whiffs of smoke into the air. Just then he heard Seth Goolve's gate close with a ring. It was Tilda Stade, who shut it sharply for his benefit. She saw him distinctly, sitting there smoking, and the triumph in her breast would not be denied, for Eirene walked by her side with a satchel in her hand. She was going to Hilltop on the evening train, and Tilda was her body-guard to the station. If Paul could have seen the expression of her face as she turned toward the gate, while she passed swiftly on the other side of the street, he would have read, "Come, if you dare;" and, seeing it, would very likely have dared, if only out of defiance of his implacable enemy. But Tilda's glance of ire expended itself in the dimness. He did not see it, yet he started with the impulse to go after them.

"What's the use, while that dragon is with her?" he thought; and he settled back on the door-step, and puffed away on his cigar in profound thought.

The afternoon of the next day Eirene sat by the open window of her own room at Hillside. Language is too poor to portray the beatitude of spirit which seemed to pervade and glorify her. To be at home—to be free—no dinging bell to command her to toil for how many blessed weeks! The sense of escape, of freedom, filled her with a joy too keen to be real. Was the weary summer, the ten hours' toil, the stifling chamber, a vanished dream? Or was this a dream—that, once more alone, at liberty, she looked forth on the beloved woods of her childhood, in all their August pomp, as they held their green crowns in the still blue air? The clouds, in great piles of fleecy cumuli, rested on the mountain-tops, or in snowy fleets sailed slowly on and on, and were lost in infinite distance. Eirene watched them as they went, and her sight drooped midway in the ocean of air; it seemed so vast, after the strip of sky which had bounded her summer. The wide earth was at rest, with its fruits ripening on its heart. With what eager delight Eirene counted the harvests—the apples yellowing and reddening in the hillside orchard—the corn with its pale green tassels—the meadow just under the window, running down to the river, now a broad field of tobacco. Was there ever before such a field of tobacco, with its languid, aromatic leaves, and flowers of amber? No; such leaves as these had never before ripened in Massachusetts' sunshine, Eirene felt sure. She leaned from the window, and tried to count every stately flowering stalk. She grew exultant over the unthought-of numbers of their waving ranks. Already she saw them lying slain beneath the September sun; saw the green leaves stacked and counted, golden-brown, in the barn; saw the trader from Busyville, who had bought it, lay the gleaming dollars on the sitting-room table—and Hillside was redeemed! Had Eirene been older, wiser, more of a philosopher, she might have estimated the probable harm which would be done to human nerves through the narcotic forces of this innocent-looking field of green and amber. But, personally, she had never seen any of the evil results born of the intoxicating plant. This field of tobacco—what did it not promise the heart of love and the imagination of youth, as both went on building dreams in the summer air! With no debt on the Hillside farm, poverty would be impossible. Her father—she saw him with head erect at last; no more shrinking away from loud-voiced Farmer Stave. He had a new hat and a new buggy; and Muggins—Muggins had retired to browse through a millennium of bliss in a field of clover, never again to be implored to "Get up." There is a new horse—a horse not unlike one she has seen arch his neck and dart away from the gate of the white house under the maples at Busyville, though she is unconscious of any relationship between the animals. Her mother has a new gown—the black silk gown which Mary Vale has so long meekly and hopelessly desired. Pansy is resplendent in another new frock, this time as pink as the June roses. Win is in college; and she—Eirene—is sitting at an old desk in the academy of Busyville, studying hard.

Thus far into the land of dreams had the field of tobacco transported Eirene. If for one instant Tabitha Mallane could have caught a glimpse of these brain-pictures, she would have set her jaw and nudged her head with a triumphant, "I told you so! I told you she was of the sort that a sixpence could make feel rich! How little it takes to make some people feel rich, to be sure!" Yes, she would study hard, and try and make up for every mental deficiency. Then, it would not seem quite so presumptuous for her to consider herself the friend of one who had enjoyed every advantage of education and society. This blissful thought pervaded every other. She had a friend! It was an utterly new sensation, this, that she had a friend—that he needed her! *Her!* How could any one away from Hillside, least of all one who had so much, who knew so much—one who was in every way so superior to herself—need her! Oh, it was delightful and passing strange!

You will perceive that our Eirene, who to this moment has been serene and sensible beyond the verge of dulness, has suddenly become foolish. More innocent she was in worldly wisdom, less wise, than the average girls of eighteen. It was not in her power to see Paul as he absolutely was. Indeed, it was not his ordinary self which had appeared and conversed with her—not the calculating, double-faced, every-day Paul, but an occasional Paul, who, at rare intervals, astonished the first with pure and genuine feeling. I am aware that, to this moment, Eirene has been very tame—a gray little dove, too sad and quiet to be any thing of a heroine. She will never astonish you, for her soul can only be harmonious with itself. But all the neutral tints in her life go out in the dawn of love. Her maiden heart, deep and still as a tranquil lake, can never go back to its peaceful calm after it has been moved and troubled to its depths by both the angel and demon of passion. For, of course, Paul is coming! While Eirene leans from her window and counts the tobacco-stalks, perching a fairy castle on every one, Paul is coming toward Hillside as fast as Fleetfoot, the horse with the arching neck, can bring him. Why he is coming, he neither asked himself nor answered. He pricked Fleetfoot's sides, and urged him up the steep and often perilous roads to Hilltop with an inconsiderate haste, which made the mountaineers, in their jogging wagons, look after him, and mutter, "That feller's a-goin' for the doctor, sure! Must be a case of life and death." Ah, it was all of life, that ardent, irrepressible haste, but not all of love—for it was in part of anger; anger goaded love, and hurried it on.

As usual, Tabitha Mallane had hastened a result which she would have made any sacrifice to avert. That very day Mother Harkwell, one of the old ladies who had remained with Eirene in the tent, came to unburden her mind to "poor Sister Mallane."

"I was lis'nin' to the preachin'," she said; "the gal was a-sittin' by the door; bime-by I looked, and the gal was gone; whar, I've no idee. I was so took up with the preachin', I hadn't seen her go. She was gone more'n an hour, I calkerlate. When she came round ag'in, it was with your son. Whar do ye suppose they'd be'n to? It's my idee that it was all a plot aforehand. It's tryin' to the sperrit to tell ye, Sister Mallane, but I must do my duty. 'Cordin' to my thinkin', you'd better look arter Paul and that ar gal."

Unfortunately for Paul, he appeared in the yellow sitting-room just after the departure of Mother Harkwell. If a single hour had intervened, in that Tabitha Mallane would have calmed down, and her sober judgment would once more have held a rein over her temper. But the sight of Paul, at this moment, was too much for it. Her rage at the story which she had just heard, suddenly laid low all the self-control which she had been building up for her own and others' management for months. So it was all a plan—a plan contrived beforehand! That girl had gone, and Paul had gone, to the camp-meeting, to meet each other! If he thwarted all her wishes and defied her—this lawless son!—at least she would pour out upon him her wrath; and she did. Paul looked her in the eyes, and listened till she accused him of the precontrived plan for meeting Eirene at the camp-meeting. Then his face blanched, and, without a word in reply, he turned, walked out of the room, and out of the house.

A very few moments after, Tabitha Mallane, from the window, saw him mount Fleetfoot and ride rapidly away. Then she knew what she had done. She sat down and rocked the cradle for an hour, with what force you may imagine; for the baby screamed with the colic for the next twelve.

During the first half of his ride, Paul thought chiefly of his mother. Without knowing it, he was glad in his heart that she had given him an excuse for just what he was at this present moment doing.

"She made me," he said to himself, approbatively. "Does she suppose that a man is going to stand and be accused of what he is not guilty, and not reward himself for such injustice? I've tried hard enough to do what she thought best, and what I tried to think best; but, hang it, I'm doing what I know is best now! Yet, I might have kept fr m it, if she hadn't accused me in advance."

The momentum of his wrath was spent by the time he reached the summit of the Hilltop road. Here he inquired the way of Farmer Stave, sitting on the station-steps, waiting for the train. In a few moments he had struck into the mountain-road. Its grass-grown paths ran on smoothly to Hillside. Now his mother seemed far behind. Every step brought him nearer to her. Every plan and project of his busy brain was this moment as void as if it had never been. All his scheming youth had receded and vanished out of his consciousness. All his future, with its dazzling pictures of wealth and power, had faded from his sight. The present possessed him. He loved her. He was near her. A few moments more, and he should see her, and tell her the truth—the whole truth. What the consequences of this truth-telling may be, he does not ask. "Consequences" he has not even the power to remember. Young men of twenty-four, who, in defiance of their own many maxims of prudence, and in open revolt against their mothers, suddenly commit themselves to an overmastering love-passion, seldom think of consequences, or inquire after them. Do they? Certainly, Paul Mallane did not. How could he minister to this life which he was seeking? If he wooed and won this girl, could he make her happy as his wife? Was he fit to be her husband? Were they together fitted, by temperament, education, and love, for harmonious, life-long companionship? These were after-thoughts. Paul had not reached the moment of after-thoughts. Youth, in the first ardor of love, never does. He was in love—utterly in love; that was all he thought or knew. That is about all most men think or know, when first struck into this blissful condition. Is it not?

Thus Paul pricked Fleetfoot's sides, and the thud of his hoofs in the soft turf grew more and more rapid. In a few moments the woods were passed, and there, in the wide space on the other side of the river, was Hillside farm!

As you already know, it was a lowly abode; yet it possessed two indispensable elements of beauty—fitness and harmony. It belonged to the landscape; it seemed to complete and perfect it. In a different mood, Paul would have pronounced it a "poor affair." You may judge of the exaltation of his mental condition, by the fact that he never thought to compare it with Marlboro Hill. He only said, "How pleasant! I should think an innocent might have grown up in a spot like this." Meanwhile, our maiden still sits by the window, building beautiful palaces in her field of tobacco—following with her eyes the sailing clouds, watching the lights and shadows which they drop along the mountain-sides and on the woods, heart and eyes overflowing with an unknown happiness. It is the story old as the earth—the maiden waiting for the man, the man coming to woo the maiden.

Here I feel inclined to stop, and tell you no more. Silence is never so golden as when it shuts from the world the supreme moments of life. Love, the sweetest ever uttered, seems to lose somewhat of its sacredness when its utterance is heard and repeated. This is why the love-scenes in novels are nearly always too hot or too cold. The lover says too much, or he says too little. The love-making never seems quite natural, quite perfect; and, while we read, we have something the feeling of a person who is listening to what was only meant for the ears of one. As for Paul, in his present mood, he is sure to say too much. I am sure that what he says will not sound well repeated.

Eirene, from her window, sees horse and rider emerge from the road through the woods. This is not an unusual sight. Farmer Stave and Deacon Smoot may be seen jogging forth from it almost any day. But it is doubtful if any thing equal to the arch in Fleetfoot's neck had been ever seen before on any horse which has preceded him. It is this which attracts and fixes Eirene's gaze. She says, "It is!—No, it cannot be! Impossible! But it looks the very same! No!—yes!—it is!—it is Paul Mallane!" There can be no mistaking him now. Fleetfoot's quick feet are striking impatiently the loose boards of the bridge just below the house with that peculiar muffled ring which has made Eirene look up from her work so many times since she was a little girl. They come more slowly along the road under the maple-trees, as if hesitating or faltering a little upon such near approach to the house.

"Has he come to Hillside for a ride? Can he be coming here? No, he cannot be!—Yes, he must be!" said Eirene in the same instant to herself; yet she moved not. Very soon she heard Fleetfoot striking his shoes against the fence. She could not see the front gate, but she heard it click, and then quick steps along the garden-path and in the old porch; then the old iron knocker sent its loud ring through the silent house, and then for the first time she started with the recollection that there was not a soul below—that she herself must go and open the door. Her father and Win are out in the fields, and her mother and Pansy had gone in the buggy to Hilltop, to buy some extra sweets for the anticipated reunion tea. She kept him waiting scarcely two minutes, but they seemed fifty to Paul; yet she kept him waiting while she did what ninety-nine maidens out of a hundred would have done —she gave a little brush to her hair, and looked wistfully at herself in the little glass, for the first time in her life moved to such an act from the desire to seem not unlovely in the eyes of one.

Paul was just beginning to ask himself if it was possible any unthought-of dragon could be lurking in the little habitation, when he heard a soft step; then, the door of her lowly home was opened to him by Eirene. Her lovely color came and went, as she frankly extended her hand and invited him to enter.

"I know you are astonished to see me here," began Paul at once; "but, Miss Vale—Eirene—my darling!—don't look frightened; I've called you so a hundred times to myself—I cannot live without you—I cannot even try to; and I have come to tell you so."

Seeing how very emphatic was Paul's first utterance, you see it is better to repeat no more that he said. Not that I am ashamed of it, nor that he had cause to be ashamed of it; for it was the first time in his life that he had uttered the words of an entire, disinterested affection—and it would be the last.

Experiences deeper, more holy, may come to the woman afterwards, but they can never repeat the rapture which runs through the maiden's heart, when for the first time she is made conscious that she is beloved. Then her life suddenly takes on its complete meaning, and for the first time she knows why she was born. We must remember, outside of her home, how little had come into this girl's life—how barren it was—in order to realize how wonderful and delicious seemed the largess of human love now poured out to her. We must not forget that Paul, though neither morally nor intellectually the god which he appeared to her to be, nevertheless possessed that charm of person and of manner, that magnetism of mind, so potent with women.

We know that women possessed of all the opportunities which fortune and society give, had passed by better men to bestow their preference upon him, solely through this force of personality. Then, what must it have been to this girl, into the whole of whose life before nothing so bright or so strong had ever come! If he was attractive when all that was best in him had been held in abeyance, how much more so was he now, while every look and word of his were transfigured in intense and genuine emotion! What a story was that which fell upon her bewildered and enraptured ears! She listened in thrilling silence, tears and smiles passing over her clear eyes swift as the sunshine and shadow on the woods without, the eloquence of her face every instant increasing the eloquence of the story. What passionate entreaty! Would she love him, and wait for him? Another year, and he would be established in his profession. He could make his own home. Would she be the angel in the house? Would she be his wife? Would she make him what she pleased—noble and good, through his love for her?

It is hard that the retributive cherubim should always be near, and always ready to drive us out of paradise. This time the avenging angel was Muggins. Paul fell straight from heaven at the near rattle of wagon-wheels and the shrill cry of a girl-voice. Nothing could make Muggins lively but the sight of the barn after a little exertion; and Pansy, seeing that her nose was again endangered, was wildly jerking the reins, and screaming to Muggins to "stop!"

Paul, looking out, saw a plainly-dressed woman and little girl drive frantically up to the house, in a very forlorn buggy, with a very remarkable-looking horse. Then for the first time he realized the disagreeable fact that Eirene had relations; and immediately he felt injured that it was possible she could belong to any body but himself. A moment before, it had seemed to him that he and she were alone on the earth—as if he could gather her into his arms and bear her away to be his own, alone, forever. And here was a mother and sister, and no telling how many more relatives, to be consulted! And what a looking horse! He was very much in love, but he could not help seeing Muggins. He forgot her, however, a moment after, when he had been introduced, and was looking into the face of Eirene's mother. She was so like her daughter! The large, soft eyes, with their tender smile and suggestion of tears, won the better Paul directly, and so entirely, that he forgot altogether that her dress was very unfashionable, and her bonnet many seasons old. It was not at all difficult to ask this mother for her child—not for to-day or to-morrow, but when he had proved himself worthy of her, and when he could offer her a home fit for her to adorn and crown.

As Mary Vale listened to Paul, it seemed to her that the enchanting pictures of her youth were all to be made real in the life of her child. She knew Paul well and favorably, through his family name. Of the world in which Paul lived, of its influences and temptations, she knew absolutely nothing. But she knew that she saw before her a handsome, earnest, and eloquent face; that the owner of this face was pleading for the privilege of making the life of her beloved child happy. She believed every word that he said—which is not remarkable, for Paul himself believed every word he said.

It was not thought necessary to introduce Pansy at once; thus she avenged herself by softly peeping through the door. "Oh!" her busy little brain exclaimed, "Oh, what a handsome man! He looks like the Prince in the fairy tale. He has come for Eirene! I know he has, by the way he looks! Why didn't he come for me? I'm so tired of this old place! If somebody don't come for me, I'll run away. I read about a girl who did."

A few moments afterwards, Paul saw this little damsel, and was made acquainted with her. "What a remarkable combination!" he said to himself; "such yellow hair, and such dark eyes—purple—black! What a beauty she'll be, some day! We'll bring her out, and she'll make a great match."

It was a fair picture that Paul saw, as he mounted his horse and looked back: the mother, the maiden, and the little girl—the head touched with gray, the head of auburn-brown, and the head of gold.

"I've seen beauty before—never beauty like this," said Paul, as he looked once more with a smiling adieu, and rode reluctantly away. But it was Eirene's face that went with him, and the touch of her hand as she had given it to him in parting. Fleetfoot paced through the woods with a slow, meditating step, so unlike that of his coming. He had taken on the mood of his rider, whose rein had dropped upon his neck. Paul felt that every step was taking him from the joy of his heart. He could think of nothing but how she had looked—how she had spoken—how incomparably lovely she was, and that, after all, in defiance of every thing, she was to be his! This condition lasted till the Hilltop station was passed. Then it was no longer Hillside, but Busyville, that he was near. Busyville! Why must he go back to Busyville—to Dick Prescott—to the world—above all, to his mother? The face that he had left behind belonged to neither. The heart that he had won beat like a captive's in his father's shop. After all, he had done it—done just what his mother, what Dick Prescott, had said that he would. He had wooed and won a shop-girl! All these together could not make him regret it. He would stand by her. He would marry her in spite of them all. He had not yet lived to the hard moment of the after-thought.

But it came: it was not possible that it would not come to Paul Mallane. We love—as we do every thing else—according to our nature. The defects of temperament, the infirmity of temper, the partial insight, the clouded judgment, the unreasonable prejudice, which distorts so much that is good in us, which mars so many of the fair actions of our daily life, extend no less to our affections. The fault of our character is visible in our love. Paul loved Eirene, but he was no less Paul. In the very glow of his passion, he saw that Muggins was a very ridiculous horse; and, as he came again and again to Hillside, he saw each time more distinctly something which the glamour of his feelings had made imperceptible to him before. It is true, he was too much in love to be moved from his purpose by any thing that he saw. Yet his cool brain asserted itself more and more, in defiance of his passionate heart. His forecasting judgment, on which he had prided himself so long, retaliated for the slight he had shown it, by perpetually tormenting him with suggestions of expediency, amid all his ardor of tenderness. He forgot them while looking into her eyes and taking into his heart the sweet tones of her voice, while walking with her along the voiceful river, or sitting with her in some sheltered nook by its side, ostensibly waiting for the fish which were so deliciously slow to bite. In all his life, Paul had never been so true a Paul as in these moments. He was delicate and chivalric. He would sooner have cut off his hand than to have taken advantage, even by a word, of the innocent and absolute trust of the creature by his side. She was to be his wife—his beloved wife! This was the beginning and end of the sweet story, told over and over in glowing words. Paul builded and furnished the house in which they were to dwell; he even fashioned the ponies and the phæton, which were to be especially her own. He surrounded her with music and flowers, with poetry, beauty, and love; and, as she listened more and more, she breathed in a realm of enchantment. This was life, and life was love, and Paul was its creator and king! It seemed so possible, so real, so very near, this story told to the maiden in white, amid the green leaves' flickering shadows, beside the laughing waters. But how remote, if not impossible, it became the moment Paul sat down in the little house! In that moment his romance suffered a fearful collapse. The thought came to him then, as a possibility, that his bearing Eirene off to his fairy palace might involve the taking with her of her entire family. His judgment assured him that he, Paul Mallane, considering the wealthy match that he might have made, had reached a state of perfect magnanimity in love, in that he was willing and glad to marry a girl without a cent; but marrying her family in addition was quite another thing, and more than could be expected even of such a magnanimous man. He knew nothing of the mortgage on Hillside, but, every time he came, he saw more and more clearly the extreme poverty of its inmates. It was written all over the little parlor in which he sat with Eirene, though there was nothing in it which offended his taste, like the parlor in Busyville. But the cheap chintz covers on the lounge and stools and chairs, and the carpet on the floor, had been made by the hands of Eirene and her mother, in their attempt to cover the poverty that would not be hidden. The effect of every thing was refined and scrupulously neat; but oh, how poor! The same story of lifelong poverty was stamped in the patient hopelessness of Lowell Vale's face, in the gentle sadness of his wife's, in the restlessness of Win's, and the peevish discontent of the little Pansy's. It was a great advance on his pleasure-loving life, when Paul Mallane resolutely made up his mind to work hard in his profession, to marry a poor girl, and to support her by his own efforts in accordance with his position. When we take into consideration Paul's antecedents and habits, it is not surprising that he was appalled at the prospect of any additional burden which might possibly devolve upon him through this marriage. His tormenting head kept reminding him of it, and asking him how he could bear it. Yet, he was so much in love, it made not the slightest difference in his actions. Almost every day, for four bright weeks, Tabitha Mallane saw him mount Fleetfoot and ride away—whither, she knew too well; but the look on his face, so like his father's when he had "made up his mind," compelled her to silence. She asked no questions, made no remonstrance. She knew that it was too late.

For Paul, all the poetry of his life was concentrated in this single month. He had never known its like before; he would never know its like again. The world of planning and of scheming and of ambition was far behind him. He lived in the benign world of nature, and in his truest affections. He uttered more words of love, created more in this little time, than a man under ordinary conditions would in years. He lived more in rich experience and in keen delight in this one month, than do many mortals in a lifetime. Perhaps he felt instinctively that its wonder of joy could never be repeated, and this was why he gave himself entirely to the bliss of the present.

The dreaded parting came. The beautiful tryst ended one starry September night. As Paul looked into the eyes of his darling, and then irresolutely set his face toward the world, he felt himself to be a very miserable fellow, and, as he couldn't have any thing as he wanted it, romantically wished himself dead. Before that extreme moment came, however, caution and prudence had reminded him that some practical arrangement must be made even by a man desperately in love, while he loved amid opposition and difficulties. Thus, when he left Hillside the last time, the definite understanding with both father and mother was, that Paul and Eirene were affianced, but that, in consideration of the fact that he was not established in his profession, and the more troublesome fact that his mother would bitterly oppose it, the engagement was to be kept secret for a year. Then, Paul declared he would be independent, and able to declare it to the whole world.

"Only a year! Only one little year, my darling!" said Paul, "and then, no more hard work and loneliness. I shall carry you from both, and you will be my wife."

#### TABITHA MALLANE'S STRATEGY.

Gouty old uncles and grumpy old aunts do sometimes die in season to satisfy their anxiously-waiting relatives. At least, old Comfort Bard died just in the nick of time to please her niece Tabitha. In midwinter Aunt Comfort passed away, and, before the coming of Spring, her share of the Bard homestead, and a very considerable legacy, had passed into the eager hands of Tabitha Mallane. Long before that hour, as she moved about her household, or as she sat before the smouldering fire, while John Mallane slept, she had laid her plans and decided what she would do with it. Once she could have had but one thought concerning it. She would simply have given it to John Mallane, with the words, "Here, father; put it into the business, and secure the interest for the children." But her anxiety for the children together was absorbed and forgotten in her passion concerning one. Paul had already entered an old and noted law-office in Boston as the junior partner. It already had its "solid man," its learned man, and was glad to add, as a special ornament, a young and eloquent advocate. All Busyville declared this to be a great opening for Paul Mallane, though it hastened to add, "He's one of the lucky ones. He always gets what he wants."

Tabitha Mallane resolved that he should come to Busyville in his summer vacation, and, for the first time in his life, find his home, in its aspect, nearer at least to what he wished it to be. She resolved on many other things, of which we shall presently be made aware. If women had spent one tenth of the time and intellect in helping each other, which they have devoted to outwitting and destroying each other, what a different world this would be! If the same talent for management and diplomacy, which they so often use to bring about positive and fatal results in trivial affairs, they had applied to noble ends, how much less cause there would be to bemoan the triviality and personal slavery of woman—a triviality and slavery for which woman herself is as responsible as man.

In the early Spring days, Eirene began to notice most unusual indications about the white house across the street. It was thronged with workmen within and without. In due time, the boxy parlor and a more boxy bed-room, and the yellow sitting-room, were thrown into one drawing-room, with graceful sliding-doors; the kitchen was enlarged into a dining-room, and a new and remote kitchen was commenced to be built in the rear of all. The little old outlooks were lengthened into long French windows opening into a veranda, which extended entirely around the house. This transformation was sufficiently wonderful; but when a strange man came and began to metamorphose the garden, the wonder was complete. Nobody outside of her own heart knew what a pang it cost Tabitha Mallane to give up her garden. It was hard enough to relinquish the yellow sitting-room, and the old cradle in which all her babies had been rocked; but it was harder still to give up that dear plot of ground, with its straight beds of beets, peas, and lettuce, wherein she had so long gathered her own fresh vegetables; wherein, when nobody was looking, she had so often turned up, with her own hands, from the moist mould, new potatoes for dinner. Through all her weary housekeeping, child-nursing years, it had given her her one pastime—this garden; it was the one bond between her and nature. It had been such a pleasure in the summer evenings, with her children about her, to weed these beds—to water her sturdy sweet-williams and hollyhocks, and watch them grow. But Paul detested them all, and they must be annihilated. Thus the plots were rolled even with the ground, covered with turf, and trimmed with narrow earth-borders, for verbenas, mignonette, and other delicate flowers. Rustic seats were placed under the old cherry and apricot trees, and garden vases for trailing plants were set out in the grass, the crowning marvel to the eyes of the factory folk. The last sacrifice laid on the altar of modern "style" and maternal love and scheming, was the white paint of the house itself. All the old mansions and homesteads of Busyville had been painted white, with bright, blinking green blinds—Tabitha Mallane's delight. But, ever since Paul had read Dickens' "Notes," the vivid brightness of red, white, and green had been an offence in his sight. Thus the painters ascended their ladders, and the white went under a pale tea-color, with heavy cappings of dark wood. When all was completed, certainly no accusation could be brought against the house and its garden. The only trouble with it now was, that it was not in harmony with its surroundings. It should have stood isolated, amid its own wide grounds. It looked out of place on a narrow street, opposite the ugly factories, and Seth Goodlove's little unpainted, unsheltered domicile.

While these changes were proceeding toward completion, Paul was surprised, one morning, by the announcement, at his Cambridge quarters, that a lady wished to see him. He was still more surprised when, on entering his parlor, he was confronted by his mother. He did not recognize her at the first glance; she looked so different, in her ladylike gray travelling suit, from the care-worn woman in a wrapper in the yellow sitting-room at home.

"Why, mother! what brought you here?" said Paul, in a really hearty tone, as, taking in her appearance, he at once saw that she really looked well, and that he need not be ashamed of her.

"You, Paul!" answered his mother, in a cheerful voice, so different from her Busyville tone. "Sit down, and I will tell you all about it."

He felt at once as if he were in the Busyville sitting-room, now he was told to sit down and to listen; but he did as he was bidden. Then, even the handsome gray travelling suit and the becoming bonnet could not keep Mrs. Tabitha from bending forward with a little swaying motion, as if she were still rocking the cradle and talking to Paul across it.

"I'll sit down, mother, if you'll sit up," said Paul, laughing; "but don't, I beg of you, rock the cradle at me in Cambridge."

"No; I'll do just as you want me to," said Mrs. Mallane, straightening. "I've come to surprise and to please you, and I'm going to do it. Of course, you know about Aunt Comfort's legacy; but you don't know what I've done with it. You'll never be annoyed again with the old sitting-room and the oak paper, nor with the shabbiness of your home, Paul. You have no idea how much feeling I had about it when I could not help it. I knew how hard it was, going in the society you do, and being invited to such places, never to be able to return such hospitality, because you were ashamed of your father's house. You won't know it when you see it. I haven't trusted to my own taste in any respect—for you know I like the old things best, because I've had them all my life—but I sent for the architect who built Squire Arnott's house, which you like so well, and for the man who laid out his grounds, and they have left nothing as it was before. It's handsomer than you can think. Father says that it's altogether too handsome for us, and that I'm crazy, or I wouldn't strike out from the old, plain way, and use up so much money, instead of putting it in the business. It's for you, Paul. I was determined that once, before you really set up for yourself, you could come to a home into which you would not be ashamed to ask any friend you have. There's Mr. Prescott, who did so much to introduce you into the law-office—you're under obligation to him; and Miss Prescott, and Miss Maynard, or any one you please. I shall be ready for them before August. And I've come down to have you select the furniture and carpets with me; you shall have them just as you like, Paul."

Paul was a good deal astonished, but did not look so supremely delighted as his mother hoped that he would.

His first thought was of Eirene. "This new splendor will only shut her out more completely—poor little girl!" he said to himself. "I've wanted it bad enough. Strange I couldn't have it till it can be of no use to me! Still, I would like to show the Prescotts that I have no reason to be ashamed of my home, as I know they think I have. It would have been a good deal kinder to have given me the money to have begun housekeeping with—Eirene and I."

"I want you to introduce me to the Prescotts, Paul," said Mrs. Mallane. "I would like to go with you to Marlboro Hill."

"I will bring Dick to see you," answered Paul. "But you are my mother, and a stranger," he added, in an imperial tone. "Miss Prescott must call upon you before you visit Marlboro Hill."

After expressing her approbation of his handsome rooms, Mrs. Mallane proposed to return to the city and begin her momentous shopping. Paul, naming an hour when he would join her, proceeded to escort her to the cars. On their way they met Dick Prescott, who was duly presented to Paul's mother. He addressed her with marked deference, adding that he would do himself the honor to call with his sister. They came, the next afternoon, in the stately Prescott barouche, Miss Isabella bringing with her her daintiest costume and most bewitching manners. She was most effusive, if not "gushing," to Mrs. Mallane. She was "so charmed, so delighted, to meet Mrs. Mallane! Oh, how much you look like your son!" she exclaimed. "I have heard Mr. Mallane speak so often of his mother, I feel as if I had known you always. And you will come out to Marlboro? Oh, do! Drive out in the early evening, and we will take tea on the lawn. It will be so lovely! Please say you will. I shall be so disappointed if you don't."

There was something in Tabitha Mallane which responded to all this. It was from his mother that Paul had inherited his love for fine equipages and stately houses, for the *éclat* and paraphernalia of wealth and place. To be sure, circumstances had held it suppressed in her nature; but, in spite of many years of drudging and of stocking-darning, it was there. With its first opportunity, the dormant passion sprang alert into life. It pleased her that her callers came in an elegant carriage, with liveried servants. But, with all this conscious pleasure, there was no vulgar betrayal of it. As she received her visitors, she looked not at all out of place, nor did she feel that she was. She felt as perfectly at home in her heavy black silk, as if Aunt Comfort had never owned it or worn it, or as if she herself had never dug new potatoes for dinner. She looked pleased, but not honored, nor did she consider herself to be. What if she did not have all the modern airs and graces? She had a son; and, while she had him, and he was both airy, graceful, and talented, she was well aware that she would never be treated as a secondary personage, at least by marriageable young ladies.

Paul drove his mother out to Marlboro in fine state. They took tea on the lawn, and it was all "so lovely!" as Bella Prescott continually exclaimed. Afterwards Dick and Paul sauntered off to smoke their cigars, and the two ladies were left together. Then, as Tabitha Mallane looked across its green spaces and down its broad avenues, she made her first real estimate of Marlboro Hill. It was one of the most beautiful and stately of those suburban homes which make the environs of Boston so charming. But it was not the red sunset through the green of immemorial elms, flushing the stone of the old ancestral house with the bloom of vivid rose, which attracted her attention. What she saw was the solidity, the age, the wealth, and vast respectability reflected in its walls. She saw also, as distinctly as Eirene beheld her mother's new gown and her father's new horse, Paul driving up this avenue of elms behind a pair of stately bays—her Paul coming home in the evening sunlight, the master of Marlboro Hill! She looked across the lawn, with its fountains and flowers, to the park, where some tame deer were grazing beside a mimic lake; and, as she looked, she wondered how, for so many years, she had thought Squire Blane's squatty house a fine mansion, his tucked-up garden "grounds," or his daughter Tilly, a match for Paul!

It was a long, long look which she had given to Marlboro with her exacting eyes. Meanwhile, Isabella Prescott had been taking in Mrs. Mallane with a much smaller but quite as keen a pair.

"I don't think that I made allowance enough for the boy," said Mrs. Tabitha to herself, "when he came home and felt so dissatisfied with all he saw there, compared with what he had seen here; but then, I couldn't have any idea of the contrast as I see it now."—"I am thinking what a happy girl you are, to be the free mistress of such a beautiful home," she said to Bella.

"Yes, Marlboro is beautiful, I suppose; every body says so. But it don't look to me as it does to other people, because I have always lived here, perhaps. Then, I get so tired looking after it, and so lonesome. Dear Mrs. Mallane, what is any home without a mother?" murmured the maiden, with two bright tears twinkling in her little eyes. "Dick is good to me—every body's kind; but oh! if you could know how I *want* a mother!"

"Dear child, you little know the feeling of a mother's heart," answered Mrs. Tabitha, in her most pathetic quaver. "It goes straight to mine to hear you say so. Being the mother of my Grace, gives me a mother's feeling for every other young girl. Yes, I see how it is: with every thing else in the world, you haven't a mother. You must see some sad hours, my child."

"Oh, very sad! It would be very different if I had a sister; but I haven't even a sister."

"Well, my dear, you must come and visit Grace. She has no sister either, near her own age. I'm sure you'd take to each other directly. She knows nothing of the world of society, and you know all about it; so you'd be fresh to each other, and I could be mother to both. How I wish you could be persuaded to visit us!"

"Oh, I don't need any persuading; it would delight me to come! I can't tell you, Mrs. Mallane, how I long to go to some quiet spot this summer! We've been to the White Hills, to Niagara, Saratoga, and everywhere, and I'm tired of all. I'd like to go and see something that I never saw before. I've been thinking of asking Dick to take board in some retired farm-house, where I shouldn't have to make four toilettes a-day in hot weather. You've no idea what a bore it is, Mrs. Mallane."

Mrs. Tabitha was sure she did not, as the outline of her old summer sacque and down-at-the-heel slippers ran before her mental eyes. Then she gave a little sigh, for she thought that, if this guest came, she must relinquish them.

"Our village is a bustling little place," she said, "but a rural country lies all around it. In half an hour I can take you to a perfection of a farmhouse—the one in which I was born. It has been in our family a hundred years."

"How I should delight to see it, and Grace! Do tell me about *her*, Mrs. Mallane! Does she look like you? Oh, I'm sure we should be like sisters! How I want to see her! How sweet in you to invite me! and how lovely it will be to go! It's so different being with one's friends, from being with people in whom one takes no interest."

"Yes, I think so," said Mrs. Mallane, "even if your friends can give you less than strangers. Of course, you know, Miss Prescott, that we are quiet country people, and live in a very plain way—not at all in your style. You will find every thing simple and homely. You must come prepared for that. But you say you want something different from any thing you've had before. You will find it with us, and a daughter's welcome; but remember, we live in a very plain way." And, as she uttered these words, Mrs. Tabitha felt an inward satisfaction in the thought that, after so much depreciation, when she did come, Miss Prescott would be astonished to find every thing so much finer than she had expected.

Dick and Paul appearing at this juncture, Bella called out, "Dear Dick, Mrs. Mallane has invited me to visit her, and I'm going. I shall see Grace, and the farm-house that has been in the family a hundred years. Won't it be lovely?"

"Altogether lovely—that is, it would be, if Mrs. Mallane had invited me too. I don't want to be left out."

"And we wouldn't leave you out for the world," said delighted Mrs. Tabitha, "if you think you could find any pleasure with us. I left Paul to decide that; he is so well acquainted with your tastes. If you like fishing, there are shoals in our river, and trout in the brooks, not six miles away."

"I doat on fishing, and so does Dick. How sweet, how kind you are, Mrs. Mallane!" exclaimed Bella, in her most guileless and gushing tone, leaning toward Mrs. Tabitha as if she were going to embrace her on the spot. Paul, looking on, said to himself, "This is the best-played game that I ever saw, if it is a game. What's the deceit of the devil to that of an artful woman? A little of this kindness of mother's had better have been bestowed somewhere else, in my opinion." And he felt bitter, as he saw, in the distance, a drooping head and a fair, sad face. Yet, an instant after, a sensation of pleasure and triumph rose in him, as he looked and saw Isabella Prescott nestled close to his mother's side. She made quite a pretty picture, sitting there under the sunset trees. Then, there was satisfaction as well as wonder in seeing his mother looking quite the lady of Marlboro, with her stately head and lustrous silk. If she had always looked like this, Paul felt certain that he never could have rebelled against her as he had done in the past.

Half an hour later, while Paul and his mother were riding toward the city, each silent with their own thoughts, Isabella Prescott still sat under the trees entertaining her brother.

"If you could only have seen it, Dick—the old lady's look! She took an inventory of the entire place, before she spoke a word. Then, she said I must be a happy girl to have such a home. I made just the reply she wanted me to: I said, I would be happy if I only had a mother! Then, of course, she offered to be my mother, with the society of her daughter Grace. It grew very affecting. Don't you see, Dick, it was just like a story-book. Yes, of one thing I may say I am certain: that the lady from the country has set her heart and mind on becoming my mother——in-law!"

"Well, if her son hadn't piqued your vanity so awfully, she would have made it out."

"That's your opinion, is it, Dick?"

"It is. But, as matters are, what under heaven is going to take you up to that furnace in the country for a visit? I saw you had some game on hand, and thought I wouldn't spoil it; but now, I'd like to know what it's all about. Mallane has gone and made an ass of himself—engaged himself to that girl. He as good as owned it to me. So you had better let him alone. I have other designs for you."

"You have? Well, I'll inquire what they are, when I've carried out my own. As for leaving Paul Mallane alone, that's just what I don't intend to do."

"But what are you going up to that blistering hole of a factory-village for? Paul does not stay there three days at a time, if he can help it."

"Well, the first thing I'm going for is to gratify my curiosity. I want to see the native surroundings of my gentleman. I want to see that farm-house. Oh, Dick, you ought to have heard the tone with which *la mère* said, 'It has been in our family a hundred years.' Then, I want to see—and intend to see—the shop-girl. What I mean to do, is, to punish her; to punish her is my object, and I shall do it."

As she mentioned the shop-girl, Bella's voice suddenly grew quick and sharp. Dick looked up. Her thin lips were white, and her little eyes were fixed and beady as a snake's.

No man is bad enough to enjoy such a manifestation in his sister.

"Come, Bell," he said, "don't look like that. The shop-girl isn't worth your spite. I'm up to such things myself; but you are a woman, and should be in better business."

"I don't care," said Bella, angrily. "Being a woman don't make it any pleasanter to be snubbed, nor any easier to bear it. Think of a Prescott ever having been put one side for a thing like that! There's no use in talking, Dick; I shall make the visit. I shall see the shop-girl, and I shall punish her. I shall catch a fish, but not in the river."

---

# A WOMAN'S RIGHT.

## IX.

WHAT CAME OF PAUL'S WOOING.

Oftener than we think, even while a man sincerely loves a woman, if he finds himself bound to her by an irrevocable vow, it chafes him like a fetter, and he instinctively begins to lament his lost liberty—at first, perhaps, almost unconsciously, and only while he finds himself restrained and held back by a moral obligation from some old pastime or pleasure, in which, until now, he has always felt perfect freedom to indulge. For Paul Mallane to come to a sudden consciousness that he had no longer a right to flirt with every woman who would flirt with him, was, indeed, a new sensation. To do him justice, through the entire winter he had no desire to do so. He had never been so thoroughly and honorably busy as he was now. His graduation from the law-school reflected great credit upon himself and his friends. He was just about entering a law-firm, which offered him the opportunity of complete success in his profession. He was going to pay his debts. He was going to be married to the only girl he had ever loved. He was going to make his own home without any body's assistance. He had never felt himself to be so much of a man, and he never had been so much of a man before. He hung Eirene's picture over the table where he sat at work, and, when he felt any of his old lawless impulses stirring him, any temptation from within or without, he looked at that face, and they all died. September, that divine September of pure love, came back; he breathed again in her presence; he saw the look in her eyes, he felt the touch of her hand; he was with her once more; and, being with her and loving her as he did, he resolutely turned from the world of pleasure in which he had so long lived, sat down, and went on with his work. He took an immense amount of credit to himself for all this. Just now, nobody admired Paul so much as Paul admired himself. He felt sure that he was making tremendous sacrifices for the sake of his love, and felt proud of himself beyond expression to think that he, Paul Mallane, was able to do it. In writing to Eirene, he took pains to impress faithfully upon her mind the great sacrifice that he made and the untold temptation which he resisted for her sake. He thought it would increase the value of his love, the more she realized the innumerable benefits which he relinquished on its behalf. Eirene, in the crowded shop and in Seth Goodlove's bare little chamber, did marvel more and more that such a transcendent gift should have come to her. Every letter that she received from Paul made it seem more wonderful and more enchanting that such a god could stoop to her lowly estate, to love her! But when, at Christmas, Paul came up to Busyville, and, with the certain knowledge that his mother was watching him from the window, knocked deliberately at Seth Goodlove's door, and spent at least two hours visiting with Eirene in the best Goodlove "front room," with the smoke perversely blowing out of the "dummy" stove till it nearly extinguished their four eyes; and when, with the eyes of Busyville fixed upon him, he escorted Eirene to church in open day, Paul's admiration of himself reached its climax. There might be more awful tests to a man's love, but they were unknown to Paul Mallane. The latter sight—that of Paul Mallane escorting a shop-girl to church—drove the mind of Busyville wild. The maidens of the mansion-houses regarded it as a per sonal injury, if not an insult. The maidens of the shops, knowing that no mortal power could induce him to escort one of them, regarded it as a base action that he should walk to church with Eirene Vale. "That was the reason, was it, that she never went with shop-people, and spent her time studyin'? She intended to catch the boss' son—the minx!"

A deep distrust of Paul Mallane pervaded the Busyville mind. It had contemplated and pronounced upon his flirtations since he was a boy in the Busyville Academy. Hitherto it had known them to be of a very unstable, if not doubtful, character; and it naturally pronounced that this one, of all others, could come to no good.

Deep was Eirene's distress, on entering the factory on Monday morning, to meet lifted shoulders, averted eyes, and scornful glances, from those with whom she had always been used to exchange daily courtesies. All day she was made the subject of mysterious looks and whisperings; the air was full of distrust and mystery; and before night, without knowing wherefore, she felt that she was being treated like a culprit. As for Tilda Stade, awful was her silence. Nothing could be more awful, except the silence of Tabitha Mallane; for, the moment that she witnessed Paul knock at Seth Goodlove's door, she resolved to be silent, and in silence to execute a strategic movement, in a small way, worthy of Napoleon. In that moment Aunt Comfort's legacy was consecrated to the annihilation of the girl across the street; the vegetable garden was sacrificed, and the white house painted tea-green.

If Paul's ardor and steadfastness of devotion suffered any diminution after his return to Boston, he was not conscious of it. To be sure, there was a difference—and he felt it—between love-making beside a lovely river on a soft September day, and love-making in a small room filled with the smell of soup, of soap-suds, and of smoke. There was a charm in walking with Eirene along the grassy road, amid the secluded hills, which he missed walking with her on the Busyville street, with all Busyville staring at him. But Eirene was no less Eirene because of the Busyville eye and a smoky "dummy." The enchantment of that last September had not yet faded so far but that he saw it and felt it, even through the Goodlove smells and smoke. He looked at Eirene's picture, and was comforted.

But a little more opposition would have been stimulating. He had been used to being opposed, and then doing as he pleased. It had a depressing effect on him to be let alone. There was nothing that he missed more than the opposition of his mother.

"If mother would only go on as she begun, what a zest it would give a fellow to take his own way!" he said.

Then, as Spring came on, after a really hard winter's work, he began to want "a little variety"—a little of the exhilaration of comradeship that he used to feel when he and his chums went off for a "high old time." If they had only come to ask him, he would not have found it difficult to have said "No" on every necessary occasion; but he wanted at least the pleasure of refusing. It piqued him, not to be invited. His self-admiration was no longer a sufficing compensation for self-denial, much less for neglect. That was indeed a new state of affairs, when Paul Mallane was neglected or forgotten by his comrades. The truth was, they had been refused so often during the winter, that they had grown tired of coming.

"Let him alone, boys, for a while," said Dick Prescott. "Just leave him to love and to law, and, if he finds himself left alone to support one by the other, he'll be glad enough to forsake both. But not if you oppose him. Oppose him, and he'll hang to both with a death-grasp. I can tell you, Prince Mallane is the last fellow on earth to submit to being left out. Let him alone, and you'll see how soon he'll get tired of it."

If Dick Prescott's words had been

false—if Paul could have gone on with the same perseverance with which he began—he and Eirene would have been married; they would have "lived happy ever afterwards," and this story would never have been written.

Alas for love, when the mind begins to assure the heart that it is unchanged—that it is as fresh, as fervent, as absolute, and as all-sufficing, as it used to be! This very assurance is born of a doubt. The all-satisfying love can neither be questioned nor assured; it is sufficient unto itself and unto all things.

Perhaps it was not Paul's fault that his mind was facile and mercurial.

"I love you, little girl, just the same as ever. I never loved you better than I do this moment," he said, looking at her picture. "I am going to spend my life with you, and, when you are my wife, I am sure I shall never feel the want of any other company. But why should I make a martyr of myself so long before?"

This would have been far from a dangerous question for a man of a more equable temperament to have asked; but when Paul put it, from the depths of a restless mind, he had no consciousness whatever that the very law of his moods was in extremes; that the blessed medium of consistency was something that he rarely touched, and never maintained.

As, in the winter, he had secluded himself from healthy companionship in an altogether unnecessary manner, and prided himself on so doing to a very unreasonable degree, now, in the restlessness of reaction, he was ready to rush to an opposite extreme, and justify himself for so doing in an equally unreasonable degree.

He was in just this state, really mentally tired with new and hard work, and personally tired of being left to himself, and anxious for the fresh excitement so indispensable to such a temperament, when his mother appeared at Cambridge.

To this moment, in the utterly new and exquisite consciousness of being loyal to one woman, and this woman his promised wife, Paul had given Miss Isabella Prescott to understand, by his manner, that he was preoccupied; whether with law or with love, he left for her to decide; but, whatever her decision, that it was perfectly useless for her to make further coquettish advances. His cool indifference piqued her till she hated him. In the privacy of her own room she indulged in all sorts of feminine rages on his behalf. She stamped her feet and ground her teeth, and, one night, after a party, frightened Dick nearly out of his wits by taking laudanum enough to make her sick, and by declaring, between her spasms, that she "wanted to die—that she would die; or, if she couldn't, that she would live only to punish him for snubbing her, and for sitting in a corner all the evening with that *old* Helena Maynard."

After Mrs. Mallane's visit to Marlboro Hill, Paul drifted slowly and insensibly back towards his old relations with the Prescotts. If their visit to Busyville had not been a settled thing, it would have been different; but, this anticipated, it was a perpetual reminder, and a most fruitful source of communication. Mrs. Mallane was continually sending messages to Bella by Paul, which, of course, involved a visit to Marlboro. Then, Bella had as many to send back; and, as Paul knew it, he would often ride over after tea, just to mention that "he was going to write," and "had she any word to send to mother?" Paul understood his mother's whole game perfectly. He could not be enlightened as to what the metamorphosed house and the Prescott visit both meant. There was a keen excitement in it. It was like a play at the theatre; and, as it was only a play, Paul enjoyed the exhilaration of being the hero, with the power to bring it to a conclusion to suit his own pleasure.

Under these circumstances, it came to pass that he went oftener and stayed later and later at Marlboro Hill. Why was it that, when he returned to his room late at night, the soft eyes looking down upon him from the wall seemed to be full of tears? Why was it that he began to justify himself to that gentle face?—to declare to it that he loved it the same as ever, and loved it alone?—that, in his heart, all he wanted was the power to flee with it to the end of the earth? Nobody had accused him of other desires or intentions, yet it seemed to reproach him more and more, until he felt sometimes that he must turn and run from it. He was conscious that a spell was cast around him. Now that he knew what love was, he knew that it was not love; yet it was no less a spell. There was fascination in the fact that Isabella Prescott had fallen in love with him. "Poor girl, I pity her!" he said to himself. "So young, with so much to live for, with such opportunities for choice in marriage, to think that she should turn from all, to really care for me! Dear little Belle! I did not think her capable of caring so much for any one. She never showed any signs of it before; and if she should never see any one else that she could love so well, if she should never marry on my account, I should feel as if I had been the cause of destroying her happiness. Well, I'll make all the amends to her that I can."

He was so assiduous in making amends, and withal felt so many self-reproaches for being quite so ardent in this direction, that at last he came to glance at the picture on the wall with an attempt at reproach. "If I had not been so unfortunate as to have loved you," he said, "I might have married naturally and happily in my own sphere. If it were not for you, poor Belle would not now be so miserable; for, if I did not love you (and I do), I could care considerably for her; she is certainly attractive."

At this distance from Eirene, it made him feel more comfortable, some way, to think that she had marred Bella's life, and, however unwittingly, was the cause of her unhappiness. As that was the case, and he loved Eirene and did not love Bella, he could and should be all the more tenderly kind to her, in consideration of the affection which she lavished upon him. The supreme September of love faded to a dream. The summer of Marlboro was an alluring reality. The stars above its park, the moonlight on its lake, its cool, luxurious halls, and their drooping mistress, pallid and lovely in the moonlight, were all of the present, and, with all the power of the present, enchained his imagination and his senses.

Potent, also, was the force of contrast. Hillside—poor, shabby Hillside, with its unfortunate inmates—how did it look, compared with Marlboro Hill?

"Beautiful June! Was there ever such a June!" said Eirene. Busyville emerged from the cold rains of a Massachusetts May a transfigured Busyville. The great elms stretched their wide arms and covered with greenery the staring sharpness and whiteness of its houses; they wove cool roofs of shadow above the village-streets; they joined the willows in the meadow along the river's side, and made a perfect embowered arcade of Lover's Walk. Almost every village has its Lover's Walk. This of Busyville was the only perfect thing in it. In this gossiping town, strange to say, it was without reproach; probably because the village-folk were too prosaic to people it with ghosts and tragedies. It was a decorous and friendly Lover's Walk, which divided its delicious shade with the young academicians who walked there studying their lessons, with youths and maidens who walked there whispering love, and with bands of shouting children who rushed through it, "going a-berrying" the nearest way. Yet, what stories it might have told, this little grass-bordered path, running in and out among the elms and willows, beginning with a village-street, and ending where the river ran dark and deep and alone!

It must be confessed that, in this month of June, Eirene neglected the study of French. It is true, she took her "Corinne" with her, and, as she wandered on, always attempted to translate it. But, with her, knowledge has ceased to be the supreme power; and as to the story, what was the romance in the book compared with the romance in her pocket, shut within the perfumed folds of that marvellous letter? What were Oswald and Lucy, or the incomparable Corinne, while Paul lived, and loved her, and wrote her letters, and was coming in August! Not much. She always began her walk studying; she always ended it reading for the hundredth time, very likely, that letter. What a letter it was! Written anew every day, its burden never changed. It was ardent, passionate, and tender, with the ardor, passion, and tenderness of a young man's first, absorbing love. It had but one object—that, to make her realize how infinitely dear to him she was. He described the life of the city—the drawing-rooms of Beacon-street and of Marlboro Hill—the gay beauties who assembled there—till they all appeared in panorama before her eyes; but it was only that he might declare, "Amid them all, I think only of you. Everywhere I am alone, because you are not here." With this letter in her pocket, its words graven in her heart, Eirene would return to the little chamber, and she no longer saw that it was low, or dusty, or hot. She no longer spent her evenings here, as she had done last summer. She knew nothing of the path by the river-side then. It was Paul who had told her of it as a pleasant retreat—one of his own from boyhood. Of course, he did not think it necessary to add, that he had carried on more flirtations in this path, told more pretty falsehoods in it, than any other young man in Busyville. It was very soothing to Eirene to take refuge under the softly-murmuring trees from Tilda Stade's reproving face; for, though she left Eirene alone in speech, with many a glance and groan she said, "You are lost—hopelessly, eternally lost." This was not a very enlivening assurance to have flung perpetually in one's face. Thus, what wonder that Eirene, beside the river, took refuge in "Corinne" and her letter? Since he had extinguished her at the Camp-Meeting, Tilda had never mentioned Paul's name; but whenever she saw a letter—and she took pains to see one as often as possible, by rushing to the Post-Office and bringing it to Eirene with her own hand—she groaned. By this groan she informed Eirene that she understood the exact state of affairs, and had in no wise changed her opinion. Eirene's portfolio lying within reach one day, as Tilda sat alone, she opened it and took from it a letter of Paul's, and read it from beginning to end. Her conscience pricking her during the process, she exclaimed, "I do it for her good. Unless I know her exact case, how can I befriend her in the end? I shall never tell any body what I know. It's the same as if it were buried. Marry her? Hum! I think I see him!" Then Tilda kneeled down, and fervently prayed the Lord to forgive her if she had erred in reading the letter, for He knew that she did it for Eirene's good!

In absence there is no barometer of love like a letter; it inevitably bears within it something of the unconscious atmosphere of its writer—one sure to be felt by the heart to whom it is addressed, although it may not be understood.

July came, and Eirene began to wonder why she felt as if she must burst into tears when she had finished reading one of Paul's letters. They were still full of protestations of love, but these were no longer coupled with bright prospects of the future. Instead, there were constant allusions to their unfortunate destiny.

Two months before, how bright and brave these letters had been! In them Paul had declared himself strong enough to conquer any fate for her dear sake; but now, Eirene was filled with a vague apprehension, without knowing wherefore. Then her loving heart travelled back to the last September, and tried to assure her that August, the dear August so near at hand, would set every thing right, and bring back once more the enchantment of life. Yet, in spite of youth and hope and love, her heart misgave her sometimes, when she looked on the beautiful house across the street —Paul's home—and realized that she was shut out.

"I wish it were all different, darling," said Paul; and as he looked into the beseeching eyes upturned to his face, that moment he did.

August had come. Paul had only reached Busyville that morning. It was evening, and he and Eirene were in Lover's Walk. He had just told her of the expected visit of his friends, who were to arrive the next day. He went on to say:

"I had nothing to do with it. It is mother's work. She came to Boston and invited them. In one way and another I am under obligations to the Prescotts, especially for their hospitality. I visited at Marlboro Hill before I ever saw you. So, when mother gave her invitation, and they accepted it, I could do nothing but second it; and now I cannot do less than make their visit agreeable in every way in my power. It is an actual debt that I owe them, Eirene."

"Yes," said Eirene, "I see how it is. I would not have you do otherwise, if I could. I am wrong, I know, to feel at all disappointed. I mean—I think—I should be glad to have you go about with them a great deal, if we could visit a little together—only a little—as we did last September. Then I shouldn't get lonesome."

"But that would be impossible, if they were not coming at all, child;" and Paul's voice grew hard, and unconsciously chilled her. "We were at Hilltop, then. I was trouting in Arcadia when I told you those beautiful stories. God knows, I wish they were all true to-day. But we are in Busyville now. I can't meet you here often, without setting a hundred scandalous tongues wagging. You see——"

Paul was going to say, "You see, they always did say such things if they saw me with shop-people;" and he might have added, "with good cause;" but he said, "You see, for some reason of their own, the people here expect that I will marry elsewhere. Thus, if they see me waiting upon any young lady in town, they always declare I do it with some nefarious design. You are to be my wife. I love you, yet at present I cannot protect you; that is reason enough why I should not bring one shadow of reproach upon you, my darling. If I walked with you here, while my mother refused to invite you to her house, you see how people would talk——"

Eirene grew pale. She was trying to accept it, to understand it—this hard fact, striking into the face of her dream. All she had actually known of Paul's society had been by the peaceful river and in the sheltered room at home; she had not realized before that she could not enjoy something of the same intercourse here. The demon of "people's talk" had never risen before her mind; but, now that Paul spoke of it, she remembered the gossip which she herself often heard in the shop, and knew that what he said was true. It was not to be; perhaps she could not see him at all; but that he was compelled to tell her that she was not recognized by his own mother, was hard. Then she remembered how he had thought that in one year it would all be different; that now was the time when he had promised to acknowledge her before the world as his affianced wife. Perhaps he read the thought on her white and silent face; for he said,

"I believed that by this time I could have acknowledged our relation to every body; but circumstances have been too strong for me. I am not yet independent. Until I am, we must wait, my darling. It won't be long. When I am fairly established, then it will all come true, the lovely life that I planned last summer."

All the light came back into her eyes as he mentioned the life of the last summer.

"I could wait forever," she said, "for ease and fortune. The luxury you told about, Paul, don't seem to belong to me. I was happy while you were away. I did not expect to see you; but to see you every day, and yet to be scarcely able to speak with you—to see you all the time with others, while I long for your society so much, will make me so lonely, Paul, I'm afraid I sha'n't know how to bear it at first; but I will try. Maybe it will not be so hard by-and-by. Only now I am so disappointed. I thought we were going to be so happy. It's so different from what I expected."

"Yet it is not so different from any thing that you might have expected, if you had taken all the circumstances into consideration," said Paul, in his most practical voice, which sounded all the harder because he himself felt annoyed by these very circumstances, and was really distressed by the pain visible on the lovely face before him. Of course, in his irritation he forgot altogether that in every letter that he had written her he had given her reason to expect every thing to be different in this visit from the present reality. She had never before heard this tone in his voice, when he had spoken to her. How full of supplication and tenderness it had always been!

It was almost as if the beloved hand had struck her a blow. The swift tears rose to her eyes; with silent force of will she held them back, and a quiver in her voice alone betrayed her emotion, as she spoke:

"I have expected too much—more than it is in your power to grant me. It is because I love you."

"You haven't expected more than I want to give you, nor one tenth of what you deserve," said Paul, passionately and penitently, feeling again the old impulse to snatch her in his arms and carry her off, away from all the world; for it seemed to him that only away from the world could he be absolutely true to her and worthy of her. "If it wasn't for my cursed life, my cursed——" position, he was going to say; but in an instant he felt ashamed to mention it. "If I was not tangled on every side, darling, it would be so different. But I'll tell you every thing. I know you would forgive me, no matter what I did. I am in debt. Before I knew you, I spent more than my allowance. I associated with rich young men, who gave suppers, made bets, and wasted their money; I did the same. Now, darling, I'm reaping the consequences. I can't marry till I get out of debt. The very day that I do, I can begin life anew, and with you. You will wait for me, won't you, precious? No matter what you see, no matter how hard things may seem, you will believe in me and love me, won't you?"

"I will." And never had the woman-gaze been so tender and trusting and entire, as it was while the girl uttered these words and looked into his face.

The influence of her spirit on his was to call forth every generous impulse latent in it. Paul Mallane never owned his shortcomings to any body else; but it really was a delight to him to confess his sins to her. It made him think better of himself while he was doing it; and, while he looked into her eyes, he felt capable of the noblest actions, and actually meant and believed that he would do every thing that he promised her. "I don't deserve such devotion, you lovely one!" he exclaimed, as all the mean thoughts and regrets of the last month rushed into his mind. "I wonder that you do, that you can, love me, when I think of myself as I really am. But I love you. No matter what happens, believe this, that I love you as I never loved before, as I shall never love again; that you are the only woman I ever saw whom I wished to be my wife. Promise me you will believe this." And, as he uttered these words, Paul snatched her into his arms, and kissed her forehead, her eyes, her mouth, with something like the prescience of despair running through each, that, as it was the first time, so it would be the last; and as the thought struck his heart, it seemed to him that he could never unclose his arms and let her go.

They had come to the end of the walk, where the river bent and ran on both sides of the great willows, which hung down to the water. It ran swift and dark and wide here towards the dam, a little further on. Its rush, and the cry of the whippoorwill high overhead, gave a weird quality to the moment, the dim moment of a midsummer twilight. Paul held the face that he loved up in the soft light. One lingering gaze, one kiss more, long and silent, then, without a word, he took her hand in his, and they walked back. When they came out into the village the stars were shining above the great elms, and hundreds of couples were sauntering to and fro under their shadows. The towering form of Paul Mallane could not be mistaken. Many recognized him, and a few the girl in white by his side.

It was told in more than one shop, the next day, that "Paul Mallane had been out walking with that Vale girl again, and it was plain enough to see that it was for no good."

The next evening, just as the last sunrays were brightening the beautiful garden across the street, Eirene sat by her window, alone. It seemed to her that she was dreaming, and she tried to think back and make life seem to her as it did before Paul kissed her. She still felt those kisses upon her eyelids, her lips, her brow. It seemed to her as if they still rested there, the seal of his love.

"This is love," she said. "How wonderful! I read of it, but I knew nothing of it. How could any one ever write or tell what love is? I only know, when I think what it would be to me now to live without it. How did I live, and not unhappily, when nobody cared for me—when nobody would have missed me or have mourned for me if I had died—nobody, I mean, but those at home. I could not be so peaceful now, if no one cared for me—if nobody thought of me and missed me, as I miss Paul. Oh, if I could only see him every day—if I could go into the garden with him and look at those flowers in the vases—if I could go into the house and look at all the pretty things! I like to look at pretty things. If I could go and come, as Miss Prescott will! And we cannot walk any more by the river! I would not, if I could not see him as a friend elsewhere. But if he cannot come here, and I cannot go into his home, we cannot meet any more. When you are so near, how can I live without you, Paul? Oh, you thought we should be so happy in August!" And her heart gave a sudden cry, and she lifted her hand involuntarily, as if to hold the remembered kisses upon her face. "I'm so lonely, Paul!" she said, in a broken voice.

Just then a span of magnificent bays in white trappings pranced up to the house opposite. The carriage which they drew was so much more splendid than any Eirene had ever seen before, that for an instant she was too dazzled to distinguish Paul sitting on the back seat with a lady, while in front was a gentleman with Grace. This moment Momo, in the further window, having just caught the name from Eirene's lips, began to cry, "Paul! pretty Paul!" with undiminished vehemence. The lady in the carriage looked up, saw the parrot, saw Eirene. Isabella Prescott immediately recognized "the shop-girl;" and the shop-girl, looking down upon that face turned full upon her, knew instinctively, without knowing wherefore, that she looked into the eyes of an enemy.

"Why, how glad this parrot is to see you! And who is that pretty girl?" asked Bell of Paul.

"Her name is Vale," said Paul, hurriedly.

Before this, the footman had opened the carriage-door, and Tabitha Mallane had appeared in the veranda of the tea-green mansion, arrayed in Aunt Comfort's best silk.

The air was full of gay words and laughter. A light, mocking laugh came back to Eirene as the party disappeared in the house. Never in her life before had Eirene heard any thing so mocking as this laugh. It struck her heart, and she felt a new and utterly unknown sensation—the pang of love, jealousy. It is not true that perfect love, if human, casts out fear. All human experience proves otherwise. Her love was complete, but the conditions under which she loved were cruel.

Immediately and intuitively she realized the immense advantage possessed by the woman who had looked up at her and mocked her with a laugh. She even overrated them, so humble was she in her opinion of herself. To see a highly-wrought, passionate woman jealous, is often a grand picture; for there may be sublimity in a mental and emotional storm as well as in a material one. But to see a gentle nature struck to the heart by this demon, is a sorrowful sight; there is no thunder and lightning and wrath to sustain the energy of such a one, but only tears, and silent, unutterable anguish. Such a woman struck by jealousy is like a dumb animal that has received its death-wound. Eirene sat silent, as if paralyzed. In an instant all joy seemed to be struck out of her life, and she to be alone on earth. But Momo, who was thoroughly wide awake, and evidently excited by the unwonted appearance of the new-comers across the street, continued to scream, "Paul! pretty Paul!" He brought Eirene back suddenly "to a realizing sense," as Tilda would have called it. "You sing for spite—you sing for doom!" she would undoubtedly have exclaimed had she been a theatrical young lady; but as she was only a simple, suffering girl, whom a new anguish had suddenly stung into a nervous irritation before unknown to her nature, she only walked quickly to the window and took the cage from the ledge, with Momo still screaming to the most piercing limit of his voice. "Hush! hush!" she exclaimed. "Momo, you shall never mortify me again; you shall go and sit in the back yard for——ever!"

Here came a long, deep sob, and she sank vanquished by the first blow of her new enemy.

"What on earth is the matter?" said Tilda, an hour or two later, when, as she returned from prayer-meeting, she stumbled over the cage in the middle of the floor, and, lighting the candle, found Momo in deep disgrace, with his head muffled in his feathers, and Eirene with her head buried in the bed.

"Nothing," said Eirene, lifting a white face from the pillow, "only I'm not feeling quite well. Momo was so noisy in the window, I set him there. I shall keep him in the yard hereafter." And with these words she arose, and quietly walked out of the room with the cage.

"Oh, no; nothing's the matter!" muttered Tilda, as she sat down by the open window, grimly planting her elbows on her knees and her chin in her hands; "nothing's the matter; only those cussed—(may the Lord forgive me!)—those *cussed* Boston folks have come. I saw 'em drive up this mornin' in a circus-coach, it looked like to me; and the snip had her hat full of feathers, and the feller looked as if he ought to be spanked; and I thanked goodness the child was in the shop and couldn't see 'em; but she has seen 'em and heard 'em, and heard the peanner goin', and the poor baby all alone in the dark! Now, we'll see what we shall see. I'll see if he'll keep the promise he made in that letter, and marry her. If he don't, may the Lord—— If he does, he'll be the death of her. I told her so. *Why* didn't she get religion! Then he'd 'a' had to have stayed with his own kind, for all of comin' to break her heart!"

It was past midnight when the music and mirth in the drawing-room across the street ceased, and Isabella Prescott retired to the apartment assigned to her for the night. It was Eirene's old room, into which two others had been thrown. Bella was seated by the same window where Eirene sat when Paul contemplated her from under the cherry-tree. But her gaze was not turned outward; she was busy scanning the furniture by the searching gas-light, which had taken the place of Eirene's tallow candle.

"Every thing smells as if it had just come out of a varnish-shop," she said, as she sniffed her nose contemptuously. "New, stark, staring new, every article in the room. I see they have taken some lessons from Marlboro—bought every thing as dark and rich as possible; but veneering, varnish, and new oils, are not to be repressed. Ugh! I shall smother. If I don't, how I shall look in the morning, after breathing such air all night! And it is quite necessary that I should look my best—languid, slightly pale, but still my best," she said, proceeding to the glass and commencing to practise her usual faces. "The shop-girl has more of a face than I was quite prepared to see," she soliloquized, as she went on putting her hair into crimps. "Not a common face, certainly—a face that I would make havoc with myself, if I were a young man. I like to do it justice—absolute justice; then I can take so much the more credit to myself as an artist, when I triumph over it and crush it; for I intend to crush it. I'll pay you, Miss Shop, for interfering with a Prescott!"

Miss Prescott was perfectly well aware what she was doing when she brought her carriage and horses, coachman and footman, to Busyville. Dick remonstrated—said it was parvenuish, and unworthy of their high estate; but Miss Isabella declared that "she didn't care;" and she didn't. What she did care for, was to impress upon the mind of a vulgar town her own magnificence, for the establishment was her own. "It is useless to object, Dick," she said; "I'm not going to be jolted about in their old country arks. I'm so delicate!" Thus the Prescott bays and barouche issued from the village livery-stable every evening, and passed through the village-street, the wonder and the envy of the natives. A European war, or the "abolition of slavery," could not have plunged the villagers into such a state of personal excitement.

"It is plain enough to see why such people visit the Mallanes. They have a son!" said the Brahmins, with uplifted noses.

"What does Brother and Sister Mallane expect is goin' to become of their souls, encouragin' such pomps and vanities, and a-settin' such an example!" said the Bustlers. But in both classes the seed of Isabella Prescott's vanity reaped an abundant harvest. For six months after, Busyville boasted that it had more dashing teams than any other town in the county.

More than a week had passed, and Paul and Eirene had not spoken since the evening when they met in Lover's Walk. Yet she saw him every day—sometimes in the grand barouche, seated beside Miss Prescott; sometimes on Fleetfoot, with Miss Prescott, in an elegant habit, with a jaunty hat full of shining plumes, on another curvetting horse by his side, going or returning from their daily ride; sometimes in the veranda, reading to Miss Prescott; sometimes in the rustic seat under the old cherry-tree, chatting with Miss Prescott by the hour; but whenever or wherever she saw him, always with Miss Prescott. Outside of working-hours there was little refuge from this sight of him; for there was neither light nor air in Seth Goodlove's front chamber away from the window.

"Well," said Tilda, one evening, looking across the stand to Eirene, sitting in her old seat with her eyes fixed upon a piece of sewing, through which the needle seemed to pass faltering and slowly, "I will declare that you are sick, and shall go home. John Mallane gave you a vacation last year; why don't he do so this? You need it now enough sight more, goodness knows. I shall ask him myself to-morrow, and tell him, if you don't go, you'll be right sick; and you will. No, I won't tell him any such thing: I'll tell him you need rest, and must have it. I *will* say to you, Eirene Vale, that I never saw such a change in any person in one week in my life. I can't bear it, and ain't a-goin' to try. I hate him so, I do. Oh, I'm losing my religion. I've lost my enjoyment. I ha'n't had the evidence for a week. *That's* the harm it's doin' me, Eirene Vale; and it's killing you. I told you so. I told you so. Heed me you wouldn't."

The face had, indeed, changed, which looked back to Tilda without a word. The roundness, the peachy bloom of the cheek, the unquestioning trust of the eyes, were gone. Experience and pain had done the work of years. It was suffering which had struck out the first fresh tints of youth. It was like an untimely frost on a Spring flower. There was a tension about the mouth, a depth in the eyes, never seen there before. The dreaming girl had gone forever; in her place was the woman.

"I am sorry, Tilda, you should feel troubled about me," she said, in a strangely quiet tone. "I am not as well as usual. I will ask Mr. Mallane myself, to-morrow, to let me go home for a week. I will go and walk a little way now. I think the air will do me good."

Eirene had been gone but a few moments, when Paul Mallane knocked at the open door below.

In the back room Mrs. Goodlove was washing the tea-dishes, amid a flock of quarreling children. The whole air of the place was hot as an oven. The heat in the front room, with the smell of the last winter's smoke and of yesterday's cabbage, was stifling to Paul; while Mrs. Goodlove, with her sleeves above her elbows and a greasy apron on, began to rattle and roll up a torn paper-curtain while she asked him to be seated, adding, that she would go and see if Eirene was in. By this time Tilda, who had seen Paul come across the street, leaned over the balusters, where, through the open door, she looked him directly in the face, and exclaimed, in no dulcet tone,

"You needn't come here, Paul Mallane. Eirene Vale is not in; and if she was, she would not see you."

"Thank you," said Paul, and walked deliberately out. As he left the house, he observed Bella in an airy robe of azure sitting in the garden veranda and joined her. Not long after, Eirene, coming down the street, saw the two sitting there, and they saw her. As she looked up, Paul bowed; but there was a remoteness that could not be measured in the recognition. Had he been on the other side of the earth, he could not have seemed further away. Still, upon her face she felt his kisses, and she said,

"One week ago he called me his promised wife. Can this be he?"

Paul, looking after her, noted the slight form, the weary step, the plain dress, the white sun-bonnet hiding her face, and said,

"She is the woman I have promised to marry, and she lives in that horrid place!"

He looked at the woman by his side, her fair hair gleaming through a net of silver thread; at the transparent robe of blue, in whose elegant fabric and fashion Paris seemed to have surpassed itself; at the delicate hands glittering with gems; at the woman whom poverty and pain and care had never touched, sitting perfectly picturesque in her summer setting of flowers and vines, and he felt the contrast. It is doubtful if the fairest woman knows how much she may owe to her graceful and gracious surroundings. It is difficult for the loveliest of women to realize how much she may lose because her beauty struggles into flower in a harsh atmosphere and amid vulgar associations. Eirene, as she stepped into Seth Goodlove's odoriferous hall, felt the pang in her heart, without knowing one half of her disadvantages. The beauty of her soul and of her face had been so potent as to command love in defiance of conditions the most repelling to a man like Paul Mallane. He loved Eirene, and did not love the woman by his side; yet her art, with the glamor of her accompaniments, were powerful enough to hold him from the woman that he loved. Bella saw Eirene, and Paul's following and returning glance, and understood it. She was perfectly aware of her own immense advantage, and made the most of it. How was Paul to know that the perfect picture which she made, with the very effect that it had upon himself, was the result of hours and days of study? for the most diplomatic of men is an unsuspecting infant before the small but occult arts of an artful woman. Paul looked at Bella, and saw only the pale, transparent skin, the shy, deprecating, appealing air which had enchanted him for the last month. She was no longer arch and tantalizing; never mentioned the shop-girl, nor teased him about "a little loveress." No; she was so utterly drooping and submissive, so pleadingly tearful. She made him feel all the time that he had done her an injury in not asking her to marry him; and he was still busy making her amends.

"It won't be long before she will be gone," he said to himself; "then I can go back and ask my little girl's pardon. I'll tell her just how it has been; and she will forgive me, when she sees how much I'm sacrificing to marry her." Paul was not in an enviable state of mind. No man ever is who is doing his best to divide himself between two women. Through all these days of utter neglect he had not been without a desire to see Eirene. While seeming utterly oblivious of her, more than once he had looked through the closed blinds of his own room to the utterly uninviting house across the street, and helplessly wished that there were some place where he could visit with Eirene, as he did during the last summer.

"What's the use of going over there?" he asked. "There's that dragon forever on the watch. And if she were not, it's enough to put the sentiment out of any man, to try and talk love amid such a clatter of pots and young ones, with more than the seven smells of Cologne pushing through the door to knock him over. I might meet her in Lover's Walk every evening, and keep her poor little heart assured, at the expense of all the slander that Busyville could concoct," he said. "But I won't. I won't be a scamp—not to her. If I don't keep her sweet heart from aching, I'll keep her pure name from blame."

I am aware that I am throwing away a fine opportunity of showing Paul Mallane to be a villain. According to the way of novels, he should flirt with Isabella Prescott, and promise to marry her by day; write to Eirene secretly, meet her clandestinely, pursue her, ruin her, and forsake her. The world has had too many of such pictures. If Paul Mallane were such a villain, I should not be writing about him. It would be sad enough for the race that he lived, without perpetuating his picture. Paul Mallane was a man with the possibility in him of a high nobility, which his mother, the prevailing power in his life, had never fed or fostered. He is a thoroughly defective character—one who has missed goodness, as in higher or lower degree we all miss it. The sorrow that he wrought came from the defects and discrepancies of his own nature, not from any deliberate purpose to do a great wrong. The consummate villain, the piercing-eyed gentleman of unutterably diabolical attributes, spends his existence chiefly in the novel. I never saw him, therefore I shall not put him in mine.

There was no end to Tabitha Mallane's projects for the enjoyment of the young people. Every day she planned some new picnic, fishing-party, or excursion, all of which Isabella Prescott pronounced to be "lovely," and most reviving to her spirits and delicate health. This was delightful to Mrs. Tabitha, who declared that the dear child must stay till her health should be perfectly restored. At the end of the week Dick took himself off; but Miss Prescott seemed no nearer departing than on the day of her coming. This evening, Paul's desire to see Eirene, quickened by many pricks of conscience, overcame his dislike and dread of the Goodlove house sufficiently to impel him to go across the street to see her. The conviction came suddenly to him, the longer he put off an explanation, the harder it would be to make it; and that moment he wished it were over, and that Bella Prescott were out of the way. But the atmosphere of the house, and Tilda Stade's reception, made him feel as if any intercourse with Eirene at present was impossible. He did not believe a word of Tilda's speech, yet something in him made him glad that she said what she did; it seemed to afford him an excuse for his actions.

Tilda, having given vent to her temper, was quite willing to believe that she did it "from a sense of duty;" but the same "sense" did not incline her to inform Eirene that Paul had called at the house and inquired for her. Presently she went away, and left Eirene alone with her thoughts, and the couple on the opposite veranda, now growing shadowy in the twilight. Eirene gave one glance at them, and then took refuge from the sight in the dimness of the room.

"How near you seemed to me in Cambridge, Paul!" she said; "but within sound of your voice, with only the street between us, it seems as if the universe divided you and me—as if I should never speak with you again."

Soon the piano sent forth the notes of the sweetest air in "Martha," and the melody drew her involuntarily to the window. All that she knew of music was in emotion; this in her was a deep interpreter; it thrilled her, moved her, filled her with bliss or pain. No music had ever seemed so sweet, and yet so sorrowful, as this, coming in to her as she sat alone. It came from him, from her; they were enjoying it together, and she was shut out. Before she knew, she felt herself moving towards it. She looked; the night was dark; no one could see her—no one, not even if she slipped into the garden and listened. There, although no one welcomed her, she would not be so entirely shut away. She stole softly down across the street, and looked around. Nobody was near. She slipped through the side-gate, on to the turf, crossed it to the old cherry-tree, and then looked up. The long windows of the drawing-room were wide open. There was no one in it but Paul and Miss Prescott, who was sitting before the piano playing. She was evidently perfectly familiar with the opera, for Paul was not turning over the leaves of her music. Instead, he was leaning on the piano near, gazing intently at her. She played on and on, air after air, and all were of an infinite tenderness, imploring, pathetically sweet. There were long pauses between the music, when Paul leaned nearer to the player in the dim light. and his low tones, with the soft, tremulous cadences of her speech, wandered out to the motionless watcher in the garden. It is a pretty parlor-picture, isn't it?—the handsome young gentleman and lady in the luxurious room, sitting in a tender attitude, certainly, discoursing of music, perhaps! It is not at all a heart-rending scene to describe. Strange it should have transfixed into a marble whiteness the girl in the garden. She was a foolish little girl, you see, and had much better have been up in the Goodlove bed, sound asleep. It is not much to tell about; it is only a true soul dying its first death in life, in its first desolation of distrust in the being whom it believed to be truth itself. It is only a young, loving, faithful heart aching out there in the darkness; that is all.

. . . . . . . . .

"Of course you may go," said John Mallane to Eirene the next morning, as she stood by the desk in his office. "Bless me, child! what's happened to you? Why didn't you ask me before, if you were sick? You need the mountain-air. Go, and stay as long as you please."

## A WOMAN'S RIGHT.

### X.

THE CRISIS

Again the Summer holds the hills in splendor. Her cloud-fleets sail down the infinite ocean as peacefully as they did one year ago; her forests sway and murmur in as deep content; her apples redden in the hill-side orchard; her corn waves its tassels; her tobacco holds up its cups of amber in the sun, just the same. Again Eirene sits by the window; but she does not watch the clouds, or count the tobacco-stalks, or build palaces in dreams. Her eyes are fixed upon the road where it emerges from the woods. Where is the horse with the arching neck, and the gallant rider, of one year ago? Sustaining the drooping spirits of Miss Prescott, probably. Yet Eirene's gaze does not wander till the white road fades in the evening shadow. With the coming morning she renews her watch, saying, "Paul, you will come to-day." So hard is it for youth and truth to let go of its faith. How many times her heart has fluttered like a bird's, at the sight of Fleetfoot and his handsome rider, coming eagerly along that road to her! How many times, with lingering, loving looks, that rider has turned reluctantly away! How could she believe that he would never come again? How could she make it seem that she should never hear more the thud of Fleetfoot's feet upon the little bridge? The scene in the garden, the last week of neglect, seems a dream—here in the spot where she has been so happy—where he once enveloped and glorified her with his love! Thus each morning she said again, "This day will bring a letter, or he will come." But the days wore on; no letter came, and no Paul. At last she unlocked the little box that held every letter he had ever written her. How well she knew each one, and just at what time he had written this, or this! Here was one in which he told her that, although surrounded by the brilliant and the beautiful, he was solitary and miserable because she was not there. Here was another, in which he wrote her that every pulse in his being trembled with joy because he was coming to be happy in her presence. She read them over, and tried to make them seem true once more. Her mind was as troubled as her heart, for its essence was truth. If these words were true—and she felt them to be true when he uttered them—how could they mean nothing now? If he loved her enough to seek her as he did, how could he forsake her to-day? This child, with her affections rooted in constancy, could realize nothing of the moods of a man moved by every fluctuating circumstance. She had not grown to that knowledge of the heart where she could say, "He had many natures. I think he loved me well with one." Soon the slender fingers began to untie the ribbon which bound the precious packet, then tremble and fail and at last falteringly tie them up again, and, without reading a word, put them back. Ardent, passionate, and tender, how would they seem to her now, in the desolation in which she sat! Herein he had said, over and over again, that he never could be happy when she was not near. Yet this very moment, while she sat thinking of him, missing, needing him, as in all her life she had never missed or needed any one before, was he not entirely occupied and absorbed by another? Already she felt through her being the keenest suffering which can come to a perfectly truthful nature—distrust of the one loved best. Believe me, there is no pang like this. More than happiness was taken from her, more than love

—faith in the man who had represented to her all that was highest and brightest in manhood.

She could not utter one word in the presence of her family that might cast the faintest reproach upon Paul. They knew her trouble was in some way connected with him; for he did not come, and they could not forget the last summer, nor that the time had arrived when he had promised to claim Eirene as his wife. But they saw the white and watchful face, and respected its sorrow too much to ask questions. Each one said, silently, "Can this be our Eirene?" and, by constant, nameless little acts of love, sought to prove the depth and tenderness of their sympathy.

Two weeks had gone by—two weeks in which every day had been a long, loving watch for one who did not come.

"She must be gone now," said Eirene. "He too, perhaps, has gone with her. I must go back; I have been idle too long!" As she said these words, she felt an infinite weariness, as if she could never take up her work again.

Yet, amid all, a faint hope awoke into life. If he was still there, waiting for her, he would explain all. Had he not begged her, whatever happened, to believe in him, to love him, and to wait for him? She would.

Never before had Muggins looked so forlorn; never before had she moved quite so slowly. Apparently she had taken on the dejection of her dearest friend; and every dragging step which she took forwards seemed a protest against bringing Eirene back to the scene of her troubles. The impulse which impelled Muggins to do it cannot be explained; but just as she reached Mr. Mallane's gate, she stood perfectly still. Lowell Vale jerked the reins and implored her to "get up," but she would not stir. A light laugh from the veranda, in the mocking tones which she knew too well, gave Eirene a fainty feeling about her heart, as if it were going to stop beating. Before they reached the house, she had seen Bella and Grace sitting there, and it seemed all that she could do to live through going past them. To be stopped, to sit there helpless, an object for them to gaze upon and to laugh at, seemed more than could be borne. "Get up, Muggins!" Muggins only stuck her feet firmer and deeper in the dust, and stirred not.

"I am paid for coming to Busyville, if it were only to see such a horse! Where, where did it come from? I know it lived before Noah!" And as she uttered these words, in a penetrating tone which she knew reached the occupants of the buggy, Isabella Prescott laughed again, more mockingly than before.

"Don't," said Grace. "That's poor Mr. Vale. He's very poor, and father feels sorry for him. That's Eirene. She used to live with us. I like her, and so does Paul; but mother don't. I wouldn't hurt her feelings for the world. She is so kind to every body. Please don't laugh, Miss Prescott! You wouldn't, if you knew her."

"But I may laugh at the horse, mayn't I? Look at it!"

There was a picture. The rusty old buggy, and its occupants covered with dust, Lowell Vale jerking the reins, and calling upon Muggins to "get up;" Muggins standing stone still, save when the warning whip came down upon her back, when she gave a jump upward and a push backward, as if she were going to back herself all the way to Hill-top.

Just then the Prescott span and barouche drove towards the door for the evening drive. The extremes in the fortune of the girl upon the veranda and the girl in the buggy could hardly be contrasted more strongly than by the two opposing vehicles. The caparisoned bays, the liveried servants, the emblazoned carriage stood beside the poor old buggy and the vicious old horse, and the contrast brought the paltry triumph to its owner so dear to little souls.

Muggins monopolized the Mallane-gate and carriage-stand, and must be got out of the way. There was no help for it. Eirene must descend before them, with that cruel laugh still ringing through her brain. She did it with a bowed head; but as she reached the ground, the tones of the beloved voice made her lift it involuntarily; the very tone brought support and courage. Surely he would silence the mocking voice.

Paul had come to the door just in time to catch one of Muggins' most ridiculous antics. He might have laughed, had he not seen Eirene. His first impulse was the old one—to catch her up and carry her far away from all her hideous surroundings; his second was to go and assist her. He had taken the first step towards doing it, when Bella exclaimed:

"See! see! that atrocious beast is backing that old box into King Ferdinand's face! Oh! oh! they are going to run!"

"Don't be alarmed, Miss Prescott."

These were the words that Eirene heard in the assuring tone. They were not for her! They were not for her, in her loneliness and poverty—not for her, his promised wife; they were for the gay and mocking stranger.

An hour later, Eirene sat in her old chair, withdrawn from the window. She had just seen her father and Muggins depart. As she watched them move slowly away, her impulse was to follow, and implore her father to take her back. It seemed to her, that she could not be left behind—as if her last friend was leaving her; but with the consciousness that there was nothing for her but to be left, she became quiet, and followed them with her eyes till they were out of sight. Thus she sat, with her still white face, and her hands listlessly dropped upon her lap. Life seemed too dreadful to be borne. She had thought that they would all be gone—that her heart would no longer be tortured with so many mocking sights. She had hoped, fondly, timidly hoped, that, after all, Paul would have remained behind, to explain, to comfort her, to tell her why she had been left alone. But her enemy was still here, and she looked as if she were going to stay forever. This enemy mocked and ridiculed her yet. Paul's words of comfort were not for her; no, they were for her tormentor. Oh, wretchedness of love, and of youth! why couldn't she die!

The sound of wheels made her look up; and even where she sat she found that she could see Mr. Mallane's gate. For her own sake she knew that she ought to retreat further into the room; but a miserable fascination held her gaze. She did not see the barouche and the bays, but a light phæton with a single horse champing his bit, and striking his feet before it. Presently Paul and Miss Prescott came out of the house together, Paul with the young lady's wraps. How long it took him to adjust them in her carriage-seat! With what infinite pains he folded and refolded the great fleecy shawl over its slender bars, that they might not come in contact with that susceptible back! Not a man among her slaves but what felt at perfect liberty to encircle it, to give it the full benefit of the muscular support of his manly arm, while he heard the young lady murmur in pleading tones, as he often did,

"Oh, my back! it tires me so to ride! I feel as if I should faint."

And as she had the art of looking as if she were going to do so, and always began toppling from one side to the other, what could the most reserved of men do but support this feeble creature, if but out of human pity? Only it was remarkable how wonderfully she revived a moment after, of course to the great joy of her supporter. If he only could have seen her a few hours later, springing about her room with the agility of a cat, it would have afforded him a study in feminine backs sufficiently puzzling to have driven to despair any masculine brain. This moment Paul was making most tender provision for this omnipresent vertebra. How carefully he assisted her into her seat, the young lady who was so delicate! How assiduously he arranged the mat for her feet! How slowly he drew on his driving-gloves, took his seat by her side, took the reins in his hand, before the gay horse darted away and bore them out of sight!

It was all too much for the eyes of

the worn-out watcher in Seth Goodlove's chamber. She had seen it all. Some horrible spell drew her toward the window and held her there. Not a gesture, not an act, not a look of his had escaped her.

"She has been cruel to me," said the aching heart; "yet see how he serves her!" She uttered no cry, but she drew her hand across her forehead, as if to brush away the confusion in her brain. "Oh! he said he loved me—loved me alone," she murmured; "that his life began and ended in me; that I was soon to be his wife, and he my husband. He said, 'No matter what you see, nor how hard things may seem, still believe in me, and love me!' I will, Paul; but to be left alone, without one word, one look, one act of kindness, and to see you give all to this cruel stranger, is hard. What does it mean, Paul, if you love me—if I am to be your wife." Then, confused in thought, desolate in heart, she crept down from the chamber, out of the gate, and mechanically, without knowing wherefore, turned her feet towards the Lover's Walk. She had not been there since the evening that she walked in it with Paul. That evening, and its bliss, now sharply defined in her memory in contrast with the wretchedness of the present, seemed to draw her back irresistibly to the old haunt. She drew her sun-bonnet close over her face, that no one might see her, and hurried on. The grass was soft under her feet; the trees bent down and whispered to her, as in the happy June hours, but she was unconscious of their ministry. She did not pause till she came to the end of the Walk. Here Paul had kissed her, and uttered his last words to her.

The light was growing dim, and, with an instinctive dread of being seen here alone, she crept inside of the curtain which a wild vine had hung from tree to tree, and sat down upon the moss inside. A great willow held its canopy over her head and fanned her face with its pendants. On the other side, the river ran with deep, swift flow. As the willow-boughs swayed and opened, she could see it moving on. It seemed to invite her, to beckon her to come to it. How easy to lie down in its cool bosom, and be borne from all this trouble forever. If this were life, she was sure she could not bear it. How blessed to end it at once! What rest, what peace, there seemed to be in those cool, tranquil waters! How many thousands before her had felt the same temptation, and had yielded to it! What had come to them then? Ah, that was the question. The girl had moved to the steep bank. Every glance of the water made more irresistible the impulse within to drop quietly down into that liquid bed, and end all. Would it end it? Even now the quick, strong conscience threw its rein over desire and weakness, and forced her to remember what her Christian mother had so often told her—that life is not our own, but God's; that we must accept its penalties, bear its pains, fulfil its promises, but that we have no right to cast it off, to flee from it, lest we should fail through it to reach that more exceeding and eternal life of glory of which it is the faintest dawn. Dim, far, impossible, seemed the other life of glory to this young and overburdened heart; but this life, how keen, how deep its pang! She had read of brave souls who conquered it; but she was not brave nor strong. It had conquered her. Still the slender feet hung over the high bank; still the white forehead, with its restraining thought, held her back from the alluring water, when the murmur of human voices divided the air with the murmur of the waves. What tone was it that made Eirene instinctively draw forward to the curtain of vines, which screened her from the walk? It drew nearer and nearer, till it came to the spot where Paul had kissed her. It was Paul, who stood here now with Isabella Prescott.

"You will always be dearer to me, Bella, for this visit," he was saying. "Indeed, I never should have known you truly if you had not come here. How could I have so misunderstood you, Bell! I used to think that you were born to trifle, and acted accordingly.

You seem to me as changed as if you were another creature. It would have saved a world of trouble if I could have known your heart before it was too late."

A deep sigh was the only response.

"Don't sigh so, Bella! Do you suppose I can ever forget what you suffer for me? It will be the regret of my life. Oh, Bella, why didn't you show your real heart to me more than a year ago? then we should not be divided to-night."

"Don't you know, Paul," murmured a broken voice, "that, when a woman loves, her first instinct is to hide her real feelings?"

"Yes; but how was I to dream of such a thing in you? Really, you played the coquette so perfectly, I never suspected you of having real feeling."

"I was too proud to betray it. I never should have betrayed it, if my feelings had not conquered my pride."

"Why did they conquer it too late? It is like all of my fate!" said Paul.

"Why is it too late?" murmured the faltering voice.

"I am bound—irrevocably bound!" bitterly answered Paul.

"To whom? I have seen nobody who has seemed to have any special claim upon you. Who has robbed me?"

"One your inferior, and mine, in position. I have loved her, but the conditions of our lives are so conflicting, I am now convinced that we ought never to be married. I would release myself if I could. But I consider a promise a binding obligation. If I could have known you as you are, Bella, it would never have been made."

"What is that?"

They both started at a sound as of something falling very near. There was a rustle of leaves, then all was quiet.

"Perhaps it was a snake!" said Bella.

Each looked, but saw nothing, save wavy boughs and vines. But a chill ran through Paul; he shivered as one does in standing near a human being in the dark without knowing it. His last words had scarcely passed his lips, before he hated himself for uttering them; he knew them to be false. The face before him receded, and another, the face that he loved, again seemed to touch his. He started with a shock as he thought that he stood in the very spot where he had kissed it—where he had said, "No matter what you see, no matter how things may seem, believe in me." That was scarcely three weeks ago; and what had he been saying? If she could have heard the words which he had just uttered, how could she still believe in him? He felt like a man enthralled by some spell which he hated, yet which he had no power to break. Had not this woman by his side always compelled him to do and say things which made him hateful to himself? Always! Yet how fair and gentle and drooping she looked now! She loved him? Then, from whence came this faint and far suspicion of her now? While he gazed, why did her face look false even amid its suffering? Was he unjust to her, even while she fascinated him and held him? In an instant the place seemed haunted. He thought that he saw something white—white, like a woman's face, in the darkness, through the swaying vines.

"Come!" he said; "that was a curious noise. It really makes me feel superstitious. Does it you, Bella? But I never heard of a ghost in our Lover's Walk," he added, laughing. "I did not intend to stray so far."

They hurried back, but Paul saw a white face close to his all the way.

It was past midnight, yet still he sat in the drawing-room, listening to that sensuous, pleading melody of Bell's, which had grown to have such power over him. It held him where he sat; yet still a white, cold face seemed to touch his.

"Where is she? What have you done with her? You have killed her, Paul Mallane! and may the Lord curse your soul!" cried Tilda Stade, as she rushed into the room, with her hair flying and her eyes filled with the wildest excitement. In his best moments, Paul hated the sight of Tilda, but she seemed nothing short of an avenging demon to him now; and, even amid the remorse and terror caused by her words, his first impulse was to seize her and thrust her out of the window. "Oh, there's no use standing there, looking white!" she went on; "and *you* had better stive your cat-face against the wall—*you!*" she cried, glaring at Miss Prescott, who had wheeled round on the piano-stool. "Where do you suppose *she* is, while you're drummin' on the peanner? Likelier than not, in the bottom of the river. Oh! oh!"

"Woman, stop your noise!" said Paul, who expected every instant to see the whole family appear, to inquire the cause of such cries. "Stop! If you are looking for Miss Vale, I will go with you." And taking his hat, he walked out, Tilda following him. He asked no questions, needed no explanations. He knew all. That was her face that he saw through the vines! That was why such a shiver struck him as he uttered those false words to Bella. She heard them. In her desolation, she had gone back alone to their last meeting-place, and that was what she heard, and from his lips. He stalked on without a word, and soon left Tilda far behind. He went straight to the end of the Walk, pushed back the heavy vines, and there, her sun-bonnet by her side, her face almost hidden in the moss, she laid, as if she were dead.

"Eirene!" he said, bending down to her. There was no answer. His hand touched the cold face, and a deeper shiver ran through him than when he thought that he felt it hours before. She was insensible—perhaps she was dead. This was his only thought, as he lifted her in his arms and carried her away, never pausing even to still Tilda's outcries, till he had laid her on her own bed.

Isabella, watching at the window, was the only one who saw him bear his burden to the house. No one had been awakened, and she sat waiting for his return, wondering what explanation he would make her when he came. She waited long. The East was flushed with morning light when he appeared from the house across the street. Then, the look on his face was so different from any that she had ever seen on it before, that even she did not dare to intrude and speak. He did not see her, and passed on to his own room without a word.

Wild and wonderful were the stories which ran from factory to factory the next morning. "A man had seen Paul Mallane come out of Lover's Walk with Eirene Vale in his arms at two o'clock in the morning!" "That Vale girl last night threw herself into the river, and Paul Mallane dragged her out, and both have been seen together in the street in a very dripping condition, with Tilda Stade crying behind." "The Vale girl had gone crazy with love for Paul Mallane, because, now the Boston folks were around, he did not notice her. She was a fool to suppose that he would. She had tried to kill herself, and there was likely more reason for her doing so than people knew. When he was seen on the street with her in the winter, every body knew that it was for no good. Paul Mallane never noticed a shop-girl yet, but to do her harm." "Eirene Vale had better go home, and stay there. In a quiet way she had held her head very high—too high; that's always the way with *such* people. The company she had slighted was altogether too good for her. She had lost her character, and had better leave. Nobody would speak to her if she stayed."

The subject of all this sweet charity returned to consciousness late that morning, to find herself in the arms of Tilda Stade, with a physician sitting near, watching her intently. He informed her that she had been overcome by physical weakness and mental distress; that nothing but an entire change of scene, and of life, could insure her from serious illness.

"I understand," she said, with perfect calmness. "I will go away this afternoon, and never come back."

She had a look upon her face as if she had just returned from a very remote country—as if all she saw was new and strange, or but dimly remembered. She put her hand to her forehead, as if she were trying to recall something, or to collect her thoughts; yet, when she spoke, her words were perfectly coherent, and there was not a touch of wildness in her manner; instead, it seemed unnaturally calm. She sat like this, propped in an arm-chair, when she heard Tilda say, in reply to a knock at the door,

"Paul Mallane, you can't come in."

"I wish to see Mr. Mallane," said Eirene; "and, Tilda, you may go, if you will be so kind."

Gentle as the tone was in which these words were spoken, there was a dignity and a positiveness in it unknown to Eirene before. Tilda was so overcome and astonished by it, that she yielded at once, opened the door for Paul, and walked out herself.

"Forgive me—say that you forgive me, my darling!" he said, before he reached her chair.

"I do forgive you, Paul."

"But do you care for me? Tell me that you care for me still; it is all I ask."

"Yes, I care for you, Paul; but I do not believe in you."

"Don't be hard with me, Eirene—don't! I did not mean a word that I said last night."

"Didn't you?" she asked, with the old, innocent wonder in her eyes. "Why did you say it, then?"

"I can't explain to you, Eirene, the conflicting and complex influences which may come into a man's life—how he may love one woman devotedly, and yet be led on to say a thousand things which he don't half mean, or don't mean at all, to another, just through the force of influences which he cannot control."

"Do men say so many things that they don't mean?" she said, bewilderedly. "Perhaps—you didn't mean what you said to me. I thought you did. I don't think I understand how a person can say one thing and mean another."

"No, *you* never will understand it," said Paul. "I am a villain and a wretch, but I swear to you I did mean every word I said to you; and I mean it now, and I will prove it, by devoting all the rest of my life to you."

"I don't want you to devote your life to me, Paul."

"You don't!" exclaimed Paul, in a tone in which incredulity, astonishment, and distress were commingled.

"No; I don't want you to do a thing for me for which you will be sorry. It was all made plain to me last night. When you first told me that you loved me, I was almost glad that I was poor. I loved you so much, I liked to think that not only love, but every good gift in life, was to come to me from you. I knew how happy it would make me, had I been rich and you poor, to have chosen you out of all the world, to have given all that I had to you, and to have proclaimed to all the world that you were the man I loved. But Miss Prescott came, and every thing changed. I never knew, till then, how hard it might be to be poor—to be left out—to be passed by by the one loved best. It was all explained last night. You said that we ought never to marry. I knew it was true—that, if we did, even if you loved me, that the time would come when you would be sorry—that, when you saw Miss Prescott, you would feel that you had made too great a sacrifice in marrying me—that you would be ashamed of my father and mother, and of Muggins; that they might trouble you in some way. I didn't blame you. Only, till I heard you, I didn't know how much there was to keep us apart. Then, I couldn't understand why you ever sought me, and asked me to marry you. But you were sorry—you told her so—because it kept you from *her*. It didn't seem to me to be Paul—not the Paul that I love. I do not know where *he* is. All I know is, that I never can marry him."

"By heaven, you *can* marry me!" exclaimed Paul; "I will give my whole life to making you forget what I have said and done."

"No, I will never marry you, Paul."

As she uttered these words, two solitary tears forced their way through the closed eyelids and dropped on the colorless cheeks; the lips quivered, then grew still. She slowly turned her face away, her head resting on the back of the chair. Her whole attitude and aspect was that of one who had given up every thing in life. There was something irrevocable in the still, white face, that could not have been expressed in the wildest frenzy of words.

It comes to every man once in his existence, the vision of a complete life upon the earth. She comes to every man once, the woman who could be supremely the wife of his soul—she who, beyond and above every other human being—might be to him what no other one could be, in companionship and love. Paul Mallane saw this woman before him, and knew that, with her going, the sweetest and most perfect possibility of his life would pass away from him forever. He saw it again for the last time, the vision that he had seen so often before in better hours—the home peopled with bright children, glorified by the presence of this beloved one, the mother and the wife, the inspiration of all his endeavors, the crowner of all his success, the soul of his soul. And there had been times—how many!—when he had felt strong to dedicate all his power, all the promise of his life, to her, and the life that he might share with her; and now it was too late. With the keenest consciousness of what she might have been, what she was, to him, he knew in his heart that he had forfeited her, and that she was not for him in time or in eternity.

He went to her chair, laid back the long bright hair from her temples, stooped down, and kissed her forehead. Her closed eyelids looked the long farewell-look in which a thousand conflicting emotions contended;—another, and another, as the soft eyes opened and looked back into his, as from another world. Then he turned, and went out of the house.

It was September. On the lawn at Marlboro were a number of persons whom we have seen before. Dick and Dolores were sitting together, and near them stood Don Ovedo, scowling darkly at a gentleman sitting at some distance away, alone with Bella Prescott. It was Paul Mallane; and he had been much astonished, during the evening, at the offensive and aggressive manner of the Don, which was full of an assurance that he had never observed in it until now. Pensive and tearful, Bella had departed from Busyville two weeks before. Paul had neither seen her nor sought her since. It had taken him the entire two weeks to lose from his own the touch of a sweet, pathetic face, and to get over that farewell look. He had done it, he thought. He could not have what he wanted—what he sometimes wanted so much; but he could have Bella, who loved him so dearly that her love had changed her character, and had made her amiable and gentle. If he couldn't have that house of his own building—for which, after all, he would have had to have worked very hard—he could have Marlboro, which in itself was well worth having.

"Bella," he said, "the bond which held me from you when we last walked together is broken. I am free. I have the right to make you happy. Will you marry me?"

"Thank you!" she said, drawing herself up, her eyes gleaming with triumph, her attitude and expression changing as utterly as if she were turning into another person. "I knew before I left that the shop-girl had jilted you. All I went to your wretched little town for, was to separate you from her. You were awfully in love with her, weren't you? and yet not man enough to stand by her and own her in defiance of *me*. We are quits now. I am paid for all you ever cost me. I would really like to oblige you, Mr. Mallane, but I am engaged already to Don Ovedo."

## CHAPTER XI.

### ANOTHER LIFE BEGUN.

WHEN Eirene returned to a full consciousness of existence, one late Autumn morning, she found herself in her own room at Hillside.

Her first sensation was that she had slept for a night, and just awakened from an awful dream, of which she had but a confused remembrance. By slow degrees it came to her what it was. It was then that she turned her face to the wall, and a numbness like death crept over her. And yet through that numbness stole the consciousness that she must arise, go forth again to life, and live. "It is all over, and this is the end," she said. "All that made my life is gone, and yet I must live on. Paul! Paul!" cried the sweet, pathetic voice; no answer broke the cold silence of the room. "Death, death in life," she murmured, "and yet I must live."

Alice Vale looked down pityingly on her grand-child. St. Elizabeth looked out upon her with angelic eyes. She looked back on them now with a new vision; she saw a meaning in their faces that she had never seen before. It seemed ages past since she looked up at them as a child, and saw them only as lovely faces. Everything in the room was unchanged: even the glass full of crysanthemums stood on the table. It seemed to her, as if far away in another life, she remembered a girl who used to sit by that table and inhabit that room; but this girl seemed to have no relationship to herself. The girl who used to sit there had a serene brow and a tranquil heart; it had never entered into her thoughts even to conceive of what a woman may suffer and yet live. What could she ever have known of the white-faced woman whose beseeching eyes now rested unconsciously on the pictured faces above her.

She slowly rose at last, and lifting the white curtain looked out of the window. There was the river, and the meadow, and the roadside maples dropping their scarlet and gold, and the field of tobacco, but not as she had watched one year before, its luxuriant leaves prophesying a prodigal harvest. It looked stunted, sickly, prematurely yellow, as if the worms had already eaten up its life. As she saw this, Eirene gave a start. The sight drew her instantly away from herself; it gave her the sudden consciousness of an interest in Life, a something which needed her, for which it was her duty to strive and live; and the soul, true to its instinct, reached out toward that which remained. "Poor father," she said, "it the tobacco should fail, everything would fail; Hillside would have to go away from us. Father and mother and Win all needing me, and I yet feeling that I cannot live, I will—I will try to live for them. My life is past, it is dead, it is buried; I must begin another, O, if I knew how to begin." Just then she heard her father's step; it sounded heavy and slow, yet irresolute, as he entered the little sitting-room below. The doors were open, and she heard him say: "Mother, old Mr. Pomson is dead, and his son has written to me that he shall foreclose the mortgage and take the place this fall." There was no answer, yet Eirene knew that her mother sat by the window below. She could see the lines tighten about her mouth, the old look of suffering and of endurance contending in her patient eyes. She saw the look of hopelessness, of helplessness, on her father's face, and her own soft, white features grew suddenly strong. These words of her father's had told her what life, *her* life meant. They had told her also how to begin. She no longer had any doubt. She felt no weakness. Her work was plain.

God would give her strength and show her how to do it.

She drew a shawl over her and went quickly down to her father and mother. They were startled at the sight of her—at the sight of this child of theirs who had been lying as silent and as white for weeks as if she were dead.

"I heard what you said," father, she exclaimed; "we have been expecting it a long while, and now it has come. I shall go away again to work, somewhere, where I can earn more than I ever have before I hope. The way will be opened I am certain. The Lord will never forsake mother, whatever he may do for the rest of us."

"No, I hope not," said Lowell Vale, in a tone of utter hopelessness, "but the only way that I ever saw is shut up; the worm is in the tobacco. If I could only have the crop I had last year, we could keep the house, but I never was lucky!"

"Never mind, father, there must be an end to bad luck as to everything else in this world. It may be my luck to go out and make a fortune, who knows? I will write to Tilda."

It seemed easy to talk bravely, standing there looking into the helpless faces of her father and mother, but a few moments after when she faced the situation alone, she was appalled by it. Hillside to be sold, the home that they had always known, nothing to redeem it; where were they to go, what were they to do? And after all, could she, work as hard as she might, could she earn money enough to support all? There was but one resource—she was writing to Tilda.

"I told you so! I told you so! long ago, and you gave no heed," said that uncomfortable damsel, as the very next evening she sat facing Eirene in her own room at Hillside. "I told you how it would be—that that man would be the ruin of you."

"You never knew how it would be," said Eirene in a calm, cold voice; "you do not now know how it has been, and you can never know. I have one favor to ask for myself, Tilda: that you will never in the remotest way speak of this to me again."

She was so unlike the trembling girl, this white-faced woman in her cold and gentle dignity, that Tilda's only exclamation was, "Well! I never saw a human being so changed."

"I am very grateful to you, Tilda, for your great kindness to me. God will reward you, I know; yet I must claim this promise of you for myself."

"Of course I'll promise; it's no pleasure to me to mention the rascal."

"There!" she exclaimed, seeing the look of pain that passed over Eirene's face. "I'll never mention him again bad as I hate him."

"I'll write to my brother to-day. He said that I was to come, or I was to send somebody I ain't going where there ain't no means of grace. *You* don't care for them, more's the pity. But you can have the place for certain. And may the Lord preserve you in that great Babylon."

Tilda had come to Hillside expressly to comfort Eirene, and to tell her that she had a place provided for her; but of course she could not proceed to administer consolation till she had first vigorously applied her, "I told you so," to Eirene, and reminded her of the great error of her life.

She said that her brother had long been the proprietor of a notion and furnishing shop in New York. The cares of an increasing family made it difficult for his wife to attend upon customers, and he had written to her to come and take her place. This was the situation which she offered Eirene, and which Eirene accepted. The one anxiety left now was whether she could out of her small wages pay sufficient rent to the person who might buy Hillside to retain it still as the family home. This now remained the one desire of her heart. She sat pondering over it the evening after Tilda left. To-morrow was to be the day of the sale. Deacon Smoot had been over the premises that day, with an eye to buying the place for his son Amzi, who was about to marry. If it passed into the possession of Amzi, there would not be the slightest chance of renting Hillside: for that very day she had heard him tell his father what changes he would make in the old house.

If he secured it, where were her father and mother, Win. and Pansy, to go? She could not think of an empty house at Hilltop, not one. O! how hard to part with this life-long home! Yet the pang in her heart at this thought sent no tears to her eyes as it would have done once. This, too, could be lived through, could be met. What could come to her now that she could not bear—that she could not meet!

Just here the gate clicked, and looking up she saw a tall and dashingly dressed young man, whom at first she did not recognize, but as he came nearer she saw that it was Moses Loplolly. He had changed from an awkward boy into an awkward man since he bade her good-by with his parrot, two years before. His dress was emphatically "loud." He wore pantaloons of a large plaid, a yellow waistcoat, a scarlet necktie, green glass studs in his shirt bosom, a blue coat, and a tall, black, shiny hat set on one side of his head. His eyes were more like gooseberries than ever, his face was covered with bright brown freckles, his pale tow hair plastered tight to his head with pomade. His bony hands looked much too large for his sleeves, and he held tightly under one arm a parcel tied up in a newspaper.

"Why Moses!" said Eirene, "you have grown to be such a large man, I did not know you."

"No? Wa'al! it seems a great while sence you knowed me, Rene," said Mr. Loplolly in an injured tone.

"Yes, I have been gone a long time," she replied in a remote voice which seemed to indicate that she had been absent centuries, "but I am glad to see you, Moses; sit down."

"I haint no objections, I cum to sit down. I don't complain, Rene, of the time yer've been gone, fur yer cum back of'en enuf if I could have seen yer when yer did cum. But it was awful tough on a chap to feel hisself forgot, 'cause he wasn't so good looking as a scrumptious feller down in town.

"But I don't harbor no hard feelins, not now."

"I hope not, Moses. My feelings toward you have never changed. I have always thought of you as a very kind friend."

"Wa'al, sometimes it's good to be thought on as a friend, and sometimes 'taint so satisfyin.

"I tell yer, you've been a mighty sight more to me than a friend when I've thought on yer, and that haint been seldom; an' I've seen no end of gals on my rounds, hansum gals, real smart gals, more'n one on em' I might a had fur the winkin'; *they* didn't seem to think me sech a bad-looking feller," said Moses, straightening up in his splendor.

"But somehow, when I looked on 'em, I did not see 'em, I saw you, and I'd say to myself, 'O, you ain't no account with all your fixens! What are all on ye side Rene, who haint even got a bosom pin!' I tell yer, Rene, I never see nobody that I sot so high by as I sot by you."

"I am very sorry, Moses."

"There, now don't say *so, don't!* Look a here, Rene. Do you know I'm a merchant now, I'm a travellin' merchant! I'm a peddlin', an' I tell you peddlin' pays. I own my team, the spankinest team on the road; I own my wagon, a perfect beauty, red and yaller; I own my stock, an there haint nothin' I haint got, from an Irish poplin, that women is sich death on, to a tin pepper box. An'"—here he lowered his squeaking voice into a sort of exultant and mysterious chuckle, "I've got a pile of money in the bank besides! You've no idear how *peddlin'* pays."

"No, I haven't," said Eirene; but as all the frauds committed by these itinerant gentlemen which she had heard of from her childhood came back to her memory, she thought that she ought to have some idea of it.

"I am glad if you are growing rich, Moses,"; she said "you are so kind and generous, you deserve to succeed. I know *you* would not make any of your money by taking advantage of people: then you will enjoy all you make."

"O! I enjoy it *now*, and no mistake,"

declared Moses, "and the truth must be told to you, Rene: I've told a good many whoppers, I had to, Rene, trade's trade. I cheat, but I strike for justice. I'll tell you who I *gouge*—them big red-faced wimen, with little round eyes and screw mouths. I tell yer I *like* to scrouge 'em. They've no end of money from their butter, eggs, and cheeses, locked up in their buros. I said to one t'other day, 'All wool and silk, every thread on't, couldn't find sich an alpacker at Stewart's for the price.' I know'd it was all cotton one way, I wasn't going to tell *her;* I sold it fur twice as much as it wus wu'th. Then I went into the kitchen, an' to the poor gal workin' there like a galler slave, I sed, 'If yer want this pink frock yer can hev it fur half it cost.' That's the truth, an' the poor gal got the frock. I cheat, but you see I'm just.

"I didn't cum here to talk trade with you," he added in disgust; "I'm cum fur su'thin' mighty diff'rent, I tell yer."

Eirene looked up as if to divine by his face what that purpose might be, but she did not ask.

"Look a he-er," said Moses, drawing a little closer, and squeaking a little lower. "Look a he-er, I'll tell you when I felt the most as if peddlin' paid; 'twas when I thought I was makin' all my money for *you.* When I sed it's all for Rene, didn't I skin close! When I sed I must hurry an git tin enough to outshine them scrumptious fellers in Busyville, didn't I spank along the road and no mistake! Why all I peddled fur was you, Rene. How'd you suppose I felt when I heerd of that other chap? Wa'al, I felt as if peddlin' didn't pay no more—all the pleasure was clean gone out of peddlin'.

"I know everything, Rene: don't look as if yer felt bad while I tell yer. When I heerd it, I sed, 'My time hez cum. Mebby now there'll be some chance fur me; Moses, screw yer courage up an' go an' see.' One thing's sartin, nobudy ever sot so high by you, Rene, as I sot by you. Don't go away! I've got money to buy the house; the family can stay on jist the same. We'll git merried. I don't ask no higher privilege on earth then to peddle fur you all my life. You'll merry me, won't you, Rene?"

"No, Moses; don't feel bad while I say so. There is no one in the world that I want to marry."

"Ther' aint? It's sum comfort that there aint no other chap you want; I couldn't stan' that, I couldn't. Do say, Rene, there'll be a chance for me sum time."

"I can't say it, Moses. I can't say what I may do some time, but I shall have to feel very differently from what I do now if I ever marry."

"O, dear! When everything might go so slick; I'll paint up the old house, an' buy new carpets an' furnitur', an' not another woman in Hilltop should hev sich frocks as you'd hev. My! I couldn't sit on my box when I'd be drivin' hum on a Saturday night with no end of presents to you. To think how it might be, an' now it can't, because you won't—and here I brought you this for the engagement present." And he began to unfold the newspaper which covered his bundle, revealing a roll of chameleon silk, crossed with soft purple and sea-green hues.

"I picked it out on purpose for yer, Rene, in Bosting," he went on mournfully. "Some how it looked as if it was made fur you; I like stunnin' things myself, but they aint your sort. See," he said, gathering the silk in his hand and smoothing its soft folds, "aint it jist like a dove's thrut? Exactly! My! how lovely you'll look in it, but I can't see yer!"

"You don't mean that you want to leave the silk now?" asked Eirene in astonishment. "I can't take it, Moses. You don't know how I appreciate your kindness to me—your life-long kindness—how keenly I feel it now, and her voice trembled, but I cannot accept obligations to you which I have no power to repay. It was very, very good of you to think of me, and buy me such a lovely dress. I thank you more than I can say, but you must take it back."

"Can't do it," said Moses doggedly, "I bought it for yer; nobody else shant never wear it. Do you think I could bear to see 'em in it! Do you think I could take and *sell* it, arter I bought it fur you? No! I can scrouge them that deserves it, but I can't sell what I bought on purpose for you, an' ther' aint nobody else I would give it to, I can tell yer. Yourn it is, an' yourn it shall be," and with this proclamation Moses' laid the silk on Eirene's lap.

She did not know what to say. Words of thanks seemed so poor and cheap. She felt her poverty more keenly than ever, because it made it impossible for her to give to Moses a parting gift in return. There was nothing she could say, except—"I shall never forget your kindness, Moses, and you know I always have been and always shall be your friend."

"Ther' aint no doubt that you are my friend," said Moses dejectedly; "I'm sure I'm yourn."

"There, don't be so downhearted. I am going away to seek my fortune. Boys always do, you know. Come! wish me well, all the more for being a girl: that will make it harder for me to find it, you know."

"Yes, a tarnel sight. I couldn't wish you nothin' but well, Rene, no matter what you did. But I must say 'tis hard on a feller when I'm willin' an' thankful to take care on yer, that yer won't be took care of an' stay tu hum. I'm sure you're too hansum to go alone to that great pesky place."

Eirene's white cheeks flushed scarlet at these words; a feeling of terror struck through her heart as she realized she was going into an unknown world alone, but she made no answer.

"I might as well go one time as t'other," said Moses, refusing to be comforted; "ther' aint no use in good-bys no how. I'll see you to-murrow, but if I don't hev no chance to say no more don't forget, Rene, now nor never, you'll never find nobudy to set so high by yer as I've sot by yer, never!"

And with this he waived his long, bony, freckled hand in the air tragically, and went down the garden path.

Eirene's eyes followed him; they took in the lank, shambling figure with its vulgar attire, but it was not of them that she thought. She could think of nothing but the genuineness of his devotion, and of the pain which she had caused, and of both with equal regret. When he was fairly in the road, and, as he thought, hidden by the maples, Eirene saw him take his bright handkerchief from his pocket and wipe his eyes. From that very spot she had seen another face turn back: how bright a face, how full of promise in its tender good-by.

"Where are you now!" she exclaimed; "another weeps for me, and you!"

Hillside was sold at auction the next day, and to everybody's astonishment Moses Loplolly outbid Amzi Smoot, and became its owner.

"Wa'al yes," he said, after the sale, to Lowell Vale, "You may pay me sich rent as comes handy, I haint no objection to take all I can git, but I shant move ye if yer don't pay nothin', haint no sech ideer. Go on a farmin', old man, jest as if daddy Pomson hed'nt kicked the bucket. Sorry yer 'baccur haint dun no better this year. But whate'er else ye do, don't let *her* know; if you're grubbin', tell me! I've got the chink, am gitten' more all the time, peddlin' pays! Come to me if times get too rubbin'. Don't keep her scrimpin' an' pinchin' till she haint a smich of nothin' left to keep soul an' body together, don't! That's all I ask, and so farewell till I come round agin."

And with these words Moses Loplolly departed without entering the house, leaving Lowell Vale in a daze of astonishment, standing in the yard.

He was not to be driven out of Hillside after all! but the one who had prevented his becoming an outcast, who had secured his home for him, was not the rich and handsome son-in-law in Cambridge, who, in spite of clearer reason, had sometimes risen before his impractical brain as the future possible savior; it was not he, but poor freckled Moses, whom all Hilltop pronounced in his humble beginnings, "Of no account!"

Eirene was to start before daylight with Muggins and her father for the early train.

She had just had her last, long talk with her mother, as that dear one put the coffee-pot on the stove and set the table for an untimely breakfast. Now, before lying down to sleep, she sat down to gather up her mental and spiritual forces, and to take another lingering look at the little room in which she had lived through all her childhood, and through the one crisis of her life. Already it had taken on the sad look of change. St. Elizabeth had descended from her shrine on the wall, and now laid face prone within the little old hair-covered, brass-nailed trunk which Alice Vale brought to Hilltop fifty years before. Her grand-daughter had just placed her last treasure within it, and pressed the old lock down, and as she did so her tears had fallen on it. Then she sat back and gazed at the quaint, old thing which was to be her only companion out into the great world. This moment she felt afraid of that world, and something like fear struck through her heart as, with the closing of the trunk, she realized that she was to go out into it alone. She would have been much more terrified had she had any real conception of its dangers and temptation to a woman beautiful, young, and unprotected. As it was, her very ignorance and innocence stood her in the place of courage. Her dread came only from the fact that to her it was all unknown and she must go out into it alone.

Even the whistle of the wind in the trees and the rush of the river in its narrow bed took on the sounds of the untried life—the roar of the far-off streets—and she wondered how she would be able to meet it.

She had already reached that crisis in life when a woman of opposite nature, disappointed and wounded in her affections, turns toward the prizes of intellect and ambition, and sallies forth into the great world in search of a crown.

It never occurred to this girl that such a thing was possible to her. Of the rich endowments of her mind as personal possessions she had no consciousness, much less that it might be possible for her to use them to build up a splendid fate for herself in the world. The realm of letters, the realm of art she knew were both in this vast world into which she was going; both in a dim and distant way had a charm for her; she had read of and worshipped the queens of women who had reigned therein. How remote and inaccessible seemed these realms. How high up and unapproachable seemed these regnant women! She could never enter one or see the other, she would have thought, but she did not think at all of this enchanted world, in which the beautiful, the gifted, and the prosperous dwell. She was only thinking, poor little sordid soul, of the furnishing shop which she was going to tend; whether she could ever earn enough in it to pay the rent and send Win to school. It cannot be denied her ideas of this shop were romantic and exaggerated in the extreme. It seemed to her a very mint in which she would coin money. Five whole dollars a week! What a fortune! Then she fell to wondering if she would feel frightened when she found herself alone in the roaring streets, till she grew alarmed where she sat, with only the river rushing through the silence.

Her heart filled with gratitude as she thought that it was Tilda who had secured this golden chance to her; it was poor, forgotten Moses, now grown so rich, who had purchased the shelter for her father and mother, two persons who not only were not necessary to her, but were personally actually irksome. Yes, it was to these two that she owed shelter and sustenance, while the one loved better than all others, the one who had promised so much, from him she had received nothing but loss and anguish.

She wondered if it was always thus in life, that the ones whom we love and lean on most are the ones who fail us at the last; and if those who support us in our need must be those on whom we have no claim, and from whom we never expected anything. Then, although she was "not a Christian," according to Tilda's standard, she kneeled down once more by the bed, where she had kneeled from early childhood, and, with silent uplifted face, with tears dropping from her closed eyelids, she prayed the Father for his blessing to rest upon those who were left, and upon the one who was to go.

## CHAPTER XII.

### THE GREAT CITY.

TWILIGHT was folding the great city in its shadow as she drew near it. How many descriptions have been written of the emotions of hope and fear struggling within the heart of a young man, as he approaches for the first time the vast world of the unknown metropolis to begin life and to seek his fortune. But who has portrayed the emotions of the young girl, pure, innocent, and all alone, when for the first time she approaches the unknown world, unless it has been to portray that for her, beautiful, young, poor, and lonely, awaits but one fate in the cruel city—suffering or ruin.

As the rocky lawns and fields of Westchester and the blue out-line of the Sound merged into dusty villages, and at last into what seemed to her to be endless streets, along which the sentinel gas lights had already begun to flame, a strange tumult of expectation and dread took possession of Eirene's heart. All the frightful stories that she had ever heard of young girls being seized and carried off to dreadful places on their entering a strange city rushed into her mind. What after all if she should miss Mr. Stade, if he should not be able to recognize her, or if he should not come at all, what was to become of her and where should she go? Her heart was almost numb with dread, and her white face was pressed against the window of the car in mute expectancy, as the engine with ringing of bells, the screaming hackmen, and pushing of passengers, rushed into the great black railroad house. Everybody seemed to be running into everbody's arms; men, women, and children, jostling and exclaiming, with bundles, baskets and babies, were disappearing in stages and carriages. No familiar face approached her out of the excited throng. Tilda had told her that she could not help knowing her brother because he looked so much like his sister. Eirene strained her eyes, but saw no one who bore the slightest resemblance to Tilda Stade. In her ignorance she had been too timid to give her check to the express agent, thus, amid her growing terror for herself, she was full of anxiety for the precious little brass-nailed trunk. How was she ever to find it, amid the avalanche of travelling houses that on porters' carts went crashing by! It was anything but a romantic sight—Eirene amid the men and flaming lanterns in the great black station-house, holding the tears back in her frightened eyes, while she vainly peered amid the piles and piles of toppling trunks for the little old box of Alice Vale.

"Here, me dear, give me your check, and go and sit ye doon while I luk for ye," said a gray-haired man with a lantern, who evidently belonged to the place. "Never ye mine them yelpin' fules, an' mine ye tek ne'er one of ther fine kerridges they shout about so loud. Go an' sit ye doon, an' I'll luk a bit."

"A stray lam', indeed," he muttered to himself as he stumped away. "It's strange to me the Almighty ever lets such kume to a place like this, craving His pardon. An' here it is," pulling the trunk out from a pile which had almost hidden it. "An' I should say I had me own gran'-mither's box, it's as like the one she kep' full of fine caps under her bed as two peas. I never see nought like it this side of the water afore, an' yet sure it's the gel's;" and giving it another pull he dragged it forth, and then after him till he came stumbling back to where Eirene sat wiping the tears from her eyes. Alas! no one could have looked less like a heroine than our maiden wiping her eyes above her fearfully beating heart in the New York station-house.

"Here, me bairn, 's ye'er box—as like me own gran'-mither's as a box cude well be. An' more, if ye can tell an owld gran'-faather jes where ye want to go, he'll go an fine an' honest man to tek ye there."

Eirene gave the number on Harlem road to which she wished to go.

"An' a long bit off 'tis," said the old man, studying the card.

"Mebby it's to Timothy Stade's you want to go to," said a shambling, slinking-looking individual, who had added greatly to Eirene's fright during the absence of the old man by walking up and down near by, eyeing her askance.

"It is to his house I want to go," said Eirene in a tone of infinite relief.

"I'm him; I thought mebby you was her, and then I thought you wasn't. But I kep' my eye on you. It's a long way to Harlem. If you'll take hold o' one end of y'er trunk, I will t'other. Can put it in front of the car, I reckon."

Eirene arose to do as she was bidden, but first handed a silver quarter to the old man.

"No! I teks my share, but nought from ye. Here man, tek it and give it to an expressman to tek the leddy's trunk. Where have ye been livin' that ye're asking a leddy to tu-g and lu-g?"

"It is not heavy," said Eirene, who that instant forgot the books in the bottom, and thought only of her light wardrobe.

She took hold of one handle while the Stade individual proceeded to take hold of the other, and the old man looked on with wondering and disapproving eyes. He gazed after them as they went down the long station-house, the young girl swaying under the weight of her burden, the slinking man shuffling and shambling along as if ready to drop it at any instant, though perfectly able to carry the whole weight upon his own shoulders.

"Weel, weel! that the like of him could come to fetch the like of her is b'yond my ken!" muttered the old man. "I'd a teken the box mysel' cude I a left this old house, for a' of that pretty bairn a tugin it."

"A lam' and a fox! an uncanny fox, sure, sure! May the gude shepherd Hi'sel' keep that pretty lam', is my prayer."

Eirene, weak from long sickness, nearly sank under her load long before she reached the Third Avenue cars. They were packed with workmen going home, and stifling with offensive odors. Eirene stood all the way, wedged into this reeking mass, and reached Harlem too prostrated to be able to take scarce any note of her surroundings. Mrs. Timothy Stade and her infants were sleeping the sleep of the abused and the dirty, thus, save the husband and father, she saw no member of the household that night.

The morning sun struggled in through speckled windows to behold the stranger in a small room crowded with children who waked her with laughter and screams, while they dragged about the bed clothes and chased each other, and fought from trundle-bed to trundle-bed.

"If you *are* to be here, it shall be to be *my* help as well as hisen," said a sharp voice, and Eirene, lifting her weary head from a soiled pillow, saw that it belonged to a very damaged-looking young woman, who had once been pretty, and who now had her hair in curl-papers. Her wrapper was soiled and torn, and she looked in every way much dilapidated.

"I am Mrs. Timothy Stade," she said, opening the door wider and coming in. "I may as well tell you first as last that I never wanted you to come here. If there's to be help, I want it *my* help, not Stade's. Goodness knows I need help with all these children! Drudge, drudge, and never a smitch of change. I want a girl for the kitchen, not one for the shop. The shop's my place. It's *my* shop. It was mine afore I ever set eyes on Tim Stade. Curse the day I ever gave him a right in my shop, an' here he's driv' *me* out of it, and has the face to put another woman in it, and shut me back in the kitchen to take care of the young ones. He'll see if I'll stay shut out of my own shop! And *you* may as well know first as last that I wont stay out of it, and if you do stay you'll be my help as well as hisen. I want you to dress the children."

The suddenness and sharpness of this unexpected tirade at first left Eirene powerless to reply. As soon as she could command her voice, she said:

"I am sorry, Mrs. Stade, if there is any misunderstanding about my coming here. I supposed that it was your wish as well as Mr. Stade's."

"Well, it aint," she exclaimed, going out and slamming the door, that ever ready relief to vulgar minds.

Eirene arose, with an almost blinding headache, and began to try to dress the children. They were like so many wild-cats. They understood the meaning of slaps and punches, of jerks and hard names, but not that of such gentleness as hers. As an expression of their approbation of her mildness, they began to teaze her, and play with her, in their way—pulling her hair, jumping on her, screaming in her ears, till with her distress to find out which particular rag belonged to each particular child, and her headache, she found herself, when she was called to breakfast, almost in a state of distraction. She could cry her eyes out, she felt sure of that, but how could she eat her breakfast? And such a breakfast, amid the screams of the children, the slaps of the mother, and the whines and grumbling of the father.

Then the shop! one-half of it might be called a small emporium of tape, pins, and needles, and cheap cotton lace; the other was devoted to a small soda fountain, to root beer, and to penny sticks of candy, for which the wretched little children in the street were perpetually coming in.

Before she had been in this place an hour, Eirene was perfectly certain that she could not stay in it. But where was she to go? Back to Hilltop? No, there was no work for her there. Back to Busyville? She could not! No, the great city must give her work to earn her bread. Even if she could stay here, how her five dollars a week had dwindled down; with her board and lodging taken out of them, what would be left!

Mrs. Timothy Stade belonged to the large race of abused women. She *was* an abused woman! To pity herself as such was the only comfort that she had left. What she said of her shop was true. It was hers, at least the cotton lace and soda fountain were her's, bequeathed to her by her dead mother. Tim Stade, the shiftless, ne'er-do-well son of his tribe, appeared at her counter on his way to the luck which he had come to the city to find: and which he felt sure was his when he drank soda-water and ate peanut candy with a black-eyed, ringleted maid in her own establishment. They were married and prospered at first. Tim sat from morning till night on a bench by the door airing and sunning himself, and gossiping with his cronies, while the shop supported him. His wife's black eyes and red cheeks still helped to attract susceptible youths from Westchester to the soda fountain and small beer bottles, and all went well. Mrs. Timothy Stade, in an undirected way, was "a business woman." Left to herself, in due time she would have drawn a small fortune out of her soda fountain and cotton lace. It was her life to "tend shop," and her misery to keep house, and she took most unkindly to the care of small children.

Thus, when at the close of seven years, six cherubs roared and rioted in the bed-clothes in the room above, when her beauty was so dreadfully damaged, and her hair refused longer to curl, she felt herself to be a deeply aggrieved woman; and when insult was added to so much injury in the form of a younger and prettier woman to attend on her shop, the wrath of Mrs. Timothy reached its climax. It was expended, not on the cause of her troubles,—the spite of an ignorant, injured woman seldom is—but on an innocent person.

"You shall *not* stay in my house, you shall *not!*" she exclaimed on the morning of the second day. Through the screaming of the children, the steam of washing suds, and the fumes of pork and cabbage, and one day more of the drudgery never done, her rage had risen to this height toward the pale, quiet young lady, who by a process Mrs. Tim could not understand had come to serve in her shop. The very contradiction between the girl's presence and the place in which she stood helped to increase the irritation of the unfortunate Mrs. Timothy. That one so fair and gentle, who looked so unmistakably a lady, even in a poor, unassuming dress, should stand in her place while she worked over a roasting stove, without a minute to take down her curl papers, was what Mrs. Timothy could not and did not endure.

Her fiat was welcome to Eirene. Where on the wide earth she could go she had not the faintest idea, but it seemed to her anywhere, if she could but see the sky above her head, and breathe for a moment God's air, would be a relief—a mercy after this atmosphere. Poverty, want even, she could bear without a murmur, but what made life seem unendurable was noise, contention, quarrelling and dirt.

"If I had known that I had been asked to come here contrary to your wishes, Mrs. Stade, I never should have come," said Eirene quietly, turning toward the bedroom above in pursuit of her bonnet. She tied it on, and came down stairs with nothing in her hands.

"I will send for my trunk as soon as I can," she said.

"Where are you going?" asked the amazed Mrs. Timothy.

"I don't know."

Like many another violent woman, Mrs. Timothy was frightened at the extent of her own execution. She intended to drive the girl away, to put herself in her place, and a drudge in the kitchen, but that it could be accomplished in such a short space of time she had not deemed possible. A girl in the shop or a girl in the kitchen was a chronic source of contention between Mr. and Mrs. Stade. The latter had acquiesced in the proposition of a girl from the country, believing that she would be just the one to banish to the cook stove. Had one dropped out of the skies she could not have been more astonished at her than she was at the aspect of the one who appeared from Hilltop. She knew that she was an utter stranger in the city, and thought that it would be a long struggle to get rid of her. To see her, without a look of anger, or a word of recrimination, turn and go, actually go down the dusty Harlem street, without one glance back, leaving her foe on her own ground, did not give that foe so sweet a feeling of triumph as she wished. Tim was down town buying a new stock of lemons and candy, to meet the increased demand which he was sure the new face would bring; for foxy Tim, lazily watching on his bench by the door, had at least acquired a keen eye for effects: he was perfectly certain that the new face would draw many a one to the soda fountain, which the dilapidated one, set amid its unwilling ringlets, never could again. So there would be a fight with Tim when he came back and found the girl gone! Under the circumstances Mrs. Tim dreaded that, in spite of her long practice, and many triumphs; for Tim was not without a latent masculine facility for taking his revenge in his own way, and Mrs. Tim had know him to take it in a way most exasperating to her feelings.

Eirene walked on rapidly toward the great city. She received no adequate impression of it through the darkness in which she entered it. It was all new to her now, as from the high ground she strained her eyes to follow its vast length, reaching far on between its two bounding rivers. She had never seen a great city before. It seemed to uplift her as it drew her on and into its vastness. Its sight gave her a sensation of buoyancy, as if she were being borne on without effort, the same which came to her, long afterwards, when she gazed on Guido's Aurora, and seemed borne on by her coursers through the clouds.

At last she faced the world! All alone, young, lovely, a woman, with nothing in her hand, and very little in her pocket. Whither was she going? She had not even asked yet. Filled with the sense of sudden relief, and the new sensation of wonder, she had not yet thought. Besides, it was morning. Even difficulty looks easy in the morning. The morning exhilaration was in the air, the morning splendor on the sky, that seemed near which would seem impossible at night. How many girls, alas! how many, young and innocent as she, enter the city as she did that morning, enter it only to meet dishonor and death. Whom should God's ministering angels follow if not these! She could not help it. At first the only impulse she felt was to hasten away from the dreadful abode which she had just left. Not till she reached Union Square, many miles from the spot whence she started, did she realize that she was tired, or that, having reached the heart of the city, she must seek shelter and work.

The little children were playing in the paths with their nurses: their very faces rested her. The willows swung over the broad basin of the fountain and made her shiver; they were so like those other willows under which she had once lain down as dead, but the gold fishes flashed in the water, and the loving sparrows hopping around her feet fed from each others mouths. "Are ye not of more value than many sparrows?" This question of the Word came to her as a promise, with an assurance unknown before, as she watched them feed by the fountain—these atoms of God, loved and nourished by Him in the heart of the great city, wherein she stood, a stranger, with not where to lay her head. Here were soft grasses to sooth her tired feet, restful shadows, and refreshing waters. The peace of nature, which had filled her heart so often in the old woods at home, touched it even here through the very thunder of the streets.

Everywhere around her in the beautiful streets running out from the park, she saw tall spires point heaven-ward, and it seemed to her that not very far away she must find some Christian soul who would kindly give her some honest work to do. It was past noon now—the exhilaration of the morning was gone. Already a chill in the air and a just perceptible shadow on the sky told of the swift decline of the brief Autumn day. She must not tarry a moment longer by the fountain among the sparrows and the children. For the first time she realized that she was tired and hungry, that she had eaten scarcely a morsel that day. She must not spend a penny for food, for, if she did not get work, she had not more than enough to pay for one night's lodging. But some Christian woman would tell her what she could do before night, she felt sure of it, she told herself that she felt sure of it, through the fear quivering in her heart. She turned her steps, which began to falter a little, now toward the nearest drug shop. There was a Directory in the drug shop in Busyville, there would surely be one here. She found one, and sought at once the benevolent institutions of the city, the refuges for needy women. She selected one, then turned to the names of its directors and their places of residence

"I will go to a good woman," she said, "tell her the truth about myself, and ask her to direct me to some employment." She asked the policeman on the corner the way to such a street and number. It was but a little way off—up Fifth Avenue. He kindly led the way, pointed to the block, and in a few minutes Eirene found herself before the house. It was of the sort that the modern New Yorker delights to call "palatial, one of the high, grim brown stone houses which make Fifth Avenue "grand, gloomy, and peculiar." A handsome clarence, with liveried coachman and footmen, waited before the door. Eirene felt her heart as well as her knees giving out as she ascended the lofty steps; she had never sought admittance to so grand a house before. Its heavy carved door did not look as if it would open easily or welcomingly to so poor a dress as hers, and scarcely did the image of the Christian lady within which she summoned to her help give her courage to ring the bell. It was a meek, faint ring which the waiter inside heard. He heard such rings at the area door often, never before above, where the rich and the privileged only sounded the ring of assurance. He slowly opened the door a little way as if only to shut it again, but when a soft voice inquired for the lady of the house by name, he opened it wider and asked her to come in. He looked upon her face, and was about to invite her into the reception room; he glanced at her dress, and asked her to sit down in the hall. In a few minutes he returned and told her, "that she might come up." While she sat there two very elegantly dressed young ladies, the most elegantly dressed that she had ever seen, swept by her.

"Did you notice that girl's face?" asked one of the other.

"Yes, I did; I'd like such a face myself," said the other. "How did it come above such clothes; who is she, do you suppose?"

"Oh, one of ma's vagrants, no doubt; that such creatures should manage to get such faces isn't fair;" and the two young ladies entered the clarence and were driven away.

Eirene, with almost fainting steps and a sinking heart, followed the servant up the stairs of polished wood, over carpets into which her feet sank like down to the door of the apartment where his mistress sat under the hands of her hair-dresser. She was a tall, high-nosed woman, with an awful manner, sitting before a toilet mirror reading a book supported on an ebony stand. She waved her hand as Eirene entered, motioning to a chair without speaking a word, and went on with her reading. She was the daughter of a mechanic in a New England village, and grew up in a pine box of a house no better than her neighbors', neither of which facts abstractly were to her discredit. Nevertheless, their memory made her cultivate a magnificence of manner which one of gentle birth would have deemed unnecessary and underbred. When it suited her pleasure she lifted her eyes from her book, and, with the air of a queen giving audience, asked Eirene what she wanted.

Eirene told her that she wanted employment, any honest work that would give her shelter and protection. In a few words and with a faltering voice, she told how the place she thought provided had failed her, and that she was a stranger and alone in the city.

"But have you no references, no recommendations whatever?"

Eirene acknowledged that she had none.

"That is questionable, indeed suspicious. Have you none from your last place of employment?"

Eirene said no, but that she could send and get one from her former employer.

"Oh! that would amount to nothing, it must be your last place of employment. Young females of proper character are seldom without recommendations; it is a very suspicious fact that you should come a stranger alone to a great city without a simple certificate of good character. You are what 'our Board' call a very unsatisfactory case. You seem to be neither one thing nor the other. You have no references, as a respectable female should have, and I am not quite prepared to say that you come within the pale of our Institution as an abandoned female. You have not yet attained the look of an abandoned female even if you are one. Our asylum is for abandoned females, and our office for young women well recommended. You do not come within the pale of our society at all, unless you *are* an abandoned female. If you are one, you needn't hesitate to tell me; I am used to them, —send them to asylum every week."

By this time Eirene had risen. Night was coming; she could stay no longer here.

"Perhaps," she said in a broken voice, "you will be so kind as to direct me to some place where they would trust me for a few days till I can get my reference. I did not think of getting one before I left, because I supposed the place that I was coming to to be certain."

"That proves you to be a very improvident person. Nothing in this world is certain but death. Adele, that twist is too high," surveying her head in the glass, "and the arrow pricks me," pulling out a gold arrow from the coil behind.

"Wait a moment," to Eirene. "I will

give you a Testament, and an excellent tract called 'Seed Corn.' I hope you will peruse them both; they will benefit you greatly. And I will give you the card of a lady up town. Your case will, I think, come within the limit of *her* society."

She slowly arose from under the hands of her hair-dresser, studied the effect of her coiffure in the mirror, then proceeded slowly to a writing-desk, took from it the Testament, tract, and card, and with an air of remote condescension handed them to the unfortunate girl standing by the door.

"Yes, I am quite sure that you are within the pale of *her* society," she said again, as if to reassure some doubt within herself. "If you are obliged to wait for a place, it will teach you a lesson which every person in your situation must learn—to be provident, provident. It is best you should learn by experience. It is a matter of principle with me that such persons as you are should always learn by experience."

Eirene was never quite certain how she found her way out of that awful presence. But she did, and herself again in the street a few moments later, with the Testament, card, and "Seed Corn" in her hand.

Again the aid of a kind policeman was invoked, ten pennies were reluctantly parted with, and Eirene, in a Fifth Avenue stage, was being jolted up town. She found the lady's house, but not the lady. She was out of town, would be absent a week or more; of her "Guardian Society" Bridget Mavourneen at the door "knowed nought," she said.

Again on the street. It was night now, and she miles from either point from whence she had started. She went on she knew not whither, only she must find a safe shelter for the night; and to-morrow, to-morrow, the sun would shine again, the world would be before her, and the promise of the sparrows would be fulfilled. But now! The awful heaven was above her, dark and moonless; the awful city, no longer bright and beckoning, but black and dreadful behind its glittering lamps, seemed to shut every door against her. And here were her fellow-creatures, thousands of them, crowding by, whether hoping, fearing, struggling, or triumphant, each alike as remote from her as if moving on another planet. Here were women in twos, walking up and down the pavement, many others alone like herself, but not like her shrinking and afraid. No, they moved on as if pacing their own drawing-rooms, many of them gorgeously attired. Some of them minced and strutted, and talked and laughed, and bowed their heads, and seemed to know many people. What did it mean? They seemed to feel more at home in the street than she could be in any house. She passed a hotel with portico and pavement crowded with men. Two women, slowly sailing on before her, turned and talked and bowed as if they knew each gentleman whose eyes they met. What did it all mean? Were these the women that she had read about; and through all her desolation a pang of pity struck her heart for *them*. "And I, I am in the street, solitary, houseless!" No man reading these words can by any effort of his mind imagine what the terror was which struck through the heart of this girl at such a thought. "Father in Heaven, take care of me!" was her silent cry.

Where are you going, Sweety?" said a voice out of the crowd; the mere human sound made her turn her head and lift her face. The man who had spoken saw it, and without another word went on.

"Ladies' Entrance," she read over the side door of the hotel. It was closed and looked quiet and solitary; any lady might safely enter here. She tottered with weakness and terror as she ascended the steps and rang the bell. She asked the door-tender for the ladies' parlor. It was easily found, a quiet, luxurious room, softly lighted, with ladies in rich evening dresses, and elegant gentlemen sitting about and chatting on the sofas. She asked a servant whom she met in the hall, if he would say to the proprietor that a stranger wished to speak with him in the parlor.

And now as she sank upon a chair near the door, it seemed to her that she could never rise again. Some of the occupants of the room noticed her homely dress and cottage bonnet, and wondered what she wanted there. Others noticed her face, white almost as snow, every drop of blood drained from it, lit with two eyes that shone like stars with the light of hunger and fear.

"Madam, your wishes?" said an important voice, a few moments later. It issued from a showily dressed young man with a dissipated, disagreeable face—the hotel clerk, who had just entered the room.

"I would like a small, quiet room for the night," said Eirene, speaking with difficulty. "I am a stranger in the city and alone."

Before she spoke it was perfectly evident to the clerk that she was a stranger and alone, and, notwitstanding the delicate face, quite as apparent that she was also poor and friendless. He answered her accordingly.

"It is contrary to the rule of the house to take in any lady who comes alone and unprotected."

"I have money, sir, to pay for a room; I hope to find friends in the morning."

Poor child! She clutched at the dying hope in her heart, that the morning might bring her friends as her only chance for a night's shelter!

"Oh! money can't secure a room to a strange woman without a protector in a first-class hotel."

"All women cannot have protectors, sir."

"Then they should stay out of New York."

Eirene had no heart to deny this at such a moment.

"I thought—I thought, sir, that public houses always afforded shelter to such when they needed it."

"Not here. When such persons come to this city, they usually have friends to meet them. If not, they don't try to get into first-class hotels."

"Only for the night, sir. To-morrow, if I can find no employment, I will go back to my home. Only to-night! surely you will not cast me out upon the street." And at the very thought, her face grew ghastly.

"Oh, no! don't feel so bad. I can't help the rule of the house, but I can take you to my sister's. You can go and stay in the waiting room till after the evening trains are in, then I'll take you to my sister's."

The words were kind enough, but the tone! She had never been spoken to in such a tone before. It made her lift her weary eyes to his face. She had scarcely seen it until now. It was an evil face. As she looked on it, it struck a terror to her heart; it seemed more terrible than all the streets,—yes, even into the street, she would flee from it.

She lifted herself up painfully. "You are *not* the proprietor. It is the proprietor of this house that I want to see."

"Oh, you do! The proprietor of this house don't run at every beggar's call. If I am not the proprietor, I am the one to decide who can enter it. You shan't, and you shan't go back to the street. I see now you want to. You shall go with me," he said in an undertone.

"Never."

She arose and attempted to move toward the near hall. The spirit was strong to defy fate; the body, tested to its utmost limit, sank; hunger, terror, exhaustion triumphed. The man knew that they would. His intention was to have taken advantage of this opportunity to have her conveyed wherever he wished. The low conversation had not attracted attention, but the looks and manner of the young stranger had.

Every hotel waiter is a spy. The one who called the clerk to Eirene was no stranger to him, and having, moreover, some personal wrongs to avenge, and being quite as conscious as the clerk himself, that the young woman who had spoken to him was beautiful, poor, and a stranger, he stood detective, in the hall near the open door, through the entire scene. Before Eirene reached the hall, before she fell, he was ready to rush to Mr. Roselle, the owner of the house, and to tell the whole story.

"Nothing but fainted," said the clerk

to a group of ladies who came running from their sofas to see what was the matter. "I will see that she is taken care of," and he hurried off to give orders of his own, while a lady took her laced pocket-handkerchief, which had never been used for so good a purpose before, and, dipping it in ice water, began to bathe the temples of the prostrate girl.

"This is not a pleasant sight to me," said Mr. Roselle, a few moments later. "I don't like to think that such a girl as this has been refused shelter in my house. But it's always the way—innocence suffering for guilt. The man who helped to bring this about shall pay for it. Tom, you go for the housekeeper."

Mr. Roselle was a powerful man. He lifted the unconscious girl in his arms as if she were an infant, and his own daughter, and, followed by the housekeeper, a little later carried her to a quiet room in the house.

Here, had she been with her own mother, she could not have been more tenderly cared for than she was in this great hotel. Widowed, and a mother herself, the housekeeper ministered to her with a mother's heart. She brought her back to life, fed her, and watched over her.

"Fear not, therefore; ye are of more value than many sparrows," said the girl, looking around, still unconscious of her condition or surroundings. The last thoughts which her heart sent up to her brain before she fell were the first to re-utter themselves when speech came back. Tears filled the eyes of the woman as she heard these words spoken in a low, quivering, child-voice. As she looked upon the face of the speaker, so young, so lovely, and so broken, she shuddered, for she knew the world as it was revealed to her in a great hotel, in a great city; and she knew the perils of this world to the innocent and the poor, as the poor child before her even now could not know or dream of them. It made the simple utterance of her faith inexpressibly touching.

"I must go," she said, slowly rising.

"Where, my child?"

"I must go and find some work. It is nearly night."

"Oh, no, it isn't. It's only just morning. You have all day before you. You needn't hurry, my dear."

"Oh, I must. I couldn't walk any faster; I tried. I was afraid it would be night before I found my work. He said I couldn't stay, that I should go with him, that wicked, cruel man! How did I get away? Oh, if I should meet him again! and it night! I did not know that night could be so terrible, when one is a stranger, and all alone."

"But it is *not* night! I'll open the blinds, and you can see for yourself. It's morning, and you are not alone, if you are a stranger. Indeed, my dear, you have found some kind friends."

"You are kind. You are *very* kind. Where am I?"

"You are in a quiet corner of a very big hotel—the one that you strayed into last night. It is true, as a rule, it is shut against all strange, lone women. But it is just as true that they are never to be insulted. And the man who took advantage of your loneliness to abuse you has lost his place for it. Mr. Roselle told me to keep you in the morning till he came."

"Mr. Roselle?"

"Yes, he owns this house, and he brought you up here himself. He is a good man. I advise you, as a friend, to follow his advice, whatever it may be, my dear."

Eirene passed her hand over her forehead, as if to smooth out the confusion of her brain. Whenever she lost consciousness, her soul seemed to go millions of miles away from the earth, so far that when she came back, it adjusted itself with difficulty to the old conditions.

In her troubled sleep, she had been traversing the great streets again, all alone in the night, with that terrible man pursuing her. Now, as it slowly came to her how it was, how she had been protected and cared for in her helplessness, in the very place where even shelter had been denied her, how her Lord's promise had proved true to her, beyond every fear, she laid her face back upon her pillow, and shed the silent tears of gratitude and thanksgiving.

It was past ten o'clock when Mr. Roselle appeared. Before then Eirene had eaten a good breakfast, and clothed, and in her right mind, with the light of a new-born hope and trust shining in her eyes, she sat, scarcely looking the same girl that was carried thither the night before.

"I have come to ask you to go with me to my wife, my child; will you go?" asked Mr. Roselle.

"I cannot express my thanks that you are willing to take me," was the answer, uttered in genuine gratitude.

Mr. Roselle's family did not live in the hotel, but in a private house in an adjoining street. Eirene soon found herself in the presence of a lady, delicate and nervous looking, but with an expression so exactly the reflection of her husband's that she might have been taken for his twin sister.

He had evidently told her all about Eirene, for she received the girl with a kindness which was actually tender in its sympathy.

"I feel quite sure that Providence has sent you to us, my dear," she said. "I have been praying for weeks that I might be guided aright in the choice of a companion for my two little granddaughters, whom we have adopted as our own. They have their masters every day, but I have not been able to find a satisfactory person to superintend them out of study hours, and to go out with them every day. I am not strong enough to do it myself, for I want them to walk, and to visit all the places of interest in the city, as a part of their education. It ought not to be a servant, nor ought it to be a person so far removed from them in culture and interest that she will not answer their questions or enter into their feelings. Don't you think that *you* could?"

"I could enter into their feelings; I am afraid I don't know enough to answer all their questions, but I would do my best. It would make me very happy if I could."

"I don't doubt it. I like your face. My husband says that I decide too implicitly by people's faces, but I can't help it, and I notice that he does just about the same himself. I really believe that Providence has sent you to me. So, if you should do anything to prove to the contrary, I should be terribly disappointed. You wont, will you, my dear?"

"Not if I can help it. I will write to-day to the clergyman of my native town, and to his wife. They have known me ever since I was born, and can tell you all about me."

"Never mind, so far as *we* are concerned. As I said, your face is quite enough for me, and I am far from believing in *all* faces, I assure you. You may write to your friends if it will be a satisfaction to yourself; but do not feel obliged to do it on our account. When you feel rested and stronger you may tell me all your troubles. And I shall believe every word you say."

"Thank you, how good you are."

"Oh, no! I'm far from good. I'll tell you now, I have a very irritable disposition. Little things fret me almost to death when I don't feel well, and sometimes you will have a very tedious time with me. Everybody does. But my friends all forgive me, for I have the hardest of it. Nothing is harder than to know that you are disagreeable, and not to be able to help it. But I shall certainly try to make your home pleasant. I'll not forget that I had a daughter once ——"

Here Mrs. Roselle began to weep in a very nervous manner, and Eirene intuitively felt wherein she was to comfort and even support her.

Eirene was a born comforter. The sight of this gentle lady's tears called all her swift sympathies into action, and when Mr. Roselle entered the room a few minutes later, he found the young stranger bathing his wife's temples and soothing her as if she had been a child.

"I told you, father, that I felt Providence had sent her to us, and now I know it. Such a touch on my aching head I haven' felt since Alice died," and she began to weep afresh.

"Don't, mother!" he said tenderly, and yet imploringly. "Don't give up to your feelings now. You know how it takes your strength, and how it troubles me."

"Yes, I know. It hurts me to think I trouble you, but *what* a comfort it will be to have somebody at last with whom I can cry as much as I please, and it wont trouble! Some one to whom I can tell *all* my feelings; what a comfort!"

"And what a comfort to me!" said Mr. Roselle. "I will pay any one a handsome salary, mother, who will let you cry just as much as you wish, who can enter into all your feelings without being worn out by them."

"Now, father, that don't sound just kind, but I know you don't mean anything, and that I *am* a trial crying so much over what you cannot help. It's a trial because you *can't* help it!" This comforting thought revived Mrs. Roselle's spirits so much that she dried her last tears herself and sat up, and smiled upon her husband a perfectly enchanting smile, which he returned with another so tender, it was proof in itself that she was the absolute queen over his heart, if she was a weeping one.

"I must tell you," she said later to Eirene, "that in about two years we intend to take the girls to Europe to study. You must know this, so that if you should not want to go with us, though I hope you will, that you may prepare yourself for a more satisfactory position. What would you like to do, dear?"

Eirene told her that she would like to qualify herself to be a thorough bookkeeper and corresponding clerk in some large establishment devoted to ladies' fabrics. That she thought such a position would command an income approaching nearer to a man's who devotes all his time and power to a business; that she had been working towards it as fast as she could, unaided, and alone; that she could already read and write French, and had studied German.

"Not a bad idea," said Mrs. Roselle, "for one who must earn her own support. It would give you great independence, my dear, and I should say that that was something that you surely need to cultivate, as you *have* to face the world alone. You will have time to go on with your studies here. Then there's the Business College, you can attend it evenings, just as well as not, and Pompey can be sent for you. I feel that I have a duty to do to you, my child, and I shall do it. I shall help you to help yourself, so that as long as you live you can carry your fortune with you, the source of an honorable competency and position in yourself. I have often thought of it, if I hadn't a husband and money, what would become of me! Why, my dear, if I were suddenly to lose both, and find myself a stranger in the streets, I should be worse off than you were last night. Nothing is so abjectly helpless as a superficially educated woman suddenly brought to want or to take care of herself. Mr. Roselle thought of this when he saw you—how it would have been with me, or his own daughter—"

Here came a fresh flood of tears, and Eirene spent at least another hour consoling her, and listening to tender reminiscences of her "dear, dead daughter."

That night Eirene kneeled long by the white bed in the neat room which she was to call her own. Forty-eight hours had not passed since she started forth in the street alone, and here she was, sheltered, protected, with the prospect of usefulness and independence before her. Already she had more than she had even dared to ask or hope for, how much more! Already she had what so many before her, alone and strange as she was, had sought, and sought in vain. And what had been their portion in this great Babylon! She shuddered as she thought. One day in the streets, friendless and houseless, had proved to her to what extremity many such days had brought her sisters. And as she thought, here on her knees, with uplifted face, and outstretched hands, she vowed to God a vow that from that hour to the last, as she had opportunity, she would consecrate it all to the help of the poor, the friendless, the struggling of her own sex; that no woman should be too depraved, nor too forsaken for her to help according to her power. She would do what she could to upbuild a self-helping, holy womanhood in the land, and she kept her vow.

"To do it I must begin with myself," she said as she arose from her knees.

Thus her new life began. Like every other phase of human life, it ran on through sunshine and shadow. Mrs. Roselle told the truth of herself. She was one of those lovely, difficult women of whom the world is full. "Her nervous system was perfectly shattered," she told her friends. And we all know that the loveliest woman on earth is to be dreaded if she has come to make a darling hobby of her nervous system, above all to dote upon it as "perfectly shattered." Mrs. Roselle's had been treated neither better nor worse than that of the average American woman of her class. Ignorance of the laws of life, self-indulgence, and the indulgence of others, with actual sickness and bereavement, had made her one of that innumerable host who torment themselves and everybody else. Mrs. Roselle's intentions were always kind and unselfish. If her "nerves" had only allowed her to carry them into action, she would have been an angel upon earth. Alas! in action she was capricious, irritable, and unreasonable. She had humored herself, and been humored by her friends, till it was indispensable to her existence that some one should live with her whose whole business on earth was to humor her whims, and listen to the story of her ailments and afflictions. This office now devolved upon Eirene. It was one which it had been almost impossible to fill by any one outside of her own family, who dearly loved her; but here at last was a stranger whose patience and sympathy had never been equalled by any mortal but her own husband. Her plan for Eirene was christian and philanthropic, but the more necessary that Eirene became to her, the more difficult it was for her to carry out her benevolent design for her welfare. Always to have one ready to bathe her head, to listen to her cry, to wipe her tears, to comfort her, to sympathize with her, was a luxury of which her shattered nerves would not willingly be denied. Thus it came to pass that, outside of the evening hours actually spent in the business college, Eirene found not an hour to study, save her old ones when everybody else slept.

The children were just what the orphaned grand-children of doting grandparents usually are—"perfectly spoiled," in many respects, and yet retaining much of the sweetness of temper and integrity of character which were theirs by natural inheritance. They were both a torment and a delight to their youthful companion and teacher, for their teacher she became, in a deeper sense than any paid master ever could become. She would weep over their impertinence and ingratitude, and forget it all the next moment, when she felt their arms about her neck and their kisses on her mouth. The brightest hour of her day was that in which she walked out with them each afternoon. Then the great city became her educator. She grew familiar with all its public and private galleries of art. She learned not only every picture shop, but almost every picture in them. She spent hours with the children at Goupil's and Schauss', studying some of the best pictures and engravings of the world. With Alice and Anna she visited her early friends the sparrows. She told them stories sitting in the sunshine by the fountain in the little parks. The very spires of the churches piercing the blue air taught her something of proportion and beauty. Her relation with Mrs. Roselle, whom she really loved, gave her deeper lessons in patience and self-control. In the business college she was laying the foundation of a solid education. Everywhere, in sky and air and earth, she saw beauty and drew it into her life. Thus her whole nature grew, and her culture had already become fine and æsthetic.

In two years the Roselles went to Europe. Mrs. Roselle had a "nervous spasm," in which she accused Eirene of ingratitude because she declined to go with them. When she came out of it, she took her into her arms and told her she had done right. She did not know how to live without her, but now her nerves would let her, she felt that she had done right in refusing to leave her own mother for so many years; if it were only for a year or two it would have been different. "My own dear child would never have left *her* mother for so long," she said, "then how can I blame you! Only I don't know how to part with you! I love you, my dear, and you wont lay up anything against my poor nerves?"

"No, indeed," exclaimed Eirene, as she began to soothe her forehead with her hand and to bring her out of another spasm.

They parted most affectionately, and with many tears. Eirene felt even more keenly than her friend how much she owed her in a thousand ways.

They never met again. Within a year Mrs. Roselle died, and those shattered nerves found rest, let us believe, in that land whose inhabitants we are told are never sick, and wherein there is neither sorrow, nor crying, neither any more pain.

Her friends were gone. Again she was alone in the city; but if alone, not helpless as she was when she entered it. She had studied diligently, and without flagging. She had won already the capital of the poor,—the assured power of self-support. To resolve in a moment of impulsive strength to labor on to a certain end, is one thing; to carry that resolve into execution, through obstacle, opposition, weariness and discouragement, is another and much more difficult thing to do. The bewilderment, the weakness, born of keen mental pain, are the effects hardest to overcome. Against these, through many joyless hours and days, Eirene struggled. Against these, while her heart cried, "Why strive!" she still had striven, just as she resolved to do in the little chamber at home, in the hour when she first came back to life, to her life--to strive, no matter how long, till she could command the highest wages of educated labor.

Now, for the first time she found herself face to face with the great and unsolved problems of daily life, as seen in a vast city with its inequalities, its misery, its temptation, its uncertain rewards! The problems of labor, of sex, of condition, confronted her. In silence she sought to work them out. Why could she receive not one-half of what a man would receive in the same place and for the same labor? Was not a part of the cause found in the fact that she had never received a man's training, and was not supposed to bear a man's responsibilities? But she *did* bear a man's responsibility without receiving his reward. How would it be if by right she could claim that? She would try. She would fit herself thoroughly to be a book-keeper. She entered the business college in advance, and such was her proficiency that, at the end of two years, she received a diploma from its President, with a note addressed to the proprietor of a famous ladies' shop in the city. Her teacher said: "Mr. Mann has applied to me for a first-class book-keeper whom I can recommend, a lady preferred. I have chosen you. Mr. Mann is a just man, but likes to drive a sharp bargain. You are fitted to fill a first-class position. You know the salary such a position commands. Ask for it, it is your due, and do not be frightened when he tells you that he can get somebody a great deal cheaper. So he can, but he will want you."

Eirene approached the counting-room of Mr. Mann with many misgivings, but fortified by the words of the teacher, she presented her diploma and letter.

"What salary would you expect in the position?" inquired Mr. Mann—a nervous, sharp-featured business man, looking over his spectacles.

"As much as you would give a man in the same position, and for doing the same work," said the calm, even voice of Eirene.

"Oh! That is what we never do. It is the reason that I applied at the college for a lady. I didn't want to pay a man's salary, when there are so many young ladies who would be glad to fill it for half of the sum that I should pay a man."

"I have studied long and faithfully to fit myself to do this work as well as a man could do it. I can translate and correspond in French, also in German, which the President told me would be a very important qualification in your business; for doing this I want all that a man would get for doing the same things, or if not, I will perform less responsible labor."

"Really, you are very exacting in your demands and ideas. Why, don't you know that *no* lady *expects* to receive the wages of a man?"

"Nor should she, unless she is prepared to render service equal to a man's. But if she can, is it not unjust to deny it?"

"It may be unjust, but we must take the world as we find it. You don't look it, child; but really, you *are* strong minded. That is a very dangerous class of women. I would advise you as a friend to keep away from them. Am sorry we can't come to terms."

Eirene felt a struggle going on within her, between her natural compliance and her sense of justice. It was hard not to yield, not to yield to her natural self-estimate and say, "I will take the situation at what you are willing to pay," but the words of her teacher, and the thought of all that she wanted money for, supported her, and made her action stronger than her impulse.

Without a word, without the slightest prospect of any other place before her, she took her teacher's letter and diploma, and walked away.

The quiet dignity of the act impressed Mr. Mann more than the most powerful argument could have done. As a business man, he depended much on the recommendation of the college principal. He was perfectly aware that such a person as the teacher pronounced the bearer of the letter to be would be invaluable to him. And as he watched the face of its bearer as she moved quietly away, he believed every word that the teacher had said.

In spite of herself, it was with a feeling of discouragement that Eirene laid down that night.

"No matter how competent or how instructed, after all, how hard it is for a woman to face the world in the shape of one rich man, to ask him for employment, without which she cannot honorably live, and to have him refuse," she said to herself.

"How can I do it over again to-morrow?" she asked, "and yet I *can*. I must go again to my teacher, and ask him to send me to some one else."

But the first mail in the morning brought her a letter from Mr. Mann, stating that her services as book-keeper and corresponding clerk in his establishment would be accepted on her own terms. At first it seemed impossible that such success could be her portion, yet she went and took her seat, and began her duties as quietly and composedly as if she had been doing them all her life, and had never made an effort to secure the power to do them. More and more it became a strangely isolated life that she lived, alone and unknown in the great city. How small her own existence seemed to her, how feeble a ripple in the mighty current of human life rushing around her. She was busy all day, she was tired at night, and for this very reason probably she felt the more keenly the need of some human presence which belonged to her.

"I am one of a great multitude," she would say, as she looked down from her high watching place, some starry night, upon the innumerable lights of the city gleaming far beneath her. "Only one! How many there must be who live and work as I do. How hard and long life would seem to go and come all through it with no one near to love. Yet this happens to many." It did not occur to her that anything different could ever happen to her. It is so natural for youth to believe that it is done with life, even before it has fairly begun it.

## CHAPTER XIII.

### THE DE PEYSTERS.

PEOPLE who imagine that all the aristocracy of New York is centered in Fifth Avenue or the streets which border it, have a very superficial knowledge of the real life of the metropolis. Many a sleepy old mansion which rarely deigns to open its securely closed eyes of windows upon the roaring and encroaching mart below, hides within its excluding and exclusive shutters the best blood of the ancient Knickerbockers.

Such an one was De Peyster House. It stood on a street which fashion had long since forgotten. All people who felt that their position in the first society needed visible support to sustain it, had left the neighborhood long before. But the De Peysters could afford to live "down town."

DE PEYSTER! There it was on the broad, bright brass door-plate. The name was sufficient unto itself, and would have been if it had glittered out from among the hovels of the Five Points. But as it was not, it only sent its long gleam athwart the sturdy warehouses which had defiantly run up beside its very door, and out toward the little triangular park before it which, being owned by the De Peysters, who were in no need of money, and who withal were very fond of their own way, and proud to show that they could afford to take it, still remained a breathing-spot for men and women, animals, birds, and little children, amid all the thunder of traffic, in spite of the enormous sums offered by corporations to buy it.

"Just like those old Knickerbockers—no progress, no public spirit in them; they want everything precisely as their Dutch great-grandfathers had it," said young New York in a pet, because he could not turn De Peyster Park into a warehouse for hams. Thus the birds sang and the lilacs blossomed, and the little old fountain spurted clear water out of its broken-nosed Neptune, and the little children came with their nurses, and the ragged children who had no shoes, and the old men and the old women from the tenement-houses, who would never have seen the bright face of Nature else, and all were happy in the little park while great New York rushed and roared around it, pausing only long enough some day to wonder and lament that such a building-spot, "worth a fortune," should be wasted. Occasionally, in the fragrant spring mornings, and in the late October, when the bright, brief autumnal day was taking its tender farewell of the world, the sleepy old mansion would open wide its eyes, which were shut often and long, and then in its great drawing-room windows might sometimes be seen a fair and wistful face looking out toward the old trees across the street, and sometimes a strong man's face would be turned in the same direction. But there were months and months that this never happened, and on its most gala days the old mansion had a rather shut-up and solitary look. No glad children ever ran up and down its high steps, no baby's face ever shone out of its windows. All its visitors came and went in stately carriages. Its door-knob was very bright, its shutters very white, its brick walls very venerable, with gray tints and tiny tufts of moss which outlined the carving on its quaintly-wrought pilasters and cornices.

De Peyster house was one of the comparatively few houses left which boast a proud historic record in this city of swift transition and eager change. When it was built in the seventeenth century, orchards blossomed about it, and meadows, musical with tinkling cow-bells, ran down almost to the Battery, where the great ships come in. Where the cows grazed and apples ripened, great warehouses now soared high in air, and pushed and almost stifled each other for room. The great garden of the De Peysters, the pride of New Amsterdam in colonial days, was now cut into lots, buried in mouldy vaults, and covered with dingy houses into which the sunshine never came. Nearly all the lands lying between their house and the bay had once been owned by the De Peysters. It was a De Peyster who had given the city the site of the old Fly Market, and the site of old Federal Hall, in which Washington was inaugurated first President of the United States, and on which now stands the vast marble pile of the New York Custom House. It was a De Peyster who gave the bell into whose metal the citizens of old Amsterdam cast their silver coins, which swung so long in the quaint belfry of the old Middle Church on Nassau street, and which by Lafayette Square still sends out the silvery chimes which have floated above the city for more than one hundred and fifty years.

Year by year, generation by generation the old house had watched its lands vanish, its race depart, to sleep in the deep vault under the pavement of Trinity; had watched the sure advance of commerce, its resistless foe; but while the very face of the earth changed, it changed not—it seemed to frown in the face of time, and to defy mutation. It could afford to smile on the narrow, shallow, toppling piles which to-day are called "palatial," this kingly old house, that tarried to tell what comfort and splendor were in colonial times. Here was its bread double door, and above it the great arched window and hanging balcony, from which on many a field-day the troops of New Amsterdam had been reviewed by colonial Governors, and from which, long after, Governor George Clinton and General Washington reviewed the Revolutionary Army in New York. Within, its great central hall, its tapestry room, its blue room, its wainscoted rooms remained untouched of time or progress. Here in its grand drawing-room were the costly furniture and works of art brought to New Amsterdam by Johanes de Peyster early in the seventeenth century. Here in the library was the portrait of the grandfather of this Johanes de Peyster, in flowing wig and robe, and ruffles, a nobleman of France, who fled to Holland with his family at the massacre of St. Bartholomew. Here hung the portraits of his wife and child, in courtly robes, and that of Colonel Arent Schuyler De Peyster, famed as soldier, diplomat, and poet, with pictures of every generation of the family down to the fair and stately De Peysters of to-day. Its spacious wainscoted dining-room was still redolent of colonial cheer; its side-board still resplendent with historic silver, the massive plate brought by Johanes De Peyster from Holland, the embossed punch-bowl and tankards—memorials of the family in France and their grandeur in early centuries. Here was a shrine sacred to the past in the very heart of the present. What did the old house, so full of proud and tender memories, care for roaring trade or young New York! Yet all left of its race to inhabit it, and to hold guard over its treasures, surely belonged to young New York, were of it, and yet not of it—a brother and sister, Cornelia and Pierre De Peyster. It is right here to call her Cornelia De Peyster, she was so truly a daughter of her race, never having merged one of its characteristics in the nominal marriage which had given her in the world another name. Mrs. Stuyvesant was the name by which the world now called her; she had borne it for years, and yet had never become used to it; even now she would instinctively shudder when she heard herself suddenly called by it. Hers had been one of those ill-fated marriages out of which so much of the misery and sin of this world are born. To be sure, it did not last very long. She had not passed youth, and was already free; and yet no less the blight that other life had cast on hers could never be effaced. And it was not wholly Cornelia's fault that she entered into this marriage; her brother knew that. Next to the rich and dissolute bachelor who coveted this lily of the De Peyster house and bore her away at last, it was unwittingly, the fault of her only brother, who, though he never sought it, acquiesced in his sister's sacrifice. At least he was negatively to blame, for, had he opposed it, it could scarcely have happened. And yet it was hardly his fault; it was the fault of his education, and the world's accepted standard of a wôman's only destiny. He was a very young man then, and had just arrived in Europe to travel, and to complete his university studies. Cornelia accompanied him, for the brother and sister were very near in heart to each other. She visited the family estates at Rouen and the ancient family fief near Antwerp; she sought to draw near in spirit to her rel tives there, and found to her astonishment that she was an American, and that more than the ocean divided her in sympathy from her European kindred. She was a star at court, and shone in the society of capitals. She studied art in famous galleries, and copied pictures in secret. But wherever she went one shadow followed her, and Philip Stuyvesant was by her side. He was twice her age, had lived one—aye, many lives, not one guiltless since that of infancy; now he wanted to begin another, with this lily maid as its flower.

"You are a woman, you know; so there seems to be nothing for you at last but marriage," said Pierre, when Cornelia came to him for advice—to this brother who had reached the astute age of twenty-one. "Perhaps you care as much for Phil. as you ever will for any one. You say that he fascinates you, and the families, you know, have intermarried for generations. Phil. seems desperate. May be it is as well to succumb to destiny first as last, as it's marriage or nothing for a woman; though I'm sure I don't want to lose you; and if Phil. would get out of the way, we might have a good time for several years."

It is but just to Pierre to say that he was unacquainted with the secret wickedness of Philip Stuyvesant's life; had he known of it, it would have aroused him to rage that such a man should dare to seek the hand of his only sister, and would have modified his ideas forever of marriage as a woman's *only* destiny. As it was, we shall see that he lived to regret these words—more, perhaps, than any that he ever uttered.

Cornelia De Peyster married Philip Stuyvesant, and only herself and God ever knew all the disenchantment and disgust and weariness of life which that marriage brought her. The men of the De Peyster house had their faults, but they were the faults of dominant will and over-strong prejudices, not of dishonor. They were true to their higher selves, and true to their fellow-men back to the days when they were driven from their native seats, for conscience's sake, by the persecutions of Charles IX. Cornelia De Peyster knew manhood only through her brother and father; hers was the highest idea of manly rectitude and of manly honor. With a soul in its inmost self pure as the snow, no words can tell what it was to her to find that the man whom she believed she could have loved —the man to whom she was already married, was the slave of low vices; to be compelled to read the record of his shameful life; to know, now that he had won her, that she was no more to him than a hundred others. Bitter knowledge to any woman, it was doubly bitter to her, so pure and proud, so young and disappointed. The years spent with him seemed to cast an irremediable blight over her nature. It was not her visible life so much, it was her soul whose bloom was destroyed. In five years he died, and the youthful widow came back to the house in which she and her father and his father before were born, and for years the brother and sister had lived together and called De Peyster house home.

Here Cornelia De Peyster, endowed with the finest natural gifts, drifted into a perfectly objectless existence. Anything more idle or aimless than her days, it would be difficult to imagine. Yet it was impossible to come in contact with her and not feel that she was born for better things than the inanities which filled her life. We see women in plenty driving about, leaving bits of pasteboard at the doors of houses, spending half of their days in dry-goods shops, and the other half in vapid amusements, and it never occurs to us that they have powers adapted to higher occupation, or were born to a better destiny.

But Cornelia De Peyster was not one of these. You felt constantly that she played with life; that she amused herself with toys upon its surface, while rich powers were lying in her soul unoccupied, and noble tasks in her life unattempted. It was often from sheer indolence that she left the latter untouched, and from fear that she shrank back from the possibilities which she felt in her own being. "It is all vanity," she would murmur to herself, "this struggle for a career, or for anything in this world, making life an endless endeavor. People can never reach their ideal; and if they could, by that time death would take them. Life is so short, it does not give one half time enough to enjoy; there is no time left for work. But what delight life withholds from me! My God! how I could love and live! But it is too late! Eulalie, come and dress my hair; make me as handsome as you can. My beauty, at least, must not be a failure." But the defrauded soul set its own seal upon those exquisite features, and told of its cheated life in every expression of the changeful face. Every glance of those eyes, every movement of that graceful form suggested the Might Have Been!

When the fine eye-brows arched, when the soft fire in the oriental eyes burned in steadfast flame—as the slight figure grew erect and stately, every curve swelling with unconquerable pride, yet alluring with irresistible grace, you said, "This woman is Zenobia; she was born an empress."

When these same eyes melted in tender ruth, growing dim with tears of loving compassion as she listened to some story of human sorrow, and listened only to relieve, you said she was born a Sister of Mercy, and no other.

There were days when she ordered the coachman to drive to the outskirts of the city, to the new streets struggling through masses of rock on which were perched the shanties of Irish laborers, where children and goats scrambled and played together. The scanty grass creeping over the boulders was a relief to her eyes after the desert of stone and brick through which she had passed; yet it was not for this meagre beauty which Nature reluctantly filtered through seams of granite that she came in search. It was the half-barbarous yet often beautiful children that she came to see. They all knew the lovely lady, and would come scrambling down the rocks in flocks, surrounding the carriage with laughter and shouts, as they stretched out ragged aprons and dirty hands for the painted primers and sugar bon-bons, which never failed to come from the coach in showers. To have watched her face at this time, radiant with happiness as she scattered her treasures among the excited children, or suffused with pity as she bent over one looking sad, or sick or neglected among the rest, you would say, "What a Madonna face! This woman was made for a mother, to find life and love, and a career in her children." Thus Cornelia, looking at the ragged, hard-worked mother in her cabin door, surrounded by her barefooted brood, would sigh, and say to herself as she turned away, "*She* is happier than I. Her life is hard, and lacks many comforts. Her husband is ignorant, and perhaps sometimes brutal; yet he loves her in his rough way, and she is happy and satisfied in him and her children. She has more to live for than I have, her life is more natural and complete than mine." Of course Cornelia Stuyvesant was the last woman in the world who would have exchanged places with the Irish mother; yet she was sincere in recognizing a charm in the other's life that her own had not, and while she pitied her poverty she envied her happiness.

Life had already taken on a very different aspect to Pierre De Peyster from that which it wore when he advised his sister to marry Philip Stuyvesant. It is the ordinary opinion that it is woman alone who feels her personal life to be incomplete until she finds her mate. This is probably true in average life. Yet there are many men, and they men of the highest type, who cannot remember the time when they did not see, if ever so dimly, in their possible future, the distant vision of their fairer self. In the proportion that they feel their own nature to be incomplete, do they sigh for its counterpart.

This had all been true of Pierre De Peyster, yet nobody had guessed it. He was a proud man, whose pride was all embodied in what he hid, not in what he revealed. Not a night of his life but, as he sat brooding in his solitary room, he thanked Fate and his own organ of secretiveness, that nobody on earth knew his heart—his real heart—that deep, tender soul of himself which could love and suffer so much. He felt a silent satisfaction in the personal reputation that he had won in his own exclusive circle of being a woman-hater. Very likely he felt a little unconscious vanity in the satisfaction that this very reputation made him a more interesting personage in the estimation of such women as he was most desirous to please. Still the chief satisfaction arose from the fact that this seemed to release him from all obligation to pay special attention to any lady. No one expected it—he was a woman-hater—that was reason enough why he should not put himself out for any lady. He rarely did. His private personal opinion was, that in comparison with his standard of what a woman should be, nearly all the women whom he knew were little more than idiots. He was intellectually arrogant, and it did not seem to him to be worth the while to trouble himself in any way for creatures of such petty lives and feeble comprehension. They did not interest him, they did not even amuse him. Every one disappointed him if in a favorable moment he was aroused to expect anything more than a surface satisfaction, a passing pleasure of sight or sound. Nor was this strange with a man of deep nature, moving in merely fashionable society. Nearly all the women whom he met lived artificial lives. They toiled not, they thought not. Others toiled and thought for them. With them existence was a brilliant, yet dreary round of mere amusement, which in its sum was toil, and which left them at last worn, haggard, and inane. The only woman he knew whom he loved was his sister Cornelia. He watched her paint, he listened to her sing, he read his favorite books with her, conversed with her on many topics; but there was one he rarely mentioned. Nevertheless, he said to her one day: "Corna, I wish you were a man, or not my sister; then as a companion I believe you would be more to me than any other person that I ever met."

"What can you want more than a sister?" she asked archly.

"What could you want more than a brother?" he asked solemnly.

"Nothing."

"There's your woman's affectation. You of all women can afford to tell the truth. You are the truest woman I know, yet even you serenely tell me a fib. You know as well as I do, that there is something more—a satisfaction in sympathy, through unlikeness, that can only be found in one not of our own blood or sex."

"Yes, I suppose that is true. Why don't you marry, Pierre?"

"More affectation. Whom am I to marry, for heaven's sake? Gimp and buttons, fuss and feathers, pearl powder and crimpers? torpid livers and turgid brains? or woman's rights and public lectures? Not one of them, thank you."

"Well, I know lovely girls, and so do you, who have brains enough, but who don't bother their heads about woman's rights, and who have nothing the matter with their livers."

"Do you? Well, they don't interest me. I have never seen a woman yet whom I would have been willing to marry, and I don't believe that I ever shall."

But the more Pierre De Peyster appeared a confirmed old bachelor even to his sister, the more he retired into himself, and into his room, and pictured the impossible woman whom he had never seen, and never was to see. What a dream of beauty she was! She was just as faultlessly lovely in cruel day cross-lights as in the evening glow. What an intellect she had; but she was to use it solely in appreciating her husband! She was full of spirit, yet she had no will; her will was to be her husband's, and her husband was Pierre De Peyster. She had exquisite sensibility, yet she was never to scream, or be afraid of things, after the fashion of modern maidens. She was intellectually the peer of any man, without a man's ambition; she was the most exquisitely feminine of women, without one feminine weakness; in fine, she was one of the loveliest and most preposterous dream-women that ever inhabited a man's brain. The more Pierre thought about her, the more perfect and impossible she became, the less likeness he found to her among the women of his acquaintance, and the more persistently he retired to his apartment, where, gazing up through a cloud of smoke, he spent his late hours building dream-palaces for her. Thus the ladies of his "set" said: "Pierre De Peyster gets to be more of an old bachelor every year; and he never was a beau." Yet they troubled their heads very little about him. He was rich and manly, but then they knew many other men who were both, and yet took much pains to please and woo them, and this was what Pierre De Peyster never did. The rising professional men of his acquaintance said: "What a pity Pierre De Peyster isn't poor! If he were, he could make his mark in the world." And the driving business men who knew him would say: "There's De Peyster! If it wasn't for that old Knickerbocker blood, he'd amount to something; with his fortune, he might make millions more out of it if he only had a little more energy, and wanted to." But he did not seem to want to do so. "I can shut my eyes and grow as rich as a man ought to be," he would say. Yet, in a quiet way, he managed his sister's fortune and his own with energy and wisdom, gathering in rents and dividends, looking after bonds and stocks, as if to do so was the supreme object of his existence. But often nothing but his pride, and sense of honor, for he regarded his inheritance as a trust, could have kept him so busy. He liked his ease, and in all that he did he felt vaguely, hour by hour, that in some way he had missed the highest and finest incentive of life. In his profession he was a skilful surgeon, but he had practised very little of late; it was too much trouble. "What's the use?" he said of that, as he did of amassing more wealth. He was not a man to put himself out much in the way of exertion, unless moved by a commanding motive. This had never come to him. A pure love of science had impelled him to walk the hospitals of Paris and London, and to avail himself of the instruction of the best American and European schools; but having become technically a master in his profession, he shrank from its practice. He saw no occasion for it, he said, and never dreamed that his occasion had not come. All around him he saw men struggling after opportunity, and he said: "Poor devils! Why don't they see that nothing they are after is worth the ado they make about it. For my part, I don't think that it pays to live. It is altogether too much trouble." I am afraid that it never occurred to him at this time to be especially grateful for his own rich endowments of mind or fortune. He was born a De Peyster, and could not realize that if he had been born John Stokes, a good many rounds farther down the ladder of life, he might have tried as hard as John to scramble up and make a standing-place for himself on a higher round. One thing is certain, with all his knowledge of science and society, at this time he was not at all acquainted with himself, and did not know that life to him, as a personal experience, was but a dawning dream, not yet a reality.

Cornelia De Peyster went to church because she liked it, because she loved the service and loved the old church. Pierre strayed there occasionally from early habit, and to please his sister. When there I am afraid that he worshipped as the men of this generation chiefly worship, enjoying the music, wandering through the prayers, listening to the sermon very little, and looking about very much. Old Trinity had always a charm for his eyes and heart ever since he sat in that same square pew a little boy by his mother's side, and watched the tall trees in the church-yard wave their boughs outside and lay their delicate tracing in waving lines of shadow against the grand window of stained glass. It seemed so unchanged to him one October Sabbath, the great dim temple, with its lofty gothic arch, through whose mullioned windows the yellow light flickered down upon the brown stone pillars.

Since he was a little boy Pierre thought that he had not seen the old church look so beautiful as it did this afternoon, with the radiance of the October atmosphere floating through the open doors and pouring through the waving boughs of the trees outside, illuminating the deep hues of the glass and hovering above the congregation in visible glory. In a sudden apocalypse of sunshine the gorgeous Christ on the great stained window seemed to stretch forth his hands in loving benediction upon the worshippers. Pierre's eyes followed the sunshine as it glinted downward till it rested on the head of a woman in the aisle. The first thing he knew he was wondering why his eyes continued to rest there; why, when he withdrew them, that they wandered directly back. It was the pure womanliness of the head and brow that attracted him, for surely the face of their owner was scarcely young. He looked as he had often looked in Rome or Venice at some rare head or face in the crowd—a peasant's, or a beggar's, perhaps, it mattered not which to him, for he was a student of human faces, and the study afforded him equal pleasure in every phase and condition in life. But now, as his eyes went persistently back to this face in the aisle, they discovered at last that it was young, although its first impression was not that of youth. At last he saw that it was youth, underlying and struggling through an expression of thought and care and weariness. The history of a long life seemed stamped on those features, and to look forth from those eyes—those eyes! He caught their expression as the girl half turned toward him to escape the dazzling radiance which fell on her face. A strange, new thrill went through his heart, and even while he felt it he questioned what it was. And who was she! More plainly dressed than the servant by her side, had she been attired in rags he must yet have recognized her as a lady—the expression of refinement and culture on the face could not be mistaken, the very choice of her colors showed it, the soft gray dress and the blue ribbon touching her hair.

The longer he gazed, the more this face took on the look of the woman of his dreams, and yet had he in his visions ever seen *her*—faded, weary, and poor? Never. "*She* had fed on the roses, and lain in the lilies of life." And whatever else were true of this woman before him, life had come to her in no gentle guise; it had strained her faculties, it had smitten her heart; he who had read many a life-story on many a human face knew this as he gazed upon this one, and the knowledge seemed to draw him toward her in a tender, an almost divine pity, such as he had never felt before.

The sweet voices of the altar-boys floated in from afar, drawing nearer, nearer, till the chancel was filled with the little white-robed choristers; the organ anthem flooded the arches; the great congregation rose, kneeled, and responded; the October atmosphere still floating in baptized them anew with its golden glory; but through all, Pierre De Peyster saw but a single face, thought of but one mortal. She, alone with her own spirit, sitting on the stranger's seat in the aisle, saw no one. The music, the prayer, the glory lifted her out of her daily condition into the holy awe of God's temple, and she worshipped. Loss, regret, weariness were nothing to her now; she lifted her face into the radiance which fell from the pictured image of her Lord, and worshipped.

Pierre De Peyster, half an hour later, entering his carriage, saw a slender figure disappear in the crowd moving up Broadway, and as it vanished he sighed.

The superlative loveliness of the Sabbath day had allured Eirene on and on till she stood at the gate of Trinity. When she came it was not time for evening service and she wandered into the ancient grave-yard. How eloquent it seemed to her, this spot shadowed by trees, lined with turf, bordered with innocent flowers—wherein the forefathers of the metropolis slept undisturbed by the tumult of the encroaching streets, by the troubled splendor of a civilization of which they never dreamed. With the deepest interest she read the half-effaced names on the old brown head-stones and mouldy vaults. Mere names had always had a singular power to attract or repel her, and as she read them over, she wondered that she liked so many of the old historic names of New York. "Cortlandt," "Stuyvesandt," "Beekman," "De Lancey," "Schuyler," "Bayard," she liked them all. And here was the name of De Peyster—she read it on the face of the ancient vault of the family; "Abraham De Peyster," "Katherina De Peyster," "Cornelia De Peyster," "Pierre Guillaume De Peyster," and many more. "I like this name better than any other," she said to herself. Thus with the name of De Peyster in her mind, she had entered Trinity Church and sat down in its aisle.

## CHAPTER XIV.

### HILLTOP.

WHAT a change had come over Hilltop. From the quietest of ancient hamlets, in a single year it was transformed into a fashionable summer resort. For hundreds of years a mineral spring had bubbled out of a rock on its highest pinnacle. The old people of the neighborhood for many generations had believed that these waters were full of health and healing. When their blood was out of order, when they had the "dyspepsy," or "rhumatiz," a wagon and a barrel were dispatched to "The Spring." The mineral water once deposited in the coolest spot in the cellar, the invalid drank assiduously every day, till new life and strength came back with the new iron in the blood. Next to the Lord, the people of Hilltop believed in their spring. They would say, "It's all on account of the spring that Grandpy Smoot has lived to be ninety, and no doctor never could get a livin' here."

There came a time in the cycles of God when the spring was not to renew the life of the people of Hilltop only, but to pour forth health for many people out in the wide world as well. It happened in this wise. Amzi Smoot, who was employed in a large hotel in Boston, one dog-day morning was commiserating a fellow-clerk on his sickly appearance. "I say, Snipe," he said, "if you'd only go up to our house and drink of our spring for a while, you won't look so pale and pimpin'."

Mr. Sharpe, the proprietor, who was sitting near at a high desk, said nothing, but listened to this remark and to the conversation which came after with the ears of a speculator and a philosopher.

The next Saturday Snipe went to Hilltop with Amzi. What with the medicinal waters of the spring, and the fascinating presence of Miss Nancy, both liver and heart suddenly became so active, that the world, from being jaundiced, all at once became a very beautiful world indeed, and Hilltop was its Paradise.

The Saturday following Mr. Sharpe said carelessly to Amzi, "What was that you were saying the other day about a spring on your father's farm? Snipe says the water is doing him any amount of good. I have a mind to try it myself; not out of his bottle, but to go up with you and spend Sunday, taste the spring, and get a sniff of the mountain air—that is if you've no objection, Amzi." Objection! Amzi never felt so honored in all his life. I dare say that it was the first and last time that the rich proprietor ever went on a social visit to one of his clerk's. Amzi drove him all about in the family buggy. Mr. Sharpe's keen eyes saw many things, and his equally keen mind came to many significant conclusions.

He saw that the remarkably wild, romantic beauty of Hilltop was still near the railroad and accessible to the great cities. He noted the pure, invigorating quality of the atmosphere. He tasted the waters of the spring, and if he had had no faith in their medicinal properties, he could still see that their surroundings would be most attractive to pleasure seekers. He was sagacious enough to conclude that here was a chance for a profitable investment, and he made it. The first result of his Sunday's seeing and planning made Farmer Smoot, by the sale of the spring-portion of his farm, the richest man on Hilltop. The second result was a host of mechanics, and the strange sights and sounds of building in the widely scattered and quiet town. The third result was visible, at the beginning of the next summer, in the form of an elegant and spacious hotel, with wide verandahs and crowning cupola surmounted by a floating flag. Blackberry bushes, mulleins, and dog-daisies no longer ran rampant on Pinnacle Hill. They had been massacred to make place for velvet turf, broad flower-bordered avenues, rustic seats and arbors.

Mr. Sharpe, with a taste remarkable in one of his class, instead of a heathen pagoda, built a quaint round pavilion over the ancient spring. Thus, while there were seats, shadow, and quiet for those who came to its side, its natural beauty remained undisturbed, its waters still bubbled up through mossy stones, and trickled through the fringing ferns as of old. The fourth result of Mr. Sharpe's visit changed Hilltop from the stillest of secluded towns into a watering-place of fashion.

Pinnacle House, its glistening cupola and flying flag on its lofty elevation, visible for miles around, was alike the pride and wonder of the natives.

The country girls on the railroad-station steps were no longer compelled to be satisfied with tantalizing glimpses of the styles through car windows, for every train of "the season" deposited on those very steps companies of miraculously dressed ladies and pyramids of back-breaking trunks, the weight of which no farmer boy in Hilltop had ever lifted.

The country roads, along which the hay-carts and buggies and old-time chaises of so many generations had rumbled without even fretting away their grassy borders, took on an unwonted aspect, now on summer evenings, crowded as they were with gay city equipages.

Down from the Pinnacle House, into ferny lanes, into forest roads, and into roads cut through fields of blossoming clover, rolled the stately coaches with their liveried outriders, open barouches filled with bevies of beautiful ladies and children, and the pretty basket phætons, their ponies driven by fair hands, while to the seat behind clung a caparisoned flunkey.

Until this day the simple Hilltopper had believed the smart teams of Busyville fine beyond comparison; it is not strange, then, that these unwonted splendors filled their souls with wonder if not with longing.

To none other did they bring so strange and deep a throb as to the heart of little Pansy Vale. The first one that she ever saw of these grand city carriages seemed to send a wild intuition through her brain. "Just such a fine carriage as that will come some day and carry me away," she said to herself. And from the moment that this thought came to her she never doubted it.

If Pansy hated anything, and it was certain that she did, she hated housework, and her especial detestation was wiping dishes. She knew nothing of the quiet pleasure which Eirene had felt in fulfilling household duties, and in making everything look pleasant. And Mary Vale often said to herself "I would do everything myself if I were strong enough; chores seem to come so unnatural to the child." Thus it was a new comfort to the poor mother, when the little maiden did everything that she was bidden to do without crying or fretting, if she only had the promise of going out to the gate "in time to see the carriages."

Tea was taken and all the evening tasks performed at an earlier hour, in order that the little girl might be dressed and at the gate in time to see the evening driving. It is true, also, that Mary Vale enjoyed a pathetic kind of pleasure as she sat by the open window or in the porch watching the cavalcade pass by. It seemed to her such a perfect reflection of the brillant, beautiful life of that world of which she used to dream. How she had longed to go out into that world, and, how wonderful, the world itself had come to her very door. Thus she sat one August evening, the low sunshine falling on her brown hair, as with anxious eyes she looked out on her child. Pansy stood by the gate,—a little princess waiting for her throne.

She had been unusually fretful over the dishes that evening, and her impatience while being arrayed in the blue merino frock could hardly be restrained.

"Dear me, I'll never get out there; they'll all be gone by," she said.

Now she leaned over the low gate and looked up the long hill far away to the Pinnacle House. It was early and she saw nothing yet of the gay people from the hotel, but she knew they would be sure to come, for the picturesque road by the dormer cottage was a favorite drive. As she watched and waited the little brain was very busy. "Mother says that Eirene is patient," she said to herself. "I don't care if she is. She can be patient if she wants to be, I don't; she can work if she likes to, I don't. I can't like to wash dishes and scour knives, and I'm not going to try. They make my fingers crack and make them so scratchy, they're hateful. I don't think I'll live here always. It don't seem like *my* house. If one of these strange ladies would ask me to go away with her I'd go. Mother wouldn't want me to go, nor father, but I'd cry and teaze them, and they'd let me. I love mother and father, too, and a couple of natural tears forced themselves into the child's eyes; but I don't want to stay here. I want to ride in a carriage with two horses, and have a hat full of white feathers like the girl from Boston. I'm a great deal prettier than she is if I am poor! O, there's my carriage! and my lady."

It rolled slowly down the hill, a basket phæton drawn by two black ponies, a dignified African in a livery of black and silver sitting with folded arms on the seat behind. A gentleman leaned back on its cushions, while a beautiful woman held the reins in her small and careless hand. She seemed to hold them still more loosely as she drew nearer, till at last the ponies walked slowly past the cottage, while the lady took a full survey of the little princess at the gate. "She stood in that same spot and wore that very dress a year ago. Don't you think that she is very pretty?" the child heard the lady say as the carriage rolled on. Amid the many which she had seen since, how well she remembered this carriage, the first one that she had seen on the road! That was a year ago, and the same beautiful lady was driving them now. How she had watched and watched for it, but it never came again till this evening. For the truth was that the phæton had rolled from the mountains down to the sea and then back to the city, and had only just come again to Hilltop at the beginning of another season. With a feeling of disappointment and unhappiness, which she could neither fathom nor understand, the child watched the carriage go down the hill and pass out of sight.

"She might have spoken to me, she might" said the little lips, with a passionate quiver. "She remembered me, and she said that I was pretty, and she looked and looked, but she didn't speak, not to me, but she will," and the little heart, which a moment before seemed to swell to bursting, gave a long sigh of relief.

Again the little princess shook her glittering hair and her whole face grew radiant—the carriage was coming back, coming much faster than it went away. Pansy watched it without moving her eyes, till the lady drove directly to the gate. Then she dropped her reins and leaning over said in the most natural tone in the world:

"What is your name, dear?"

"Pansy Vale."

"Pansy Vale! What a pretty name. It's just like you, too. She looks like a Pansy, don't she, Pierre, with such dark purple eyes and yellow hair?"

"She is a marked style, ve–ry," said the gentleman thus appealed to."

"Do you live in this pretty little house?"

"Yes, madam."

"You like to live here, don't you?"

"No, madam."

"What dignity! Who taught you to say 'madam' with such an air?"

"Nobody."

"Nobody! Well, she hasn't the manner of a country child, has she, Pierre?"

"Perhaps you have not always lived in this little house, and that's why you don't like it?"

"Yes, I've always lived here, I was born here."

"But you have a good papa and mamma, haven't you?"

"Yes, *indeed*," said Pansy with emphasis.

"Yet you don't like to live with them?" said the lady reproachfully.

"I *do* like to live with them, but I don't like to live *here*," said Pansy.

"Why don't you like to live here?"

"It's lonesome."

"Is that all?"

"No, madam, I don't like to go so far to school; the sun burns me and makes me red."

"O, Pierre, hear the child! Who would think that she was born in the country!"

"Now, you have told me every reason why you don't like to live here?"

"O, no! I haven't told you the reason of all—I don't like to wash dishes and scour knives, I hate it."

At this announcement the gentleman laughed outright.

"What would you like to do?"

"I would like to ride in a carriage like this with two horses, and wear a hat full of white feathers like the girl from Boston. I would like to learn to dance and sing, and paint pictures, and talk French, and live in a great city where I could see a great many people, and where they could see me."

"Well, you certainly know what you want; that's more than most of us grown people do," said the gentleman with a look of amusement.

The large soft eyes of the lady looked down into the child's face with an inquiring gaze.

"You have very strange notions," she said, "for a country child. Does your mamma let you read novels?"

"No, I only read the stories in the newspapers. I've read UNCLE TOM'S CABIN," she said musingly.

"Then you know all about little Eva. Don't you want to be like her?"

"O, no indeed."

"Why not?"

"She was too good. If I were like her I'd have to die."

"Do you want to live?"

"O, yes. I'm sure this world is a great deal pleasanter than heaven. I don't want to go there at all."

"You don't? Why not?"

"My Sabbath-school teacher is always telling me that if I am a good girl I can go to Heaven and sing forever and ever. I think that it would be dreadfully tiresome to sing forever and ever, and I shouldn't like it any better walking up and down by a river."

Again the gentleman laughed. "What stupid ideas good people have of Heaven any way," he said, "But we are none of us so sure of getting there that we need worry about it, Puss."

"I don't believe that there is enough in this world or in the next to satisfy you, my little Pansy," said the lady as she slowly lifted her eyes from the child's face; but thereis one thing that you can have without waiting—a ride. Would you like to go?"

"Oh, how much! Thank you," said the excited Pansy.

"Go and ask your mother, then, and if she says yes, we will take you up to the Pinnacle House."

"But stay," she added, "that is hardly the way to carry off a mother's child. Will you introduce me to your mother, Pansy?" And gathering up her delicate draperies, she stepped out upon the grass and followed Pansy to the house.

Mary Vale, who had witnessed the conversation from her seat by the window, rose to meet the tall and lovely stranger whose airy robes filled all her narrow doorway.

"Mother! this is *my* lady—the one that I chose from all the rest last Summer."

"I did not know that I had been so honored, Mrs. Vale," said one of the softest voices in the world; "although I noticed your daughter last Summer, and remembered her. I am Mrs. Stuyvesant, of New York, and have made myself very well acquainted with your daughter. I am very fond of children, of little girls especially. If you will be so kind as to let me drive Pansy to the Pinnacle House, I will bring her back safely before dark."

"It is you who are kind," said Mary

Vale, as she offered her easiest chair to the stranger, while Pansy flew up stairs for her best hat.

"Pansy has tried to describe you to me many times, and has so nearly succeeded that it seems as if I knew you and had seen you many times before."

Ere these simple sentences had passed between these two women, they had felt intuitively attracted toward each other. The one was young and of rare loveliness, carrying with her the unmistakable insignias of wealth and rank; the other was faded, and bore on her face the sign of a life repressed and unfulfilled, as well as an expression of endurance and tender patience. But there was that in each which appealed to the other; and when Pansy came down in her shabby little hat which she had privately punched, because it dared to be her best one, she found her mother and the lovely stranger conversing as if they were not strangers. She entered the door just in time to hear her mother say, "I think it is beyond my power to make the child contented or happy; yet I often reproach myself for it all: her habits and state of mind are the reflections of what mine were before she was born!"

A few moments more and Mary Vale watched the phæton roll away, with Pansy seated on a stool before the lady and gentleman. She noted the look of almost wild delight on the child's face as the ponies darted away. There was such a difference between them and Muggins!—such a difference between the gliding phæton and the shaking old buggy, a difference which Pansy felt fully now for the first time.

"It is the first time that they have come to take the child away, it will not be the last," said Mary Vale with a sigh as she turned to go back to the house. "But have I any right to complain if the very life comes to my child which I longed for so much for myself, when she has inherited from me that very longing? Nobody likes to take the consequences ot what is worst in themselves. I will try to take mine without complaint."

No one of the four slept very well that night. Pansy dreamed all night of the girl from Boston. In the evening she saw her on the great piazza of the Pinnacle House, and she laughed at Pansy's shabby hat with its faded ribbons—Pansy was sure that she did, and that she ridiculed her shabby looks to the girl in flounces by her side. Thus Pansy's sleep was full of wounded vanity and wrathful pride; she talked and cried and ground her pretty teeth in her sleep. Mary Vale slumbers were filled with fears. Cornelia Stuyvesant could not sleep at all for the multitude of air castles that kept shooting up from her brain. "O, what if it could be! If she could take that child home with her, adopt her, and educate her, who could tell, after she had moulded her over to her own heart, but that she would be the wife predestined for Pierre from all eternity. What a life work that would be, to mould a wife for Pierre!"

Pierre himself was puzzling *his* brain in a very misty and unsatisfactory way, trying to expound to his own satisfaction the natural law of resemblances. Why did the girl at the gate resemble the girl in the church? rather why did she suggest her? For there could scarcely be a greater contrast than between that blooming young girl and the lovely but almost faded young woman of his memory. "If it were possible, I should say it were blood, the mysterious out-raying of a family look," he said to himself; "but of course that's impossible, at least it's very unlikely that the solitary face I saw in Trinity and lost on Broadway ever sprung from the blackberries and mulleins of Hilltop. There was a history written in *that* face if I ever saw one on a human countenance, but then she *did* look like the girl at the gate." There was no getting away from this fact, and no solution for it. Thus, in a very unsatisfactory and puzzled state of mind, Pierre at last departed for the land of Nod.

It was two weeks later. Pansy in the meantime had had many drives and talks with Mrs. Stuyvesant, each one of which confirmed the latter more and more in her desire to adopt the bright child, and to give her the opportunities of a life which she seemed born to adorn.

She had been very shy of talking of this project to Pierre. Doubtless the fell design upon his future which she was conscious of cherishing in her purpose made her less disposed to shift any responsibility upon him.

She informed him, however, that if she could persuade Mrs. Vale to give her up she was going to take Pansy home with her.

"What for, pray?" inquired the unimpressionable Pierre.

"Why, don't you think she will be a great deal of company for me, now you have resolved to go again to Europe?"

"Yes, I suppose so."

"And don't you think it worth while to give such a bright beautiful child better opportunities and fit her for another sphere in life?"

"I am not so sure of that. Very risky business, I can tell you, taking such a miss out into the world which she is so crazy to see. She would be a good deal safer if you would leave her among the blackberry bushes."

"No, Pierre, not half so safe; not when so much of the world goes by her gate, and all that she knows of it is through her imagination. She is too pretty to leave here, and think, Pierre, what I can do for her; what a woman I can make of her!"

"Hum! A perfectly material nature, measures everything already by what it will be worth to herself. Don't like calculation in a woman. What's a woman without spirituality?"

"But do you think it quite fair to measure a woman's spirituality in a child of twelve years?"

"Well, perhaps not. Of course you will do as you please, Corna. I only wanted to tell you that I don't hanker after her company, and think it will be a good deal of a nuisance when we sit down to talk together to have her always around."

"O, I'll take care of that. She shall never interfere with our chats, never."

Corna was so in love with the little romance which she had nursed in her heart, that in this instance twice as much objection on her brother's part would not have moved her from her purpose.

They were to leave the next day, and Mrs. Stuyvesant, Mary Vale, and Pansy were in the cottage sitting-room, while the phæton and the black servitor waited without.

"Pansy, you shall make your own choice," said Mary Vale in a broken voice. "Will you go with the lady, or stay with your mother?"

There was a pause. Pansy stood between the two. She looked at her mother, and her lips quivered. She looked at Cornelia Stuyvesant, and her eyes kindled, and a glance akin to triumph lighted her childish features.

"I will go with *you*," she said. "When I am rich and have my own beautiful house, mother, I will come back for *you*."

It could not be unsaid. The child had chosen, and her choice was to go with strangers. The next morning a tearful little group stood once more at the gate, watching out of sight the youngest member of the house. Not as Eirene went did Pansy go. No jerking Muggins, no rattling buggy, carried her off. No little brass-nailed trunk went behind her holding her possessions. She owned nothing fine enough to take with her to her new estate save her blue merino frock, and that she wore. Beside Cornelia Stuyvesant in the pretty phæton, with the black ponies and the black footman in silver bands, the little princess went forth to her kingdom in the world. As they had watched Eirene before, they watched her up the hill—a teazing, dissatisfied child, who had ever brought more of care than sunshine to the household; but they thought not of that. Had they not all come to feel that it was a privilege to wait on her and to try to make her happy. Was she not Pansy, the baby, and so lovely to see! Tears were in their eyes as they turned back to the house, but not a word was spoken. There was nothing to be said. Had she not chosen to go!

Thus it came to pass that for the first time in a generation a bright young face became visible in the great windows of

De Peyster house. While Eirene sat within her little iron railing, poring over ledgers, and casting up accounts, and writing business letters from morning till night, Pansy had nothing to do but to be dressed and to drive out beside Mrs. Stuyvesant, or to learn her lessons for the masters who came every day to the house to teach her. To be sure she felt this to be very irksome, yet she studied bravely and made rapid proficiency; for no one realized more than Pansy how indispensable were culture and accomplishments to fine lady-hood. One sister laid down on an iron cot in her bare attic room, and if her eyes were not too weary or her heart too sad, would try to study past sleeping time, as she did of old. The other sister, in a lofty chamber, which had once been the nursery of the De Peysters, laid down on a couch curtained and covered with embroidered laces, amid pictures and flowers and every appliance which affection and wealth could devise, and dreamed of still richer and rarer gifts waiting in her future; and neither sister knew where the other was. Mary Vale's last injunction to Pansy had been, "Go and see Eirene as soon as you get to New York," but Pansy had not gone, nor was it wholly her fault. Cornelia Stuyvesant, generous in almost everything else, failed here. It was not pleasant to her to think that Pansy had a sister, least of all that she had a sister in the same city. By so much she seemed less entirely hers. Few of her class were as free as she from the prejudice of caste, yet she could not forget that she was educating Pansy for a sphere far above that in which she was born; that a sister in a shop in the same city and on visiting terms, to say the least, would be inconvenient. Even Cornelia De Peyster was not entirely noble —how many of us are.

Yet she was incapable of deliberately separating two only sisters. She fully intended when it was convenient to take Pansy to see her sister, yet she involuntarily without knowing wherefore put off the day.

"Is your sister pretty?" she asked one morning of her pet.

"She used to be," said Pansy.

"Used to be! Then why isn't she now? She must be young."

"Well, she was very sick. We thought she would die, and she has never looked the same since," said Pansy meditatively, guarding Eirene's secret with a touch of true sisterly feeling.

"Sick! I'm sorry; but does she look like you?"

"I've heard mother say that we both had the family look, but Eirene's hair is brown."

"I am glad of that; I don't want any one to look like you, Pansy. But *is* your sister like you?"

"No, indeed; I wish I was like *her*, or I would if she wasn't so quiet. It would tire me to death to study, and be as still as Eirene is. If I tried it would make me scream right out."

"You needn't try, my darling. I don't want you to be like any one but yourself. Although it is very proper and commendable in your sister to study and make the most of herself, poor thing!"

Cornelia De Peyster instinctively felt a touch of pity for the unknown girl, whose distant image rose faintly before her, wasted by sickness, silent and alone, yet she found herself resolutely turning away from it, why she knew not, unless it was because she could not bear the thought that Pansy had a sister.

Meanwhile that sister had long since learned by a letter from her mother of the change in Pansy's fortunes, that she was in the very city with her, that she would soon come and see her. Day by day she waited, but no Pansy came. In the morning when she went to her desk, she would say, "She will come to day." And at night when she went to the lodging-house that she called home, "She has been here, I know, and left word where I can meet her;" but the long days wore into weeks, and no Pansy appeared. As the hope too long delayed wore out, Eirene's yearning to see her sister became almost a sickness—the sister whom long ago she held in her arms, whose hair she had combed and played with, whose little bumped nose she had so often bathed with camphor, and whose scratched and pounded fingers she had so many times cured with kisses. It was Pansy from home, with the freshness of the hills on her face, and the sweetbrier scent in her garments, and the mother-touch on her head, but where? Shut up in some great New York mansion where she could not find her! The conviction fixed itself on her mind at last that the rich lady who had adopted Pansy did not intend that she should associate with a sister whose lot in life was to be so different. Then she thought, "I will not intrude, I will not do anything to mar her prospects, but I will find the house, and perhaps from a distance I can see her go in or come out."

Thus if Pierre De Peyster had been at home, and had sauntered to the drawing-room windows as he sometimes used to do, he might have seen just at early dusk a slight figure hovering amid the shrubbery of the little park before the house, and a face sometimes wistfully lifted toward the windows, which, if it were not too dark, he would have recognized as the one that he saw at Trinity. He was not there, but away beyond the ocean, studying science, and trying to persuade himself that he was very much occupied and living a very complete life.

Eirene, when her day's work was done, would turn her face toward the mansion of the De Peyster's. It was rather late, and she sometimes felt timid when her pausing in the park seemed to attract the attention of a passer-by. But no one ever accosted her. The subdued dress, the shrinking face, were enough to command respect from any one who noticed them. The most depraved man, had demoralized habit moved him to speak, would have paused and have remained silent with one look at her face. It would have been offering insult to his sister, or the young mother whose smile made the heaven of his childhood.

She never lingered long. Sometimes she would go for days and not catch a glimpse of any one within the great curtained windows. Once she saw a young girl come to one of them and look out, and then go away. It was Pansy. At the sight of her sister's face her heart gave a bound, and forgetting everything she started toward the house; she reached the stone steps and began to ascend, when her heart failed her. Pansy would be glad to see her—she was sure that she would, but the lady, the lady who owned this grim old house, who had made Pansy a daughter in it, she rose before her in overpowering state and majesty; she could not meet her, not in her own parlor, into which she had never been invited, and where she could only appear as an unwelcome intruder. With an anguish and desolation in her heart for which there were neither words nor tears, she turned and fled from the house as rapidly as she had approached it.

As she looked up from her books one morning, she noticed a lady buying goods at an opposite counter. She wore a suit of black velvet trimmed with Russian sable, and the costly elegance of her costume and the remarkable type of her beauty both attracted Eirene's attention. Soon a young girl came from another counter and took a stool by the lady's side. She also wore black velvet releived by bright blue ribbons and plumes, her yellow hair glittering like a fleece of gold around her head and shoulders. No human being would have thought that the dainty little fingers tossing about the costly fabrics on the counter had ever been made red by hot dish water, or rough with a coarse dish towel,—and yet they had both, for these were Pansy's fingers. No one would have dreamed that she had ever been a princess without a throne to have seen her seated on that high shop stool. Not that she said much, she left Mrs. Stuyvesant to do the talking, but she "had an air," and was not the coach with its outriders waiting outside. They were just turning to go, they had nearly passed the young book-keeper's cage on the other side of the shop when Pansy half caught the gaze, the intent, eager, questioning gaze fixed upon her. She did not turn to look, but walked straight on. If it was her sister, and she felt that it was—the passing glimpse had told her that—but here was no place to meet her. Had she not been playing the grand lady in miniature, and now before all the shoptenders to rush into the arms of one of them and call her sister! This thought lasted Pansy as far as the door, when a deeper and stronger feeling overthrew it altogether, and she exclaimed to Mrs. Stuyvesant, "O, I must go back! I saw somebody as I came out who looked so much like Eirene!"

She returned to the desk more swiftly than she had passed it, and leaning over the wire railing,—there were but two words—

"Pansy!"

"Eirene!"

They embraced, then gazed into each other's faces.

Just then Mrs. Stuyvesant came up.

"It is my fault," she said to Eirene, without waiting for an introduction. "I have been very selfish. Yet I have not deliberately separated two sisters. Come and see Pansy? Will you come this evening. If so, I will send the carriage for you."

Eirene, who realized nothing now but that she had her sister back again, gave her assent, and Cornelia Stuyvesant, wishing to avoid all the public notice possible in the shop, hastened forth with Pansy, every clerk in it gazing after her. It all seemed so sudden and unreal to Eirene, such a meeting with her sister and such a sudden termination of it, that it was with great difficulty that she brought her mind back to her duties for the remainder of the day.

The stately carriage came to the lodging house for her at an early hour in the evening. The sisters had a long visit alone in Pansy's beautiful room, in which they exchanged many confidences, and another visit in the presence of Mrs. Stuyvesant in the great library. It was not the great pictures, Johanes De Peyster's grandfather in his mighty wig, nor the handsome Colonel Arent De Peyster with all his gold stars and lace, nor even the massive carved cases filled with books, which overawed Eirene and made her trembling soul dumb within her,—it was the slender and stately lady who sat their with the soft sad look in her beautiful eyes, but with a manner so remote and cold even in its kindness that that it made the stranger before her feel that she was shut out from her sympathy forever. Every moment it seemed to Eirene that she must burst in tears, she knew not wherefore, and she felt so no less at her departure, when Mrs. Stuyvesant politely invited her to come again, and promised that Pansy should visit her, and in addition proffered the carriage for the two to ride together to the Park some day.

With Cornelia this was her superlative effort to do right, to "do her duty" by Pansy's unfortunate sister.

Being in no wise a hypocrite with all her polish and grace, she performed an insincere act ungracefully, from the mere fact that her gracious words expressed nothing of her real feelings. Eirene felt quite as much like crying as if she had not been invited to ride. Nothing could have added to her exquisite consciousness of the immeasurable distance between herself and the foster mother of her sister. Time did not bridge this distance. It widened it. Cornelia Stuyvesant did not cease to make efforts to be kind to Eirene, but not one of them could hide the truth from her—that Pansy's friend was sorry that Pansy had a sister. Under the circumstances Eirene thought this very natural. She at least taught herself to accept the fact, that in the complete sense her sister could be her sister no longer.

She avoided De Peyster house, and never went there except on special invitation and occasions. These occasions were rare. In them her intercourse with Mrs. Stuyvesant never passed the bound of formal politeness and kindness. She never heard her mention her brother's name, and did not know that she had a brother—Mrs. Stuyvesant, as we know, for her own reasons taking pains to keep such knowledge from her.

Meanwhile, Pierre De Peyster did not hasten back. Two years went,—but when the third came, it brought him the opportunity of his life, as it brought it to so many Americans who till then had never dreamed of their destiny.

The first gun of the civil war brought

him home. He was as true to the principles of constitutional freedom and as eager to defend them as were the De Peysters of the seventeenth century.

He equipped a regiment at his own expense—started with it as its surgeon and when Eirene wrote her first letter of the war to her mother, Pierre De Peyster was already at the front with his regiment.

# CHAPTER XV.

THE WAR.

*Eirene to her Mother.*

NEW YORK, *June*, 1861.

SATURDAY.—*Dear Mother:* This is war. Now it seems as if life never meant anything before. I stood on the steps of a house overlooking the vast crowd at the meeting at Union Square, and as I listened to Colonel Baker, the most eloquent of men, and watched the new-born army of American citizens below, in their silence more eloquent than he, and thought of the great sacrifice for liberty just begun, I wondered how I had ever been so absorbed in my own little life, or had cared so much about it. The whole city has blossomed out in banners; they float from every house; they line and canopy Broadway. Under those banners, amid waving handkerchiefs and streaming eyes and beating drums, the whole nation seems to be marching to war. The rudest men of the town swarm up from the lower streets arrayed in uniform; they are going to the war. The most cultivated men of the town march out from their splendid homes in uniforms, amid tears and prayers; they, too, are going to the war. Alas! already they are beginning to come back. Funeral pageants follow quick upon the triumphant march. Day by day Broadway is walled on either side by a mass of humanity tearful and silent. All its roar is hushed; wailing music, the measured stride of horses, the muffled footfall of marching men smite the silence with a stroke of pain. Then we see mounted cavaliers with bowed heads, long lines of infantry with reversed arms, a hearse with nodding plumes, holding a coffin wrapped in a flag and covered with flowers, followed by a riderless horse, and carriages filled with mourning friends. Mother, this is war.

MONDAY.—Every train brings in new regiments. O mother, they all seem boys from home, these bright-eyed, brown-cheeked men, fresh from the hills and valleys of the land. The men from Vermont, how big they are; I did not know that even the Green Mountains could send forth such a regiment of giants. To see them march down Broadway, to know that so many are marching only to death, how strange and awful it seems; and this is war!

MONDAY.—I was going to my dinner, when I saw a regiment coming, and the crowd on the pavement was too near for me to escape it. It pressed me to the very curbstone, and I stood there leaning against a tree, although it seemed more than I could bear to see *another* regiment go by. I had seen so many, and my heart felt so wrung. But this one marched so proudly, its banners were so bright, its men so young, their uniforms so gay, that, as cheer after cheer went up from the street, I felt their enthusiasm, and forgot everything but my delight and pride in my countrymen. I looked up and read the name on their flag. It seemed as if my heart leaped out of my body. "Rene!" I heard a voice say. It came out of the ranks. The outer line was so near I could have touched it. "Rene!" I heard it again. Before my very face marched Win. He stepped out of the ranks. He stretched out his hand—wrung mine—marched on; before I could speak he was gone, gone! O mother, why didn't you write that his regiment was coming? Or didn't you know when it would reach New York? Or did you think that it would only pass through? I went directly back to the shop, and to the counting-room. I said to Mr. Mann, "I am going to the war!"

"Are you insane, Miss Vale?" he asked.

"No," I said, "but I *must* go."

"But you can't fight."

"No," I said, "but I can nurse those who do. My brother; if not him, the brothers of many others."

Mother, I am going.

Mr. Mann didn't think me crazy after all. He has two sons already at the front; the thought of them makes him tender. "If it's a man's right to fight," he said, "it's a woman's to nurse I don't deny; only, Miss Vale, don't go in an undirected, hap-hazard way. Don't go on your own responsibility. The enthusiastic foolish girls who are rushing to Washington to nurse, though they haven't the sense or nerve to nurse a chicken with a broken toe, are doing a great deal of harm. They are creating a prejudice against women nurses which thousands of trained nurses can hardly overcome. Nursing is a business, and requires training like any other. Go to Church Hospital," he said, "and join the Sisters of St. John. They are being very thoroughly prepared for their work; they will go out under the care of a superintendent, with a regular commission from the War Department; they will have their work assigned them, and due honor in doing it. It's their ridiculous way of doing a thing, often, not their doing it, that makes half the opposition against women's work. Cultivate common sense, Miss Vale, and you can do whatever you see fit to do.

I thanked him for his excellent advice and started. But he called me back.

"What are you going to live on?" he asked. "The sisters of St. John receive nothing but their rations."

"I have a year's savings in the bank," I said, "and I will write to my friend (Moses) to give me an extension on my payment for the house. I feel sure that he will do it."

"I only wanted to know if you were losing your reason in your enthusiasm, and growing improvident. Charity does begin at home, Miss Vale," he said.

"Yes, sir," I answered, "I know that it does; but, with the little farm, what I have saved is more than will be needed at home for a year."

"I wanted to be certain that you had thought of it, before I told you that your salary can go on, while you are a nurse, the same as if you were here. What you have in the bank can stay there."

"You are too good to me," I said.

"No. If you do your share, let me do mine," he answered, and gave me his hand in token of approval.

TUESDAY.—Mother, here I am. The hospital seems so strange, but it is very bright and clean. I see such strange sights here. Splendid carriages are continually being driven up to the door, filled with ladies of every age. If you could see what they bring! Money, stores, delicacies of every kind, to be sent to the front. They bring piles on piles of sheets, of the most costly linen, the most delicate fabrics; and some of them sit down and tear them up in the most frantic manner. We have great rooms filled with linen bandages all ready to be sent. Dr. Mott says there will not be war enough to use up half the bandages now in this hospital. I can't help being amused by some of the young ladies who apply to be nurses. They come so beautifully dressed—they have such wonderful little caps on their heads, with such ruffled and fluted aprons. From what I can gather, their whole idea of nursing is to sit in this beautiful attire by a handsome officer's bed, rolling bandages, or reading to him. When our Sister Superior asks them to lay aside this elegant costume, and put on the plain black dress of the real nurse, it seems very hard, and some of them refuse. Then, when they have to take their turn in the wards to watch all night—to nurse some one old, and ugly, and poor, their last glimpse of romance vanishes, and I notice in a day or two a carriage comes and takes them back to their home. I understand now what Mr. Mann meant. Some rush on to the army without any preparation or knowledge of what they are doing whatever, and I am afraid do much harm. I'm under training, as Mr. Mann says. I'd just as lief be trained as not. I like it. One company of sisters has already gone, ours will go the first of August. I can scarcely wait. O, mother,

I know how you felt when you kissed Win, and said good-by, and saw him go out of the old door—go to the war. I know by what I felt when I saw him march down the street with the men, a soldier. He couldn't kiss *me*, nor say good-by; yet I watched him march, march out of sight, to—what? This is war, the war that he dreamed of so long ago in the old barn, when we were children. He said then that he would some day be a soldier—and he *is* a soldier. To think that I lived to see him march away!

*August*, 1861.

DEAR MOTHER:—To-night we go. I have just been to bid Mrs. Stuyvesant and Pansy good-by. Mrs. Stuyvesant was very kind. How lovely she is. I never felt so drawn, and yet so repelled, by any one before. I could not put into words the admiration I feel for her, yet when I try to say the simplest thing, she seems so remote, so inaccessible to me, that I can scarcely speak to her at all. I fear in her heart that she cannot like me. I am sorry. The love of such a woman would be so much to me, for her own sake, and because she is so much to Pansy. Sometimes, for a moment, I think that she does feel kindly towards me. She will look on me so sweetly, and her manner will seem almost affectionate; then, in an instant, such a cold look will cover her face, and her manner will grow so remote, as if in heart she had withdrawn from me the whole width of the earth. But I mustn't care for this now, not when I have so much more than myself to care for. Still I find that it makes me almost happy to remember that her last words were very kind. She put a little netted purse in my hand and said: "Here is a trifle for the wounded. If at any time you want money for any purpose, don't hesitate to send to me. Give me the privilege of doing some good at least with that." When I opened the purse, I found in it a hundred little gold dollars.

It was hard to part with Pansy, and yet in one sense it seems as if I parted with her for life long ago. She was very affectionate. It moves her more deeply than she owns, to think that Win is a soldier. The gentlemen whom she knows here who have gone are all young officers, who went away with shining swords and beautiful uniforms and prancing horses. It hurts her to think that her *own* brother must suffer all the hardships of the common soldier. I wish myself, mother, that he had a horse. Pansy has grown to be very elegant, and is as beautiful as ever. I looked at her in her costly dress, and tried to make her the little Pansy who wore the blue merino frock that I made myself, and couldn't—not until she threw her arms around my neck in the hall and whispered: "Change that into money for you and Win," and she put into my hand her diamond ring.

When I write you again, dear mother, it will be from the South. As far as I can, I will keep a little journal, and tell you everything that happens.

I'll not say good-by, for I am coming back. I know you will pray for your children.

Your loving child,

EIRENE.

## CHAPTER XVI.

EIRENE TO HER MOTHER.]

Maryland Heights, *August*, 1862.

Dear Mother:—A part of our corps of nurses is detailed for Pleasant Valley, Maryland, the rest of us are to go into the Valley of Virginia and are now on our way. As we had an escort we came up this old mountain rather than around it, for none of us were willing to miss the sight from its summit. Our flag is flying from its highest peak, our batteries are bristling all around its crown, we have a strong garrison here to guard the valley below. In an hour the ambulances are to come to convey us down; thus you see, dear mother, I have nothing to do till then, but to sit on this rock and write to you. If I could only tell you what I see, so that you could see it! I can't, I fear. On one side I look down into Pleasant Valley, a lovely rural valley, the white tents of war gleaming through its foliage;—it stretches away toward the beautiful valley of Frederic with its environing hills, so blue they remind me more than any others of the hills of home. Before me is the great Valley of Virginia, walled by the Blue Ridge and the distant Alleghanies, and watered on either side by two rapid rivers, the Shenandoah and Potomac, which rush together at the base of this mountain. It is a vast valley. Now it stretches away an embattled plain. I can think of nothing but the hosts of Xerxes as my eyes travel over the cities of tents which line the river, climb the heights, and spread on through all the valley out of sight. Across the Shenandoah, above Loudon Heights, beyond it, I seem to see the peaks of the Delectable Mountains. I am on a high mountain myself, but beyond, other and other mountains range on range lift their lovely green crowns into the clear blue atmosphere. Such an atmosphere! There is the bright tenderness in it that Ruskin talks about, a bright softness I should say, it is so crystal clear and yet so suffused with warmth. On, on far as my eyes can travel other mountain tops notch the brilliant sky. A poor wizened old woman lives in the hut yonder. She told me all about John Brown. On this very mountain top only a few rods away he lived in a little log house with his daughter the whole winter before he matured his plan and descended upon the arsenals at Harper's Ferry below. I try to make it real to myself, the life that he lived here through that long winter on this mountain top. Without, no voice spoke to him but the screaming winds which in winter must sweep over these summits in hurricanes. Nothing about him but the freedom, the isolation, the vastness of the mountains. Such a sense of power, of vastness comes to one in such a place. How much mightier one feels to do than he ever can on the levels below. I never thought of it before, but what a sanctity rests on the mountain tops of the world. The law was delivered on Sinai. From an exceeding high mountain Christ, beholding them all beneath Him, rejected the kingdoms of the earth. On a high mountain He took upon himself the ministry of death. On a high mountain apart He was transfigured.

Yes, this lonely summit seems a fit place whereon a solitary nature might nurse a sublime purpose. What a study of the mental and spiritual influence of mountain scenery on a deeply imaginative and religious man the life of John Brown affords. Long before he came here he dwelt amid the solitudes of the Adirondacs. I look at his ruined hut so torn and silent, so far behind him now if his "soul is marching on," and feel that here by its isolated fire, here on this mountain top, the awful war for freedom began, began in the heart and purpose of one solitary man; and now this whole army before me is but part of the result. Here where the floods had torn the very mountains asunder, where nature holds her fiercest conflicts, was it not meet that the conflict of human races should begin? Where will the final triumph of liberty be won!

Harper's Ferry, *September*, 1862.

Friday.—One sister is on the island below, the others have gone up the valley and I am here in the stationary hospital on Camp Hill. The hospital itself is a large square brick house, once the abode of the superintendent of the arsenal here. It stands on the summit of the hill commanding a view of the ruined town below, of the rivers, the valley. It has been well riddled by shells, and yet it is possible to make the men very comfortable in it. A little brick house near has been set apart for the reception of my stores, and for my own especial use. My duty will be chiefly to prepare food for the sick and wounded, as ordered by the hospital surgeon, and to take care of such patients as he shall deem proper. He has received me very kindly, and has done much to help me in the beginning of my labors. My only fear is of a superintending surgeon who is soon to have his headquarters here. It is said that he is very averse to women nurses in the army, also that he is a very haughty, stern man, of whom very few people like to ask favors. My only hope is that he will not think me worth noticing at all. When he comes I shall cover my face with my big bonnet and hide in my little soup house, so that he can scarcely ever see me. And as I obey orders as strictly as if I were an enlisted soldier, I trust that I may never incur his personal displeasure. If I don't, surely he will let me stay and make broth and sago for my boys; don't you think that he will, mother?

I found some old books in the little closet over the high Virginia mantel-shelf this morning, in which I was making room for some of my stores. One was a copy of "Jefferson's Notes on Virginia," which I have glanced over with a strange interest. It is said that there are chapters in it which he wrote just below these windows, seated on that great plateau of stone yonder overhanging the valley which the people call Jefferson's Rock. I believe that he did. I have copied what he wrote as he sat there, for it is the most perfect picture of the scene which I now see from this window that will ever be written. He says: "The passage of the Potomac through the Blue Ridge is one of the most stupendous scenes in nature. You stand on a very high point of land. On your right comes the Shenandoah, having ranged along the foot of the mountain for an hundred miles to seek a vent. On your left approaches the Potomac, in quest of a passage also. In the moment they rush together against the mountan, rend it asunder, and pass off to the sea. But the distant finishing which Nature has given to this picture is a true contrast to the foreground. It is as placid and delightful as that is savage and tremendous. For the mountain being cloven asunder, presents to your eyes, through the cleft, a small catch of smooth horizon, at an infinite distance in the plain country, inviting you, as it were, from the riot and tumult roaring around to pass through the breach and participate of the calm below." If the eyes of Jefferson sought repose on this far-off "catch" of blue horizon when the tumult and riot of the elements were all that disturbed his senses, what is it not to the eyes of one weary and worn with the bloody sights of human war? That "catch of blue" is this moment just what it was that day. If ever I step to the window or cross the hill my eyes travel on towards its rest. Afar off in that peaceful blue it seems as if I caught faint glimpses of the hills of home. If there comes a moment when I can look away from the suffering and sorrow around me, all I can say is, "Yonder lies my home." It is such a comfort to look at the getting-out place the great open gate of the mountains, and think that some time, when my work is done here, mother, I may pass through it and go home to you.

Never did rail cars reach any spot with such a weird, wild cry. In a dark night the sight is wonderful. Afar down the river you catch glimpses of the great gleaming eye of the engine through the opening and closing mountains. Then it seems to go out in blackness, when suddenly, with a piercing cry, it shoots from behind yonder precipice, and, vibrating between it and the river, rushes over the great bridge and into the little town, but only in another moment to rush through the blackness before it, on into the mountain passes.

It seems as if this strange place was doomed by Nature before it was doomed by man. Jefferson thinks that here these two rivers were dammed by the Blue Ridge till they formed an ocean that filled the whole valley—that they rose till they broke over the spot and tore the mountain from its summit to its base to make its passage. The savage piles of rock which rise and topple beside each river are the relics of the disruption and avulsion in the mighty conflict. I tremble even now when I think how these two rivers might rise in their beds, meet in one terrific flood, and sweep away all life in their awful passage. This has happened. In the black night no sound was heard but the roar of the flood and the crash of houses and the cry of human beings going down into swift destruction. Remembering it, this scenery is awful to me. Often I see it touched with tender beauty. But the suffusing sunlight on the flood, the wild flower in the mountain cleft, cannot win me to forget its frightful possibilities.

Saturday.—Troops are coming into the valley by forced marches. I saw a regiment come toiling up the hill this afternoon. As I knew they would stop at the spring by the road to fill their canteens, I sent two contraband boys down with—buckets they call them here—filled with coffee and a third to come back and tell me the name of the regiment. It was Win's regiment. I was not surprised. I knew that it must pass through with others before long. I filled my hands with every thing I could carry and rushed down to the road. You know that I saw Win many times last year, but have never seen his regiment on the march before since I saw it go so proudly through Broadway. That bright, bright flag! If you could see how faded and riddled it is to-day, you would be proud of it, mother. And the boys so fresh and young that morning—to-day ankle deep in the dust of the road, gray as the dust under their feet with the dust that covered them, haggard and worn, for they had marched thirty miles since they broke camp. They stopped just long enough to drink, to fill their rusty canteens, or little black coffee pots, then marched on. Win—I could scarcely see him for dust—he was haggard and brown, but he had the old smile in his eyes, our boy! I stuffed his haversack—I filled his canteen—I— It was only a moment—

Forward! March! was the cry.

He went on—he went on.

I stood in the road alone.

## CHAPTER XVII.

### THE ARMY NURSE.

"You can't tell me anything, Fay, about army nurses. I object to all of them, and I don't want one in my hospitals. I wish you would send the one who has installed herself here a polite request to leave."

"Really, De Peyster, I can't. She comes from Church Hospital, New York. She is one of the Sisters of St. John. There is a whole band of them scattered through the Valley. I can't meddle with one of St. John's Sisters. Besides, this one has a regular commission from the Secretary of War, and it would not do any good if I did meddle; to tell the truth, I don't want to do so."

"Confound the Secretary of War. No wonder nothing goes right, with both Secretary and President nosed around by old women. But I tell you, Fay, I am not going to have female nurses imposed upon me, Secretary or no Secretary. This nurse shall go, and if there's a row about it, I'll resign."

"Oh no, you wouldn't; your heart is in the army, and you would not let so small an object as a female nurse drive you out of it! Do you know, De Peyster, I think you are prejudiced? I share your opinion concerning the class; but come, now, just lay your finger on one atom of harm that this Sister Eirene has ever done, and I will lay mine on a hundred good and blessed things that she does every day."

"You will! Spare me. I don't object to her personally. I don't know who she is, and don't care. I never heard her speak. I never spoke to her, I never saw her face, and never expect to, inside of that tunnel of a bonnet that she wears. I object to her on principle. A hospital full of men is no place for a woman. I saw no end of mischief come from it in Alexandria."

"Not from good women nurses," said Dr. Fay; "you saw mischief come from women who were not nurses at all, although they pretended to be,—women who came there in fine array to beguile the officers, and with them to drink up the wine which the Sanitary Commission had sent to the patients. But I saw some good devoted nurses even in Alexandria, and perfect ladies they were, too."

"Well, perhaps you did, but where you saw one such, you saw a dozen of the other sort. Any way, I did. Even your goodies don't know anything; they have killed more men than ever wounds did, feeding them with candy and cake. I came into the ward one day, and found one administering peanuts to a man just out of typhoid fever. I tell you, Fay, there is not more than one woman in a hundred who has sense and judgment enough to be an efficient nurse, to say nothing of those who play the devil with their actions."

"I admit all that you say of many, but I know more of whom it is not true, and this Sister Eirene is one of them. I tell you, De Peyster, there is no end to the good that she does. And she is never obtrusive, never in the way; she knows when to come into the ward and when to go out of it; she has the knack of doing the right thing in the right time and place,—and such broths and soups and sago as she does make in the little house out yonder! My! when I sat down to a bowl with parsely in it, I thought I was at home again."

"Oh! so she feeds *you*, does she? I see why you are so anxious to have her stay. The old story! the female nurse feasting the officers instead of nursing the men! You rascal, you make me want a bowl of soup myself. Hard-tack and pork and army cooking have made me feel like a cannibal." And Pierre remembered ruefully the delicious soups served every day in the week in De Peyster house, for which he had an especial liking.

"If she makes good soup she can stay," he said. "But don't mistake me, Fay, I object to female nurses on principle. You may convince me that she is a soup maker, but you cannot that she is a nurse. Select the most troublesome men in the ward that you would about as lief have die as not, and let her take care of them and kill them. But bring me a bowl of soup the first time you have a chance, without saying that it is for me. I could eat some soup with parsely in it; but remember I don't believe in your female nurses."

Eirene heard this conversation through the thin board partition which separated the little linen-room in which she was from the office where the two surgeons sat. She drew her bonnet closer about her ears to shut out the sounds, and went on rolling the bandages which she knew these same surgeons would want to use before another hour. They went out presently, and she was left alone with her work and her meditations.

"I don't know why I should take it so much to heart," she wrote that evening in the journal for her mother, as she sat before the wide hearth in the little Virginia house, stirring her sago for evening use as it simmered in two iron pots over the fire on the hearth, writing with her pencil in the little book on her knee in between. "Why should I feel it so keenly," she wrote, "the opinion of this gentleman, who is a stranger to me, unless a desire for personal approbation is mixed with my desire to do good? I can do my duty no less if I am not approved. Still, the pain is something more than a personal one. It hurts me to hear women spoken of in such a way, especially a class of women whose devotion to duty should lift them above all reproach. It shows me how women harm each other, how one woman, false to her higher womanhood, can cast reproach upon an entire class in which each one is humbly striving to do the work their hands find to do. And so some of the poor men are to be selected for *me* 'to kill'" (and here the pencil dug a little bitterly); "there is nothing in my broth or sago to kill any one; they are very nourishing" (and here the pencil rose proud and stately). "I am not learned, I know; but I have studied faithfully the laws of life and of health, and so far as I attempt to do a thing, I know how to do it. I know how to take care of my boys" (with an air of maternity). "I think that I don't like this Dr. De Peyster. I am very sure that I do not. He has a way not at all American, as if he was born to rule, and all around him were his subjects. I dislike him the most when he walks through the ward, and all the lame soldiers and all the sick soldiers who can rise have to stand up during the entire time that he is in the room. Of course, respect is due to an officer. After they have risen and bowed, it seems to me, if he were really kind-hearted, he would tell them to sit down. But no, he don't; he lets them stand as long as he is in the room. It is cruel. I shall never enter a ward when I know that he is in it; I would rather not meet a gentleman who thinks me out of my place, and to whom I am an object of contempt. I never did but once, that was before I knew that he had arrived. Then as he marched down the ward, so grand and stately, there was something about him which reminded me of Mrs. Stuyvesant—it even seemed as if he looked like her. Very likely I fancied it because his name is De Peyster, the name on the door of her house—a name I liked the first time that I saw it—that was in Trinity church-yard. I have never glanced at him since, and feel as if I would never dare to, or want to again. I will try to do my duty even more faithfully. The army will soon move on, these fine surgeons will go, and then you, left behind, will need me, my poor boys." Here the tears began to drop at the thought that her boys would have no one much wiser than herself to take care of them. She shut her little book, and leaning forward slowly stirred the sago bubbling over the low fire. This was the picture that Pierre De Peyster saw through the open window. He was coming from the tent hospital, where he had just amputated a gangrened limb. He had tried hard to save it, tried hard to send the young man who owned it unmaimed back to mother and wife; but it had been impossible. Cruel as Eirene thought him, punctilious and exacting as he was in official etiquette, he was unmindful of no human being's pain. "Will this butchery never cease," he said dejectedly, with the smell of blood and the cry of anguish still lingering with him. Just then looking up, he noticed a single white half-blown rose looking forth unsullied and fragrant in the evening air, the only one amid a cluster of unopened buds on a bush, near the open window of a little old brick house.

"I will send it to Corna," he said, with the thought coming instantly into his mind, "what man but I would have only his sister to send it to?" and stepping toward the bush he glanced through the low open window, and for an instant stirred, not but gazed. He had heard often enough of Sister Eirene's soup house, but had never troubled himself to inquire which of the numerous little Virginia houses scattered about the hill it might be.

Was this the nurse? Yes, for there was the tunnel bonnet which he detested hanging at the back of her chair. Sister Eirene slowly stirred the sago simmering over the fire. Then she laid her head upon the back of the chair, and seemed to watch it. She folded her arms, and the little book on her lap slipped upon the floor. The sun, dropping down the valley, shone through the opposite window, and its splendor fell upon her face. Its glow was welcome to her, she shut her eyes and basked in it. It was the same sun which shone through the rafters of the old barn years and years before, and this the same face which it shone upon—a young girl's then, a woman's now. And this the same sun which glinted downward, through the waving boughs and illuminated windows of old Trinity, upon the woman's face in the aisle, and this was she—yes! A look of bewilderment, then of recognition, passed over Pierre De Peyster's features as he gazed. The hair waving out from under the close muslin cap was gold in the sun; the face, worn and pallid in an ordinary light, in the radiance which touched it now, wore the halo of a saint. "MY WIFE," said the soul of the man, though his lips spoke not. With a trembling hand he gathered the white rose and went on.

At last he had seen the face of her for whom till now his whole life had been a fruitless quest.

The next morning Eirene found upon her table in the ward an envelope on which was written: "For the Sister Eirene." She opened it, saw a wilted white rose, nothing else. She thought that some lame soldier hobbling about had gathered it for her, and laid it here a token of his gratitude. She looked upon it with a tender smile, and cutting out the superscription placed it over the rose in a book filled with souvenirs of battle-fields, of soldier's graves, and of her life in Virginia.

About noon Dr. Fay appeared in the little office of Dr. De Peyster with a bowl of fragrant broth in his hand.

"Here, you scamp," he said, "you don't deserve this from the one who made it; but I begged it without telling whom it was for. May it refresh you mightily, and modify your prejudices against women nurses."

Pierre received it with a single solemn, "Thank you." He waited till he was alone, and then sat down to it as if it were a sacrament. Never before had he tasted such a bowl of broth as that.

At midnight Eirene walked the ward alone. The men-nurses, worn out by the excessive labor of many days, had retired for a little rest while she watched. With noiseless steps she moved to and fro—here pausing to adjust a pillow for some aching head; here to administer medicine or cordial; here to utter some word of faith or cheer. Many a human heart, fluttering to death in a wounded body, thanked God for her ministry, and that he was not left to die alone. Many mournful eyes, longing for sight of wife or mother, called her toward them with wistful entreaty, and silent tears and broken voices blessed and thanked the woman's love which in its unselfish devotion made each man a brother.

Eirene's lips quivered as she walked. Here were men with the damp of death upon their faces to whose mothers and wives she had written words of hope and consolation. Those mothers and wives had written to her till she had made their love and sorrow her own. How she had watched and nourished their wounded ones, how she had hoped for them, what stories she had told them of their coming convalesence, of their furloughs, of their visits home, of the glad and prosperous years afar on! And yet in the face of her love, and care, and prayers, they were dying! Only another morning and she would see the stretcher with its dead body borne out to the half-made grave on the open hill. A long sigh of anguish arose from her heart; but the suppressed lips shut upon it before it escaped. Silence, patience, and self-restraint, she owed them all to the sufferers around her. And her heart swelled with gratitude that God in his love permitted her to minister to her brethren. "It might have been so different if I had had my own selfish way," said the faithful heart. "God knew best. He saved me from myself, and from a life of selfishness. In his mercy He permits me to comfort the afflicted, and to bind up the wounds of those who have fallen."

These thoughts, with her surroundings, the midnight, the long dim ward filled with wounded and dying men, seemed to lift her into a state of exaltation. As she passed the last couch, she drew the curtain which covered the window at the end of the ward, and for a moment stood transfixed with what she saw. They who have never seen the full moon suspended above the Blue Ridge in September have missed one of the consummate sights of nature. Tens of thousands of brave men, could they see this page, would bear me witness that the earth never bore more transcendent nights and days than those which trailed their splendor along the Valley of Virginia, through the September of 1862. The great mountains rose on either side in sombre shadow. The two rivers, pouring down the valley, rushed together at their feet.

Above their heads, out of the heaven's unfathomable blue, the moon hung a globe of flame, flooding the embattled valley with a mellow half-day, like that in which it lies in the sun's eclipse. Around the base of the hill, from whose summit Eirene looked, clung the ruins of the fated little town. Perching on a side precipice, one solitary church which both armies had spared lifted up its glittering cross in mid air. Right before her on the hill-top was the old grave-yard of the natives, while in every direction, running far down its sides, were the new half-covered graves of dead soldiers. Between the house and the grave-yard a solitary sentinel paced. From the side hill she could hear the steps of other sentinels, and hear their solemn challenge breaking the silence. Above her, along the heights of the Shenandoah, a vast city of white tents gleamed in the moonlight. Below, on the great bridge spanning the rivers, she caught the glitter of bayonets, then the slow tramp, tramp of marching men. Another regiment coming, and another! a forced midnight march! the men were coming from below to reinforce the men lying on their bayonets on Bolivar Heights. Her heart fluttered with a sickening sensation, as she saw them drawing nearer, nearer, the heavy laden, weary, marching men. Silently, solemnly on they came beneath the midnight sky, beneath the very window where the stood.

"A battle to-morrow! Win is up the valley; the end nears," she said with a shudder as she dropped the curtain and turned back. Another moment and she walked the ward again, and no eye saw the deepened pallor of her face. Yet amid all the sickening fear in her heart was born an unspeakable gratitude, that she was where she was.

"O, to think that God has spared me," she said, "for the sake of others. When I prayed that it might be taken, how could I know that my life could ever take on so rich a value; it seemed to me emptied of all joy and worthless. O, my boys!" cried her heart, and she looked up and down on every couch as if each man on it were her son. "To think that God lets me live for you. And to think what you are—the roughest, the rudest! Never by word, or look, or deed have one of you ever made me feel that I overstepped my place in serving you. Had I been born a queen you could not have been more reverent than you have been to the simple womanhood that seeks to serve you; never by word or look have you made me regret that I am here. I never heard but one such word, and that was the surgeon's. He is proud and rich—he does not know what your life is or mine! How can he know that my place is here with you who die for our country. Win! To-morrow!"

Whose eyes will follow these lines who saw those days in the Valley of Virginia! How our lines grew less and less. Winchester, Martinsburg, Charlestown, Bolivar, one by one possessed by the foe

## CHAPTER XVIII.

EIRENE'S DIARY.—THE SURRENDER OF MARYLAND HEIGHTS AND BATTLE OF HARPER'S FERRY.

September, 1862.—We had been expecting to hear the rebel guns for a week. From the moment that we learned certainly that the Confederates were in possession of Frederick; that they had destroyed the railroad bridge at Monocacy; that they had entirely surrounded us, we knew that they were only awaiting their own convenience to attack Maryland Heights. "If we can only keep the Heights," we said, as we looked with anxious eyes to this green fastness above us, "if we can only keep the Heights, we are safe." We could not forget that Jackson said when last here, "Give me Maryland Heights and I will defy the world."

Of what avail would be the force in battle-line on Bolivar Heights, three miles away; of the array of infantry lining the road to Charlestown; the earth-works, the rifle pits, the batteries—of what avail all, if from the other side Jackson ascended Maryland Heights and turned our own guns against us!

I had just given the boys their breakfast last Saturday morning, September 13, when the quick, cruel ring of musketry cutting the air made them start up in their beds. I ran out upon the hill in the rear of the hospital overlooking the town. On one side was the Shenandoah bound by Loudon Heights, on the other the Potomac, with the Heights of Maryland, a high, green precipitous wall, towering above its opposite shore.

Jackson had come; come to the only spot where he could effectually besiege our stronghold. I strained my eyes through the blue of that transcendent morning to the sunlit woods upon the mountain-top echoing with death. Volley after volley shivered the air, and with it the bodies of men. At first the report was far up on the very mountain-summit, then it drew nearer, rattling louder, and I knew that the enemy were advancing. I heard their dreadful war cry and caught the flash of their bayonets piercing the green woods.

Suddenly the cry grew fainter, the resounding guns seemed muffled in the thicket, and a loud shout from the soldiers of the Republic told that they were driving back the foe. The sounds of battle palpitated to and fro, the double line of bayonets glanced advancing, retreating, while I listened with suspended breath. The fight on the mountains was to decide our fate. Below the artillerists were at work. The great guns pointed upward. Shells screamed and hissed, tearing the green woods, poisoning the pure ether with sulphurous smoke. Ambulances began to wind down the steep mountain road with their freight of wounded. Many of these brave soldiers were so shattered that they could only be carried on blankets, and the sad procession was swelled by the bodies of two of our artillerists shattered to death at their guns.

Traitors gathered upon the crest of Camp Hill to watch the fight; cravens squatted on stones and stood in groups, with their hands in their pockets, estimating the probabilities of the battle.

"The Yankees can never lick our boys, 'taint no use tryin'; we'll get the hill, of course we will. Don't our boys go where they have a mind to? Didn't they march into Maryland; who hindered? Haven't they walked into Pennsylvania? Yankees can't stop 'em!" they said. Beside these creatures stood women, watching, trembling for the safety of their homes; little children frightened by the fight; young girls to whom the fortunes of war had given temporary abode in this besieged spot;

loyal old men who sat lamenting over the troubles of their country.

It was just noon when the sudden cessation of the musketry firing called me away from my work to the open window. The batteries were still sending shells thick and fast into the woods; the men at their guns seemed as eager as ever, when for the first time in my life I doubted the evidence of my senses. Without warning the firing suddenly ceased. Tents were struck. Cannon were spiked and sent tumbling down the mountain gorge. Bayonets flashed out from the woods; long columns of men began moving down the mountain defile. O, saddest, most disgraceful sight of all, the flag which waved from that mountain top, our signal of freedom and hope, they tore it down!

"They have given up the mountain! They have given up the mountain!" rang from mouth to mouth in every accent of terror, joy, and despair.

In fifteen minutes Maryland Heights were deserted, dumb. The gleaming tents were prone, the exultant banners gone. Far down the mountain side our hurrying hosts were flying from the spot, which at the utmost cost of life they should have defended. Already the pontoon bridge was black with returning thousands. The street was alive with the wildest excitement. Men, women, and children were running in every direction, with only one sentence on their tongue.

"The Heights are surrendered!"

Three thousand soldiers were marching back in disgrace and defeat. As they came wearily on, they heard from every direction:

"Is this the way you defend us?"

"Do you want women and children killed in their homes?"

From the ranks came one curse, long and deep, "If we had not had a traitor for a leader, we should not have surrendered!"

In less than an hour after, quick and sharp from the lower ridge of Maryland Heights sounded the enemies' rifles. Their cannon were not ready, but they came and fired volley after volley down into the narrow streets of the town, upon unarmed citizens, upon women and children. Thus the Southern chivalry began their work. We knew that they would erect their batteries in the night, that the Sabbath morning would dawn with the missiles of death pouring down upon us from each side, from both mountain tops.

It dawned, that memorable Sabbath morning, September 14, 1862, in superlative splendor. Sunshine, balm, and beauty suffused the august mountains and the blue, ether which ensphered us. All were unheeded while we awaited the terrors of the day. We had lost the Heights. Cowardice or treason had caused the surrender of our only stronghold of defence. All night the enemy had been erecting batteries on the hills of Maryland and the heights of Loudon. We were surrounded. There was no corner of safety for unarmed men, for women or children, or for the sick or wounded. They could do nothing but look toward the frowning mountain walls uprising on either side and await the storm of fire about to burst from their summits.

Through that long, azure-golden morning—a morning so absolutely perfect in the blending of its elements, in its fusion of fragrance, light, and color, that it can never die out of my consciousness, I sat by this open window making bandages. Directly before me across the Shenandoah towered the Loudon mountain. Where the great trees had fallen on its summit I knew that the enemy was at work ranging his batteries. The red flags of our hospitals, hoisted high above their chimneys streamed toward this foe imploring mercy for our sick and wounded ones. The stony streets of Camp Hill throbbed with unwonted life. Many soldiers were hurrying to and from the hillside spring with their black coffee kettles, eager to get their day's supply of fresh water before the bombshells grew thicker in the air. Many strangers, refugees from Martinsburg and Winchester, paced up and down the street. Citizens at the corners discussed the probabilities of the day with troubled faces. Young girls and matrons toiled up the steep Camp Hill side to our hospital laden with baskets of delicacies, mindful of the suffering soldier amid all their fears. Poor contrabands stood in groups talking in incoherent terror of Jackson, and of the certainty of their being "cotched and sold down South." In a high yard opposite a company of little children were rolling in the grass amid the late-blooming flowers, utterly unconscious of the impending storm about to burst upon their innocent heads. The atmosphere was pierced with the deep trill of insect melody. Golden butterflies flickered by me on flame-like wings. The thistle down sailed on through seas of sunshine. The spider spun his web in the tree beside my window. The roll of the rivers rhymed with the music of the air. Nature rested in deep content. The day, serene enough for Paradise, murmured, "Peace." God from the benign heavens said, "It is my Sabbath."

Whiz, whir, hiss, roar, bang, crash, smash!

Helpless men started in their beds. The house shook to its foundations. Heaven and earth seemed to collapse. The deafening roar rolling back to the mountains died in the deeper roar bursting from their summits. All the rebel batteries opened on us at once. Those on Loudon faced us, and our hospitals were under their heaviest fire. The shock of the tremendous cannon near the house sent me off my chair, in spite of my aspiration after a sublime courage. I am not a hero. I wish that I were. It is extremely mortifying upon a stupendous occasion to find oneself unequal to its sublimity. I was pervaded with horror even more than with fright. The profanation of man seemed awful. God's Sabbath, the divine repose of nature, invaded, outraged by the impotent fury of men. I am afraid of bombshells. I am more afraid of them now than I was before I heard or felt their sulphurous current hissing near my very head. If there is a sound purely fiendish this side of the region of the lost, it is the scream and shriek of a bombshell. No matter how many tear the air, each demon of a shell persists in a diabolical individuality of its own, and refuses to hiss or shriek precisely like any one of its neighbors.

I suffered most through my imagination. Each dreadful thing that tore the air I thought must burst into the room and take off the head of one of my boys. They poured into the garden beside us, they struck the pavement before us, they tore up the earth beneath us, they threw the sacred soil upon the very beds of our wounded, but they did not hit us. O, futile rebel shells, what rare restraining angel withheld your fire and deadened your destruction beneath the eaves of our lintel!

Two hours! and I had grown so accustomed to this unwonted thunder that I was able to go from cot to cot as if no battle were going on. Another hour, and I had nearly ceased to be conscious of it amid the newly wounded, moaning for succor in the ward.

How royally that day died. How supremely nature asserted her divinity high above the roar and smoke of battle in a holy hush of twilight, which man could neither reach nor destroy. I saw it and rested in it for a single moment, as I turned from the smell of human blood to the open window for air. Then faint from South Mountain came the muffled roar of distant artillery. Then nearer, nearer, and I knew that it was the thunder of another battle beyond the hills. It is Franklin! It is Sumner! It is McClellan! They are coming to our help! If we can hold out two hours longer, one of them must come to our aid, and we shall be saved.

It was night, no helper had come. From the moment in which Maryland Heights were lost, we knew that the disgraceful penalty would be surrender, unless reinforcements saved us from such a hapless fate. It was the night of the second day and no helper had come. At dark the cannonading ceased and the infantry fight began. The enemy tried to storm the breastworks at Bolivar, but were repulsed by our brave boys. Quick and sharp through the night we heard the crack and rattle of the musketry. It was then, under the protecting stars wrapped in protecting darkness, that I watched nearly three thousand of our cavalrymen ride swiftly away down the rocky gorge out into the night, resolved to cut their way through the enemy's lines at any hazard, rather than stay to surrender their swords to traitors. "Let us cut our way through, let us fight our way out," was the utterance of each one. O, brave men, I can never forget you, nor that moment! The dim lights of the hospital flickered out upon their faces white and resolute, as they sat in their saddles holding the reins of their restless horses. I lifted to Captain M. the brace of pistols which a few hours before he had committed to my keeping, and as I saw what a dauntless face he turned toward the darkness and danger before him, I could but say:

"How grand a thing to be a man!"

"How divine a thing to be a woman!" he said in the gentlest voice, pointing to the open window of the hospital, extending his hand in farewell. With these words he rode on. Then I saw the vast, dark-moving mass of living men, each one with a high heart of courage in his breast, pass silently and swiftly out into the night.

"How divine a thing to be a woman," I repeated, as I entered the ward, thanking God that, if He had denied me the material power of my brother, he had granted me the healing hand and devoted heart which could minister to him and help to save him in the hour when material force was as impossible to him as to me.

On Monday morning I drew my curtain and looked out. The dense fog above Maryland Heights was already splintered with the sun rays darting up from behind the Blue Ridge. Curtains of violet mist hung along the green sides of Loudon mountain. The sulphurous smoke of the cannonade enveloped its summit, spreading dense and blue above our heads, broken here and there into rifts of blue sky. In the stillness of the early morning, the awful roar of yesterday seemed to be a dreadful dream. It could never happen again. The tops of these mountains could never cleave together again in such an apocalypse of sound. The poor old hospital, the very foundations of Camp Hill, could never be thus shaken more, "No, never," I said, half asleep. The next instant I stood in the middle of the floor, sent thither by the shock of forty batteries. The cannonading of Sunday had been terrific, this of Monday morning was appalling. The enemy fired upon us from seven different directions, while our own guns from below replied with great spirit and effect. The fight was unequal, hopeless, but the soldiers at our guns never faltered.

Just then Colonel M., the commander of the town, rode past. He was going to the front—to surrender, accompanied by his handsome young aides in glittering uniform, followed by an imposing retinue of mounted "orderlies."

He was going to surrender, mounted for the last time on the petted, prancing horse which had carried him through the campaign of Mexico. He rode to the front of the battle-line amid torrents of bursting shells, and saying to one of his aides, "I have done the best I could, I have done my duty," he waved a white pocket-handkerchief as a flag of truce. But the cannonaders upon the mountain tops were too eager with their fiendish firing to see this feeble signal of surrender. In vain Colonel M. rode up and down the line, waving the white flag, the storm of death seemed only to deepen. Half an hour later, hearing the swift fore-running triumphant shriek, he bowed his head to save it, but the avenging shell would not be defrauded of retribution. Its sole errand was death to him. It struck low, it tore the very artery of life, and he fell. His attached aide-de-camp, after trying vainly to staunch the profuse bleeding of the wound, placed him in a blanket, and with great difficulty found a soldier willing to help carry the fallen commander from the battle-field. This was a young officer of a New York regiment. He had scarcely taken hold of the blanket, when another bomb-shell, almost grazing the fallen head of Colonel M., struck this young man and shivered him to atoms.

The announcement of the surrender

and of the fall of Colonel M. passed along the ranks simultaneously. Then the lion-hearted Captain McG., of New York, who sent shell after shell from his battery into the enemy's ranks, whose splendid shots and rash bravery were the admiration of all, being told that the town was surrendered, threw up his arms, burst into tears, and cried, "O, my boys, we have no country!"

It was then amid the resounding shells and the cries of the wounded and dying, that imprecations and curses broke from the ranks.

"After all to surrender, what a shame!" was the cry. Yet there was no help for it now. Our ammunition was gone—there was not enough for another round, while the enemy had reserved his most deadly fire until to-day, and his store was unexhausted. Now his firing upon a foe utterly at his mercy was appalling. We ought to have had ammunition, we ought to have had help, but we had neither, and the end was surrender.

I saw them bring him back, bleeding and groaning, on a blanket, the man who had passed my window so proudly mounted two hours before! It was a sad, sad sight, this bleeding gray-haired soldier. Whatever his faults, he expiated them with his life.

Another day, and a rough pine box, on the floor of the hall of the house which had been his headquarters, held all that was left of him mortal. Young rebel officers, in grey jackets richly embroidered with gold lace, sat chatting upon this box, clicking their swords and striking their spurs against it as careless of its contents as if it encased a dead mule.

No one but a few personal friends honored the dust of this unfortunate man, doubly unfortunate in that death could not retrieve his clouded honor. It could not annul the fact that he had failed as a commander. The guns on Maryland Heights were not properly mounted for defence. Loudon Heights were left utterly open to attack. The pontoon bridges were left for the enemy to pass over. Stores, ammunition, arms, were held intact for Jackson to seize on. The only key was turned, the only door opened, through which the rebels could escape from Maryland, or Jackson rush from Virginia to reinforce Longstreet,—the war prolonged, the pæan of another rebel victory shouted in the face of Europe, the most disgraceful victory of the war.

Surely, this man had every personal incentive to do differently. A clouded brain, an overwhelming foe, must have made him incapable of seizing his chance for immortality, and have sent a brave soldier into a dishonored grave.

Not half an hour had passed after the surrender when the rebel army had entered the town. It was a sad, a humiliating, a disgraceful sight. While the bombardment lasted hope did not quite die. Help might come; the last thrill of hope kept us from despair. I saw the first mounted ensign pass the earthworks which had been guarded so long by loyal soldiers. I saw him flaunt aloft the bloody stars and bars and the palmetto flag; I saw him drag the banner of the Union in the dust. It was a sight that I could not bear. After it came Jackson's entire army. No waving flags, outstretched hands, no murmurs of joy, no woman's welcome greeted it.

They peered into the windows with curious eyes,—some of these mounted cavaliers, but the few faces which they saw were tear-dimmed: the bitterest tears of a lifetime greeted them in at least one house. If I were to live a thousand lives, that moment in its poignant conciousness of shame, defeat, degradation, could never be repeated,—that moment in which for the first time I saw the flag of my country dragged in the dust of the road, followed by a triumphant host, that host my own countrymen.

First came the cavalry, the "flower," the "chivalry," the aristocracy of the South, spurred and mounted like the knights of old, each man in his spirit and person, in his dauntless daring, in his insane devotion to one idea, repeating the princely crusade of the Middle Ages. They look what they are, high-blooded, high bred, infatuated men. Every eye burns with passion. Careless, reckless even of life, all that they value risked on a single stake, they ask only to win or to die. Unlike the infantry, they know what they are fighting for. They will tell you without the asking. "I am fighting for Southern rights, for my home, for my niggers." Their intercourse with those whom they consider equals is marked by a lavish generosity, a courtly courtesy, but to inferiors they are supercilious, tyrannical, and often brutal. They hold a slave as scarcely more than a beast, yet they rate him higher, and would choose him as a personal associate sooner than they would a Yankee.

After these imperial leaders marched their slaves, their white slaves, true serfs, fighting in their rear for eternal serfdom, which they are taught to believe is Southern rights. On, helter skelter, crowding the street, swarmed a worse than Egyptian plague! Barefooted, half-naked, foul, flouting their dirty banners, gazing eagerly about with their starved faces, intent only on plunder, and on finding something to eat. Thus the deliverers of Maryland, regenerators of the nation, entered Harper's Ferry, September 15, 1862.

While the officers were dashing down the road, and the half-naked privates begging at every door, General Jackson stood sunning himself, and talking with a group of soldiers across the street,—a plain man in plain clothes, with an iron face, and iron-gray hair. Only by his bearing could he be distinguished from his men. He stood as if the commander of all, marked only by the mysterious insignia of individual presence, by which we know instinctively the genius from the clown. No golden token of rank gleamed on his rusty clothes, none of the shining symbols of which, alas! too many of our officers are so ridiculously fond, that they seem unconscious how disgraceful is this glitter of vanity. They were nowhere visible on old Stonewall's person. When General Jackson had drank at the pump, and talked at his leisure, he mounted his flame-colored horse, and rode down the street at the jog of a comfortable farmer carrying a bag of meal to mill.

As he passed I could not but wonder how many times he had prayed on Saturday night, before commencing his hellish Sabbath work. His old servant says that, "when Massa prays four times in de night, he knows de devil'll be to pay next day." And I am very sure that there was a large number of devils at work above Harper's Ferry on Sunday, September 14, 1862.

## CHAPTER XIX.

EIRENE'S DIARY.—DEATH OF WIN.

*October* 1.

Dear Mother:—All is over. I will write down on the pages of this little book every thing that you want to know, but which I cannot send you now. I knew that Win's regiment was at the front, but tried to think of him as unharmed—in the thickest of the fight, and yet untouched. If I thought of him otherwise I knew that it would unfit me to serve the many who really needed me. Yet a feeling of dumb terror seized me with every fresh ambulance that I saw coming down the winding road from Bolivar. Who might be in it? Alas! I was forced to say: "Somebody's brother!" Then I served him but the more faithfully because in my selfishness I had been so glad that he was not my own.

At last all the wounded had been brought in they said, all but those who had fallen between the battle lines; they had lain longer, and there was less hope for them.

You cannot imagine the look of the ruined town that Monday evening, September 15. Thirteen thousand of our own men wandering about idle, unarmed, paroled. Thousands of Confederates swarming the hillsides, the roads, the yards and houses, ragged, often bare-backed, bare-footed, abject, worn-out men. Their little camp-fires were flickering in every direction along the roads and over the hillsides, and over them they were cooking their suppers. And yet where could you look without seeing their stretchers standing in the yards and in the road, filled with their dying and dead. Far down in the gorge great tongues of fire leaped up into the darkness where they were burning the Government arsenal, and firing the grand railroad bridge doomed so often to destruction. It was by the light of these flames that I watched the last line of ambulances approaching the hospital. It was a power above and beyond myself that helped me to stand there. It seemed as if my heart broke anew in my breast with every cry of human anguish which smote it. Their moans and cries as they were lifted from the wagon I can never cease to hear. Dr. De Peyster and several other surgeons were there to superintend their removal to the hospital tents; for the main buildings were filled to overflowing.

They were lifting from the last ambulance a slender, fair-haired boy whose face to me seemed already struck with death. In the very midst of my pity I was thanking God that *he* was safe when I saw them lift another from the same ambulance. Mother, it was Win.

"O my brother!" I cried.

"Rene," he said "Rene!" as if he dreamed, then shut his eyes.

I saw Dr. De Peyster and Dr. Fay lift the stretcher on which he laid with their own hands and carry him away. I followed close behind.

"My brother, O, give him to me," I implored.

Before I had thought whither they were going, I saw Win laid upon Dr. De Peyster's own cot in his own room leading off from the great ward.

"Sister Eirene," he said, "you shall have your brother. Where could you care for him better than here?"

"Where is Davy?" murmured Win, slowly opening his eyes.

"Who is Davy, brother dear?"

"The boy—the South Carolina boy who was brought here with me. We fell—together—we've lain together since yesterday. He gave me the water in his canteen—all he had, can't *he* come?"

I looked at Dr. De Peyster.

"A gray back?" he said, "and yet—

yes! let him come. Fay, will you tell them to bring the South Carolinian here?"

A few moments more and another couch was brought into the room and placed beside that of Win's.

The boy in blue and the boy in gray face to face looked into each other's eyes. Twenty-four hours they had lain in their wounds; this was the thought which agonized me as I washed the grime and mud of the roadside from their pallid faces and hands. I had not shed a tear since I saw the rebel host march defiantly in—not one since then. I had only had time for my duty, but now, now bending over my brother, my only brother—at last, at last, it seemed as if my very being were dissolving—as if all I could do was to take him into my arms and implore him to live.

"Sister Eirene," said Dr. De Peyster, "I must ask you to go now for a little time while we examine their wounds. You will need all your strength and all your fortitude to nurse your brother afterwards. It pains me to ask you to go, but I must."

He saved me from an outburst of grief which must have unfitted me for all service for hours after. I felt at once how wise and kind he was as I lifted my head and went. At first it seemed to me that I must go to my room, throw myself upon my face, and sob and cry to God to save my brother. I was helped to do otherwise. Just as I was rushing on to do it, I caught the mute appeal cast upon me from the eyes of one of my boys, one who had been under my care for weeks. I stopped and went to him, from him to others, and thus in mercy was once more saved from myself.

Yet it seemed long, it *was* long before I was summoned back.

"Your brother is very dangerously wounded—we will be prepared for the worst," said Dr. De Peyster, as he met me outside of the door.

Dreadful as his words were, I knew that even they did not convey the full import of his thought. He did not know it, but his voice said: "Your brother will die."

I felt as if my own heart had stopped beating as I stole softly back into the room. I sat down between the two cots. Both boys were still under the influence of the ether which had been administered to them before the examination of their wounds. I don't know how long it was, but at last Win opened his eyes.

"Rene," he whispered, "I know now what it is to be a soldier. Do you remember in the old barn years and years ago—I dreamed about it? All that has come to pass, and more, so much more."

"Yes," I said, "so much more, and it seems as if it were away in some other life that we talked about it, Win. We won't talk about it now, it will *tire* you; but we'll think of nothing but of your getting well, and going home to see mother."

The sweetest smile passed over his face, but he shook his head.

"I shall never see mother again in this world," he said. "Let me talk, Rene. It's the last time—the last time. I've thought so often in my tent at night, and when lying in the trenches, and under the guns, if I could only see Rene, if I could only talk with Rene once more—this is the *once more!*"

I did not answer him. I knew if I tried that I could not.

"It has been hard sometimes to be a soldier," he went on—"not in battle, not when we were marching to an engagement. There was excitement in that—a fire in the thought that forced one on beyond and above every thing in one's self; but day after day to build corduroy roads in the snow, to march and countermarch in the beating rain, in the Virginia mud to the knees, to wait in trenches and under guns for *nothing*, as the Army of the Potomac has so often done—that *has* been hard, Rene."

"Yes, I have felt so many times, how hard it was."

"Rene, I have seen so many dear comrades drop and die by the road, and felt that their lives were thrown away. *Then* it was hard to keep up one's faith and principle. It seemed sometimes as if we were only puppets

—the puppets of incompetent or unprincipled men; and when men no better born or bred than ourselves were cruel to the common soldier then it was not pain of body only, it was anguish of heart and torture of spirit. Then it was hard to keep hold of the grand idea of country."

"O Win!"

"I've felt so different, Rene, ever since I *knew* that you were in Virginia. I've never doubted for a moment since then that if anything happened I should be brought to you. I knew that you were thinking of me."

"Yes, every moment. I knew you were up the Valley. At last I thought that all had been brought in, and that you were safe."

"It was not to be, Rene. That was all that there was in life for me—to be a soldier—and to give up my life."

"Had you lived ages you could not have given more. But I feel it hard," I said.

"No, Rene, what can one have more than their destiny; this is mine, the destiny of so many young men of my generation, to die for my country. I never could struggle on like you day by day as if I had a future. I *knew* that I had no future; but I could do my duty, and I did it gladly."

"You did it bravely, and you will have your reward somewhere—*somewhere*, Win."

"It is reward enough, Rene, that you are satisfied with me, and that I am with you. Tell mother that when I laid in my blanket—when I marched in the road—when I stood on guard at night under the stars—when I went into battle, I always thought of her. Every unkind word I had ever spoken, every naughty thing that I had ever done, came back to me, and it seemed if I could only live to see her once more I would be a better boy. Tell her so. Tell her how sorry I am for every wrong thing I ever did. Tell her that I—I love her."

A low sob broke from the other cot. God forgive me, in hearing Win's voice I had forgotten the other boy.

I turned to him, it helped me hide my tears. I laid the hair wet with cold sweat from his forehead. The death pallor was on his face, his lips quivered in its chill. I had seen its sign too often not to know that he was dying.

I took his hand, I bent over him and kissed him.

"Thank you," he said, and the tears trickled through his closed eyelids.

"O, to think there is no one to take my message to *my* mother!"

"I will send it to her," I said. "Tell me her name and where she lives, and I will write her any word you say."

"Will you! thank you! How good you are! And *you* are a Yankee! My mother lives near Aiken, South Carolina. Tell her I love her, just as your brother loves his mother—that I die trusting in the Saviour in whom she taught me to trust."

"I will write it just as you say it, Davy."

"O, how I thank you! Could you—would you mind pushing me a little nearer to him?" And he opened wide his blue eyes and looked wistfully toward Win, whose face was turned towards him.

"He spoke to me so kind in the trenches. I loved him if he was a Yankee. I knew no harm of Yankees only what they told me. I never saw one till in the fight. I was at school when the war broke out. I'm only seventeen. I had no slaves to fight for—never had any. My father was a minister, Scotch-Irish born. I was a Carolinian, and when they conscripted me I would have gone cheerfully if mother had not cried. Poor mother! a widow, I her only one! If I could only see you, mother, just for one minute—just to kiss you before I die—what a comfort! Please push me closer to him. We fought—we shan't again."

I pushed the cots together. Each boy stretched out a hand.

"It was for my country," said Win.

"I thought it was for my country," said Davy. "I didn't know what it was for; I don't now."

They smiled into each other, the blue eyes and the brown. I leaned over their heads, and noticed for the first time their jackets left inadvertently upon the foot of their cots—the blue and the grey, each soaked with the blood from their wounds.

* * * * * *

I don't know when it was. I heard Win say: "My love to Pansy. Mother, my love to mother. Kiss me, Rene."

He threw his arm over my neck, drew my head down. It seemed as if it was the same instant that the other voice said: "Mother!" and the other's arm was thrown about my neck. There I kneeled with my head between the two. I felt their quivering breath. I felt their souls departing. I felt them as they went out in their passage to eternity. Then I knew no more.

Some time, I don't know when, I heard Dr. De Peyster say: "Come with me, Sister Eirene."

Then I looked upon their faces—they were dead—both of the boys were dead.

I kissed them both. I said: "I must stay with my brother."

"By and by; now you must come with me," he answered, in a voice gentle and yet compelling.

He took my hand and led me away to the door of my room.

"You will sleep now," he said. "To-morrow you can stay with your brother."

That night Pierre De Peyster went the rounds of the hospitals as usual. Then he came back to the door of the room within which Eirene sat alone with the two dying men. Little did she dream, as she sat there, of the pity and sorrow and love which throbbed in one strong heart for her. Little did she dream that the man who had seemed to her both haughty and unfeeling, now paced up and down before that closed door, too sensitive and too delicate to intrude personally upon an interview sanctified, in his thought, by love and death. Accustomed as he had become to every possible sight of human suffering or mental anguish, his step and hand both faltered whenever he essayed to cross the threshold of that room. At intervals a low murmur of voices, a broken sob, would reach his ear, and his heart would impel him to enter, but in the silence that followed he could not; he felt that he could not meet the look of mute appeal upon that face. He knew what it would say: "Save, oh, save my brother!" He knew that he could not—knew that he must stand there and behold the sorrow that he could not alleviate, and the knowledge made him a coward.

"My God, I could never deny her anything if she looked at me," he said; "but death is mightier even than love, and now she would appeal to me in vain.

"Everything that could have been done has been done. If she needs assistance she knows that it is within call," he said, again resuming his watch.

Time wore on — the dead silence within at last became unbearable, then he softly opened the door and entered. As he approached the bed, at first he thought that all three were dead. The girl kneeling at the head of the low cots seemed to have fallen forward; an arm of each man was thrown over her neck—they were dead, and she lying there looked as white and motionless as they. Yet it was not death. As Pierre De Peyster lifted the unresisting arms which encircled her, and held her up, she opened her eyes and looked into his face. There was no swooning, no crying, no ungoverned excitement. It was a simple coming back to life and to an utter consciousness of it.

"He is dead. They both are dead," said the pathetic voice, and the unutterable grief expressed in tone and gesture was more moving in their pathos than the loudest cries.

It was then that Pierre De Peyster said: "You must come with me."

He saw that she must find present oblivion from sorrow, or that in her very silence she would break under it. He used the will which was the strong underlying element of his character, and mentally compelled her to go. Worn out and broken as she was, there was rest in the very fact that another thought for her and told her what to do. When he left her he came back to his own room, shut the door, and sat down alone with the dead. He was used to death, in some respects had become too used to it. He had come to meet it in its most hideous forms outwardly unmoved. The wholesale human slaughter by which he was surrounded had had the tendency to make the life of any one man to seem comparatively but a little thing. He had no time and no rest now to think of men individually.

Neither was he free from the faults of his class, nor the spirit of caste so constantly fostered by the discipline of the army. A private in his thought meant a poor ignorant Irishman or Dutchman, one of the city rabble who risked his life for fifteen dollars a month, and then received more for it than he could under any other possible circumstances. He knew, if he thought of it, that there were tens of thousands of exceptions in boys well born and gently reared, from the farms, the shops, the schools, the professions of his native land, who marched in the ranks, and who had given up all that they held most dear to fight for their country. He recognized them when he saw them, and sympathized with them, and yet no less the average private in his mind was a fellow always getting drunk and into the guard-house at every possible opportunity, who consequently deserved to be balanced on a pole, or to receive any other inhuman punishment which his superior officers chose to visit upon him. Yet here upon his own bed was stretched the dead body of a common soldier, no finer, and no truer than tens of thousands of his comrades who had died as he died. And here was another common soldier—Pierre De Peyster turned with a look of repulsion from the gray uniforms so hateful to him, lying on the foot of the bed, covered with dust and pierced by bullets,—but it faded as it fell upon the face of the wearer, so little more than a child, a fair-haired, blue-eyed boy, with an infantine smile hovering about the sunken features, so wasted by hardship and suffering. It was impossible to regard this face as the face of a foe, although he had not heard a word that the boy had spoken. The face of the other dead soldier smiled back upon his friend. It was embrowned by many months of exposure, yet it was no less beautiful in its fresh young manhood. The soft brown eyes, looking forth from the half-closed lids, were so like *hers*, the seal of blood and birth showed so plain in death; for an instant he seemed *her*, and Pierre De Peyster started. There were the two outstretched arms just as they had been unwound from her neck. Pierre, seeing them, realized all, and again sat down and gazed at the dead faces before him.

"I am converted," he said slowly, aloud.

"Either all life is changed, or I am. At last, I seem to see everything as it is. You, my poor boy—I should have hated the sight of you six hours ago. Looking upon your face, I see that you are not to blame. And you! If I had come to you in a ward amid a hundred others, I might have seen no difference, and now—both are holy in my sight."

Dawn was flushing red above the mountains when Pierre De Peyster went forth from this room. Then he went into the old graveyard, which, a few rods from the hospital, stretched over the hill.

"It is as I thought," he said, standing by an open grave almost covered by bushes near the old stone wall.

"Poor Erwin's body was taken up and sent to his friends before the surrender. The bushes have hidden this grave, and here is room for another. They can be buried side by side."

EIRENE'S DIARY, OCTOBER 3.

Mother, in the quiet of the early evening, when even the torn mountains and the ravaged valley took on a look of peace, we laid—not him, but his body, down to rest, and beside it that of poor little Davy. Everything had been done that kindness could do to make their burial home-like and Christian-like. I could not but think of it, even in my grief, how different were the neat caskets and attire in which they rested, from the rude box and the rough coats in which I had seen so many of our boys buried—

yes, so many without coat or box at all, just as they fell. It was Dr. De Peyster who did this for them. It was all done before I awoke. I came out of that sleep as if I had come back from another world; I was so worn out, I suppose. I remember I wrote you I didn't like Dr. De Peyster. I should be very ungrateful if I could write that now. He seemed stern, even hard. I think still that he has this nature—but he has another which has covered me with a kindness that I can never forget.

It seemed as if a tender Providence had saved this sheltered corner in the old over-crowded graveyard for these two boys. I don't know who found it, but I see it now, hidden from the highway by rose-bushes, close to the stone wall on the very hill-top. I have much to do, but no day so much but I take a few moments to visit these graves. I cannot weep for Win now. I never shall weep for him again, till I come home and see his old haunts, and sit down once more in the old barn where he told me when a boy that he should some day be a soldier. I cannot weep here. The suffering that I see, the dying eyes that I close, would make it seem too selfish. He is a part of the vast sacrifice—the sacrifice which began on yonder mountain-top—when that heroic old martyr, insane with a holy idea, came down its sides, undaunted and alone, to be the saviour of a race. But, mother, while I realize what freedom costs, at what a price this Republic is preserved, I feel as if it would break my heart if its government is ever again administered by unholy men.

When the war is over, and I come home, I shall bring the body of our boy to rest in the spot that he loved, where we shall all rest some day. When it seems hard that we gave him, our only one, we will remember that every hillside and valley of our land is sown with the dust of its most precious sons. In almost every home some one weeps as we do. At every table there is a vacant place that can never, never be filled in this world. So many, O, so many, will watch and wait for the boy who will never come back—and they will never know where he fell, or where he lies—or if he were ever buried. This will be so much harder to bear, and yet it must be borne.

## CHAPTER XX.

EIRENE'S DIARY.

*November* 1, 1862.

Dear Mother:—The army has gone. The entire army of the Potomac marched down Camp Hill days ago. All the regimental hospitals are broken up. The regimental and brigade surgeons have gone. The convalescents have been transferred to Washington and Baltimore, only the very sick and the dangerously wounded are left behind. If I could live a thousand lives I doubt if I should ever witness again such human suffering as I see here every hour. No matter what I behold hereafter I believe that I shall record at last that nothing ever equalled the suffering of the sick and wounded left behind by the army of the Potomac at Harper's Ferry, October, 1862. The greater portion of them lie in the hospital tents which line the meadows between Bolivar and Harper's Ferry. It does not seem like the same land from which I wrote you last. The equinoctial rains have flooded the valley for more than a week; the two rivers have risen to a great height and pour down in two overwhelming floods, which rush together below. All the meadow land between is soaked with water. In this, on the ground, our soldiers lie. The daily increasing number of dead bodies brought past our hospital, to be buried on the open hill, convinced me that something was wrong in the hospital tents, and I went to see. When I lifted the curtain and entered, the sight that I saw made my heart sink within me. On either side, the entire length of the tent, lying as close as they could be packed upon the ground, were wounded and dying men. As I went to one near the door, he lifted up the corner of the blanket spread under him, and he was lying nearly body deep in water.

"Lady, do you remember me?" he asked.

I looked at his sunken features, out of which the last hope of life had gone, and could not recall that I had ever seen him before. I would not pain him by saying so, but asked, "Where did I meet you?"

"Don't you remember the Sabbath afternoon that you brought cordial into the little brick house on the hill, filled with a new Pennsylvania regiment? I was one of the nurses, and hadn't thought of getting sick then. Nothing ailed any of the boys then, but a touch of the chills. We thought that we were all going on to victory. Here we all are, all that's left, and we can't be here long. My wife wouldn't know me. Will you be so kind as to write to her, lady?"

For an instant I felt too shocked to reply. I did remember him now, and his regiment, and that Sabbath afternoon. Dr. Fay told me that there was a part of a regiment in that house just getting acclimated for whom my cordial was the thing. When I entered I thought that scarcely since the war had I seen so pleasant a sight. There sat, or rested on their cots, all the convalescents in clean attire, and nearly all of them had their Testaments or some book in their hands. They were from the farming districts of northern Pennsylvania, not one of them had lost their rural home-look, and the sight of these men was like a glimpse of home before the war. I can never forget how their faces brightened, nor how they smiled upon me. And there was not one but what spoke to me of his mother, sister, or wife, and many thanked me in their names as I handed them the glass of cordial.

Here all that were left were dying on the wet ground.

"I don't understand it," I said, "when I saw you last not one of you were very sick. It seemed as if you would all be as well as ever in a few days."

"It seems to me that we might have been," said the man, "if we could have stayed in that dry house; but we've been moved and moved from one wet place to another, till here we are. I took the fever; our regiment and doctor have gone, and I had given up our last hope till I saw you, lady. We've always called you *our* lady since that Sunday afternoon. So many times the boys have said: 'If our lady only knew how we were, she would help us.'"

"If I could only have known before," I thought, but I did not say it.

"I will write to your wife and do everything in my power for you all," I said.

I saw him shudder as his back came in contact with that of his next compaion.

"He is dead," he whispered, with a look of horror.

I bent down and lifted the cape of the blue overcoat which covered his comrade's face. It was true; he was dead. On the other side so close that he touched him was another soldier dying.

There was nothing to be done but to go and to discover the condition of all. It was the same to the end of that long tent; feet to feet, closely packed, devoured by vermin, and lying in the water of the soaked ground, were two long lines of the soldiers of the Union dying and dead. Gray-haired men, men in their prime, boys almost children, so many of them rosy and beautiful in their youth, a few weeks ago—here they were lying upon the ground in the last extremity of neglect and suffering.

To me these are the saddest days of the war; there is so little alleviation to the awful suffering which surrounds me. These men are dying for lack of physicians, nurses and care. If twenty other women were as busy as I am, preparing broths and cordials, walking and watching from morning till night, there would not then be enough to care for these men. We hear much of the rights of women. It seems to me no woman need question her right or ask what her work is in days like these. I do all that I can, and it is so little. I feel as if I would give my very life for these men, and yet I cannot save them. I can scarcely look up without seeing one carried forth on a stretcher, wrapped in his blue overcoat, without a coffin, without a prayer, laid in a shallow grave scooped out from among the stones on the hill. They die so fast there is scarcely room for any more. Their graves reach from the hill-top down to the road. Their names are all given to me, even when I cannot attend them personally. The most heart-breaking duty comes after they are at rest. The vestibule and closets of the little Lutheran church standing mid-way between Bolivar and Harper's Ferry, and now filled with wounded, are piled with the knapsacks and haversacks of dying and dead soldiers. I go to these and open them, take out every treasure they contain, and with a letter send them to the friends of the boy who owned them. A little drummer boy died yesterday. I have found his haversack; it contained a picture of himself, taken with his mother when he enlisted. Such a rosy boy! I thought as I looked upon him yesterday, wasted and dead, that I was glad that his mother could never know how he changed before he died. I have sent his last message and all his things to her. The eloquence of these worm-eaten, mouldy bags cannot be written. Here is the piece of stony bread, uneaten, the little paper of coffee, the smoked tin cup in which it was boiled over the hasty fire on the eve of battle; here is the letter sealed, directed, never sent; here is the letter half written, never ended, beginning "Dear wife, how I want to see you," "Dear mother, my time is almost out;" and the rusty pen just as it was laid in the half filled sheet by the brave and loving hand which hoped so soon to finish it. Here are scraps of patriotic poetry carefully copied on sheets of paper tinted red, white, and blue; here are photographs of favorite generals, and photographs of the loved ones at home; here are letters full of heart-breaking love and of sobbing loyalty to duty and of holy faith and cheer written to them from home; and here is the Testament given him by the woman that loved him best. Mother, these are all mementoes of brave, loving life gone out. The boys who owned them will never go back. To one unfamiliar with the soldier's life these relics might mean little. To me they mean all love, all suffering, all heroism. Deeds of valor are no longer dreams gone by. We live in knightly days; our men are dauntless men. Will there ever be one to write the life of the common soldier. His blood buys us all that we hold dear—country, home, a free government, the endless privileges of a free people. I ask no higher privilege than to serve him living and to honor him in his grave.

It is after I have been the rounds of ward and tent that I come into this old vestibule and sit down to this sacred task. Sometimes I make up many packages. Sometimes I take up some mother's or sister's letter, and it brings so much back to me that I can't go on. This was so last night. It must have been late, but I did not know it. I looked up from the contents of the knapsack which had moved me so much, and for the first time realized the appalling loneliness of my surroundings. There were the high walls of the vestibule all torn with bombshells, its dark open closets; its wide floor piled high with old knapsacks and haversacks, I sitting in the midst of them on a box, with no light in the place but that given by the one tallow candle at my side, which threw its feeble and flickering rays over the open bags and their contents. My own feelings, I presume, made the place seem more weird and desolate than ever before. It was then I was startled by the sound of horse's feet without, and it seemed the same instant that the door opened and Dr. De Peyster entered. I thought him many miles away, and cannot tell whether I felt more astonishment or joy at seeing him.

"Sister Eirene," he said, "my brigade leaves Pleasant Valley to-morrow. Before it moves I have come to say farewell. I did not feel as if I could go on till I had seen you once more."

And as he said these words he came forward, and looking down upon the open knapsacks amid which I sat, I thought that his face grew grave.

"I have missed you much since you went," I answered. "Every hour it has seemed if you could only have staid you would have lessened the awful suffering of the men in the tents."

"Yes, I could have done something. It is the result of the army moving and of the medical staff being broken up. But I could do nothing but obey orders and go with my brigade."

"I know it."

"I certainly could have worked with more heart if I had staid behind," he replied. "It did me good to know that you came after me to do what I could not do."

What I once heard him say of the army nurse *would* come into my mind, mother, and yet it was the same to me as if he had never spoken it.

"The chances of war are many," he said. "They make it more than probable that we may never meet again. What I wanted to say is, that while I live I can never forget you."

"While I live I can never forget you," I answered, and I gave him my hand in farewell, for he had already turned to go.

Without another word he departed. I held the candle in the open door as he mounted his horse, and by its little light flaring out into the night I watched him ride away.

As he went up the hill which rises between the church and the town below, the sight of him brought back more powerfully than I can tell, the image of the man who used to ride away from the little house at home. Mother, I have never spoken to you of *him*. There was a time when I thought I never could. But this outward resemblance forced upon me the real contrast. What did that man live for? For what this? As I looked after him so swiftly passing out of my sight, perhaps forever, he seemed to me to be the realization in himself of all that I had once dreamed another man to be. He is my kind strong friend, whose life stretches far away from mine. Probably I shall never see him again, and yet I thank God that I have seen him and known him, and that he is my friend, that he was so kind to my brother, that he has been kind to me, that I can always remember him and pray for him. He is the manliest man that I have ever known. I reverence all men more because I know him, and yet I remember I wrote you that I did not like him, and I did not when I wrote you so.

## CHAPTER XXI.

THE BEGINNING OF THE END.

AND was this the end? No one was gladder than she that the war was over, that the great guns whose echoes still seemed to float out from the mountain tops, had sent forth at last the reverberations of peace. And yet the consciousness that here her work was done, forced her thoughts back upon herself. She who had lived so long and devotedly for others, knew not now how to begin to live for herself. The work that she had been doing made all mere personal work seem poor and selfish. She was no less glad to live for her loved ones than she had been years before, but it seemed to her now that while her life would encircle them, that it must also reach out toward something more. It was a moment of reaction. The unfailing. the unflagging power to do which had never left her while there was anything to be done, now that the last task was almost accomplished, seemed gone from her forever. An inexpressible weariness crept over her. She had lived through two lives: the first, life of youth and of love; the second, life of devotion and of moral heroism. Now for a moment came weakness, and a vague, undefined yearning for protection and rest. "I am tired," she said; "it would be sweet to rest if I could." The dream of her youth came back—a memory, it was nothing more. And what is sadder than the memory of the very sweetness of life lost? What more mournful than the knowledge that you have survived life's fondest illusion? It swept through her like a shock that after all these years, after all that she had suffered and outlived, if she could have it all back, that early dream, it would be nothing to her now. What could such a love as Paul Mullane s be to her to-day? Nothing. What seemed for the moment too hard to be borne was the desolation which it had left behind. Since the moment in which she renounced it she had lived as solitary in heart as if she alone inhabited the universe.

She had just left the two graves lying within the old stone wall of the graveyard. She came down the hillside a little way, sat down under the shadow of Jefferson's Rock, her feet in the new grass, her head leaning against the rude pillar of stone which supported it. She had been gazing toward "the getting out place," as she called it, the great gate of the mountains and the blue vista of sky far beyond. It seemed a long way off, this country of hers—this old-time home, this far back life! She was tired, she was lonely, she was unloved! Suddenly the thought came to her that beside her father and mother she was necessary to no one; her eyes closed over this dreary thought, and the tears dropped upon her cheeks. Thus the May sun dropping down behind the mountains left her, covering her face in its going with tender light. Thus the south wind floating down the valley came to her, rippling through her hair as gently as through the grasses at her side. Thus the wedded rivers sang to her in glad music as they moved in concert together to the ocean, and thus Pierre De Peyster found her, for he had come far down the valley to find her—and her alone. He went to the hospital and for the first time found her absent, not at her old post. Her work was almost gone. Nearly all the sick and wounded who had survived had been carried to their homes by near friends who had come after them. The remaining convalescents in a few weeks would go, and the hospital be broken up.

"Are you looking for Sister Eirene?" asked one of the invalids who, sunning himself on the great portico, had seen Dr. De Peyster tie his horse to the tree at the foot of it, enter the house, and then come out with a disappointed look upon his face.

"There she is down yonder, Doctor, down by Jefferson's Rock; I saw her go down there more'n an hour ago."

She was taking one of her last looks at the wonderful picture that she might carry it away the more perfectly to hold it in her memory forever. Thunder of battle, moving armies, the dying, the dead, *her* dead, all were with her again as she looked down from her rocky pinnacle, and home, her home awaited her at last, far on beyond the dreamy blue.

"I am going home," she said aloud. "Yes," said a voice behind her, and she looked up into the face of Pierre De Peyster.

"I have been looking for you, Sister Eirene," he said, "in the hospital. I think that I have been looking for you ever since I was born."

The last tinge of color faded out of the lovely face as of old; but not as of old did it rush back in rosy bloom. The deep heart drew it downward and held it fast in its deep and silent current.

She answered not.

"Now I look upon your face again it seems as if my whole life had been a search for you," said the strong man in a voice sweet and solemn. "I never found my highest self till I found you; I never dreamed how holy and how precious this life could be, until I knew you. Are you glad that I can tell you this?"

"I am," and the woman's eyes looked up and the woman's soul, looking through them, realized how rich and wonderful a thing is the gift of a good man's love.

"May I sit down here and tell you what is in my heart?" he asked. "It seems to me that the moment has come at last when I have the right to tell it. I did not think so three years ago. During the war I thought that neither men nor women who had devoted themselves to their country had the right to turn aside to seek their own personal happiness. I thought so the night that I said good-by to you in the old church. The future looked so dark it looked more than doubtful if I could ever tell you how very dear you were to me, in this world. Yet I thought as I rode away that if it was denied me in this life, that I would tell you in the other; if not until eternity, that I should somewhere seek you out and say that it was you, and you alone, whom I had sought through all my mortal years. Tell me Eirene, have you thought of me since I went up the valley?"

"Now I see you I know I have scarcely ceased to think of you since that night," she said. "I remember as I watched you ride away in the darkness, that for a moment it seemed to me as if everything in the world had gone, and when I went back to the knapsacks as if everybody in the world was dead."

"Eirene, can you realize what it is to me to find you at last, at last? What it is to me who have sought you all my life?"

"I realize what it is to me to feel as if I had found that which I have sought all my life, in you! truth, honor, high manhood. *I believe in you!*"

"What a compensation for everything I have ever wished in this world I find in your words. Can I ask you without intruding what is your plan for the future?"

The old look of pain crept over her face. She looked up to him as if his question had suddenly removed her far from him. The joy of seeing him, the exquisite happiness which his undreamed-of words had brought her, the new rapture springing above weariness and loneliness to find herself once more beloved, had in their birth annihilated her past. It was as if she had had no past. Life and love were born anew in the perfect present. All went out as suddenly while his inquiry brought back her history. She was not ashamed of it. It was not pride which made her shrink from telling him her exact position. It was the wound of the old injury.

Even now she could not forget that another had turned from her, had been ashamed of her because she was poor. If this could be so now, she wanted to know it; and yet—yet if this man, who seemed so noble, so lifted above all littleness, if he could see her differently, treat her differently because she was below him in social condition, no other could fill his place in manhood; but she must know it at once.

She was silent an instant, and when she spoke her voice had lost all the sweet tones of companionship which it had when he and she had greeted each other, as two souls might have done who were alone in the world.

"I am very poor," she said. "I have always been poor. My only support comes from the labor of my hands. I was a book-keeper in a furnishing shop in New York when the war began. My employer has been very kind, and holds my position open to me on my return. As soon as the hospital here is broken up, I expect to go back to my old place."

She made this revelation in a clear, cold voice, but with downcast eyes, which she lifted as she ceased, fully prepared to see a frightful look of revulsion if not of repulsion on the face of her listener.

Instead, the expression of his eyes, full of mingled mirth and delight such as she had never seen there before, filled her with astonishment. It was perfectly plain to see that Pierre De Peyster was both amused and delighted.

"You speak as if I could never forgive you for being poor," he said, "as if it were a crime for which you are horribly to blame. I am glad that you are poor. I am glad that every one belonging to you is poor. I am glad that you have nothing but yourself. All my life I have been searching for the woman who held in her own nature the only treasure that I wanted. What can I say to you to make you believe that you are needed very much more somewhere else than in your old place? In another part of New York, in a dingy old street, there is a dingy old house. It was pleasant once, full of children and home cheer. That was a long time ago. Now the greater part of every year it is shut up. Sometimes a lady and her adopted daughter occupy a portion of it. Before the war an old bachelor had his rooms there. He used to have wonderful visions in those old rooms of somebody who would come some time and brighten up the old house, and brighten up him, and do something towards civilizing and making a man of him. He looked among all the ladies whom he knew, and he knew a good many, to find one whom he thought would be willing to spend her life in the old house and do this missionary work on him, and there was not one. No, he did not believe that there was one in what was called 'his set' who would be contented with the old house; and when it came to the final test, there was not one whom he was willing should try. Nobody cared for it as he did. Even his sister wanted to leave it and go up town. All his friends thought him a fool because he did not sell it and make tens of thousands of dollars by the sale. But he was born in the old house, his father and mother lived and died in it, his grandfather and grandmother lived and died in it before them. Although it was very un-New Yorkish to care at all for such associations, he could not shake them out of his fibre; there was not a brick or rafter or cobweb in the old place that he did not care for; and as for the musty old trees in the little park before it, he would not part with one of them for all Wall street. Can't I interest you in the old place? Now, wouldn't it be as pleasant to go there and brighten its old rooms up, and develop a warped old bachelor into something more human, even though you took his name and found out all of his faults, as it would be to cast up accounts in a furnishing shop year after year? Can't you say that it would be? I'm awfully lonesome, Eirene."

The blended forlornness and humor in his look and tone were irresistible.

In spite of herself they made Eirene's answer a gay laugh. The idea of this proud man pleading in such a way to her was comical as well as delightful.

"You make the old house seem very pleasant," she said. "I like old houses full of histories. It seems as if I had seen yours. It is just like the one in which my sister lives. I did not finish what I was going to tell you, Dr. De Peyster. I have one young sister; she is very beautiful, and has been adopted by a rich lady who lives in New York. The lady's name is Stuyvesant. I've been to her house to see Pansy, and the one you tell of seems like it."

"Very likely. Pansy! Hum! Stuyvesant is *my* sister's name. It seems that your sister and mine already know each other well."

As he made this declaration, certainly in an annoyed tone, all the light of happiness in Eirene's face died.

He could have said nothing scarcely which would have seemed to have divided her from him so completely.

Then Dr. De Peyster, who in the ruined old hospital and in the field tents had gone in and out among the sick and wounded for months, till he had come to seem like a brother in the same work; who on the battle-field had shared the dangers of the soldier; who had worked hard and fared rudely; he *was* the brother of the lofty lady who had separated her only sister's life from hers! The face of Cornelia Stuyvesant as she saw it last—remote and cold in its very kindness—made her shiver sitting here now. A moment before he had seemed so near in his simple manhood, his sympathy, his humanity, his tender love—but now so far from her in her low estate. This lovely and implacable sister, what would she say when she heard his story? The very look in her eyes would be sufficient to divide them forever.

But Pierre De Peyster's present annoyance sprang from a cause undreamed of by Eirene. He was not a saint in patience, and like many another brave man who could meet death without flinching, he would be perfectly fretted by a very little matter. While Eirene, in silent woe, was surveying the image of *his* sister, he with much irritation was recalling the likeness of *hers*.

"Well, it's some satisfaction to have it explained," he said. "I've always been tormented by the resemblance, because it was unaccountable. I didn't want you to look like her, or anybody else. But it's only a faint family look; I think I can bear it, now that I know what it is. Why on earth didn't Corna tell me that her adopted had a sister," he was going to say, but did not, out of regard to Eirene.

"I understand it quite," he said to himself. "Much good your plotting has done you, Mrs. Corna. It will teach you that a De Peyster should never plot."

"Then you have really seen the old house?" he asked, with the look of irritation still on his face, which Eirene thought sprung from a very different cause than the true one.

"Yes, sir, I went there a few times to see my sister. It was there that I bade her good-by. Mrs. Stuyvesant was very kind. She adopted Pansy as her own daughter. This removed her into a sphere of life very different from mine. I thought—I thought it might annoy Mrs. Stuyvesant, although she was so kind, if I came often to suggest the contrast. You know there *was* a difference?"

"A decided difference," answered Pierre, still intent upon his own view of that difference.

"Dr. De Peyster, it is hard, but I want you to realize all that difference. It seems as if you could hardly know what a struggle life may be to a woman, poor, imperfectly educated, with a natural shrinking from publicity and responsibility, who yet has no way, and no right to live in the world save by her own unaided labor. *Do* you know how hard and meagre life may be to such a one?"

"I begin to know it," he answered.

"I have walked the street hungry because I feared debt even for bread. But good help came, and, for me, I am rich now."

"How rich?"

"When the war began I had a little money saved for Win. After I became book-keeper, I had good wages, as women's wages. My employer's two sons went into the army. This softened his heart beyond expression. When I told him that I must go, he said to me: 'Go; God bless you! Your salary shall be the same as if you staid.' I have never been paid as a nurse—I could not take it; but for myself I have needed almost nothing. My salary has gone to my father and mother, and toward the payment for the little homestead which had passed into the possession of a friend. It is ours again. The money that made the last payment was the money saved for—Win."

"Then you are really a property-holder," answered Pierre, with the merriment coming back into his eyes. "I hope it isn't worth much."

Eirene's impulse was to feel injured at such an unfeeling remark, but the brightening face before her forbade it.

"It could not seem worth much to you," she said, "but it is worth more than all the rest of the world to me."

"Then I can't interest you in *my* house?"

"O, yes," was the reply, with a quick blush and laugh. "When I saw its great pictures, and all its old family relics, I thought it was the most interesting house I was ever in."

"Thank you."

"There is such a contrast between your house and ours. Ours is so low and small and poor. Yet there I was born; it is the only home I ever had. But you can't know the difference between it and yours."

"Why, I know all about it. I've seen your house," he said. "And I did not see anything so dreadful about it. You could not have had a better place to have been born in, Eirene. You took in the strength and freedom and freshness of the mountain-tops with your baby breath; don't you know it?"

"No. But *you* never were there!"

"O yes I was; I was there with my sister at those much advertised springs, and I saw your sister waiting at the gate for her fortune to come to her, and I sat in the carriage considerably fretted while my sister talked with yours."

Eirene was covered with confusion at this information. She was afflicted because she did not understand at all why he should have been fretted while his sister talked with Pansy.

"I can tell you something more stunning still. I saw you before I saw your sister."

"O, no! you couldn't. I was never at Hilltop after the Pinnacle House was opened."

"I did not see you there. I saw you months before at Trinity Church. You seemed awestruck and rapt in the service. It was this that first attracted my notice. I am sorry to say that I was very undevotional myself, and was gazing about after the manner of undevotional men. The apparition of an absolute worshipper in a New York church was enough to fix any man's gaze. Do you remember the time, Eirene?"

How well she remembered it! How often she had shut her eyes till all came back, the organ's anthem rolling through the nave; the altar-boys' chant flooding the arches with sweet reverberation; the trees swaying against the stained windows; the hush of the atmosphere; the thrill of worship which she felt.

"I can't tell you how often that hour has come back," she said, "nor what it has been to me amid these awful Virginia Sabbaths. But I could not recall any person that I met there."

"I know it. You didn't see anybody. You were a worshipper. But I was a godless fellow. I only went to church to please my sister. As a slight compensation, after the reading of the service I would study the people sitting on the benches in the aisles, settle on their nativity, temporal condition, etc., as they were usually strangers. I could not place you at once. At first, all that I saw was that you were weary and worn; that your clothes were plain, if not poor. I did not even think that you were young. The light from the great window falling on you seemed to bring a whole history out upon your face. At once it interested me because it baffled me. I could not read it, but the longer I looked the more I wanted to. At last I grew almost annoyed, for in spite of myself it seemed as if something within me said, 'It is she.' No, I declared; and yet answered my heart, 'It is *like* her. It is what she would have been had she passed youth and missed every human joy.' I knew you, and yet I knew you not. My spiritual perceptions were half blinded by a thousand traditions and fancies. I was a sceptic of women, of all the women whom I had met, through my very worship of one imagined woman whom I longed to meet but had never seen. One thing I can't remember of that afternoon, that is one word of Dr. H.'s sermon; but I do remember how absolutely absurd I seemed to myself as I stepped into the carriage with my sister, and was conscious of a slight pang of regret as I caught my last glimpse of you in the crowd."

"What you say sounds like a story," said Eirene."

"You in the church," said Pierre De Peyster, "were just like a passing vision. One sees hundreds of them in the great city if you study the human life around you at all. If I had never seen anything to remind me of you again, your face might have faded out at last. As it was, I only thought of it among a thousand other things. But the next June, when I went to the Pinnacle House with Corna, there I was confronted by a reminder of it at the gate of a little out of the way house hundreds of miles from Trinity Church. Yet the face there was so much younger, fresher, and unworn than the other, that in some unaccountable way, instead of being better pleased I was provoked by it, as if (I could not explain how) it was doing the first face an injury. I think this was at the bottom of my opposition to Corna's adopting Pansy. The resemblance always irritated me."

"Why don't you ask me where I saw you next?" asked Dr. De Peyster after a pause which Eirene spent in deep meditation, instead of asking a single question.

"It must have been in the hospital, she said.

"How was I ever to see you in the hospital under that trough that you had on your head? I felt angry every time that I saw you in the ward, and attributed it wholly to my hostility to female nurses. I believe now it was really because you always wore such a poke of a bonnet that I never could see your face to make up my mind about it."

The tone of injury in which this declaration was made amused Eirene more even than Pierre's mirth had done.

"That bonnet was a good friend to me," she said. "I can't tell you how many times I blessed it for hiding my face."

"Won't you ask me where I saw you the next time? Is it possible that I live to behold a woman without curiosity?"

"Where *did* you see me the next time, Dr. De Peyster?" said Eirene in an amused voice.

"Where! but stirring soup in that little hut upon the hill. The bonnet had really fallen off as far as the back of the chair, and that was the first sight I ever had of the nurse's face against whom I had been making war. I did not like army nurses. As a class they had made me much trouble. They defied discipline, they flirted with the officers, in many instances they injured the men. It was the last class on earth in which I should have looked for her, the only one whom I could have prayed to be my wife. Yet, when I saw her, she *was* an army nurse! Yet it was before I saw you at all, that I told Fay that you could stay."

"Yes, you said that I could stay because I could make soup," said Eirene with that touch of perversity inherent in the loveliest of women.

"O Eirene! How can you bring a man down from the most beatific vision of his life to such a contemplation of his baser self. I was hungry. I did want the soup. But when I saw you, it was not of soup that I thought, though I am sure you were stirring it."

"No, it was sago."

"Which I detest, that very moment did I not pick a white rose and send it to Sister Eirene? Could I have done anything more romantic if I had never hungered for soup in my life?"

"Then it was *you* who sent the white rose. How glad I am. I have it and shall keep it all my life," exclaimed Eirene in supreme delight.

"Then you are appeased! But how on earth did you know that I said you could stay and make soup?"

"And kill the men?" added Eirene. I was rolling bandages the other side of the partition, and heard all that you said to Dr. Fay. Even the pasteboard in the bonnet was not thick enough to shut it out."

"And you thought me a brute; and very unreasonable?" asked Pierre in a discomfited tone.

"No, I thought you prejudiced and tyrannical. I—I did not like you then, Dr. De Peyster."

"You didn't (forlornly)? I hope your opinion and feelings have changed?"

"My feelings have entirely."

"And not your opinion? That comes of loving a woman strong minded enough to have an opinion. See what a direful thing it is when it is turned to one's own disadvantage."

"But my opinion is very much modified. I think still that you *could* be prejudiced, *could* be tyrannical, but that there is a nature in you so noble and kind that you very seldom are."

"Thank you for the opinion modified. I begin to breathe again. Truly, Eirene, it seems now as if the most dreadful thing that could happen to me, would be to lose your good opinion. Hereafter I shall live to deserve it."

"And I to deserve yours."

"Imagine how you will have to work for it. But let us decide about that army nurse, the average one I mean. My opinion of *her* is not even modified. Thus you will think me prejudiced still. Shall we agree to differ? I protest that I believe only in the exception, and her name is Sister Eirene."

"May I say that I think you mistaken?" said Eirene, with deep feeling. "You are too generous to me, and not just to others. I have tried to do my duty, Dr. De Peyster, and have loved it: many thousand women during all the war have tried to do the same, and have done it, and it seems to me true that daughters give up more than sons, for they give up their brothers."

"Yes, in your sense they do. But we must agree to differ. You cannot make yourself in my eyes but the exceptional woman, the flower of all your race. Your very name signifies 'peace.' In the simple thought of you I find it."

"I wish I could tell you how you bless me in your words. I wish you could know what they will be to me hereafter, when I cannot see you. How I shall bless you for them. How I shall find it easier to reach out toward every good, however weak or lonely I may be, because you have believed in me and have cared for me."

"Eirene," said Pierre De Peyster, and he fixed his eyes upon her in a searching gaze, "I used to say that no woman lived who was free from affectations in her dealings with men. I should say now that you were trying me thus, if I did not see that you mean and feel every word that you utter. Yet I cannot understand you; if you cannot love me, I do; but if you can, I cannot imagine any reason on earth why we should finally be separated."

"Pardon me, Dr. De Peyster. Have you yet taken time to think of all that separates us? For nearly four years you have been in camp and field. When you find yourself in that great proud city again, you will see life from a different position; then you can realize how much there is to separate us."

"You disappoint me, Eirene," he exclaimed passionately. "I thought—but I was a fool—that you would understand me better. I thought, presumptuous as I was, that I had only to present myself to the woman whom I love, and that she would read my heart as I knew it, by a divine intuition. I thought that the mere conventionalities of surface society would look as poor to her as they do to me; that when I said it is for you that I have sought all my life, that she could say: 'It is for you alone that I have waited.' Surely you don't take me for a boy filled with a sudden fancy. Your image has grown into my heart hour by hour, day by day, and year by year, till I should not know where to begin to tear you out, and I have no power to do it. What disappoints me in you is this, Eirene, that against such eternal facts as these you can put the poor little facts of external condition. I hold that if a man and woman believe in each other, and love each other, and have chosen each other out of all the world, that in their manhood and womanhood they are equal, that no condition of wealth or poverty can make the one greater or the other less. I thought that this would be as true to you as to me. And yet I will not blame you if you accept the average standard of the world."

"How can you blame me when I say to you that I know I am *not* your equal," she declared. "I am not your equal in strength, in intellect, in culture, nor in power of any sort. I am not your equal in anything save in my purpose to do the best I can, and to make the most of all my little life."

"O, how blind you are! Then I am not your equal in any attribute that can lift a human creature near to God. Yet I am disappointed that I seeing all this so plain you do not seem to perceive it at all, that it is our opinion and feeling toward each other alone which must determine our relation, not the conventional judgment of society on our relative external positions."

"I do see this as you do," said Eirene, slowly and painfully. "There was a time when the thought that any one might feel differently, could not have entered my mind. I believed that truth and honor and devotion could make a man and woman equal, through their love. I believe this still, and yet I must tell you—I have tried to tell you from the beginning that I was engaged in marriage once to one who thought differently. He came to be ashamed of that engagement, to regret it because—I was poor, because he was ashamed of my associations and surroundings. I could never live through such an experience again—it seems as if I could not. I would rather live as I am—alone all my life. I feel as if you could never fail any one who trusted in you," she said, lifting her large confiding gaze full upon his face. "I believe in you, and yet I shrink from ever putting any man to such a test again for my sake."

"Now I understand," he answered. "This is hard, Eirene—do you know how hard?—for a man to feel that he has saved his whole heart and life for one woman, only to have her tell him that at any time in hers there was another who had a claim upon her affections and her hand?"

"Yes, I know how hard it is for you to hear it by the pain I feel in telling it. Yet I want to tell you every thing, every thing about it," she said.

"Tell me," he answered. "Now is the time to hear it."

She told him all—all her life, from the hour that she left her father's house to the moment when she shut her eyes in farewell upon Paul Mallane,—told him without one word of exaggeration or reservation, the simple truth in a voice quivering with the tears that she would not shed. As she ended she leaned a perfectly colorless face against the blue rock beside which she sat, and looking up to him once, the lids closed slowly again over the large eyes with the old look of renunciation.

"It makes no difference," he said, looking upon her face. "It seems to me that nothing in heaven or on earth could make any difference, because I love you."

As she heard these words she opened her eyes wide and looked upon him as if she were listening to him in a dream.

"And you loved him! You loved him, Eirene. How could you love him and I in the world?"

"Yes, I loved him. I was scarcely seventeen. Then I must have loved any one who seemed so far above me, and so kind to me as at first he was. And yet I loved, I learned at last, not him, but that which he seemed to me to be, that which he in the end showed me he was not. It almost broke my heart, it almost took my life—not the loss of a lover, but the loss of the man in whom I had believed. I had believed that I loved truth and honor and all nobility in him. When he proved that they were not in him, not for me, I loved them still, though I did not know where they had gone. It was another Paul that I loved, not the one whom I saw, or whose voice I heard. I have always known that I must love again what I thought I loved in him, if I ever found them again. But I have never sought them; I have never found them, not for me, not till now. I feel as if they had come back to me again, all glorified with your true and tender love, and it seems too much. I am like one dazzled, and afraid as if this great gift could not be for me. All that has gone before, all that I have suffered, seems but a preparation and a discipline for it. One must grow through loss and loneliness and suffering to the capacity for affection which I feel now. I cannot trifle. There is room in my nature and my life but for one supreme love—I love you. I could love no mortal more. I must say this if I never look upon your face again."

"My wife!" he said, with reverent tone, as he took the hand which rested by her side, and his own closed over it in silence.

Thus beneath the twilight skies, upon the mountain top, above the floods, the holy compact was sealed.

The thrill of speech through the silence at last was the sign of these two souls coming back to earth.

"It shall be as you say," he murmured. "Put me on probation; make me serve for you as long as Jacob, but never speak again of final separation."

"Then may it be like this," she answered: "I will go to my father and mother, then return to my desk in the old counting-room. You will mingle freely with your world. Then, if at the end of one year we see each other as we do to-night, it shall be as *you* say."

"But the very thought of the old house makes me feel as if I could not wait. That's hard—a year! a whole year! think how long a year can be, Eirene!"

"But you just said you would wait seven years!"

"And I would; but you could not be so cruel as to make me, Eirene? I submit, you are wise, and yet I feel—I can't help it—as if you were making me pay the penalty of that fellow's double dealing. It's the only bitter drop in the joy, his cursed memory—and the impulse I feel to thrash him. I would if I could see him. I wouldn't shoot him like a brave man, I'd thrash him, and let him go for a coward all the rest of his life."

"O, no, you would not," said Eirene, smiling at the ludicrous picture presented. "I am afraid you would never look the same to me again if I were to see you thrash a man."

"Then I will never thrash him."

But the deeper and sweeter consciousness in the man's soul could not be banished by any badinage.

"Mine," he murmured, with all a man's unconscious triumph.

"Thine and mine," said the woman.

"Forever and forever."

Hand in hand they walked up the stony hillside, and without a word went to the two graves within the old stone wall.

"I feel that you have been dear to me ever since the moment that I saw you carry him," she said, pointing to the spot where the body of Win rested.

"I know that you have been dear to me from the first moment that I looked upon your face," was the answer.

The convalescent soldier still sat on the veranda as they walked from the graveyard toward the house.

"I had my eye on 'em," he said to a comrade a few moments later, after he had watched Pierre De Peyster ride down the hillside out of sight. "I had my eye on 'em. A mighty time they sat by the stun. I'd say they'd been a courtin' only they looked so awful solemn, and they went and stood in the graveyard, and people don't gen'ally go and look at graves after they've been making love. . But it's kind o' queer they sot there so long by the stun. I never saw Sister Eirene with a feller before. But now, I think on it, I know it's all up with that Dr. Pi-ster. Never saw anybody look disappointed as he did when he came out of the house fust and couldn't find her."

Pierre De Peyster wrote from the hotel at Harper's Ferry that night to his sister:

"*Dear Corna*:—I have found my wife. She is the sister of your *protégée.*

"Your satisfied brother,

"PIERRE."

The next morning he started for New York to begin his probation, Eirene remaining behind till the hospital closed. Pierre De Peyster retained all his old horror of love-making in a hospital.

"Then I must go at once," he said, and he went.

Not many days after Eirene caught a brilliant gleam from some object moving up the road which reminded her of the old glitter of bayonets. She looked and saw a bright red peddler's wagon driven by a man sitting under a chaise cover high upon its top. She saw also that the glitter came from rows of tin pans, dippers, and other culinary utensils strung behind. The sight struck her oddly; it was a new one for Virginia. It could remind her of nothing but Yankee land, and Moses Loplolly.

"Poor Moses," she said kindly, remembering how he saved her home for her so long. "How good he has been; I hope he is well," and with this thought she returned to her work. But in a very few moments she was summoned to the little office leading off the great hall. The "orderly" said that there was a man there who wanted to see her. As she descended she saw the great red wagon before the door, and entering the office there stood Moses Loplolly.

"Eirene, I swan! Wa'al, wa'al!" and he rushed toward her, and extended the well-remembered hand.

"Why, Moses, where did you come from?"

"From hum straight—that is, straight as the road would bring me; rode all the way; peddled lots."

"Then you are peddling still?"

"Peddlin'! I guess—I am; peddlin' pays. I thought so 'fore wartime; tha. warn't nothin' to what it pays now."

"But I hope you didn't peddle all through the war," she said, reproachfully, as she looked at Moses, grown big and brown, and thought of Win, the brother for whom she had hoped so much, dead, dead by yonder wall.

"No, not all through the war; I driv three months an army wagon. My! the difference 'tween drivin' your own team and drivin' six tarnal pesky army mules, all backin' and balkin' in the middle of a river—runs they call 'em here, every river 's a run—and not a bridge over one on 'em. Wa'al, I never swore till then! —till my mules backed me and a wagon load of bread all down hill head over heels into Snicker's Run. Then I did cuss. I cuss'd till I was so tired I couldn't cuss no more. Then I rested, and cuss'd again. That was the last time that ever I driv a mule. You oughter seen the bread a poppin all over the run, an' me almus' drownded, and those pesky critters standin' stock still in the water enjoying on it. 'Twus nuff to make a parson cuss. My! I could cuss now when I think on it. But I wont. I didn't come here to cuss, that's sartin."

"How have you happened to come here, Moses?"

"'Taint no happen! cum on purpose. An't it likely that I want to see yer after all this time? I set just as high by you, Rene, as ever I sot. I don't see no great change, sech as I've he'rn 'em tell about. Ef you was faded clean out, you'd be handsomer 'n any on 'em. I wouldn't care ef yer eyes was green, and your hair was blue, or if you hadn't a hair on your head, you'd be Rene, that's enuff for me. But it cuts me up to see you're 'as agin peddlin' as ever. It pays lovely. And I'll give—wa'al, I'll give half to you of all it pays if—"

"O Moses, I don't object to honest peddling, or to any honest way of earning a living. But look there," and she pointed out of the open window to the mounds stretching far over the hill. "Look there, Moses! every grave holds a man as young or younger than you, who died for his country. I don't think that any young man had a right to be peddling for his own gain during the last four years."

"Now don't be hard on a chap, Rene, 'cause he didn't hanker arter the cannon's mouth. I never cheated on my pies, not a soldier. Ef I told him they warn't spiled, they warn't. I never cheated nobody on pies but the trac' men, who peddled religion when there wasn't no danger round. They didn't love gunpowder no more'n me. I was jes as much a patriet a-peddlin' pies, if they wan't too tough, to the hungry soldiers. Besides, some of them fellers that went round with pious books in their hands, peddled pies on the sly. They'd pay another feller to do it for 'em and they'd clap on the profits. That wan't *me!*" said Moses, proudly, "I peddled jack-knives and pies above board, an' on my own hook. When a poor soldier was hungry or wounded, he wanted suthin' more'n a trac', I reckon."

"He certainly did," said Eirene, "and more than jack-knives or pies. I can't help it, Moses, the only men that I can honor now are the men who fought, or the men who served those who fought."

"Aint I a-servin' on 'em!" exclaimed Moses triumphantly, "with the very money I saved out of pies? Afore I cum away I started a monerment on Pinnerkel Hill for our Hilltop boys, 'by 'scribin' a hundred dollars. And there's Rhody Tanner, Seth's widder, I said to her: 'Rhody, you'll have ten dollars a month till your pension comes round.' It all cum out of pies."

"You were always generous with your money, Moses. No one has more cause to be grateful to you than I," said Eirene, mollified by the remembrance of his kindness.

Moses thought this his moment to strike, and exclaimed:

"I heven't been half as kind to yer as I wanted to be, or as I would a bin ef you'd a let me. But I thought by this time you'd be tuckered out, an' I'd come an' see. You know you need never hev left your own hum, if ye hadn't a-wanted tu. You might a lived there all these years as snug as a bug in a rug. Aint you tired totin round? Cum, Rene, won't ye go back along a me? I'll go up the valley and peddle off my tins and notions; they are clean wiped out of everything up there, sech as they had, which wa'nt much. Say, jest think of heathens that never had no cook-stoves, or a kitchen nigher nor handier 'an one of our barns, callen 'emselves Amerikins an' our ekels, an' sayin' one of 'em could lick ten Yankees. I've hearn 'em! guess they'd better try (buttoning up his coat ferociously). My! how they'll buy my pans. I'll take old picturs or any old granders and make money sellin on em over agin. If they look lumberin', I'll put 'em all inside the box, an' you can ride on the top with me, jest as easy! We can go to Frederic in a mornin' and get merred, and then jog along back to Hilltop jest as slick. Say now, Rene, won't yer? *Do!* Do let a poor feller peddle for yer all his life, yer needn't do nuthin' but spend the money."

Moses' darling plan, on which he had doted every moment of the way from Massachusetts to Virginia, looked so easy of fulfilment in the light of his imagination contemplated from his wagon-top—Rene would be so "tuckered" out that she would be glad to go back with him, he was certain of it then. Several keen bargains along the road sharpened his sense of happiness; his two ruling passions seemed nearly gratified, his passion for gain and his passion for Rene. But now the eager tones with which he began his appeal died before the look in her face, and he ended in a piteous tone of whining entreaty.

"O Moses," said Eirene, in a tone of actual distress, "I hoped that you would never oblige me to appear ungrateful again. There is nothing, nothing in my power that I will not do for you, but marry you I cannot."

He looked at her sharply.

"I know it! There's another feller 'round, I know it! You didn't speak like that afore. It wa'n't so hard to bear when there wa'n't no other feller on the carpet. I might a knowed it—that some infernal shoulder-strapper would be a pickin' on you up. Where is he?" he cried, in the shrillest tone, pulling up his sleeves, showing eagerness to fight at last, if never before.

"This is not *you*, Moses, and you forget me," said Eirene. "You are in a strange house, full of strange people. I know you don't want to disgrace yourself or your friend."

"No, I don't," he said, drawing down his sleeves and growing calm. "But, O, to wait and hope all these years for nuthin'. Aint it hard?"

"It *is* hard, Moses. Life is hard for all of us in some way. I would make it easier for you if I could."

"I believe you," he said, looking in her face. "Ef yer only could a lov'd me, Rene—if yer only could! Yer can't. I give up tryin'."

"I shall always like you, Moses, always," said Eirene, with emphasis.

"Will yer?" his face brightening. "That's suth'en—but not much to to'ther. I find there's a mighty difference 'tween liken and luvin. 'Taint no use tryin'. I'm going for good and all."

"O, no; I'll see you settled and happy, some day, at Hilltop."

"Likely," in an injured tone. "I shan't see *you* settled and happy, for I wont come wher yer be."

"Do, Moses!"

The sweetness and the happiness of her tone struck Moses. He looked at her keenly again.

"I KNOW IT!" he exclaimed, and started for his wagon.

Eirene followed him to the door. And as he pulled up the chaise-cover over his head and looked back, the sight of his early playmate gazing after him with gentle farewell, stirred within him all the tender regret of which he was capable.

"O Rene," he said, mournfully, "to think how peddlin' pays; and yet 'taint no account if it can't bring a feller what he cares for most." Thus, in epitome, telling the story of life without knowing it, he and the red wagon moved away.

## CHAPTER XXII.

### THE WEDDING AT HILLTOP.

You have seen Hilltop in June, dear friends, but that was years ago. What has not happened since then to you, and to me, and to the land that we love? Thrice ten thousand graves grown green upon her breast tell something of the harvest that war has gathered in! The brown-eyed boy, who, in his dreams in the old barn, so dimly foresaw the future, has been brought back to sleep with his comrades in the soil of their fathers. The white shaft pointing skyward on Pinnacle Hill tells where they rest together—these sons of the hamlet whom nature nurtured in her solitude for the holy holocaust of human freedom. From how many of her homesteads a bright, brave man went forth who never came back. By how many of her firesides doth the heart of woman ache for her lost, who are not. Great nature, as if she took no part in human loss or sorrow, as if it were her's to lift humanity to the consciousness of immortality in herself forever renewed, wears this moment all the youth of her first June morning. Still her white cloud fleets, undimmed, sail towards her vast horizon. Her encircling mountains cover their faces under veils of tender green; her pine forests distil their frankincense, life-giving with the tonic of perpetual health; her maples that line the roadside flutter their breezy garniture unsullied and young as ten years ago. How is it with the woman who sits once more by the old window? Time and sorrow that have not marred the landscape, have they spared her? Do they ever spare that which is human? We try to soothe ourselves with the fiction that we do not change, but other eyes see that the experience which has transformed the very thoughts and feelings of the soul is reflected upon the countenance. The emotion surging in the blood of the heart ebbs to the face, and the line which it leaves there is never effaced. Yet it is is only meaner natures which grow ugly under the hand of time. For the finer soul, loss and grief, renunciation and yearning, fruition and joy, are but the sculptors who, touch by touch, remould the face and make it beautiful; not with the untouched beauty of youth, but with that outraying illumination of the spirit which may glorify the plainest features.

Life, the consummate artist, has remoulded the face of Eirene till it shines forth with a vivid lustre of expression which mere youth can never possess, for whose lack no glory of tint or outline can wholly compensate. Large intelligence and thought, deep feeling, with an exquisite refinement and an undefinable tenderness and gentleness hovering over it like an atmosphere, combine to make the charm of this face; each in turn seems evolved from it, and to transfigure it. Yet there is a serenity in her attitude, a repose pervading her entire presence, which never belongs to first youth, for it is the repose of a being grown strong through discipline and trial. The girl who once sat here was lovely, but the woman is lovelier. She is thinking of that girl to-night as she would think of another person. She remembers her, but in the journey of life she has come on and left her far behind. The girl was bewildered and dazzled with her anticipated happiness. The woman in her serenity calmly awaits her crowning joy. It seems too much at times, the fulfilment of her early dream, this rich love of a deep and true nature, which had come to complete her life at last. And yet the very wealth of her womanhood forces her to feel that this is not a gratuitous gift conferred upon her. She gives an equivalent in return; she gives herself, her truth, and her devotion, her life and her soul to the man whom she honors and loves. It is not the first dream of youth and of love. Like youth itself that can never be repeated. The later morning has a splendor that the dawn has not, yet it has lost one thing that day can never restore—the freshness of the dew. Our life has but one youth, and its promise can never be renewed. Noon may fulfill, but it does not re-utter the prophecy of the morning.

A year has passed since we looked upon Eirene last, in the half-ruined Virginia hospital. It has been spent as she promised—at her desk in the counting-room. Never had the moral strength of purpose which she had gained through years of painful discipline been so tested as during this twelve months of probation. For she worked now in the face of undisguised opposition.

"It is very annoying, Pierre, it is perfectly outrageous," Cornelia Stuyvesant would say, "to have the woman, who in twelve months is to be your wife, perched from morning till night at the desk of a furnishing shop. The Livingstons, Beekmans, and Van Dykes, and all the rest go there and take their very bills from her hands, and in twelve months they are to meet her as an equal."

"Equal! In twelve months! as if she were not their equal *now*, and ten times more. Let them go there every day and learn a lesson, that a true lady honors her employment whatever it may be, and that no honorable employment can make her less than a lady."

"O, you men can talk such fine sentiments, but they are not practical to women. You know very well what I mean by equal. Of course, Eirene is their equal and more personally, but she is not their equal socially, and she can't be till she is your wife. Then I don't want them to have the advantage of pointing to her former position. That she will stay in that old shop is very obstinate and provoking, as she *is* to be your wife."

"Fudge! on your fine female distinctions. A woman has a right, a perfect right, to earn her own living as long as she chooses. Now, I am sorry that Eirene does it, but honor her for it."

Nevertheless he would walk away and feel that it *was* provoking, that after all Eirene *was* in this regard obstinate. Few sisters, wives, or mothers work in private on a man's prejudices and feelings in vain. Only God knows the harm they have wrought in the world by sending forth from their presence to its work irritated and exasperated men.

Pierre honored Eirene for her industry and womanly independence, yet Cornelia's incessant criticisms combined with his own impatience had their effect. He could not pass the furnishing shop and see the Livingston carriage outside with its livered lackeys, and think that its idle occupants were perhaps at that moment being waited upon by his affianced wife, without a feeling of inward wrath. All combined to make him seek Eirene at last with expostulation and even fault-finding, although he had fully intended to remain a monument of resignation and patience until the end of the year. More than once Eirene had rushed to her little room, plunged her face in her pillow as of old and shed bitter tears. After all the saddest thing on earth was loving! She loved a strong, noble man, yet even he found fault with her and had spoken, it seemed to her, unkindly. He was once more the first Dr. De Peyster, whom she had not liked; he was tyrannical, and, and he had called her "unreasonable," whereupon would flow a fresh tide of tears. But always joy came in the morning, in the shape of a basket of fresh flowers, a dear book that she had wanted, and a note so full of loving contrition, for having been severe, but it was so hard to be rich and to have her work, so hard to wait in a home without her—it was all because he loved her so much, but he would begin anew the patience of Jacob—if she would forgive him? which she always did, by writing him in the evening that it was *she* who was unreasonable, and that he must forgive her. Whereupon she would kiss her flowers, devour her new book by gaslight, and feel in her heart that she loved him more than ever.

Nevertheless the furnishing shop was a standing cause of "little misunderstandings" to the end of the year. Pierre resigned himself to the conclusion that even his lovely ideal woman was in one thing obstinate, not to say unreasonable. He sighed, but loved her no less. Eirene sighed because he thought this of her, yet felt that she could not explain the deepest cause that made her so.

"He says that he is glad that I am poor, that everbody belonging to me is poor," she would think silently. "And I have no feeling about it for myself, not with him. If his wife, I could take any treasure from his hands without humiliation. But those who need me should receive their independence from *me*, not from my husband. This year's salary with the old place will make them comfortable at home. This is my first duty. If there were no other cause, I must work on to the end of the year, no matter what is said to me." But the year has gone, her object is accomplished. Eirene sits by the old window, and to-morrow is her wedding morning.

In the old sitting-room below, Lowell and Mary Vale await the guests expected later in the evening. The table is spread, and by the mother's side is set the plate and chair for the boy who will never return to use them. With Mary Vale's joy there is blended an undefinable loneliness. She rejoices in the return and prosperity of her children, and yet she is conscious that in one sense that prosperity divides them from her. The world that she longed for in her youth has come to them, and she in her old life is left behind. Her's is the mother's loneliness which in this country must come to the parental heart with a keener pang than in any other. For it is not the inevitable separation only which soon or late must come to almost every parent and child, but it is separation in condition. Some day the father and mother wake to the consciousness that the children to whom they have given birth belong to another race and time, and come back to them almost as strangers. Their humble belongings, their homely ways, their simple faith, are all foreign if not repugnant to the younger generation. In Europe, with but few exceptions, the child is born to the station of the parent, but in this country, with equally few exceptions, the reverse is the rule. The most illustrious often rise from the lowliest beginnings. The man of millions, whose home is a palace, could scarcely stand erect in the low house in which he was born. The haughty woman of fashion would feel more shame than if convicted of crime, if any one of her "set" should ever be brought face to face with the lowly abode in which she spent her childhood. It was perfectly plain to the eyes of Mary Vale that her children already had passed away forever from the daily life of their parents. She would not have it otherwise, yet the fact left her no less alone. "It would have been different with Win," she said with a sigh. "Poor boy! he would never have outgrown the old house or the old life."

"No," she said while talking the future over with Eirene, "it is too late for father and me to be grafted onto the life of a great city. We can come and visit you, and we will keep the little house open, always ready for you. But we are too old now, child, to change our ways. We couldn't feel natural in the great house that is to be your home, and I dare say we should look very awkward and old-fashioned there. Though ever so small we shall be happier in a home which we can call our own." Eirene knew that she was right, and, with all her longing for her mother, did not try to shake her opinion or resolve.

In the meantime at the Pinnacle House, a bridal party of three had arrived. Cornelia Stuyvesant sits in the old room to which she came years ago, and ponders over the strangeness of human life. "Talk of novels!" she says to herself. "The most remarkable things in them we say are unnatural, not like life. The most remarkable thing that I have ever found is life itself." When she received Pierre's letter from Virginia announcing the fact that *he* had found his wife, her first exclamation was, "I might have known it!" and her next, "Thank fate, she is a lady!

"I might have known it, that of all men Pierre De Peyster would choose his own wife, and that he was the very last one who would take a creature to mould, or a kitten to play with. Above all the men whom I have ever seen, his wife must be his equal, companion, and friend."

"I've not been very noble myself," she says now with a sigh. "Nobody knows it better than Cornelia De Peyster. I know what Margaret Fuller means when she calls on the woman of the nineteenth century to reclaim herself from 'littleness.' This must be the first enfranchisement—I feel it! I feel myself bound by a thousand fancies and customs which in their result amount to meannesses. Perhaps it is something to know it, and to feel it. Perhaps some time I may work my way out and on to something better and nobler. I know I have not been thoroughly kind to this girl, to this lovely, struggling woman, who had a claim upon all my sympathy, if only as the sister of Pansy, whom I had made as my own daughter. Then what a claim she had in herself. That was the rub! She and her condition were so at variance. And I was not noble enough to take her, and ignore her condition No, not ignore it but honor it, because she honored it. But it *was* provoking, and she was obstinate to stick at that old desk. Besides it was not in human nature to give up at once a darling plan! But Pierre has settled it all. I might have known that he would—I did know it. I knew by instinct that if he ever met that woman he would love her, and nothing on earth could hinder."

During the last year she had shown Eirene many lovely attentions. Nothing in her manner to her personally could possibly have suggested to any one who did not feel it that a constant struggle was going on in her mind concerning her brother's future wife—a struggle between the affection which she really felt for her and all her deep-rooted prejudices of caste and custom. She reiterated over and over to herself how weak and foolish it was in her to care at all if all the Livingstons, Stuyvesants, Van Cortlandts, and Beekmans in her drawing-room recognized in Pierre De Peyster's affianced the quiet young woman who cast up their accounts and handed them their bills in the great furnishing shop, and yet a cold perspiration would start upon her at the very thought. On this marriage eve the woman of family and of fashion ponders over it all, and it seems stranger to her than ever. "To think whom he might have married," she said, as a long and fair procession moved through her memory. "Wealth, birth, and beauty, how many would have laid them at his feet. To think that he turned from all, to take his wife from such a home." And the little house in her thought stood forth lower and smaller and meaner than ever before. "How strange! And yet is it so strange? Eirene in herself is more than them all to *him*. I allow that. Even I chose Pansy, but that was different; Pansy is Miss Stuyvesant now."

As Miss Stuyvesant, Pansy herself dressed for the evening drive which was to convey her to her early home, walks up and down the great piazza, with her snowy draperies and azure ribbons fluttering far behind her.

If the girl from Boston could but see her now! Where was that girl from Boston that she did not walk the piazza as of old, to behold the fresh beauty and splendor of the young beauty from New York, who bore such slight resemblance to the little mountain maid at whose old-fashioned dress and faded ribbons the girl from Boston had once dared to laugh!

"I would just like to see her once. Would I notice her? No!" (with superb scorn,) "but she would notice *me!* She would not laugh to night," says Pansy, the grand piazza bringing back her early resentment in all its first force. "Mother will hardly know me, nor father," she goes on, stepping through the long window into the parlor, and surveying herself from head to foot in the mirror. "I knew I would never end my days here where I began them. Yet *he* chose Eirene! I don't care. But I know something that he don't—I was intended for him. Mamma don't know that I know—

I'd like to see her hide anything from me. He had seen me, and he chose Eirene! I don't care. I'd have to live in that old house all my days. He says he wont sell it, and he wont leave it, and Eirene don't want him to, how stupid! But he *is* splendid. I have not seen his equal yet, but I will. Mamma and I are going to live on Park Avenue. I'm to be brought out, and I'll see the best, and they'll see *me*, turning slowly, and scrutinizing her own beauty. In half an hour, I'll see the old house; how odd it will seem, and how natural, how old and low and shabby! And to think that I was born there! What would Berta Von Beekman say, if she could see it! I don't care, I'm more stylish than she, and a great deal handsomer. Everyone says so. But I want to see mother and father, and ——; dear Win, how sorry I am, that I ever quarrelled with you. And Muggins! Poor Muggins is dead, dropped dead in the road. The only horse we ever had. What would Berta Von Beekman say to Muggins! I don't care, I liked her. I always shall, though I believe it would kill me to ride after her now. Half an hour! And I'll see mother, dear mother! Will she know me? Will she think me fine?"

Pierre De Peyster paces his room in intense impatience. Every man on the eve of his marriage is made subject to some woman who takes charge of his proprieties. Cornelia has named the proper hour to go to the cottage, and he waits for it, but in no acquiescing mood. Yet impatient as he is to see her, the very thought of his wife soothes him while he waits. Many a man, as blindly in love as David Copperfield with Dora, on his marriage eve finds himself in a state of incoherent bliss with a feeling running through it as if he were about to leap in the dark. He is in love, dreadfully in love, there is no doubt of that, but what he is really in love with he is by no means certain. He has called his love "a darling," "a blossom," and "a mouse." She is the sweetest creature in the world, he is sure of that; but through all the chaos of his joy shoot random fears tacked to stray cookery books and long lines of accounts. When he faces her with these and says, "My love, let us reason," will she be the sweetest creature still! Poor fellow, he does not know, though he is sure to find out afterwards. All that he is certain of now is that he is in love, and there's his wedding suit. Pierre De Peyster is haunted by no such doubts. He is perfectly sure that he has found what he has sought through all his life, and never found before—his wife, his true wife. It is she, and he has nothing to fear. He can never be mistaken or disappointed in her. He even dwells fondly on her faults. They have teazed him some, for he is a man, and the sublimest man ever made can be teazed and tormented by the faults of the woman that he loves. And yet some way now he is delighted to think that he knows them and that even she has them. This moment her very infirmities seem to bring her nearer to him. "They go against mine," he said, "and how miserable I should be with a wooden angel. She is wilful, in a quiet way, she is certainly very wilful. If not, she never could have held out through the year against all my feeling and opposition, yet she was right. She is too sensitive, and too proud—a little inconveniently so sometimes, yet I would not have her different. She is so true and devoted in her own nature, it will make her exclusive in love. She leaves a wide margin for friendship, but love in her life stands sacred and alone. I must make up my mind to be an absolute Benedict. Suppose I should want to flirt and amuse myself with other men's wives, or with women not other men's wives, as I see men constantly doing, how would it fare with me? Bless me! I can see her shut her eyes upon me as if she were shutting me out forever. If I ventured to say, 'I didn't mean anything,' she would open them then with such a strange look of wonder, and ask, 'How can you do or say what you don't mean? I don't understand it.' And I should walk out of the room feeling like a culprit and a villain, which would *not* be agreeable. Lucky for me I've no such proclivities.

I see wherein my Rene could be an intolerant wife. Worse than all, she believes in Women's Rights—at heart I know she does. Not that she talks them, thank Heaven. I could not stand that, but she acts them. What else has she been doing the last year, indeed all her life? If left alone, while she had head or hands, she would never think of being dependent. She would support herself and others too, and work out her own future like—not like a man, never, always like a woman, the quietest, gentlest, and most lovable of women. Yet wherever she was hampered by inequality of opportunity or of reward by legal oppression, or injustice, she would quietly ask, 'Wherefore?' She would say, 'I ask for justice, not as a woman, but as a human being.' Yet her demand would not be in words, but in herself and in what she is. A few more such women would make public speech unnecessary. They would make all men ashamed of themselves and of their laws. This is I, Pierre De Peyster, talking, the born foe of strong-minded women, and the embodiment of man's supremacy. I—I'm subjugated already," and he laughs aloud, as if the idea were delightful. "But she don't talk politics,—if she did —well if she did—I haven't a doubt I'd be the same idiot that I am now. Nothing can make her other than Eirene, the dear Sister Eirene, the wife Eirene—

" ''Tis *she*, or none on earth.'

"I feel what Schiller felt when he wrote that, and why does that tedious Corna keep me waiting like this!"

Meanwhile Eirene's mother had called her from the old window where she sat looking across the tobacco meadow, now beautiful with the tender green of early wheat. She went down, and there in the porch sat Moses, brave in holiday attire as when he came wooing years before, but with an unmistakable look of happiness in his eyes.

"Glad to see yer, Rene! Jes' stopped in to say it's all right."

"Thank you, Moses. It makes me happy to hear you say so," said Eirene, who at once by no means comprehended how very right it was.

"Wa'al, I knowed t'would. Yer so kin' hearted, I know'd you'd like to know aforehand as I was cumf'table. I am, and a lee—tle more."

"I'm glad of it, Moses. I'd like to have you tell me that you are perfectly happy."

"As *you* be," said Moses, with a touch of the old reproach in his tone. "That can't cum right off; mebby 'twill arterwards. Arter all the tuckerin' I been thro' its sum'thin for a fellow to say he's cumf'table, and a lee—tle more. I jes' stopped in to say that I set by you, Rene, as high as ever I sot, only it's t'other way, *your way*, I reckon, when you said, 'Moses, I'll allus be your friend.' Rene, I'll allus be *your* friend—that's what you've wanted, aint it? Now I've sed it."

"Yes, it would make me unhappy to think you would not always be my friend, Moses."

"Wa'al, I will, allus. Thar aint no wipin' that out. I've seen him. Good lookin' feller, tu. High an' mighty! 'taint no wonder, with sech lordish lookin' chaps arter you, yer took no shine to me, leastwise to merry. I know I aint no how uncommon, an' you be; so is he, but he can't be no prouder on yer nor I'd ben, that's sartin. I seen him up to the Pinnerkel. Deacon Stave said: 'Kingdom come! that's the man that's going to merry Eirene Vale; he is a New York mill'onar; that's what comes to the folks' children that haint a mite of kalkerlation now an' never had.' You better b'lieve, Rene, I looked, an' had my look out. Arter all I couldn't help sighin' when I said, 'So *that's him!* lookin' so happy.' When I thought what fur, I almos' forgot I was happy myself. Why don't you ask nuthin' about *her?*"

"About whom, Moses."

"Why, about Rhody! Rhody Tanner, Seth's widder, which she aint agoin' to be long. Me an' Rhody's made up to take one another for better and wus."

"Now I *am* glad. Why didn't you tell me at first, Moses."

"Wa'al, I meant ter, but the sight on yer put so many other things inter my head. That's what I cum fur. I know'd you'd like to know that if you *was* gettin' merrid it might be wus. I might agone and drownded myself," said Moses, with a quaver, growing self-pitiful at the thought that at this moment he might have been dead. "I thought on it. I knew 'twant no use to trouble yer no more, an' I said what's the use o' livin'? I went an' stood on the bridge arter I cum hum, and said, 'I'll drownd myself, *then* Rene'll feel sorry.' I look'd at the stuns in the bottom, at the poliwogs a skipperin' on top, an' thought how creepin' the water felt when those tarnel army mules tumbled me an' the bread into the run, and the longer I looked the more I thought I *wouldn't* drownd myself. 'What's the use?' I sed, 'arter the first Rene'll go on enjoyin' herself jes' as if I hadn't gone an' drownded myself, an' there I'll be dead, an' can't enjoy nothin'—leastways it's by no means sartin' I could. I wont drownd myself, I'll live an'—peddle. I'll—thar's Rhody, how thankful she looked when I took her the money. If a feller can't git what he wants, why shouldn't he take what he can git? I'd like to know?' So I didn't drownd myself, but yer see I might'er; it might a been wus, I might a been dead. You'd a been sorry, wouldn't yer, Rene?"

"You know that, Moses, but think what a foolish fellow you would have been to have done that, and how wise you were to think of Rhody, and how happy she will make you."

"Wa'al, Rhody might be wus. She's mighty taken' in her own way, which aint yourn. I couldn't bring myself to make up to her, at fust, no how. It warnt her, but 'twas *you* I'd wanted allus. 'Twarnt likely I could give yer up in a minnit, was it, if I had gi'n up drowndin'? But I tried. Fust the more I tried to like Rhody, the more I didn't. Her ways warnt yourn. They made me think o' yourn, and like 'em more'n ever afore, I sed, 'taint no use, Mose, you're struck clean dead with luv to the roots c yer marrer for Rene; 'taint no use, your heart wont go pit-pat, not a pat for nobody else, 'taint no use a tryin'. I stopped tryin,' an' gin clean up. But I took Rhody's money to her jes' the same. 'It's all fur Seth,' I said. 'Peddlin' pays, Rhody, but what's the use if it don't make nobody cumf'table side a me.' Purty soon it seemed to me she looked a leetle more fixed up every time I cum, tell one night—wa'al, as sure as you live, she had a leetle curl a hangin' aside each ear, and a red rose stuck in the bosom of her black frock. I never *did* see her look so takin'. Mebby I kind o' looked, for she said, 'What's yer hurry, Moses; stay and take a cup o' tea.' So I staid. Arterwards, while her mother was clearin' up the dishes, we went and sot in the porch, an' it was all covered over with red roses. Purty soon Rhody put the corner of her white ap'on in her mouth, an' looked down awful solemn."

"'What's the matter, Rhody?' ses I.

"'Nothin', Moses, that you can hender,' ses she. 'I'm dre'ful lonesome.'

"'That's nat'ral, ses I, but don't cry. I'll do all I ken to chirk ye up.'

"'Nobody cares for me, no more,' ses she, an' cried the harder, an' patted her ap'on on her eyes.

"'Yer ma dus, an' I du tu,' ses I.

"'O, no, yer don't,' ses she, 'you care for Eirene Vale; I've allus hearn so.'

"'Wa'al, I said, ye cared for Seth, didn't yer; why don't *I* cry for *that*?'

"''Cause yer don't care, and yer know yer don't,' ses she, and wiped her eyes the harder; 'an' I'm so lonesome, and yer don't care.'

"'Yes I du,' ses I, 'an' I'm lonesome tu, awful lonesome, Rhody; an' peddlin' don't pay, nor nothin' else, when a feller's so mis'able. Let's make up!' An' wa'al, I kissed her. She peaked out o' the corner of her ap'on—I saw her eye. Lor! thar warnt a tear in it! Sech a luvin' look. You never gin me such a look, Rene. I'd a gone on my knees to yer if ye had. Such a luvin' look! My heart went pit-pat afore I knew it. That's how it wus. Now, I know you may try to death, an' it won't pat because you tell it, an' all of a sudden it'll give a jerk when you're least a lookin'. That's how Rhody and I made up, an' you see it might be wus."

"Worse! I don't know how it could well have been better," exclaimed Eirene, laughing in perfect delight over Moses's picture of his courting. "You see what I said will come true, and I shall see you married, settled, and happy at Hilltop."

"Well, what you say is allus true. Arter all I believe you put the ideer inter my head. I'll allus be glad to see yer, Rene. Can't say as much fur Rhody, till she gets it out of her head as I wouldn't a had *her* if *you'd* a had me. One woman wouldn't nat'rally hanker arter another on sech a principul. But I'll allus be glad to see yer callin' round. I'll set jes as high by yer as long as yer live as ever I sot ef 'tis t'other way. My blazes! he's cumin'! The sight on him don't improve my sperrits arter all. But it's all right. Good-by, Rene. And with a touch of the ancient quaver in his tone, Moses turned and hurried down the garden path, while a carriage, containing two ladies and a gentleman, was driven up to the gate, and Eirene with radiant face arose to meet her husband of to-morrow.

A perfect morning in perfect June saw their marriage and departure to the old De Peyster house. Eschewing the modern barbarism which gives to the vulgar gaze cf hirelings and strangers, and to the discomforts of rail cars and hotels the most sacred month of life, Pierre and Eirene went to spend their honeymoon in their own home.

The feelings of Hilltop were deeply perturbed by this wedding. They were injured also, for not a Hilltopper was invited to it And the dainty box of cake with its snowy cards, which found its way into every household was not a compensation for the fact that no one witnessed the marriage ceremony outside of the two families concerned.

The Smoots said, "That if the feller was so rich, a perfect mill'onar as *sum* said, *why* was the weddin' such a poor affair in the little old house without a spec of new furnitur? That Eirene Vale could go from sech a place to a grat house in New York was by no means likely—they didn't believe a word of it, or that the feller was rich or in any way oncommon!"

Red-cheeked Nancy Drake, who long before had succumbed to destiny in the form of a brown-faced farmer, and settled on the old mountain after all, felt occasional twinges nevertheless of her old desire to get off it and achieve a splendid fate in some great city. She declared that *she* would like to know what there was about them Vale girls that they should have sech luck? she couldn't see anything so dre'full taking about 'em for her part. Eirene was well enuff—very well—pious, and pokin', but as for Pansy Vale, she was a stuck up little minx, an' allus had been. My! when she hadn't anything but a crust of rye bread for her dinner at school, she'd eat it as if she owned the hull earth, an she couldn't do no more when she cum back and strutted up an' down the piazza of the Pinnerkel House, all covered with Indy muslin and blue ribbons; for *her* part she thought Indy muslins and ribbons very unekally divided in this world,—and she looked with disgust upon the ninepenny calico in which she was doing her morning churning.

Farmer Stave said, "Wa'al, I never thought I'd see the sight! Neighbor Vale's barn mended and painted, an' his house painted stun color, an' everything fixed up spic and span. Why he's jes as well off as we be who've grubb'd an' laid by all our days. That aint what I call ekal compensation—that him that haint laid by should have as much as him that has. I jes say it aint fair that a man's got jes as much in the end, as if he'd been a kalkeratin all his life, when he aint kalkerated none. For ye all know," he said to his cronies, and he struck the bright red settle of the fine new station-house with all the vim that he ever did the old bench of thirty years before—"you all know as neighbor Vale haint a mite of kalkeration, and never had."

## CHAPTER XXIII.

### ONE DAY OF HER LIFE.

"What are you thinking of, my love?" asked Pierre De Peyster of his wife, as he came back to her sitting-room, to say good morning, before going to his office, where she sat with her boy, looking over a morning journal.

"Thinking of what I have found in the *Tribune*. It always gives me something worth thinking about," she said. "It is an editorial. Here in another paper is an advertisement. Both interest one. They set me to thinking till I forgot that I had anything to do to-day."

"Read them to me?"

"The advertisement says: 'Mrs. Helena Maynard Mallane will lecture to-night at Cooper's Institute. Subject, "The Husband of the Period."' You remember the name?"

"Yes indeed. You see what you have missed? Personal experience with the 'husband of the period,' and the chance to tell the world all about him in a public hall. Do you think that you knew him once?"

"Yes, the name is unusual. I never heard of it in another family. I never heard the lady's. Yet my impression is that she is Paul Mallane's wife. Will you go with me to-night to hear her?"

"Then you will ask me to do one of the things that I feel perfectly unequal to doing, to listen to a woman lecture in public just to gratify your curiosity, and yet I have always thought you remarkably free from curiosity of any sort."

"Perhaps it is curiosity, I don't know; but then it is something more. I do want to hear what the wife of Paul Mallane has to say on such a subject."

"Well, I'll go; but on one condition, that you wont ask me to listen to another woman for a year! It's no use, Eirene! it's in my grain—I can't *like* to hear a woman preach."

"I wont ask you to go again. Thanks for your willingness to do penance to-night."

"Perhaps it wont be penance after all. I'm perfectly willing to hear Paul Mallane berated myself, and to be with you is ever delightful, even in the catacomb of Cooper's Institute."

"Hear your papa, baby! Isn't he a gallant gentleman?" said the happy Eirene, lifting up her two-year old boy. His father seized him, seated him on his knee, and began to tickle his nose. "My poppa is a gallan' gemon," cried the boy.

"Your papa is a ten-gallon gentleman," said Dr. De Peyster. "What about the editorial, Eirene?"

Oh, it's one of the *Tribune's* best on marriage. Don't you think the *Tribune* very true and consistent on that subject, Pierre? It never swerves in its defence of marriage, as the one sacred, eternal unity which must bind man and woman and society together forever. No man living is truer to this faith than Mr. Greeley, no one would suffer more for it. Why do some journals accuse the *Tribune* of being a nest for every crazy ism? It is not true, and it is too bad, isn't it Pierre?"

"Very likely. You know I'm not up to you in enthusiasm for the philosopher; but I believe in him. What has he been saying?"

"I'll read the editorial this evening; you will say it is too long for now. What set me to thinking is this quotation in it, taken from another paper, the text which the editorial preaches against. This is it: ''Tis true that women can and do exert great influence over men, after swaying them into courses they would not otherwise pursue; but it will be found this influence rarely proceeds from the wife. . . . The influence of the wife as such forms no part of the power of society.'"

"Do you believe that, Pierre?"

"No, I do not."

"I was thinking how much power was your own before you married me,—the power of your manhood, the power of your wealth, of your intelligence, and of your goodness; and if to all these anything could be added through the influence of your wife?"

"My wife is my inspiration, and my help every moment of my life. I am twice the man that I was before you married me," and Pierre De Peyster leaned over the head of his boy and kissed his wife.

"I am twice the woman that I was before I loved you. It comes to me every day, a fresh sense of new power, sweet and strong. Why, Pierre, I think more clearly, I do more, I love the whole human race more, because I love you. I was thinking when you came in, how it would be if you were a poor man and had to build up your own fortune in the world, how we would work together and in what ways I might help you. But if, in addition to what God has given me, so much strength comes to me through you, how can it be that my influence as a wife can form no part of the power of society?"

"Why, it cannot be. That is one of the extreme statements which the tearers down of society make every day, and which every day refutes, and yet, Rene, even I admit that woman's power in society as a wife has not been and is not all that it might be, or ought to be. I don't believe in the English Common Law in all its bearings upon women, if I am down upon ranters who are trying to turn women into men. Why, what makes you open your eyes so?"

"With wonder! when did you come to such a conclusion?"

"I came to it long ago. Am I a heathen if I am a fogy? Suppose you were in the furnishing shop still, and I was a drunken 'cuss,' and yet the law gave me the right to take up all your wages and spend them for liquor, you don't believe in my sober senses, I would uphold such a law against wives as that, do you? You can't think of the time, Rene, that you ever heard me even excuse the diabolical disabilities in law which men have heaped upon women. Since you have been my wife, I have felt it more and more keenly, so there's one proof of your power as a wife. And I candidly believe that when a whole race of wives just like you rise up from a new basis of womanly education, thought, and feeling, there will be a whole race of husbands as thoroughly ashamed of mannish tyranny as I am."

"Oh, how grand you make me feel! We will try to do better than ever before, won't we, baby?"

"Well, both of you may try. But now speak *your* piece, Rene. In all the time that I have known you, I have never heard you *say* what you believe to be *your* 'Woman's Right.' Come, tell me now. I'll give you five whole minutes for it, and Pierre looked at his watch.

"Oh, I never could do anything, just because I was told to do so, and to time me puts everything out of my head."

"Proof you are not yet prepared to go to Congress. Suppose a subject of life and death to the nation was being discussed under the five minutes' rule, and the result on the lovely member from New York was to make her sink down in hopeless confusion with nothing in her head!"

"Stop, Pierre, I don't want to go to Congress."

"Nor do I want you to go. Pretty fix baby and I'd be in, with nobody to take care of us or to make us behave. But come now, the 'Rights!' Listen, baby! mamma's going to expound her rights.

"Mamma's 'ites!" cried baby.

"The first, to love and take care of you, blessed boy!" exclaimed Eirene, seizing him.

"No! the first is to love and to take care of *me*. I will not play second to such a mite of humanity."

"No, nor to anything on earth with me," said Eirene.

"But come, Rene, won't you explain your rights? The next time Livingston asks me what *my* wife thinks about all this outcry, I want to tell him. When he asked last, I said that I had never heard you say what you thought your rights were, but I noticed that you went on and took them, so I thought you knew. We have changed our minds, haven't we, baby? Mamma don't know her rights; couldn't tell us if she tried."

"O yes, I could, and if you really want me to—"

"I thought that would fetch them," said Pierre, laughing.

"Well, Pierre," Eirene went on, look-a little like a culprit, "if you *will* know, I think, as a human being, that I was born with every right that you were. That as a human being there is no right dear to you that is not equally dear to me. My humanity, with all its possibilities and privileges, is worth just as much to me as to you. And I have the right to equal opportunity to develop through it every power that God has given me—the right to equal justice before the law."

"So far true, what next?"

"Yet I remember that I am a woman as well as a human being—that my womanhood involves many second considerations. As a man, you might question the fitness of a course which, as a human being, you have a perfect right to pursue, but no woman could decide it for you, or lay down the lines of being or of action for you. So I think of myself. I suppose I have the natural right to do many things which, as a woman, I may not even wish to do. My personal obligations are more to me than my abstract rights. What I owe my husband and child is the first and deepest obligation of my life, but not my only one. If I had no husband or child, if I were a solitary force in the world, I deny the right of any man to set a limit to my advancement, as I deny mine to set a limit to his. There is where I find fault with you men, Pierre. You take it upon yourselves to say just in what way and how far a woman shall be educated —just how far she shall have any chance to make the best of herself. Equal chance! Why, men never thought of such a thing, and then they pronounce on our inferiority. Darling, I never had an equal chance with you since I was born. As a woman, I could not have had it if I had been born to the same condition in life. George William Curtis never spoke truer words than the other evening when he said, 'There is nothing so barbaric as for one human being to say to another, "Thus far you shall be developed, and no further," and that there is no other subject on which so much intolerable nonsense is talked as upon the sphere of women.' Why, Pierre, how can anybody, man or woman, get very far out of their sphere? God and Nature have set bounds in every individual which cannot be overpassed. Only no one can decide for another. I never can give up that. Power is the measure of function in any human being. Circumstance or custom may curtail its exercise, they cannot destroy its right."

"My son, the deed is done!" said Pierre with mock solemnity. "Your mamma has spoken her little piece which I have waited to hear for four long years. It would have won her applause in a Woman's Suffrage Convention. All the sisters on the platform would have clapped their hands could they have heard it, and here it has all been expended on one big unbeliever and one small boy with a ridiculous nose."

"Pierre, don't laugh at his nose. I have pinched it up this very morning, and its bridge grows higher every day."

"Nevertheless, you will not be out of occupation for several years if you are determined to pinch it into a respectable nose."

"Now, Pierre!"

"Well, I wont teaze you, Rene; he has his mother's eyes—they are enough for me if he had no nose."

"He has his father's head, that is enough for me. He looks like his father, and his father is the handsomest man in the world."

"Certainly he is! And he is the image of his mother, and she is the loveliest woman in the world. And now, pet, I *must* go."

"And you are not vexed with me, Pierre?"

"What about?"

"Why, about what I think."

"What do I care what you think? You're a' the world to me."

"You know you would make me say, and I couldn't say anything but what I believe, and you don't think I'm so very wrong?"

"Wrong! I think you are very right, according to your century; only, Rene, it's the slow old blood in me that rebels against 'the resistless tendency of the times,' as Curtis calls it. I stick to it, some of the women who go about in conventions say and do the craziest things, yet, as a thinking man, and a man who desires to be just, I cannot deny that the immutable law of human growth underlies this universal uprising of women. Only it's a trifle formidable, you must allow that, to us poor fellows, the prospect of our sisters getting *all* their rights! We are such selfish dogs, we like our comfort so much, that I'll own to you, Rene, and you wont tell anybody (laughing), that it is the mere selfishness and prejudice of the man usually that speaks when he makes such furious objection to woman's advancement, and lays down anew the old limit of his sphere for her. If a man is half a man, Rene, his wife is more to him than all the earth beside; imagine his distress, then, at the bare thought of her vanishing away in the scholar or reformer."

"Yes, Pierre, but think of the thousands upon thousands of women who have hungered all their lives for knowledge, and died with the hunger unsatisfied, accepting ignorance to please their husbands."

"Well, there is no danger of *my* wife dying of that hunger, I've that consolation."

"Yet, Pierre, how little I know compared with you! Think of all the colleges, and universities, and everything that you have been to, and I know nothing but the little I have picked up here and there without any one to tell me how."

"Yet I have found out that such patient and persistent picking up as yours has been amounts now to quite a formidable pile. All the universities and everything can scarcely be put against such an absolute and unending habit of study as you have attained. What astonishes me is that it is increasing, and that you find just as much time for it as ever. You dreadful woman! with all I have to think of, do you intend to compel me to drag forth my old exercise books, or else feel like an ignoramus compared with my wife? Do tell what it is all for?"

"For baby! Bless him!" exclaimed Eirene, drawing her boy tight to her heart. "Oh, Pierre, how could I bear it to have him grow up and grow away from me in his thought and pursuits, and perhaps secretly scorn his mother because she was a woman and didn't know anything; how dreadful!"

"How dreadful if he should grow up, jump into the fire, and burn himself to death. Scorn your mother, young man! That would be a sorry day for you, if your father had life enough left in him to thrash you!

"I think of giving up all out-door pursuits, and of spending the entire time at home with my wife," said Pierre, in his most humorous tone, looking once more at his watch. "How would you like that, Eirene?"

"I wouldn't like it at all. You would hinder me, and I should lose the happiness of thinking of your evening return all day, and you wouldn't be so much of a man."

"I would not! then it's just possible *you* might hinder me! Come, Master Vale De Peyster, escort your father to the door," and he hoisted the boy with "a ridiculous nose" to his shoulder, who shouted with glee at his elevation.

His wife took his other hand, and thus the three came through the broad hall toward the street door.

Let us look at them as they come.

Four years have passed since this husband and wife entered the old house. A glance is sufficient to see that they are not only happier but handsomer than they were then. To this woman has come the fulness and perfection of existence and she shows it. To the man has come the fulness and completeness of his being and he shows it: shows it in the firm, free step, in the clear glance of his eyes, in the blended consciousness of power and happiness which radiates from him in every glance and gesture.

There are two types of American women. One at thirty is hopelessly old. With first youth vanished the last vestige of beauty, nothing has ever come to take its place. To the other, with wifehood and mother-hood begins rejuvenation, a second youth, riper and more lustrous than the first. This has come to Eirene. She looks fuller and taller than when we saw her last. Love and happiness, the only real beautifiers of women, have done their best for her. There is the sweetness and purity of health in her fine contour. There is the ever-increasing light of an ever-growing soul shining through her eyes. She was never so lovely a woman before.

It is difficult to write of such happiness as theirs. The pen, rarely failing when it depicts woe, falters at the very threshold of joy. Sorrow is so real, there is relief in its very cry. But bliss is so subtle, and spiritual, its finest essence is rarely caught and imprisoned in words.

William Morris tells us of this in lines whose melody is rarely surpassed:—

> "Of their bliss
> Nought may we tell, for so it is
> That verse for battle-song is meet,
> And sings of sorrow piercing-sweet,
> And weaves the tale of heavy years,
> And hopeless grief that knows no tears,
> Yet hath no voice to tell of Heaven.
> Or heavenly joys for long years given,
> Themselves an unmatched melody,
> Where fear is slain of victory,
> And hope held fast in arms of love."

The husband goes forth to the business of daily life; the wife turns back to look after the ways of her household. There is no department in it that she does not supervise, and no room in the old house that she does not enter. Her boy goes with her; sometimes he sits beside her, sometimes he is in her arms, sometimes he is tugging at her skirt. It is a fair sight! If the old De Peysters in their frames could but see it,—or if in the air invisible they look down upon it, grand Johanes De Peyster in his curled wig, lace ruffles and gown, or the gallant, handsome Colonel Arent Schuyler De Peyster, whom her husband so much resembles, or Cornelia De Peyster, his mother,—it is a fair sight for their eyes, which now must measure all things by immutable measure, and weigh all things in absolute balance, the vision of this mother of the nineteenth century and her child in the old house—and that child a De Peyster.

Noon had not come, when Eirene and her boy and his faithful little nurse entered a quiet carriage and drove up town. Her days held no happier part than this toward which she was going now.

Most of us at some time lie and dream what we would do if we were only rich. This had been Eirene's solitary pastime in the old days before the war, when her work and her lessons were over, to sit or lie in the dark and ponder on what she would do if she were rich. After portioning each member of her family, her darling project was to build a large house of rest and help for women. She meditated long on the name of that house. She turned instinctively from all which in their dubious significance were a hurt and a discouragement to the erring at the very beginning. "The Woman's Help," that should be its name, and no woman should be too old, or too young, too needy, or too fallen, to be helped within its walls. The moments which she gave to devising and planning its interior were incredible. Herein should lowly women rest if they were weary, and be nursed if they were sick. Here womanly handicrafts should be taught to girls, and places of employment be provided for the worthy. The vision of this Woman's Help vanished during the war under the stress of a mightier need, and yet now she was driving toward it this morning, a reality in brick and mortar. Like all realities it failed of the utmost splendor of its dream, yet it was already a prosperous and practical house which, without loud ado, provided actual help and encouragement to many hundreds of women in a year. Her husband had given to her two brick houses which had been thrown into one large one Every nook and corner in it had been utilized to practical service. Other ladies had gladly co-operated, and the "Woman's Help" was a nucleus for the daily illustration of a woman's highest right to minister to the needy and afflicted. Certain hours of certain days of every week found Eirene in this beloved spot. And now she was devoting a portion of the morning, as she always did, to the stories of the lately arrived, before deciding on just the thing to be done for them. It never wearied or fretted her to hear of the troubles of others, where she had the slightest chance of alleviating them. Yet it was not always a perfectly easy thing to do, to adapt every thought or suggestion to the entire satisfaction of the story-teller. This morning, a poor girl, dirty, wayworn, who had lost her situation through sickness, who had taken refuge with "a cousin," who had at last been turned off to want or vice, who had hovered on the border of both, and had been rescued before it was too late, and who now held up a sickly face and wasted hands to her more prosperous sister—she, in the little parlor of the "Help," looked first at the beautiful boy, playing at a table with his nurse, then at the lady before her, so plainly dressed that nothing she wore could arouse envy or jealousy in the mind of the most unfortunate, and yet carrying on her face a light of happiness that a queen might envy—she looked at the child, then on this happy face, the poor girl, and burst in tears.

"It's no use; I can't tell *you*, lady, what I've been through; *you* couldn't understand how a poor girl like me has been tried. You don't know what it is for a girl to come to this great city poor and all alone. How could you? There's a great difference between the like of you and me. I can't tell you—you don't know anything about it," and she sobbed anew.

"I know *all* about it," was the answer; and the gentle sympathy of the tone seemed to hush the girl's sobs at once.

"My dear sister," said Eirene, leaning forward and taking the wasted hand, "years ago I came to this city alone. I was young, and poor, and unprotected I had seen nobody in it. I did not even know my way through the streets. I did not know then, but as I look back I see how many dangers the good Father helped me to escape. A great many difficulties and dangers beset a young woman trying to earn an honest living in a great city which never trouble a young man; there is so much peril in it that I should dread beyond expression to have one I love exposed to it, and yet I believe that if a young woman is honest, industrious, patient, faithful, and modest, and prays to God day by day for protection and wisdom, that she is always protected and saved to the end. Kind friends are raised up for her, new opportunities are opened to her, and though she may not attain to just the condition that she would wish, yet she may achieve independence and success."

"You believe it! and you know!" said the girl with a look of amazed incredulity.

"I believe it, and I know," said Eirene.

"You don't look as if you had ever been poor, or sick, or unhappy."

"God has been very good to me," said Eirene, with the old tremble in her voice; "He has given to me so much more than I have ever earned, or can ever deserve. Yet I know what it is to be sick and unhappy and very poor."

"How strange! and you feel for me!"

"I feel for every creature that God has made who suffers, but nothing seems to come quite so close to my heart as a struggling and a suffering woman."

"And yet you believe that a poor girl like me can work her way up to something better?"

"I do. No honest industrious girl need go unprotected in this city. There are thousands of homes open to-day to any good girl who would enter and identify herself with their life and service."

"Oh, but you forget, not many ladies speak to the like of us as you do; if they did there would be better girls in service."

"Yes, mistress and maid both owe more to each other. There is not patience, forbearance, and sympathy, or willingness to teach on one side, nor fidelity, truth, and industry enough on the other. But come, you will trust me?—and I will trust you. I have a friend who wants a faithful girl to take charge of her only child. Such a one will have time given her to study, and when the child ceases to need her to learn any business to which she feels adapted. I will tell my friend that I *believe* you will do well for her; that what you do not know now, you will take pains to learn. If you adapt yourself to it, you could scarcely have a better home. Shall I tell her this of you?"

"Will you, can you? Oh, lady, look at my clothes; nobody would take in such a looking creature as me."

"Never mind your clothes. Before I leave we will go up stairs to a closet full of clothes, and we will look for a suit that will fit you. Besides, you are not ready for anything just now but rest. Your body is not half so sick to-day as your poor worried mind and heart. Here is a ticket for a quiet little room in this house, which will be yours till you are rested and ready for a new life. Here is another for the table, where you will find good, nourishing food. I'll not set any time. When you are able, I know you will come to my home some day before noon, and I will go with you to my friend. I feel quite certain that it will prove satisfactory to all."

"How could I fail any one who looks at me as you do! Why, lady, I feel as if I would rather die than disappoint you. Why has nobody in all my life ever spoken to me like you before?"

"Oh, you could not have lived till now without meeting kindness. You are tired and worn out. Life always seems harder to us at such times."

"Oh, I don't say nobody has ever spoken kindly before, but not feeling, not like you."

"To feel anything we must have experienced it. It is not easy to be sympathetic always with what we do not understand. Many kind ladies know nothing actually of what you have lived through. I know it all, thus how can I help feeling for you? Now, if I can truly help you, I shall be satisfied."

"Help me! you have saved me. Another day of want, of homelessness, and hopelessness and it seems as if there were nothing that I might not have done. God has given a friend even to me!"

The thought seemed more than she could bear in its wonder and joy, for as she spoke she sank forward on the table.

The tears started to Eirene's eyes, but she brushed them away in an instant.

"Come," she said in a cheerful tone, "we will go and see how nice a frock we can find." And without giving the girl another moment for grief, she took her hand, and led her away.

Many months have passed since then, and the friendless and hopeless girl of that morning, in a happy home to-day is working her way surely toward education and honorable independence. God bless, and help her! And the thousands of American women, who like her, poor, young, and lonely, in the beginning, through their own powers and by the labor of their own hands, must measure the utmost arc of success which can be earned by the self-supporting woman.

Eirene came through Park Avenue on her way back and stopped and lunched with her two sisters. There was no semblance of a shadow between her and Cornelia now. Nothing troubles a naturally noble soul so much as a suspicion that itself has stooped to something like littleness if not meanness. Cornelia survived all the "oh's" and "ah's," the shrugs and glances of "her set" at her brother's marriage, and wondered when over that they had been so few. After all, we must do something startlingly eccentric, or "awfully" shocking to become the objects of absolute interest to our neighbors. Our little tame *outré* affairs cannot make more than a passing ripple in their daily comment, overtaken and swept out by the first wave of something "perfectly dreadful." If Pierre De Peyster had only married his sister's ignorant cook, that would have been worth exclaiming over, but to marry a book-keeper, who in spite of that was a lady and better educated than themselves, though they wondered at his taste, it was his own affair and in no degree interesting to anybody but himself. Nobody need be surprised at any act of independence in Pierre De Peyster. Had he not always done precisely as he pleased!

Therefore comparatively no surprise was shown, to the infinite relief and self-shame of Cornelia. There came a day when she could bear the pricking of her conscience no longer, when she appeared alone in Eirene's room, and sittting down confessed the worst feeling she had ever had concerning her; how she had always liked her, and yet what a coward, what a mean coward she had been, for the fear of her world and her set, and the overthrow of her first darling plan.

"It was perfectly natural," said Eirene; "how could you feel otherwise, as the world looked to you. You must have seen hundreds who seemed better adapted to be your brother's wife than I. I have only wondered how you could be so affectionate to me."

"Then you don't mind, you darling?"

"How can I when you are so good to me. How can I help loving Pierre's sister for his sake, and her own?"

"I love you, Rene, better than any woman that I ever knew, I do!"

Whereupon the two women looked into each other's eyes, and then threw their arms around each other's necks, and from that hour had been sisters indeed. There could be no happier sight to Pierre De Peyster than this. He did not tell his wife yet, it was true, that the comparison of Cornelia's superficial and objectless life with the intellectual activity and spiritual freedom of Eirene's had forced him almost against his will to modify his opinion of woman's education and work. He reproached himself in silence for the part he had taken in his sister's early loveless marriage; and for the arrogance and prejudice with which he had curtailed her education, and given her to understand that marriage and nothing but marriage could be her destiny as a woman. "If I had left to her," he said, "the same right that I claimed for myself, to wait, solitary and free, till she had met the one she would have chosen out of all the world, and who could have loved her as she loved him, how different, how much more complete would be her life now. I know that I am in part responsible for what it is."

This thought was the bitterest that Pierre had ever had. Cornelia did not dream that there was a touch of remorse in the very tenderness of the kiss with which he left her now. It made her quite happy, and she would say, "How lovely Pierre has grown. I feared his marriage would take him from me, and he is tenderer to me than ever before. To think of his urging me to paint a picture for the exhibition, the dear boy. He never used to have any ambition for me, and now, by the way he talks and acts, I should think there is nothing he thinks I could not do."

None of our little group either mentally or spiritually have stood still in the last four years.

Pansy is Pansy still. She loves the world, its pomp, and its splendor; but not with that entire zest which early poverty and privation are sure to goad to passion in such a temperament as hers. Already it is apparent, the first touch of the palling of its pleasures which soon or late is sure to come to the world's devotee, who holds in her deeper soul a longing, however latent, for better things.

Here's a hundred dollars for your tiresome old "Help," Rene, she said one day, handing her sister the money. "Mamma gave it to me for a chain I fancied; but come to think it's not becoming, and I don't want it. Give it to the most dreadful creature up there, but don't tell me about her. How you *can* sit by the hour and listen to such stories is more than I can fathom. I shall never love anybody enough to listen to their troubles. I am in this world to enjoy myself if I can, not to listen to anybody's miseries, so be sure you don't tell me. I never shall get over what you *have* told me for the rest of my natural life. There's Railroad Jane, her ghastly face haunts me even when I am riding in the Park—and there's a bundle upstairs I have made up to send her whenever you say."

The first time that Lowell and Mary Vale came to visit in New York, Pansy spent a week in making them presentable, *i. e.,* fashionable.

"It's no use," she exclaimed to herself in despair at last. "They could not be better dressed, yet any one can see at a glance that with it all they are only plain country folk, and no amount of broadcloth and silk could make them look anything else. I don't care, they don't look vulgar, and that's enough. They shall ride on the back seat through the Park, and if Berta Von Beekman don't like their looks, she can look another way. They are my father and mother, and that is enough."

This fact from that moment was all sufficient for Pansy. She bore off the plainness and simplicity of her parents, as Nancy Drake said, "as if she owned the whole earth." Her very sensitiveness lest some of her friends might smile at her kindred, and by their manner remind her that she was lowlier born than themselves, made her instinctively assume unnecessary hauteur. Her father and mother did not escape comment any more than the rest of the human race. The Von Beekmans wondered how such very plain people could have a daughter with *such* an air, a beauty, and a belle, nevertheless in their hearts they honored that daughter the more for doing just as she did, and as it was impossible to patronize her they did not even try it.

Pansy and Eirene went everywhere with their parents, who were in a perfect daze of delight. In Central Park Lowell Vale thought that he had reached Paradise, that the Arabian Nights were made true for him; and Mary Vale, who had waited so long for a sight of the Celestial City, came to the conclusion that she had seen many fair and wonderful sights before reaching it. Every summer Pansy went home with Eirene, and year by year the dormer cottage took on a more gala look, and Farmer Stave grew more deeply troubled, stumping his cane the harder over the unequal results of the law of compensation. How it could bestow a new horse and buggy, new furniture, and new fences "on a critter that hadn't a mite of kalkerlation, while it left to be contented with old traps a man that had been kalkerlatin' all his life," was more than he could understand, and was something to which he had not the slightest idea of being reconciled.

To-day Pansy took her little nephew with his nurse to her room to amuse her while she dressed for the drive an hour or two later. Cornelia and Eirene were left to one of their "talks," of which they never seemed to tire, but which Pansy pronounced "perfectly tiresome."

"There!" she said before she started, "you two are going to discuss the mysteries of the universe again. Why don't you leave the universe to take care of itself, and spend the time that you devote to it in the shops? There would be some variety in that. I declare, Eirene, I think your life is perfectly prosy and poky,—housekeeping, your old woman's Help, books, baby, husband,—and you are so awfully in love with Pierre, I believe you begrudge every moment that you give to your evening visitors."

"Oh no," I don't, said Eirene; "I must own Pierre's society is so perfectly delightful to me, that if I had it three hundred and sixty-five evenings of the year all to myself, it would be just as fresh and charming to me the last evening as the first; but that would be too selfish.

"You must own, Pansy, that the old house sees some very bright evenings, especially when you and your friends come to play and dance."

"O, I don't find fault with your evenings, 'tis your days; but they are no concern of ours, are they, baby?" And with these words she seized her little nephew and departed.

"Your days are my envy," said Cornelia, "always doing, yet never worried or hurried; how do you manage it, Rene?"

"O, I am nothing at managing, only I have so much more to do than I can possibly accomplish; it is only by being regular and constant that I can do anything at all! But you, dear Corna, have so many gifts, I often think if they had only satisfactory occupation that you would be happier!"

"Very likely; yet do you know I doubt if any mere occupation of the faculties can satisfy anybody who has a soul. You know Life is many-stranded, one may fill in a long way, yet all the same there is the empty space below, warp without woof."

"Yes, but the occupation fills our time and our thoughts, and that is filling so much of life. Don't you think it helps to make one happy to be very busy?"

"I'm sure I can't say, Rene, I was never very busy in all my life."

"What a story, Corna, your heart and your thoughts are constantly busy. That is part of what I mean. Every day you give me some idea or suggestion which I remember. I carry it away—often it assists me more than I can tell you, and I can't help thinking that it might comfort and give pleasure to many others. Why don't you write them down and publish them? Wouldn't it make you happy to know that you were helping other people to be so?"

"Utility! Utility! I should know you were born in New England. And you would set me to writing for the newspapers, with every other woman in the land doing the same already. No, I thank you, the writing devil has not caught me at least, though the demon of discontent has."

"You may be sure that I have never thought of your writing as a source of fame," said Eirene. "It seems to me no person of common sense could do that in this day when so many people write well, and so few superlatively. But it must be a pleasant way to do one's little share in the world to those who can—this breaking forth with a good word and a God speed. You send your little message out, and the one who waits for it receives it, while you behind your door can be as sheltered and shut away as if you had never spoken a word. How proud I'd be of you!"

"O Rene, if any one could tempt me to go and make a goose of myself it would be you. But you overrate me; I have not the power of embodying ideas which you think I have, and if I had I would not write, dear. I should only add another voice to the thousands echoing the prevailing spirit of the age. I am not willing to do that. No, I would rather be dumb forever."

"There are so many opinions of the prevailing spirit of the age, many call it progress, so many infidelity. What do you call it, Corna?"

"I call it a compound of unbelief, discontent, unrest, ambition, and aspiration. I find it all reflected in myself, but I will not give public voice to it."

"I am sorry that you are troubled."

"Of course you are, but that can't help me. You said true, so many people write well, so well that I find myself astonished over it every day. I can't take up the commonest book or newspaper without finding some subtle or new idea in it, or some old one presented in entirely new relations. This seems to me pre-eminently an age of thought, but it is thought without unity. Everybody is proclaiming his *ipse dixit* upon his own authority. Each one seems to be afraid that he wont have all the chance he wants to declare his own individuality, no matter how awry it may be. Individuality is one of the cant words of this country at least. For my part, I would like to lose a little of mine. There is nothing but doubting, questioning, denying, and aspiring—so little realization—that lies far on, Rene, in a golden age that you and I will never see. Mind, I don't say that all this upturning is not necessary for the far fulfilment, but I'm dreadfully tired of it all. This spirit of the age, as people call it, makes fearful discord in my temperament, which is as slow as an old Dutch canal."

"But it is well with you, carissima," she added, leaning forward and kissing tenderly the sunbeam which changed to gold her sister's hair. "It is well with you, and you rest me more than any mortal that I ever knew. You are never restless or anxious, and yet it is not because you have not felt all that a human heart can feel. There must have been a time, Rene, when you ceased to anticipate anything for yourself in this world, then you ceased to be restless or anxious. Fruition came to you unawares, and now you are filled with a heavenly content. All that you have ever suffered has deepened and enriched your nature, and made greater your wonderful capacity for giving."

"O Corna, why will you say such things to me?"

"Because it's true, my dear, and I'm not of the sort who believe that we are to tell no truths to our friends but disagreeable ones. I believe more people are harmed by fault-finding than by praise in this world of ours."

"I *like* it, I can't deny that, Corna, only it makes me feel ashamed."

"I'd like a chance to feel ashamed in the same direction, but I've the horridest set of duty-doing friends who always feel that they *ought* to tell me every hateful thing that they can think or even hear of me. It has hurt me so much that I say every pleasant thing I can think of to every one I care for. Nobody comforts me like you, Rene."

"If I could only see you happy. You have so much to make you happy, if you only have a little more faith."

"Aye! If I could, but I can't, that is what is the matter with me. I'll confess the truth to you, carina. (I never did to any one before.) All that my heart has really craved on earth I have 'missed or itself missed me,' as Robert Browning says. *Now*, what I really want most in this world is to *believe*. I often wish that I had lived in the old mediæval times when people took every thing for granted. But I don't. I question every thing. A blade of grass baffles me. I cannot look upon the sky or upon the earth, or feel the beating of my own heart, without being conscious of the mystery of life. I find no satisfactory solution anywhere. And yet I feel sure that only the fruition of another and perfect life can explain the incompleteness and disappointments of this one. I am always peering into the dark beyond, yet I never see my way!"

"Have you never thought of one thing, Corna; the most famous men and women, no matter how much they have doubted, no matter how completely they have lived for this world, when they draw near death, then they think most of their souls, and turn to the very Bible that they have neglected or despised for consolation? Long ago this fact impressed me so deeply, that I resolved not to wait till I had passed by the best of this life's joy, to live for the coming life, which must be a continuation of this. If we think at all, I suppose we must all question many things, there is so much that we cannot understand. But there is a comfort in believing in God's love, in resting in it, in living for it, which is beyond every thing."

"Yes, I suppose there is for those who can, but it don't rest me much. Even the Bible is a fearfully contradictory and unsatisfactory book to me."

"The grand, the blessed old Bible. At least its promises are not contradictory. How many go to them for consolation when every thing else on earth fails."

"Yes, I go to them myself, and if I could only make them real—if I could make the future life as real to me as this one is—if I could only feel that it holds a compensation for all that fails me here, *that would be enough*. I never should utter another murmur. No matter what happened I could wait content. But I can't; it's all vague and myth-like. I moan for what I have missed and lost as if they were all. Yet I know they can't be all, not all, else why should I long for something higher and more perfect than I have ever found, or ever can find in this world."

"No, not all. With your glorious faculties how could it be all, the dwarfed life that they have here; and yet I believe in *this* life, in this age. Dear sister, how I wish you could feel their possibilities and privileges as I do."

"I wish I could; and yet, Rene, you must have seen moments in your own life when you did not feel it to be such a privilege to live this life."

A swift shadow passed over Eirene's face.

"You are right," she said. "I have seen moments when I was willing even to fling it away. How wicked I was. Yet I should be more wicked now if I did not thank God for letting me live on this beautiful earth in a life so complete. As Pierre says: 'Life is a big thing.'"

"It strikes me that death is a bigger one. What you said of everybody being anxious about their souls at last, makes me think of the last night of the Girondists. You remember how they sat around a table full of wine and flowers and discussed the immortality of the soul till day dawned? Then Ducos said: 'Let us sleep, life is so trifling a thing it is not worth the hour of sleep which we lose in regretting it.' 'Let us watch,' said Lasource. 'Eternity is so certain, and so terrible that a thousand lives would not suffice to prepare for it.' I often feel like that, yet who would believe it that knows me only by the butterfly life that I live?"

"No, who could believe it of those who know you only in your worldly guise," said Eirene to herself half an hour later as she saw the beautiful woman enter the carriage for her afternoon drive. The gorgeous cavalcade had already started parkward. Many were the hats lifted and the heads bowed to the beautiful girl, and no less beautiful woman, as their elegant equipage moved slowly on. Not one of all those worshippers probably thought that this queen of fashion and beauty had a desire beyond the homage which she received as her birthright. That moment she had not. She liked it, and it was her life to take it, but it was the life which had come between her and the higher life which she longed for in solitary moments, but which yet she had never won.

Eirene went home with her boy. Later he slept by her side in her own room through her own hour, to her one of the dearest of the day, when she shut all the world out, and herself in with her child, her books, and her own soul. No soul can grow that is never nourished in solitude. It is in silence that its deepest springs are fed from the secret sources of life. Like other American households Eirene's was not always free from invasion even in its most sacred moments. The demands of others sometimes took from her the hour which she had set apart for her own improvement, but she always came back to it again, and perhaps another day gave her two; thus unobtrusively and almost unknown, save to her husband, even her scholastic education went on. Now she looked from her book to her boy. The morning conversation had centred her thoughts even more than usual upon him. "Yes," she said, gazing on the slumbering child. "In one sense your mother must be your teacher and friend always. The mother of a man cannot afford to rust or to go back. The time will come when you will leave me. Alas! I would not have it otherwise. You must be a man, a free man, to do a man's work in the world. If you can come back to me, if you can love me and honor me always, *my boy*, it will be enough." She was looking upon her child when a servant came in and handed her a card, while she said, "I told the gentleman that you were always engaged this hour, but he said he could not come again." Eirene took the card and read:

PAUL MALLANE,
BOSTON.

She read the name as she might one dropped to her from another life, or another world. It seemed such to her, so far was she removed in circumstance and association even from its memory. She gazed at it till a crimsom tide swept over her fair face at the recollections which it brought back.

"Bettine, tell the gentleman that I will see him," she said quietly, and the happy-faced German girl departed with her message.

Below waited a gentleman who bore slight resemblance to our early acquaintance. He had changed greatly, yet we should know him by his eyes, which alone retained the beauty of his youth. If I obeyed the stereotyped law of novels, I should portray him in a very sorry condition, but as I began this book not "to tell a story," but to tell the truth, the truth compels me to say that he looked precisely what he was, a "high liver," a fashionably dressed prosperous man of the world. One can see hundreds of men of precisely the same type in a single walk down Broadway, or on any other grand thoroughfare in any city of the world. You catch glimpses of them at the open windows of fashionable club houses, lounging in groups about the doors of grand hotels, rolling in ease through parks, driving four or six in hand along the corsos of fashionable watering places, everywhere that money, luxury, and self-indulgence meet; men whose material life has triumphed over the intellectual and the spiritual, and made them its slave.

He was handsome still, but his good looks were suggestive chiefly of turbot and capons, of strong liquors and fast living. Seeing him anywhere you would say: "There is a rich man, prosperous as the world goes, but neither satisfied nor happy." He had the nervous movement, the abrupt manner, the restless glance which indicate a dissatisfied mind, and which combined form a presence peculiarly American. America produces thousands of such men. In their youth their mothers and their native towns believe that they can attain to almost any greatness possible to man. But they reach the acme of their power in early manhood, and in maturity never fulfill the promise of their youth. There were none of the probabilities of Paul being President of the United States now, that there were when Deacon Nugget prophesied that dubious honor for him in his old shop door, when Prince Mallane was the pride of Busyville. Yet, as the world goes, Paul was a prosperous man. He had only missed the highest success in his profession in himself. When he allowed himself to think of it, no one knew this better than he. It comes to all men, certainly to him whose higher nature is but partially obliterated—glimpses of the best and highest life to which humanity may attain. But it takes more than mere ability to win it, to ensure even temporal success. It requires a motive and an object, whatever they may be, powerful enough to command every force. These Paul Mallane never had. Without them he had the impulse, but not the steadfast purpose which conquers success and commands even fame. Thus as a lawyer he achieved his most brilliant position as a young man, when he believed that he was going to earn his own fortune, and make a home and a name for the woman of his love. The grandest men who have won renown have esteemed this joy and triumph enough. Lord Jeffrey writes at the death of his young wife: "I took no interest in anything which had not some reference to her. You know how indolent I was by nature, how regardless of reputation and fortune. But it was a delight to me to lay these things at the feet of my darling, and to invest her with some portion of the distinction she deserved. Now I have no interest in any thing, and no object or motive for being in the world."

What purer human motive can inspire a man than the faith and devotion of the wife who holds him next to God! All that was best in Paul Mallane went out to Eirene; had there been enough of it to have preserved her in his life, his whole fate had been different. As it was, he had been gnawed by the daily canker which has eaten away so many men's lives in secret—an unhappy home. No children were born to bind the discordant pair together in one common hope. He settled down to a lucrative but mediocre law business, carried on chiefly by assistants, while he reaped the profits. He gained at least one of the supreme objects of his desire—money! He spent it at clubs, races, in feasting and drinking. He lived in a great mansion—in one half of it—while his wife opened the other half to *her* clubs, her societies, her re-unions, and reigned there in undisputed possession of her "rights"! Paul was what society terms a "hard drinker," not a drunkard—that is, he was rarely or never intoxicated, and just as rarely free from the stimulus of liquor. Without it nothing could have tempted him to appear in this house; but he had seen something that goaded him that morning—had drank a double potion, which made him feel equal to anything, and here he was.

You remember his early weakness for grand old rooms? He had not lost it; and as he looked down the great drawing-room of De Peyster house, such a contrast to the narrow vault of the modern New York parlor, as he glanced at its antique furniture, at its sacred souvenirs of the past, at its exquisite forms of art, the well-remembered glories of Marlboro Hill faded in comparison.

"Compensation," he exclaimed, with a half bitter smile. "I am glad of it."

In the library beyond he caught a glimpse of a painting which seemed to draw him irresistibly. He yielded to the impulse and stood before it. It was a recent picture of Eirene and her boy, which Pierre had had painted—a masterpiece by an American master. His finest art and inspiration were infused into it, and the subject, if only as a rare type of womanhood, motherhood, and childhood, were worthy of the genius of the master. Life-size, there she sat with her boy, all surrounded by the grand old De Peysters, this guardian angel of the later destinies of their house. The vision struck all the fever out of Paul Mallane's veins, all the illusion out of his brain. He was sober in an instant, with the soberness of absolute realization.

"My God!" he exclaimed, "how like! I should have known it in Timbuctoo. Yet how changed. What am I here for—an ass after so many years!"

Suddenly the man became a coward. He could not meet her. What could he say to her? How could he behold her eyes? After all, he would go away without seeing her, and he turned towards the door. As he did so, he saw her coming toward him out of the depth of the great drawing-room—not the Eirene that he saw last, the wan and faded half-dead girl whom his duplicity had made but a lustrous woman with shining hair, and eyes lit with a soft splendor, and a gliding motion as if she were not walking, but borne on to him by the white draperies which floated around her; the face and the form of her who had made heaven seem possible to him on earth in the days of his youth—that denied and defrauded youth lying so far back in his past.

It was the man who was moved to emotion, and who showed it, not the woman. There was no triumph, no regret, no pain in her aspect, as she approached; there was nothing but the outraying peace of her own being, and the unconscious kindness which was the impulse and law of her life. She came forward with the gentleness of a gentlewoman to receive one who had asked to see her in her own home, as she might have come had she never seen him before. Since she shut her eyes upon him—so far away in another existence—the realization of a perfect life had come to her in the place of that early dream. A man whom she revered and loved with a reverence and a devotion which Paul Mallane could never have inspired, had superseded him in her affections. It was different with him. In his heart no one had ever taken her place. No evil in his life had ever touched the shrine whereon he had placed her, and where in thought he worshipped her alone.

He had lived his man's life according to his nature. He had run the whole gamut of a fast man's pleasures, but as one by one each palled upon him and left him more dissatisfied than before, more and more distinctly came back to him the angel of his youth, and more and more bitter grew his regret for all that he had lost in losing her. There was always just good enough in Paul Mallane to make you like him, and to make it seem that there must be a great deal more. You may say that Fate was cruel to him, that Eirene could have saved him? No. She could never have changed his nature, and yet all that was good in it was hers.

She came out of the depth of the great drawing-room as in fancy he had seen her come so many times out of the silence of the past, lovelier than ever before! Forever inaccessible to him, never had she seemed so dear to him as at this moment.

"I have been looking at your picture," he said in a hurried tone, before she had time to speak. "You have changed as well as I, but not *as* I have. Mrs. De Peyster, pardon me for coming here uninvited. I realized the extent of my intrusion a moment ago, while gazing on this portrait and its surroundings, and was going away without seeing you."

"I am glad to see you, Paul," she said, simply. "Will you come into the library?" And she led the way into the room which he had just left. She had not had the faintest idea of what she would say, nor how she would greet him a moment before. Now as she looked upon him it was not triumph, nor bitterness, nor love that she felt; it was compassion. For it was not his fine clothes, nor his prosperous (and under ordinary conditions his still important) air which she saw; it was the face, the face once so beautiful and dear to her, now so clouded, heavy, and dark with the traces left on it by long sinful years. Her subtle spiritual sight looked through this face as the thinnest mask, and read the stormy, unsatisfied, unhappy heart below it as an open book, and she out of the depth of her perfect happiness pitied the man whom she had once loved, even while she could wonder now how she had ever loved him. And he who would scorn pity from any other mortal could receive it from her as a priceless boon.

"Then you don't hate me?" he asked, gazing upon the gentle face before him.

"I never hated you, Paul, I only lost you."

"Lost me! You never lost me. It is I who lost you," he said bitterly.

She meant "I lost you when I lost my faith in you; when you deceived me and made me the victim of subterfuge and falsehood." She saw that he did not understand her meaning, and in mercy to him she did not explain it.

"You have been avenged, ten times avenged, Eirene, for all I ever made you suffer," he said. "To tell you so is all that I have come here for. I am willing that *you* should triumph over me, and you are the only one on earth I am willing should. I even like to punish myself by coming to look upon your happiness. It's a comfort to see that *you* are avenged, even in the face of my own misery. That if I've spoiled my own life, that I could not yours. Just two things I am sure of in this world—retribution and compensation. You have your compensation, I see," he said, glancing from the portrait to herself, and from herself back to a magnificent portrait of Pierre De Peyster, "and I, my retribution. I've been ten times punished for every sin I ever committed. I am as miserable as you could ever possibly want me to be, and I am willing that you should know it."

"I never wanted you miserable at all," she said, and as he heard her tone he believed her. "I have never even thought that you deliberately caused me unhappiness: that grew out of many circumstances and conditions."

"It grew out of my cursed nature and ideas," he exclaimed. "But bless you for what you have said. It's something. Have you ever seen my wife?"

She looked up in astonishment at this question.

"Oh, I see you haven't. But I wonder that you look surprised. She *can* be seen by any stranger who wants to look upon her, or listen to her lecture on 'Woman's Rights.'"

"I never knew her name till—this morning. I thought it might be she whose name I saw advertised to lecture."

"And you saw it! I knew that you would. *I* saw it, and it made me so—so mad—that the result is I am here! That is one of her lovely tricks. Wherever she knows I am—if I go off with a party of friends, if I am anywhere, where she is sure that the sight will be particularly unpleasant, there she alights. And in the first newspaper that *I* pick up I see my wife's name, with my own appended to it. She announced to lecture on 'THE HUSBAND OF THE PERIOD.' Isn't it a precious morsel for my cronies? She knows it. She knows nothing could gall me more. If she would only stick to the truth in her—lecture, it would be a little less maddening."

"You don't mean that she *can* tell truth or untruth about her own husband to a public audience, do you?" asked Eirene, striving to take in the monstrous idea.

"I mean that she does, d——n her. Pardon me!—I humbly ask your pardon. You will think I deserve it, but I don't, not that *lecture*. In it she goes on and portrays an ideal wife, a lovely, neglected, suffering woman, makes her an angel, a creature full of seraphic gifts and graces, all of which are sacrificed to a brute of a man. She tells a touching tale of how this brute robbed this angel of every chance to use her talents—'repressed her,' 'robbed her of her individuality,' those are the pet phrases—while the devil has gone on making whatever he chooses out of himself, with nothing on earth to hinder, squandering his own and his wife's fortune, and that now she supports not only herself, but him! The inference of all this is that *she* herself is the seraph, and I the demon. I'd forgive her everything else if she did not go about hinting that she supports me!"

There was something comical even in the distress of the tone in which the last sentence was uttered; it made Eirene smile.

"If you were a man, you could not smile at *that*," he said reproachfully.

"But even if it were true," Eirene said, "you would have considerable company. I am told that many women do support men in this land and generation," and her thoughts went up to the "Help," and to the pitiful stories that she heard there.

"*Do* they!" said Paul. "Then Mrs. Mallane is not one of them. I support myself and her too—not that it is a very gracious task. I wouldn't if I could help it. She is rich. If she had not been—well, she *is* rich; but her father took care before we were married to secure it all to her, so I couldn't touch a penny of it. I don't want to touch a penny of it; but as things go, I wouldn't support her if the law didn't compel me. So much for men's rights! If you could look into that great desolate house (it's hers), and see the man and woman who inhabit each the remotest corners of it, then if you could hear that house called a home, you would realize how you are avenged."

"I pity you both," she said earnestly.

"Her too? Well, you may. I pity her myself sometimes. And you never heard of her?"

"No, not until this morning."

"Yet I knew her, and she cared for me before I ever saw you."

"Didn't you care for her?"

"Yes, in a way; I did not love her—I see you smile; I suppose you think that remark sounds like old times."

"Well, I didn't—I never did! I've got through with all those early lies. I can afford to speak the truth now. I always *did* speak the truth to *you*. I declare again that I never loved but one woman, and that woman is you. I admired Helena—very much then, which is a good deal more than I do now."

"How could you wish to marry her if you did not love her; that was doing *her* a wrong in the beginning, if you made her believe that you did," said Eirene.

"Not changed after all! I see you don't understand now, any more than fourteen years ago, that a man may act from more than one motive even in marriage. Several entered into mine with Helena—one you can commend. I felt that my attentions had been sufficient to cause her unhappiness, that I had helped her to love me. I could make no other amends."

Here he struck beyond the limit of her pity, beyond even the large white margin of her charity. A look of icy coldness, touched with contempt, stole outward through the soft features and covered her face. She was trying to measure the duplicity of his youth. Then she herself was not the only woman whom he had caused to suffer after he had wooed and won her love!

"It was before I knew you *that* happened," he hastened to say; "you won't hold me a sinner for what I did before, will you? I see you despise me. That's hard, when I'm more than punished for my sins already. I am glad to have you pity me, but I am not so far gone as to be willing that you should despise me. What a dolt I am to sit here confessing every thing!—you thought me mean enough before. I told Helena long before we were married that I did not love her as I ought to love my wife. You will give me credit for that?"

"Gladly. It makes it seem a little less wrong. For what could be harder to a wife than to find out that the husband that she married for love married her without it? I could not help pitying her."

"You make me pity her myself. Poor Helena! I think we might have gone on well as the world goes, for I did admire her and she had splendid traits, and she *did* love me if it had not been for that—devil. You look! The word's too good for her. More than seven devils live and flourish inside of her pink and white skin. How anything can look so fair and be so false, so innocent and be so wicked, is more than I can understand," said the man hopelessly, for the most treacherous man feels like innocence itself, when he attempts to measure the subtlety of an evil woman. "It was not enough that she came between us, robbed me of *you*, destroyed the last chance of good in my life. She waited till I was married to Helena Maynard, then went to her and told her everything—all about you, all about herself—that she had jilted me, that a shop girl had jilted me, and that Helena had taken their leavings. And as if the truth was not bad enough, made up any number of falsehoods, of how I had ridiculed Helena to *her*; how I had told how long she had been in love with me, how she had worked for me, and even proposed to me—everything that could torture and insult a proud woman and wife. I came home to dinner one day, and found a Niobe, a marble woman, dressed in black, sitting at the head of the table. Helena liked high tragedy and stage effects, but she was not acting then. She came to life once, blazed upon me, told me what she thought of me. The opinion was not flattering. I have never forgiven her, and she has never forgiven me. She is as proud as Lucifer. She would have forgiven me many things, but not my ridiculing her to a rival whom she had always hated,—not my seeking her only when that rival had refused me. She met Belle Brescott's stories everywhere. The charming Madam Ovedo told them all through Boston as delightful jokes.

"Helena went her way, I mine, and the way has been from bad to worse. We live in one house, but we do not meet now even as friends. She will never forgive me for some things that I have done. I will never forgive her for what she is doing. As for the other one, the ——, I'll never forgive her in time or eternity; my curse follows her in life and in death. She *can't* escape forever, if she does flourish and fatten on sugar at present,—that is my consolation."

"I was sorry for your wife when you spoke of her first, now I am sorry for you both," said Eirene. "I only wish it were in my power to help you in some way, to bring you nearer together."

"Thank you; but *you* could not help us. We are past being helped, there are injuries on both sides that can't be forgiven. My child (with the air of a patriarch), *you* don't know it, but it is true; when people, through a long process of mutual injuries, have grown to hate each other, they can't un-hate at any one's mediation. If you were to attempt it, Helena would wither you at a glance. She likes to face the world. She likes to face great audiences, to strike tragic attitudes, and to sweep the platform amid a roar of applause. She has troops of admirers, followers, and friends, any one of whom could tell you all about her awful husband. If she hasn't a husband, she has 'a career!' You have heard of such a thing, haven't you? What is your opinion of careers? Mine is, that when a married woman is in such violent pursuit of one that she goes lecturing through the land, there is usually something the matter at home. Happy wives and mothers don't go about the country lecturing on suffrage, or anything else, do *you* think so?"

"As a rule, no," said Eirene; "yet I know some exceptions—women very happy at home, and in all the relations of life, who yet feel that they have something to say in public, and say it."

"But you wouldn't lecture, would you?"

"No, I couldn't to an audience larger than one," said Eirene, laughing.

"Did you go to the war?" she asked, anxious to turn his thoughts from a subject evidently so disagreeable. "The awful reality of the war must have helped you to forget your own troubles."

"No. I don't look like the sort of man that would go to the war, do I? I am just the sort to send a substitute, and I sent one. I staid at home and let *you* go. Wasn't that manly?"

"I deserve no credit for going. I followed my brother, to do the little that I could. I couldn't do less."

"Nor more. I know all about it. Hilltop is not a thousand miles from Busyville."

"Then you still go to Busyville?"

"Yes, and shall every year while mother lives. Mother and I are nearer together than we used to be. Father is dead. Father was a good man. He was always *your* friend, Eirene."

"I know that he was, and I have always remembered him with gratitude. He was very kind to me and to my father."

"Mother is a good deal broken. She goes away in corners and cries and talks to herself. Will you believe it, she sometimes talks about you? If she could see you she would cry, and ask you to forgive her. You see she is disappointed in me. I am rich enough, but I am not great, and she wanted me to be both. Because I am not, some way she thinks that she herself is to blame; that if she had let us alone, if she had not interfered as she did, that I would be happier, and greater, and better now. She said so to me once. She spoke of my unhappy home, and said that if she had her life to live over that she would do so differently; said she was sorry for the way she treated you. This made mother and me nearer together than we ever were before."

There was real pathos in Paul's voice as he uttered these words. The tears arose to Eirene's eyes as she heard them.

"Thank you for your kindness," she said. "Please tell your mother I have nothing to remember but this."

"You have a son," he said, looking up at the portrait. "If you live to see him a man, think of me. And if he really sets his heart on any one, don't try to thwart him. Whatever else you try to keep him from, don't try to keep him from marrying the woman that he loves, if he can get her. It is he who is to marry her, not you. Not that I hold mother to blame for my own meanness, not I."

"Do you never go to Busyville?"

"Never. I supposed there my very existence was forgotten."

"What! not know more of a Yankee village than that! The mind of Busyville never forgets anybody that it can gossip over. Did you suppose a marriage like your's could take place within thirty miles, and it not be deeply exercised over it? Why, I heard all about it in the summer when I came up to see mother. Poor mother! She don't know herself how many degrees you have risen in her estimation since she has heard you spoken of as the wife of a rich and influential man. I have long known of Dr. De Peyster through acquaintances. I have walked by your door a hundred times, meditating on compensation, and retribution, and you! Yet I dare say you thought I had forgotten you as well as Busyville?"

"No, Paul, it is not so easy to forget one's own life."

"I haven't found it very easy. The meanest man can't forget quite. My domestic bliss at least has not been sufficient to obliterate the only happiness that I ever knew. Your fancying that Busyville had forgotten you makes me think of Viner. You remember Viner, don't you? He left there years ago, yet you should hear those dear sisters go on about him."

"Why, what did he do!" asked Eirene.

"He committed an unpardonable crime."

"Crime! He seemed like a very good young man."

"Well, he was, but that's not the thing. He committed a crime for which the united sisterhood of the Bustler church will never forgive him—he married outside of it."

"Oh! that was all. I'm quiet releived. I remember him as such a good man and delightful preacher. I should certainly be very sorry to hear that he had done anything worse."

"As if that were not bad enough! It was rich, the whole thing. The man hasn't got to the bottom of the trunk yet, filled with slippers, tidies, and book-marks embroidered for him by the young sisters of the church. He has been away for his health, but his health was well enough till the doting sisters stuffed him with pies and pickles, and 'ris' cake. It was, 'dear brother Viner!' '*such* a lovely spirit,' 'such a gifted young divine,' till one morning, sudden as a thunder-clap, he was a demon, a hypocrite, a villain! how *had* they been so deceived! He was not at all what they thought he was,—no, no!—he had married the squire's daughter, Tilly Blane, and not a sister in the church had ever suspected that he was even acquainted with her."

"'Why,' I said, 'mother, you wanted *me* to marry her; if she is good enough for me, isn't she good enough for Viner?'

"'That's nothing to the point,' she said. '*He* is a minister, and should have married in his own church, and a pious girl!'

"'You have always told me that Tilly was pious,' I said.

"'In their way,' she answered. 'What can she do in class-meeting, or female prayer meeting? She is good for nothing but to play the piano and crochet lamp mats. She knows no more than her mother before her.'

"'I'm sorry you should have insisted on such a wife for me,' I said, 'or else that you should have so changed your opinion of dear Tilly.'

"'Why *will* you aggravate me Paul,' she said; 'you are *not*—Viner—my brother in the Lord; he is no more. To think of his deep deceit. He did show an uncommon interest in your sister Grace, there's no denying *that*. He has trifled with her young affections. He has fallen in my estimation as far as the earth below the sky,—he is a hypocrite and a deceiver.'

"'Oh! he is neither,' I said. 'You were always getting him to pray with Grace—praying was his business, he couldn't do less; I never heard of any further attentions. Let her marry Simpkins. She has no style, and never had any. She'd be a world happier feeding the chickens on Simpkins's farm than in dragging around the country worrying her life out in trying to please several hundred sisters in the Lord like you. Tilly Blane is just the one. She will play on her piano, and please her husband, and the sisters may sing or howl, and it'll be all the same to her.'"

"But Busyville has never forgiven Viner. If he were to go there to-day to preach, the united sisterhood would arise in one virtuous body and leave the church."

"But has kind, good Grace married?" asked Eirene.

"Yes, married Simpkins, and lives in the big white house on the farm. She is as happy as she can be among her chickens and babies, with a husband just adapted to her. I went out to see her the other day, and as we were sitting in the piazza after tea, Simpkins exclaimed: 'There comes the presiding elder, and the elderess. I hope your pantry is ready for inspection, Grace.' As he said this, I saw a little dapper old gentleman, with a conceited smirk and a white choker, proceed from an ancient chaise, followed by a gaunt woman with a high nose and round, sharp eyes, looking red as coals through her spectacles. Even they could not hide my ancient enemy, Tilda Stade, on a visit of church inspection with her spouse. I had no intention of speaking to her, and didn't expect that she would to me, but she did; she walked straight up to me, and said, 'I told you so! The Judge of all the earth *will* do right.'

"'Yes,' I said, 'and if he has hit a fellow enough already, why do you come and strike him another blow. Do you call *that* Christian?'

"She thought a moment, then said, 'No, I don't.'

"I added, 'Follow your master, then. If a man is punished enough already, let him alone.'

"She set her eyes on me, extended her bony hand, lifted up her voice, and said, 'Paul Mallane, I believe there is some good even in you.'

"'Thank you,' I answered. 'I presume there is *some* good even in you, but I have had a very disagreeable time in finding it out.'"

"If you can do as much as Tilda, Eirene, give me your hand in forgiveness, and say that, in spite of my sins, you believe there is some good even in me. I will go away a little happier, and never trouble you again."

"You do not trouble me, Paul," she said in her sweet, tremulous voice. "It is the good in you that I will remember. I pray God to give you peace, and a happier life."

"Thank you."

These words were on his lips as the street door opened, and in a moment Pierre De Peyster entered the library, glancing with a look of surprise from his wife's face to the stranger's, on both of which were visible signs of emotion not joyful.

Eirene introduced the two gentlemen, and in the same instant each measured and estimated the other.

"You have a perfect right to kick me out of your house, Dr. De Peyster," said Paul in his old brusque way, "and I presume that your opinion of me would justify you in doing it. I apologize to you, as I have already done to Mrs. De Peyster, for coming here uninvited. I came partly because I was unhappy, and partly because I didn't just realize what I was doing, to catch a glimpse of the happiness which I knew must be yours and *hers*. I felt that it would be something from my load to see for myself that it had not been in my wretched power to mar the life of the truest woman that I ever knew."

"You are welcome," Mr. Mallane, said Pierre De Peyster, extending his hand. "You have disarmed whatever resentment I might have felt. Any one whom Mrs. De Peyster welcomes is welcome to me. Will you stay and dine with us?"

"No, thank you. Even I am not saint enough to want to see too much happiness. I am witness already to all that I feel able to bear. You wouldn't dine in *my* house if you stood in it as I stand in yours! The club house is the place for men like me to dine in. When you come to Boston, Dr. De Peyster, I shall invite you to mine, and do the little in my power to prove to you that I can appreciate both hospitality and a true gentleman."

He was turning to depart, but just then there was a knock at the door, and the nurse, who had heard the street door open, appeared as usual bringing the boy with the "ridiculous nose" to see his father.

"I kiss him for his mother," said Paul Mallane, pausing on the threshold and bending down to kiss the smiling child. "I have lost and you have won," he added, turning to Pierre De Peyster. "I deserved to lose, and you deserved to win. So I could not hate you if I tried."

"There is that in you which deserves a happier fate. I could not hate you if I tried," answered Pierre.

"If any man living was so to triumph before my face, I am glad he is a gentleman, and a noble man, that's some comfort at least to me," said Paul, and he looked from the grand man to the lovely woman by his side.

The eyes of both men rested upon her face. In the same instant both realized, the one all that he had lost, the other all that he had won.

"Farewell," he said, extending his hand to Eirene, and in another moment the door of De Peyster house shut upon Paul Mallane forever.

As it closed husband and wife turned instinctively toward each other. Pierre drew Eirene to the window, and they stood in silence till the tall form of Paul Mallane disappeared in the twilight through the shrubbery of the park.

"I don't want to go and hear that lecture this evening," said Eirene.

"I am glad of it, my love, for I am sure that I don't want to go."

"So I have seen that man, and could not hate him. Now I understand how it was that you cared for him. If you had married him, you would have loved him always."

"Yes, and have doubted him always. Can you think of more absolute torture than to love and distrust the same person? My only refuge would be to flee from such an one forever. Where I love I *must* believe."

"Do you believe in me?"

"Without a doubt and without a fear, you are truth itself. I trust you as I trust God."

"Bless you! You give me the purest happiness that a man can know."

"And mine is the highest right ever won by woman," said Eirene, kissing the face bent down to hers "to be the honored and beloved wife of the one man I would have chosen out of all the world."

www.ingramcontent.com/pod-product-compliance
Lightning Source LLC
LaVergne TN
LVHW050529100826
845148LV00002B/498

* 9 7 8 1 4 2 5 5 1 9 4 8 3 *